The
Pursuit of
Happiness

The Pursuit of Happiness

Government and Politics in America

John A. Moore, Jr.
California State Polytechnic University, Pomona

Myron Roberts
Chaffey College

Macmillan Publishing Co., Inc.
New York
Collier Macmillan Publishers
London

Macmillan Publishing Co., Inc.
866 Third Avenue, New York, New York 10022

Collier Macmillan Canada, Ltd.

Library of Congress Cataloging in Publication Data

Moore, John A
    The pursuit of happiness.

    Bibliography: p.
    Includes index.
    1. United States—Politics and government—Hand-
books, manuals, etc. I. Roberts, Myron, joint
author. II. Title.
JK274.M67   320.9'73'092   77-4254
ISBN 0–02–383310–6

Printing: 2   3   4   5   6   7   8   Year: 8   9   0   1   2   3   4

For Our Students

Preface

The Pursuit of Happiness attempts to place the study of American government and politics within a human perspective. We have tried to relate the traditional content of courses in American government and civilization to the efforts of people to live their lives in society.

We believe we offer the reader both structure and content, ideas as well as facts, and we have not hesitated to borrow widely from the broad range of humanist studies, including literature, philosophy, sociology, and popular journalism. For our title we have borrowed Thomas Jefferson's phrase "the pursuit of happiness" because we believe it best expresses what politics in America has been and is about. Moreover, it reflects our working definition of political life: not merely the business of going to the polls periodically to elect officials, or the day-by-day functioning of the governmental and party apparatus, but rather the sum of the ideas, ideals, passions, and actions that engage the whole nation.

We have tried to show what the government is and does as well as how this government affects the rest of us and how we affect it. Also, we have tried to meet the strict demands of sound scholarship in a style not bound by the limits of conventional academic prose, a style catching not only the words but also the music of an exuberant democracy.

The book lends itself to as flexible an approach as may be preferred by the instructor. There is no necessary sequence of chapters or topics. For example, it is possible to begin with Chapter 3 ("The Constitutional Framework") and end with Chapter 2 ("The Pursuit of Happiness").

We are indebted in a variety of ways to several people who helped us. John Korey, Charlotte Weber, and Walter Coombs of the faculty at California State Polytechnic University and Robert Latham of Chaffey College offered advice in their special areas of American government. Professor Robert S. Marcus reviewed the entire manuscript and made several helpful criticisms that we believe improved the final product. Without the help of Vicki Smith, Judith Cooke, and Chris Kukulka and their typewriters the task of completing the book would have been much more arduous. Editors

A. H. McLeod, Clark Baxter, and Susan Greenberg provided the proper mixture of urgency and encouragement so that the sometimes painful author–editor relationship was both pleasant and educational. Finally, we should like to thank our wives, Linda and Estelle, for their advice, patience, and assistance.

Needless to say, the end result is the responsibility of the authors, who continue to debate and discuss the major themes and ideas of this book. We would hope that the excitement and pleasure thus generated are transmitted to the reader.

Our aim is not to press upon the student a certain view of life or a given political philosophy. It is, rather, to provoke the student to think, to examine his or her life, ideas, and society, and to engage in an excursion of the mind that will lead to a broader view of both the problems and possibilities of civil life.

J. A. M.
M. R.

Contents

Congress and Its Critics   101

The Courts: The
Search for the Just Society   127

The Art of Politics:
Parties and Elections   151

Who Rules America? The Elite, the Interests, the Bureaucracy, and the Voter   181

Media, the Shadow Government: Power and the Press   211

Economics: The Prevailing Smell of Money   237

America in the World:
Big Brother or Brotherhood?   263

Politics and the Pursuit of Happiness   287

Appendix   299

Index   339

Introduction

Thus we presume to write, as it were, upon things that exist not, and travel by maps yet unmade.

> *Walt Whitman*
> *Democratic Vistas*

In a letter to John Adams, his political foe but personal friend, Thomas Jefferson defended the American government both men had helped to create on the grounds that it provided the best means of elevating what he called "the natural aristocracy" into the offices of government.[1] Jefferson defined the natural aristocracy as one based upon "virtue" and "talent" rather than upon wealth and birth.

In a world where "talent" is associated with the arts or show business rather than with politics, and where the word *virtue* takes on a somewhat quaint, priggish, and old-fashioned connotation, Jefferson's definition may require some additional explanation. By *talent* he meant, simply, the ability to govern well and effectively, "to manage the concerns of society," as he put it. What Jefferson meant by *virtue* is not so easily understood. It had to do with certain qualities that today we might associate with statesmanship, qualities such as wisdom, self-control, vision, and perhaps most importantly, the ability to provide moral leadership to one's fellow citizens. Moral leadership does not require or even imply that a person must live as a saint. Certainly Thomas Jefferson was not a saint. He owned slaves, although he himself often denounced the moral horror of slavery. There is evidence that he may even have had children conceived outside of wedlock. And there are other charges that could be and have been leveled at Jefferson the private individual.[2] But it is quite another matter to fault Jefferson the statesman, who, with the power of his imagination, his words, and his deeds, helped create "a new man and a new earth." Moral leadership implies the ability to postulate ends for a society, whereas "talent" is largely concerned with finding means. In the Jeffersonian sense, the moral

---

[1] The question of a natural versus a hereditary aristocracy is the subject of a letter to John Adams, written from Monticello on October 28, 1813. The Jefferson–Adams correspondence, comprising more than 150 letters between the two old political foes, began in 1812 and continued until both men died on the same day, July 4, 1826. The letter to John Adams on true aristocracy appears in Scully Bradley, Richard C. Beatty, E. H. Long, and George Perkins, *The American Tradition of Literature* (New York: Grosset, 1956), Vol. 1.

[2] Gore Vidal's novel, *Burr* (N.Y.: Bantam, 1973), presents a most unflattering view of Jefferson as an unscrupulous politician and hypocrite.

leader is one who enlightens and ennobles, as opposed to a leader who merely administers society.

If today there is "no virtue in the Republic," as *Harper's* editor Lewis H. Lapham has suggested,[3] Jefferson would grieve to know it. He relied upon the common people because he believed that such people would demand "virtue" from their leaders. He knew, of course, that there were ambitious individuals, then as now, who might lead the country into defeat, disgrace, and failure. But he believed that the people, aided by education, would find the wisdom to reject the blandishments of the "pseudo-aristoi" and to select leaders who belonged to the "natural aristocracy."

In a certain sense, the 1976 presidential campaign was contested on these grounds. Specific questions of public policy seemed less important than did the character and personality of the candidates. Jimmy Carter swept to the Democratic nomination under a banner proclaiming "Trust me." President Ford was chosen to lead the Republican party into the campaign despite a powerful challenge from former California Governor Ronald Reagan, less because Ford had provided the nation with brilliant leadership in the two years since President Nixon resigned than because Ford was perceived as a decent, honest, sane man. Indeed, an Election Day poll of voters by CBS News found 54 percent of the respondents listing "trust in government" as the most important issue of the campaign.

This could be contrasted with the 1972 campaign, when Senator George McGovern captured his party's nomination largely because he took a position on controversial issues, such as the Vietnam war, that agreed with that of many Democratic primary voters. McGovern was then soundly defeated by Richard Nixon in November, partly because of his (McGovern's) stand on these same issues.

The 1976 campaign focused on questions of morality and the personal integrity of the candidates, in part because of Watergate, Vietnam, and a steady barrage of scandals involving highly placed Congressmen and once-sacrosanct institutions such as the FBI and the CIA. There may also have been something deeper at work: a dimly perceived and largely unarticulated belief that all of the blunders, scandals, and stupidities that had made the very word *Washington* into a kind of epithet were merely the tip of the iceberg and America was the Titanic. Had events and the passage of time brought the nation to a point where decency, moderation, common sense, ordinary civility, and competence were the exception rather than the rule? Was there some fatal flaw at work among us, in the people or the system or both, that made high tragedies such as Vietnam and the fall of Richard Nixon or low comedies such as the Congressman Wayne Hays–Elizabeth Ray fiasco absolutely inevitable? Was the United States destined to follow Greece, Rome, and the gilded aristocracies of nineteenth-century Europe,

[3] *Harper's* (Aug. 1976).

3

into decline and fall? Marxists throughout much of the world believed this and acted with a growing certainty of impending triumph. But it was not a foreign enemy that frightened most Americans, as had been true at the height of the Cold War or when Hitler was on the march in the 1930s. Rather, it seemed to be something here at home, something happening to ourselves. Clearly it was an era of introspection. That America was, to some degree, turning inward and away from the world was a common-place observation in the post-Vietnam era. If political activism and the quest for a better world and a more rational society at home characterized the college generation of the late 1960s, what Tom Wolfe called "the age of Me" [4] surely dominated the late 1970s. The decline in political activism among the young was offset by a sharp increase in religiosity. Along with rising church attendance among the more traditional faiths, a thousand strange new spiritual flowers bloomed (scientology, transcendental meditation, Hare Krishna), most stressing in one form or another the quest for a purely personal peace or happiness rather than social justice. Many of the erstwhile radical leaders of the 1960s became celebrated converts to the more exotic new faiths. The popular governor of the most populous state, California, and a strong if tardy candidate for the Democratic presidential nomination, Jerry Brown, was a self-proclaimed mystic, answering reporters' questions with Buddhist-like questions of his own. Religion became an issue in 1976 in a way that it never had been before in American political history. For while the question of John Kennedy's and Al Smith's Catholicism had been an important factor in previous national campaigns, never before had a candidate's personal religious views been as central to his candidacy as Jimmy Carter's "born-again" experience. In a sense, the Carter campaign seemed to suggest that America must be "born again."

Thus the 1976 campaign may have represented a nation attempting to regenerate itself morally and spiritually and to find its roots, roots that had been attacked by defeat and self-doubt.[5] When Ronald Reagan (who, incidentally, also claimed to have had a "born-again" experience) conceded defeat to Gerald Ford before his tearful supporters at the Republican National Convention, he invoked a phrase originated by Puritan John Winthrop: a vision of America as "the City on a Hill." Like a city on a hill, America would be "the light of the world," "the New Jerusalem." This idealistic vision of ourselves is a recurrent theme in American life and history, from Winthrop to the abolitionists, from Walt Whitman to

[4] "The Me Decade," *New West Magazine* (Aug. 30, 1976).
[5] The Louis Harris Poll of August 24, 1976 indicated that in a cross-section of the voters, nationwide, Carter was given high marks by the voters (73–11 percent approval) for "not being part of the Washington establishment." Fifty-three percent agreed that he was a "deeply religious man, and this is important to me this year in choosing a president."

Woodrow Wilson to John Kennedy. Through much of our history, we seemed to believe that we had a duty to serve as a kind of beacon for an errant mankind. Thus in his campaign for the presidency, James Earl Carter stressed his determination to make Americans "proud" of their government. From time to time, he went so far as to point out that if elected, he would be the first farmer to occupy the presidency since Jefferson, hinting, perhaps, that he hoped to revive the eighteenth-century Jeffersonian tradition.

In 1933 Franklin Roosevelt perceived that the central challenge facing his administration was a restoration of confidence in an American economic system badly wounded by the Great Depression. He set about to rebuild and restore that confidence with a burst of legislation that, for good or ill, has permanently altered the shape of American society and that changed the life of many Americans. In 1977 President Carter perceived a similar crisis, no less real and perhaps even more threatening because it was spiritual rather than material. He sensed that his task would be to restore and rebuild America's faith in herself and her government and in that nebulous notion of "virtue" that Jefferson believed indispensable to the survival of the republic.

It is against this background and with these premises that we have undertaken to write still another book about American government and politics. Believing, as we do, that the issues of our time have less to do with the structure of institutions, including the government itself, than with the ideas that these structures reflect and that politics is less often a struggle for ends pursued by rational means than it is an embodiment of the complexities, passions, and ecstasies of the human mind and spirit, we have tried to create a book that mirrors the human realities of American political life as we encounter and deal with them in the streets, in the media, and in the voting booth, as well as in the classroom.

If it is the burden of the politician to act and of the voter to decide in the face of ambiguity, the student, we believe, has a different role, a role that is both easier and more difficult. For the student, the problem is not to act, or to decide, but to understand. How does this American government work? Is there an American political system? How is the system supposed to work? Who decides and how and why? Are we "free"? Is there a "power elite"? How did our government get to be the way it is? What could it be like in the future? And if we can help shape that future, how shall we do so and to what ends?

The problems of politics, we believe, are the problems of civil life. From a certain perspective, man is not a very impressive creature. He is not as strong as an ape nor as quick as a cat. He is not particularly well endowed to withstand extremes of heat or cold or to survive without food, water, and rest. "The weakest and frailest of all creatures is man," said Montaigne, "and withal the proudest." Yet through politics, by learning to live and work together, human beings daily accomplish miracles, building oil pipe-lines across frozen Arctic wastelands, erecting great cities in the midst of inhospitable deserts, walking on the moon, filling the very air with the sound of music and human voices. All of this, in a very real sense, has been done through politics, that is, through the organization and direction of human thought and energy for the achievement of certain specific social goals. At the same time, we see much of the world's population continuing to endure extreme poverty, ignorance, and injustice. In the entire history of the world, there have rarely been times when a large part of the human race was not intent upon destroying another part through war. And even today the most "advanced" and "civilized" societies continue to devote much of their wealth and many of their finest minds to building, improving, and using instruments of mass destruction. That too is politics.

The study of government is the study of humanity. Focusing as we do upon one nation, America, means that we are studying ourselves, our past, our present, and perhaps our future—what we have been and what we hope to be, not as individuals, necessarily, but as members of a society that nourishes and shapes us all.

Shine, Perishing Republic

The American Success Story: Is It Over?
•
The Positive Argument
•
The Negative Argument

Epochs sometimes occur in the life of a nation when the old customs of a people are changed, public morality is destroyed, religious belief shaken, and the spell of tradition broken, when the diffusion of knowledge is yet imperfect and the civil rights of the community are ill secured . . . the country then assumes a dim and dubious shape in the eyes of its citizens; they no longer behold it in the soil they inhabit . . . nor in the usages of their forefathers; nor in religion, which they doubt, nor in the laws, which do not originate in their own authority; nor in the legislator, whom they fear and despise. . . . The country is lost to their senses . . . and they retire into a narrow and unenlightened selfishness.

Alexis de Tocqueville
Democracy in America

While this America settles in the mould of its vulgarity; heavily thickening to empire,
And protest, only a bubble in the molten mass, pops and sighs out, and the mass hardens.
I sadly smiling remember that the flower fades to make fruit, the fruit rots to make earth.
Out of the mother; and through the spring exultances, ripeness and decadence; and home to the mother.

Robinson Jeffers
*Shine, Perishing Republic**

James Earl Carter's path to the American presidency confirms one of the central myths of American life, that ours is an "open society" in which almost anyone can accomplish almost anything given talent, hard work, determination, and boundless faith in oneself. It is difficult to imagine the Carter phenomenon happening anywhere else in the civilized world. In most countries it is all but impossible for an individual to become the head of a major government without the approval and support of the established party and governmental bureaucracies, the ruling interests, and/or the mass media. An obscure farmer–politician from a remote area, largely unknown to the people, unrecognized by the media, on the fringe of his own party's power structure, simply could not take power in England

A modern skyscraper captures the image of an older style of architecture near Lafayette Park in Los Angeles. "First we shape our buildings," Winston Churchill said, "then our buildings shape us." [Photo by Dean Immenschuh, Upland, Calif.]

or France or Germany or Russia or China without leading a successful revolution. Virtually the only path to power, short of armed rebellion, in any of these nations lies in decades of hard and patient service to the party. Normally, a successful politician gradually wins the respect and approval of his party's leadership.

Carter's victory seems to confirm the fundamental premise of democratic government, that power to select the leadership of society shall be vested in the people.

Beginning with virtually no national power base or recognition by the public; relying mostly upon the support of his immediate family and friends; speaking at first to small groups of people, often numbering no more than five or ten at a time; building support; fighting his way through thirty primary campaigns and a national convention and then defeating an incumbent President who was widely respected and almost universally liked, Carter's election was a textbook example of democratic theory carried into the realm of practical politics. Whether his administration is successful or not, his manner of winning the Presidency will be a source of study and amazement to historians and politicians, here and abroad, for many years into the future.

Moreover, in a world where a transfer of political power from one regime or faction to another is often accompanied by civil tumult, mass arrests, and imprisonment or execution of the leaders of the defeated faction, the manner in which power was transferred from Gerald R. Ford to James Earl Carter is worth noting. After a long, close, and sometimes bitter campaign, the civility and mutual expressions of respect that marked the actual transference of power from one man and regime to another represented a kind of unspoken testimony to the stability and success of the American political system.

But despite an auspicious beginning, it was by no means certain that the Carter administration would be able to deal successfully with the problems that seemed about to tear America apart during the turbulent 1960s and early 1970s. Racial conflict, unemployment, inflation, and the energy crisis were no less serious matters because Jimmy Carter enjoyed high ratings in the public opinion polls in the early months of his administration. Nor were world affairs any less complex or menacing. And if the problems were not dealt with, sooner or later the polls would reflect these facts.

The American Success Story: Is It Over?

John F. Kennedy often made the point that the United States, although a relatively young nation, was the world's oldest democracy, with an unbroken tradition of two centuries of representative government. The young President reflected a pride in the past and a confidence in the immediate future shared by most Americans in the early 1960s. There indeed seemed to exist ample reason for this confidence. The United States was, it seemed, unquestionably the strongest, the wealthiest, and the most stable democracy on earth. While some Americans may have remained abjectly poor (largely as the result of their own indolence, it was commonly argued), the great majority (about 80 percent) were enjoying the benefits of the most affluent society in human history. [1] Automobiles, television sets, packaged foods, and stylish clothing poured out of the seemingly bottomless cornucopia. Our military forces, scattered throughout the world, defended not only our own borders but much of the non-Communist world. And after eight years of leadership by President Dwight Eisenhower, domestic political strife had muted to the point where scholars were writing about the "end of ideology" in America.[2] Said sociologist C. Wright Mills:

> Underneath this style of observation and comment there is the assumption that in the West there are no more real issues or even problems of great seriousness. The mixed economy plus the welfare state—that is the formula.
>
> *C. Wright Mills*
> *White Collar*

Moreover, in the midst of this unprecedented material abundance, the ordinary United States citizen enjoyed personal freedom, high mobility, and easy access to education and information. Thus a case could be and often was made that the United States was the most successful society in human history, at least in terms of Jeremy Bentham's classic statement on the proper aim of government (published, incidentally, in 1776, the year of the Declaration of Independence): "the greatest good of the greatest number." And it was widely held that at the core of the American Success Story was the political system created by the unsurpassed wisdom of the Founding Fathers, who had created the framework that made possible the freedom and stability President Kennedy celebrated.

Today, more than a decade later, we should be hard-pressed indeed to find a national leader who could summon up the soaring confidence that characterized President Kennedy's First Inaugural Address.

A succession of bitter and largely unprecedented blows has shaken American confidence and forced us to question ideas and institutions that seemed faultless only a few years ago. The Presidency, the armed forces, public schools, colleges and universities, the mass media, the CIA, the Congress, even the Postal Service, all of which seemed so serenely benevolent, have come under unprecedented attack and suffered a clear decline in public confidence. The mere listing of some of the more traumatic events of the past decade and a half leaves little doubt as to why this has come about:

[1] Michael Harrington, *The Other America* (New York: Macmillan, 1962), challenged the widespread assumption that affluence in America was universal and is said to have influenced President Kennedy (and later President Lyndon Johnson) in the formulation of the War on Poverty programs.
[2] Daniel Bell, *The End of Ideology* (New York: Free Press, 1960).

11

President Kennedy was assassinated. His murder was followed all too quickly by the assassinations of his brother Robert Kennedy and the nation's most eminent civil-rights leader, Dr. Martin Luther King, Jr., and by an attempt upon the life of leading presidential candidate, Governor George C. Wallace of Alabama, which left the governor crippled.

The United States fought a long, bloody, unpopular, and—in the opinion of most Americans as measured by the polls—largely useless war in Southeast Asia.

The Watergate affair, the greatest political scandal in the nation's history, culminated in the resignation of President Richard Nixon in the face of impending impeachment by the Congress. Earlier, the Vice President, Spiro Agnew, had resigned in a separate and unrelated scandal, so that for the first time in United States history the Presidency was occupied by a man—Gerald R. Ford—who had not been elected by the people.

Urban riots swept almost every major city in America in the late 1960s. Crime rates soared to unprecedented heights, to the point where President Ford's Director of the FBI (Clarence Kelley) spoke gloomily about the possibility that the nation might be compelled to create a national police force and former Attorney General William Saxbe predicted that if means were not found to reverse the trend, vigilante groups would start taking the law into their own hands. The Attorney General called his own administration's highly publicized War on Crime "a harsh, bitter and dismaying failure." [3]

The same or similar words were used to describe the results of President Lyndon B. Johnson's equally heralded War on Poverty. A decade after the start of a multibillion-dollar crusade to eliminate poverty in America, unemployment rates among blacks and other minorities were substantially higher than when it began (jobless rates of 25–50 percent among minority youths were common in the mid-1970s), and the nation's ghettos were simply ten years older. [4]

Many of the nation's colleges and universities became battlegrounds as resistance to the Vietnam war centered in the educated young. A substantial number of alienated intellectuals concluded that only radical change, not excluding the possibility of armed rebellion, could cure "American imperialism."

The dollar was twice devalued in the early years of the Nixon era. The stock market plunged to levels that created paper losses as great as or greater than those accompanying the 1929 crash. Commenting upon the economic impact of the Nixon years, liberal economist John Kenneth Galbraith noted that no one since Lenin had presided over so great a

---

[3] *Los Angeles Times* (Sept. 25, 1974), Part 1, p. 1.
[4] For further information see *New York Times* (Oct. 1, 1974), for a report on President Ford's economic summit conference.

[Editorial cartoon by Paul Conrad. Copyright ©
1977, Los Angeles Times. Reprinted with permission.]

liquidation of capital. "A costly lesson, probably unlearned," he concluded in the pessimistic style of the day.[5]

A foreboding undercurrent to this economic decline was that in the
early 1970s the real income of the average American worker began to go
down rather than up as a consequence of the worst inflation in the nation's
history.[6] To complicate further the apparent economic crisis of the 1970s,
Americans were confronted with an energy shortage that seemingly would
make things only worse. The unusually severe winter of 1977 underscored the problem of limited sources of natural gas and oil, two resources used in ever greater amounts by Americans. In April 1977, President Carter warned the American people of a possible "national catas-
trophe" if the nation failed to cut sharply its consumption of energy.

This litany of horrors could be continued almost indefinitely; widespread
drug abuse among the young, the growth of an alienated "counterculture"
and an ominous counter to the counterculture from "hard hats" and gun-

---

[5] John Kenneth Galbraith, *Newsweek* (Aug. 19, 1974), p. 52.
[6] Robert J. Donovan, *Los Angeles Times* (Sept. 16, 1974), Part 2, p. 7.

13

loving "mid-Americans," soaring welfare rolls, and repeated warnings from eminent scientists of an impending ecological Armageddon. All of these combined to transform the image of an American "demiparadise" into that of a troubled, impotent giant. In the late 1950s a transplanted French intellectual spoke of America as *God's Country and Mine.*[7] By the early 1970s another French intellectual, counting himself an admirer of American society, was forced to conclude that "America is suffering from what strikes this European observer as a nervous break-down."[8]

Other Europeans described our difficulties in less sympathetic terms. Thus when President Ford granted private citizen Richard Nixon a "full, free and unconditional pardon" for any and all unspecified crimes committed during Nixon's incumbency, the London *Times* noted that in the United States, after all, "There is one law for the powerful and another for the ordinary citizen," and the Paris *Le Monde* noted, "The most powerful democracy in the world, which once commiserated with the poor Europeans for not liquidating their traces of feudalism, has given us a masterly lesson in princely absolutism."[9]

While some of the individuals who presided over these events found themselves under attack and in some cases driven from political power, many Americans, witnessing a nation seeming to reel from crisis to crisis— where in Thoreau's words, "Events are in the saddle and drive mankind"— began to raise questions not about this or that specific leader or policy but about the very nature of the system itself. Some of the basic American institutions, not excluding the Constitution itself, which had been venerated for most of our history, were being examined as candidates for revision and/or liquidation.

Former New Deal braintruster Rexford Tugwell, of the Center for the Study of Democratic Institutions put forth a formal proposal that the time had come to draft a new American Constitution.[10] At the height of national anxiety about the impending impeachment of President Nixon, the Congress was deluged by proposed revisions in the nature and power of the Presidency, most of them aimed at moving America toward something akin to a European parliamentary system. It was suggested that the President be compelled to resign upon passage of a "no-confidence" motion by two thirds of both houses. Various members of the House and the Senate advanced proposals for giving Congress the right to call a new national election. Historian Barbara Tuchman proposed that we get rid of the Presidency and substitute a six-man council of state. It was even suggested

[7] Jacques Barzun, (Boston: Little, Brown, 1954).
[8] Jean Louis Servan-Schreiber, *The Power to Inform* (New York: McGraw-Hill, 1974).
[9] *Los Angeles Times* (Sept. 9, 1974).
[10] R. G. Tugwell, *Model for a New Constitution* (Santa Barbara, Calif.: Center for the Study of Democratic Institutions, 1970).

14

that Congress abolish both itself *and* the Presidency, in the spirit of fair play.[11]

Moreover the underlying assumptions of a democratic society, upon which the legal system of democracy rested, were themselves under critical attack.

Ecologist and political scientist William Ophals reflected an idea increasingly in vogue among environmentalists when he wrote:

> In a crowded world . . . the grip of planning and social control will become more and more complete. The random behavior of individuals cannot be permitted. In the new era of scarcity . . . the inalienable right of the individual to get as much as he can is a prescription for disaster. It follows that the political system inherited from our forefathers is moribund.[12]

The *New York Times*'s James Reston brooded about the difficulties and dangers that were in wait for a democratic society forced to adjust to "a revolution of falling expectations."

Maybe these fears would prove to be too pessimistic, as has been the case (thus far) with those intellectuals who once predicted nuclear annihilation as the inevitable result of the Cold War.

Since prophecy is outside the province of this work, it might be useful to summarize the arguments of both sides of this debate, that is, of those who hold that American society has entered an era of crisis leading to dissolution of the republic and of those who hold that the American system, for all of its recent trials, remains viable and is still, in Lincoln's words, mankind's "last best hope."

The Positive Argument

Those who take a positive view of the future often argue:

1. Despite all of our problems, it remains true that the American people continue to enjoy one of the highest living standards in the world's history and the greatest degree of personal freedom to be found anywhere on earth, in this or any other era.

2. Education and opportunities for cultural and intellectual advance remain abundantly available, and the percentage of young people (eighteen to twenty-four years of age) who go on to some form of higher education

[11] Barbara Tuchman, "Should We Abolish the Presidency?" *New York Times* (Feb. 13, 1973); also see Arthur M. Schlesinger, Jr., *The Imperial Presidency* (Boston: Houghton, 1973).
[12] *Harper's* (Apr. 1974).

is about 50 percent of the total population, whereas early in the century it was closer to 4 percent.[13]

3. The threat of imminent nuclear annihilation, a very real one through most of the past three decades, has now significantly receded as the result of United States–Soviet and United States–Chinese detente that has replaced the policies of the Cold War. In the long run, this cannot but have enormous positive consequences for all mankind, and particularly for the American people.

4. Although many serious problems, such as inflation, energy shortages, and racial conflict, have not been successfully resolved, these problems have their counterparts in one form or another in every industrial society on earth. Instead of racial problems, Western Europe still struggles with the vestiges of class conflict. Communist countries may not experience much inflation or unemployment, but they tremble at the utterance of an unauthorized thought or the writing of a critical book.

5. Although persons high in the Nixon administration may have perpetrated serious assaults upon traditional American freedoms and values, the system proved equal to the challenge. Mr. Nixon and dozens of his associates were brought to disgrace, ruin, or imprisonment. Put to the test, the American system, unlike some European counterparts in the 1930s, did not collapse but rallied and brought to heel those who had overstepped the bounds of constitutional power. Perhaps only in the United States could there have been such an investigation of corruption at the *very highest level.*

6. In this test, the press, the courts, and finally the Congress worked well. Subject to immense pressure, the television networks and the newspapers insisted upon their right to criticize the President and were ultimately justified. The courts, challenged by an unprecedented extension of the doctrine of executive privilege, compelled the President and his men to obey the law. The Congress, while moving cautiously, nevertheless brought forth a bill of impeachment after a serious and thoughtful public debate watched by tens of millions of Americans on television. At no time during this process—despite the great passions involved, the high seriousness of the consequences, and the lack of any real precedent—was there even a suggestion of public disorder.

7. Despite the numerous traumas of the past decade, only a few Americans have abandoned their traditional preference for political leaders who at least appear to be moderate middle-of-the-roaders.[14] Fringe movements, such as the Black Panther party, the Klu Klux Klan, and the American Nazi party, have microscopic support at the farthest fringes of American

13 *Time* (Nov. 7, 1967), p. 33.
14 Richard M. Scammon and Ben J. Wattenberg, *The Real Majority* (New York: Coward, 1970).

16

society. A Gallup Poll released October 6, 1974 indicated that only 3.9 percent of the voters supported minority parties. In the 1976 presidential election, only 1 percent of the electorate did not vote for one of the two major candidates. Other polls show that despite public concern over crime and political instability, about 80 percent of the people remain adamantly opposed to the introduction of totalitarian techniques for maintaining order, such as wiretapping, mail monitoring, or search and seizure without a warrant.

8. Although "justice for all" remains more an ideal than a reality of daily life, minority groups, such as blacks, Mexican-Americans, and Indians, and victims of traditional prejudices, such as women, have become more militant, more visible, and to some degree more powerful than ever before. At least problems once swept under the rug of American life have been brought out into the open, a necessary first step to eventual resolution.

9. Culturally and intellectually the United States remains the most dynamic society on earth. Whether in pop arts, like music, or advanced scientific technical achievements, such as landing a man on the moon, the United States is still preeminent. In 1976 Americans swept the field among Nobel Prize winners, a sign of the society's continuing creativity and scientific preeminence.

10. Finally, abuses that have undeniably crept into the American system during three decades of unparalleled power and affluence are being recognized and dealt with. Congress has moved to reassert its constitutional balance with the executive branch. Serious corruption of the political process by private corporations and individuals, revealed as the result of the Watergate investigations, has led to a host of reform measures. The tone of skepticism, particularly toward politics and politicians, that has come to dominate public affairs in recent years is probably far healthier in an avowedly democratic society than the tone of reverence for any and all things American that characterized the 1950s.

Despite much talk of apathy and alienation in the mass media, the election of 1976 generated a substantial vote among the people (by modern American standards) and proved to be, on the whole, a spirited and clear-cut choice between a moderate conservative and a moderate liberal, very much in the traditional American pattern. There was little in the campaign, the candidates, or the results to suggest that the system had broken down. On the contrary, President Ford proved to be a well liked and fairly articulate exponent of the more-or-less traditional conservative view of society (governmental spending should be limited; inflation is a greater threat to society than unemployment; taxes should be cut; free enterprise should be encouraged), and Governor Carter represented a fairly traditional mainstream-liberal viewpoint (the government should use its power to stimulate the economy and reduce unemployment; the threat to the nation's cities and to the physical environment must receive a higher priority; the tax

17

system should be fundamentally changed; the public must be protected from the abuses of private corporations). Both men, while apparently lacking the "charisma" of a Kennedy, an Eisenhower, or a Roosevelt, were at least respected by most Americans. Apart from a handful of those who clamored for fundamental, even apocalyptic change, the candidates were sufficiently different to offer a clear and coherent choice. Had the candidates been Governor Ronald Reagan and Senator George McGovern, the choice would have been clearer; but in all likelihood the campaign would also have been far more bitter and divisive.

The Negative Argument

Let us now turn to those who make the counterargument:

1. Not since Dwight D. Eisenhower left the Presidency has an American President succeeded in serving out two full terms. President Kennedy was cut down by an assassin. Both Richard Nixon and Lyndon Johnson were, in effect, driven from office by a nation they could no longer hope to govern. Gerald Ford was defeated. After four successive Presidents failed to serve out their terms under anything like normal circumstances, some began to wonder if the nation had not become so complex, overgrown, and bitterly divided as to be ungovernable. Indeed, public confidence in politicians has fallen to an all-time low.[15]

2. Decades of unbridled affluence and power have produced a level of both spiritual and physical pollution that may well be irreversible. Along with filthy air, rivers so polluted as to constitute a fire hazard, and foodstuffs so adulterated by potentially poisonous chemicals as to produce a standing threat to the health of every American, there has come a mass explosion of pornography, crime, drug abuse, and generally declining standards of personal conduct and public morality that suggests the last days of Rome.

3. Despite the best efforts of do-gooders and liberals, the American people have not been able to solve their most urgent domestic problems: racism and poverty (and their deadly offspring, crime and urban decay). Rather than face and deal with these problems, most middle-class Americans have fled from the city to the suburb, erecting walls in the form of zoning ordinances that effectively prevent integration. American cities in the North are more segregated today than they were when the civil-rights movement was launched in the late 1950s. Furthermore, the cities are dying, that is, becoming places where almost no one would choose to live and raise a family if another choice existed. In New York City, one in

---

[15] A Gallup Poll of September 1973 listed politicians ninth in a field of ten in the matter of personal trustworthiness. Only used-car salesmen ranked lower.

18

every five families is on welfare. There are said to be at least two hundred thousand heroin addicts in the city. One result has been the much-publicized danger that the city will go bankrupt. New York's fate awaits virtually every major American city. And as its cities go, so will go the nation.

4. The middle class, traditionally the bulwark of American society, is being systematically denuded of its sources of material and spiritual strength. As an illustration, private-home ownership, long a cherished American ideal, is in general decline. Given a continuation of prevailing trends in the cost of financing and constructing a home, responsible authorities in the home building field estimate that 80 percent of the nation's families will be denied the opportunity to buy a home by 1980.[16] Even in Los Angeles, a city where home ownership has traditionally been very high, in 1974 there were more people renting apartments than buying homes for the first time in this century.

As inflation continues to erode the practical ability to afford the highly publicized "good life" that Americans have come to expect, the middle class may abandon its traditional preference for "middle-of-the-road" politics and attend more carefully to demagogues promising desperate remedies.

5. As measured by the most fundamental act of citizenship in a democracy—voting—Americans are growing steadily less and less enchanted with "politics as usual." From a historic high of almost 80 percent participation in the voting processes in 1880, the percentage of Americans of voting age bothering to exercise the franchise has dropped in recent years to around 50 percent.

6. In 1971, according to Pentagon figures, 7.3 percent of all U.S. Army personnel deserted, a rate many times greater than that during either World War II or the Korean War. Authorities in the military have placed the number of heroin addicts returning from Southeast Asia as high as one third of total returnees. What is happening to the army is occurring to a greater or lesser degree to many if not most of the fundamental institutions of society. Traditional churches are losing ground, particularly among the young, to exotic cults such as flourished in Rome during the dying days of the empire. Courts are jammed beyond belief, with some counties faced with as many as thirty-five thousand criminal cases awaiting trials, which may take years before being heard. Major railroads and airlines are in or near bankruptcy, and public transportation gets worse and worse. Prisons are riotous. In the winter of 1973–1974, Americans were confronted with the unthinkable: inability to buy enough gasoline to keep their automobiles running. By 1976 we were even more dependent upon foreign supplies of oil than in 1974.

16 *The Nation's Housing Needs, 1975 to 1985,* (Cambridge, Mass.: MIT–Harvard Joint Center for Urban Studies, 1977).

7. Although much has been made of the positive elements in the nation's response to Watergate, the fact is that this unprecedented scandal did occur, and moreover, it occurred in an administration that had won the electoral vote in 49 out of 50 states, one of the most overwhelming endorsements by the people in American history. Richard Nixon was well-known to the American people. With the possible exception of Franklin D. Roosevelt, he has probably been the most widely scrutinized politician in this century. (Nixon ran in five national campaigns and was four times a winner.) Moreover, many of the essential facts about Watergate were known before November of 1972, when President Nixon received his "mandate." They were published in the *Washington Post* and broadcast on national television. Even Spiro Agnew's curious financial dealings had been described in the *New York Times* prior to the election. But the people simply were not very interested. It was not public demand, but a handful of individuals in the press, the courts, and the Congress who forced the nation to face up to Watergate and its meaning for American democracy. After the Senate Watergate committee's televised revelations had laid bare most of the facts about Watergate and the ensuing "cover-up," *Newsweek* magazine found few Americans who believed the President should resign or be impeached. Almost until the very end, there was no great public pressure for either Nixon or Agnew to resign—certainly no demonstrations or public protests such as have accompanied the bussing of school-children to achieve racial balance. One could make a case that the average citizen, upon whose judgment and concern the American system must ultimately rest, simply does not care about political corruption unless it touches his life and income directly and that he often fails to complain even when it does. He has, in fact, retreated, in de Tocqueville's phrase, into "a narrow and unenlightened selfishness."

8. Reference has already been made to the fact that from 10 to 20 percent of the American people—as many as 40 million people—continue to live in poverty despite three decades of unparalleled national affluence, a much-publicized national War on Poverty and incessant official boasting about the blessings of America's free-enterprise system. In fact, many countries, such as the Scandinavian nations, have succeeded in virtually eliminating slums and dire poverty, whereas America's ghettos and Appalachias continue to fester and breed crime, disease, and appalling waste of human life and potential.

The persistence of widespread poverty—and unemployment rates generally much higher than those that most Western European states regard as socially acceptable—raises a question as to whether or not the American ideal of equal opportunity for all must in fact remain meaningless rhetoric for tens of millions of Americans who happen to be born with the wrong pigmentation or in the wrong part of the country. And just as President Lincoln once asked, "Can this nation endure half slave and half free?" to-

20

day some people are asking, "Can this nation endure four-fifths affluent and one-fifth poverty-stricken?"

9. America's self-image as freedom's global champion and righteous defender suffered an agonizing blow as a result of the Vietnam tragedy. Those who have argued that Vietnam was not just a mistake, however terrible, but the inevitable fruit of the "arrogance of power" can point to such events as the disclosure of the CIA's clumsy and brutal interference in the domestic affairs of Chile, helping to pave the way for the overthrow of a legally elected government, coupled with support of fascist dictatorships, such as the regime of the Greek colonels, to make a deadly argument: the United States, once the embodiment of human aspirations for personal freedom and a decent material life to much of the world, has now become a reactionary power actively conspiring through force and guile to suppress precisely those ideals of a better life that led to our own Revolution.

By, in effect, shedding its historic role as a model and an inspiration to other developing nations (North Vietnam's 1945 Declaration of Independence, for example, closely paralleled the wording of the 1776 American Declaration) and assuming the burden of global policeman, the United States has too often placed itself squarely in opposition to the legitimate national and social aspirations of much of mankind. The consequence is that America, only a few decades ago the most widely admired nation in the world, is today at least a serious rival of the USSR for the role of the most feared and hated. And despite unprecedented generosity in some areas, such as the gift of over $25 billion in free food to needier nations over the past two decades, the United States often finds itself almost isolated in times of international crisis. (An example of this was the 1973 Mideast war, when efforts by the United States to supply its ally, Israel, were seriously hampered by the refusal of most of its allies on the European continent to cooperate in staging operations and, indeed, to follow the lead of the United States in support of Israel.)

10. The shift of capital from the United States and Western Europe to the Arab states as the result of a sudden quadrupling of oil prices in 1974 threatens to undermine the economies of many of the major non-Communist powers and could conceivably result in the destruction of the international system of mutual trade and economic interdependence supporting the non-Communist world, a system ultimately based upon the preeminence of the American dollar and the strength of the American economy. In 1976 three of America's closest allies—Mexico, Italy, and England—were faced with a collapsing currency, growing unemployment, falling production, and rampant inflation. If this pattern is not reversed, or if it should spread, there is, according to some political, social, and economic leaders in Europe and Asia, the possibility of a reversion to the pattern of the 1930s, when nation after nation embraced totalitarian solutions to the

21

problems of the Great Depression and, when these solutions proved illusory, proceeded to the final solution: war.

11. Finally, there is evidence that the moral underpinnings of American society are in danger. The ideals implicit in the Declaration of Independence—equal justice under the law and the right to life, liberty, and the pursuit of happiness—were in Carl Becker's words:

> founded upon a naive faith in the instinctive virtues of human kind. . . .
> [This was] a humane and engaging faith. At its best it preached toleration
> in place of persecution, goodwill in place of hate, peace in place of war.
> It taught that beneath all local and temporary diversity, all men are
> equal in the possession of a common humanity.[17]

The idea of a "common humanity" has been severely strained by the events of the past decade. In place of "goodwill and toleration," we have had "enemy lists" and paranoia.[18]

The new critics of American society insist that it is superficial to believe that we have arrived at the present impasse because John Kennedy was murdered, or because Lyndon Johnson foolishly escalated an unwinnable war, or because Richard Nixon and some of his aides were wicked.

Closer to the truth, they insist, is that American society is under a profound pressure of a new, terrifying, and perhaps unresolvable kind and that in the face of these new conditions, our traditional way of life and the political system that evolved from the Constitutional Convention of 1787 is indeed becoming moribund.

A loose but practical test of these two viewpoints was provided by the 1976 presidential campaign. President Ford, as the incumbent, took a generally optimistic tone about the nation and its problems, as reflected by his campaign theme song, "I'm Feeling Good About America." Governor Carter, on the other hand, although stressing his faith in the soundness of the people, charged that the government had lost all sense of direction and leadership. The closeness of the result and the uncertainty and confusion that existed in the minds of many voters, reflected by the very high number of "undecideds" measured by the polls right up to the eve of the election, probably reflected a certain ambivalence within the minds of the American people about the future of their society and the direction they would have the nation take.

Even before taking office Jimmy Carter began to unfold a strategy clearly aimed at a restoration of confidence. Carter well understood that the "credibility gap" that had opened between the American people and their President in the Lyndon Johnson administration as a result of the Viet-

[17] *The Declaration of Independence* (New York: Vintage, 1958).
[18] John Dean, *Blind Ambition* (New York: Simon & Schuster, 1976).

22

nam war had widened to a veritable chasm during the Nixon years. Carter undertook a series of largely symbolic gestures: walking down Pennsylvania Avenue on Inaugural Day, taking random phone calls from the people on a radio talk show, and dispensing with much of the pomp and ceremony that had grown up around the White House (announcing, for example, that he intended to sell the presidential yacht). That the new President's efforts to signal an open administration were understood and appreciated by the American people was clearly indicated by public opinion polls, and by the fact that they virtually deluged the White House with an average 87,000 letters and 20,000 to 30,000 phone calls each week. (The Ford administration had received an average 15,000 to 20,000 letters each week.)[19]

However, the President's substantive proposals, ranging from his "human rights" initiative in foreign policy to proposals for stimulating the economy, energy conservation, and tax reform at home, ran into powerful opposition at home and abroad.

Whether or not the new administration will succeed in reversing the dismal chain of events that has engulfed the United States since the Kennedy assassination remains to be seen. But the question of whether the American republic will emerge from its trials a wiser and a stronger nation, or whether it is destined to follow a historically well-marked path of gradual decline, will not be answered by one President or by one administration. The answer ultimately must lie in the American people themselves and in their capacity to respond to the burdens and opportunities that their wealth and power have created.

[19] *Los Angeles Times* (Apr. 16, 1977), p. 1.

23

The Pursuit of Happiness

What Is an American?
•
The Puritan Thesis
•
The Frontier Thesis
•
The Melting-Pot Thesis
•
Popular Culture and the American Character
•
Materialism
•
Racism
•
Mobility
•
The Cult of Youth
•
American Values

This is what you shall do; Love the earth and sun and the animals, despise riches, give alms to everyone that asks, stand up for the stupid and crazy, devote your income and labor to others, hate tyrants, argue not concerning God . . . take off your hat to nothing known or unknown . . . re-examine all you have been told at school or church or in any book, dismiss whatever insults your soul, and your very flesh shall be a great poem.

Walt Whitman
Preface to Leaves of Grass

Although the Constitution defines the legal framework of American government, and documents such as the Declaration of Independence set forth the principles of the American political system, there remains another factor that critically influences the practice of politics in this nation: American culture.

Culture refers to a given group's common ideas, values, attitudes, beliefs, and behavior. The definition includes the material and technological state of a given society. Culture is normally passed on from generation to generation, although it is sometimes subject to rapid change. The language we speak is part of our culture, as are the clothes we wear, the machines we use, and the ideas we believe to be eternally true.

Government does not consist wholly of passing laws and making speeches. Inevitably it shapes, and is shaped by, the culture of the society. The Declaration of Independence may proclaim that "all men are created equal" and Congress may legislate and judges issue edicts designed to enforce this principle, but if the people do not in fact believe in equality of races, racism will persist.

Nothing in the Constitution precludes a woman or a black person from being elected President. But our culture has in fact prevented this from occurring, thus far at least.

What Is an American?

People speak, imprecisely, of "German thoroughness" or "Italian devotion to family" or "the Englishman's sense of fair play." Such phrases assume, despite obvious exceptions, that it is possible to generalize about the values and the behavior of a given people or nation. But is it possible to speak sensibly about an "American culture"? For America is a relatively new nation made up of people from virtually every race and culture on earth. Germans, generally, are fair-skinned and Italians, generally, are dark. What is the American complexion? Was Jack Armstrong the "All-American Boy"? If so, what about those Americans whose names are Morales or Epstein? What about females? Who and what decided that they cannot be "All-American"?

> Almost every conceivable value or trait has at one time or another been imputed to American culture by authoritative observers.
>
> *Lee Coleman*
> *"What Is American: A Study*
> *of Alleged American Traits,"*
> *Social Forces, 19 (1941)*

It may be impossible to define "the American character," but we nevertheless seem to find it necessary to try. Or so at least it has seemed to innumerable writers, sages, politicians, newspaper editorial writers, and sponsors of high-school essay contests that begin with the phrase "I am an American because . . ." The phrase "the American way of life" has become a cliché of our political, commercial, and ceremonial rhetoric. What does it mean? One is tempted to conclude that one way to define an American is that he is forever trying to define America.

Most of the studies made of American character and culture have tended to focus upon one of three epochs in our history: the Puritan period, the conquest of the frontier, and the mass migration of Europeans that occurred in the late nineteenth and early twentieth centuries and that is symbolized by the Statue of Liberty. Most people who write or speak about America tend to focus upon one of these three eras and then argue that this was the crucial element that defined the American experience. Such arguments can be labeled as: the Puritan thesis, the frontier thesis, and the melting-pot thesis. The Puritan thesis tends to emphasize that period of our history from the landing at Plymouth Rock (1620) until the Revolutionary War era. It stresses the religious and idealistic motivations of the early settlers of New England, the notion of America as the "New Jerusalem," John Winthrop's belief that America would be like a "city on a hill" to become a model for older, more sinful Europe.[1] From this standpoint, America can be seen as a newer and perhaps better extension of an old idea, the idea of a distinct Western civilization that used to be called Christendom. The frontier thesis stresses the "winning of the West," roughly from the time of the Louisiana Purchase (1803) to the closing of the western frontier, which occurred about the end of the nineteenth century. The melting pot thesis dwells upon late nineteenth and early twentieth-

---

[1] "A Model of Christian Charity," in Perry Miller (Ed.), *The American Puritans* (New York: Anchor, 1956), p. 83.

century America and the millions who came here seeking refuge from poverty and oppression in Europe, seeking to find a "land of promise."

While each of these ideas expresses a certain truth about our national development, none of them is, by itself, adequate to explain the full range and complexity of American life. It should also be noted that the historical divisions implied by each of these theses are somewhat arbitrary. People were moving out into the frontier before the Louisiana Purchase and are still doing so today, in Alaska, for example. At the same time that the Puritans were developing a theocratic society in New England, other very different kinds of civilizations were emerging in places like New York and Virginia. And many critics of the melting-pot thesis still argue that it never really melted the various races and ethnic groups coming to America into "one nation indivisible, with liberty and justice for all."

Which of these ideas one chooses to cite as the "American heritage" is likely to have practical as well as purely theoretical consequences. Opponents of gun-control legislation, for example, often cite the frontier experience as providing a rationale for the idea that gun ownership is a natural "right" of Americans. Proponents of the Puritan thesis often invoke an essential element of that idea, the Protestant work ethic, as the basis for an attack upon the "immorality" of welfare.

On the other hand, those who argued in favor of federal aid to New York City when America's largest city faced imminent bankruptcy usually invoked the melting-pot thesis in one form or another, while those opposed to such aid usually responded by invoking the Puritan ethic.

In short, what we do today about the nation's problems is inevitably influenced by how we choose to interpret yesterday. The present is the hostage of the past.

The Puritan Thesis

Many nations have a "creation myth" that suggests that the beginnings of that particular nation were accomplished with the active assistance of the Almighty.[2] That the Pilgrims—and their later descendants, the Puritans— came here seeking to escape religious persecution and to found the "New Jerusalem" probably helped to make this particular group of European immigrants a more popular and likely choice for the role of America's "forefathers" than other groups that were settling other parts of America at about the same period. For the mundane fact that many Europeans

---

[2] An example is the story of Moses leading the Hebrews across the desert to establish the nation of Israel, which is the subject of Exodus in the Old Testament. Another example is the story of Romulus and Remus and the founding of Rome.

came to America seeking free real estate or to avoid military service or to escape imprisonment for crimes or debts is not the stuff of which national myths are made.

Implicit in the Puritan thesis is the belief that Puritan values, ideas, and customs explain much of the development of America historically and constitute the basis for the first truly American culture. The Puritans are usually credited with having given us the "Protestant work ethic," which laid the moral basis for America's economic growth. It is often argued that the city of Boston and Harvard College were the intellectual and cultural leaders of the nation, for Harvard was not only the nation's first university, it has remained the most eminent university in America. (For example, six of our last seven Secretaries of State have been Harvard men.) New Englanders like William Bradford created the nation's first literature, and later others like Nathaniel Hawthorne, Ralph Waldo Emerson, Henry David Thoreau, Henry Wadsworth Longfellow, and Oliver Wendell Holmes lifted that literature to a place where it could seriously rival the work of Europe's finest writers. New England's "Boston Brahmins" later proclaimed themselves the nation's cultivated, educated, and wealthy elite, and to some extent the claim was justified [3] (although the heirs of Jefferson and Washington, products of another kind of culture, would surely have disputed the point). From John Adams to Calvin Coolidge, the Calvinist belief in hard work, self-reliance, and stern morality heavily influenced the familiar image of the "hard-working, hard-driving American" hot in pursuit of what Henry James (another son of Harvard) once called the "Bitch Goddess of America, Success."

At the core of the Puritan culture was the notion of individual responsibility for the well-being of society. As one of the "elect of God," the Puritan bore a heavy sense of duty (which Wordsworth labeled the "Stern Daughter of the Voice of God") to improve not only himself but his neighbors, particulalry in matters of morality. This sense of duty can be seen in the dilemma of John Winthrop, who had serious misgivings about leaving England for the New World in 1630, even though Puritans were being heavily persecuted in England by Archbishop Laud. Winthrop finally convinced himself that in going to the New World he would be helping ultimately to reform English society rather than abandoning it. For when he landed in Massachusetts Bay, he is reputed to have said "men shall say of succeeding plantations: 'The Lord make it like that of New England.' " [4]

[3] Oliver Wendell Holmes, Sr. argues, in the novel *Elsie Venner,* "There is, however, in New England, an aristocracy, if you choose to call it so . . . it has grown to be a caste—not in any odious sense . . . which not to recognize is mere stupidity." Holmes goes on to argue that the Boston Brahmin is the natural intellectual and cultural leader of the American race.

[4] See Edmund S. Morgan, *The Puritan Dilemma* (Boston: Little, 1958), and Miller, p. 83.

In a sense, Winthrop's prophecy may be said to have been fulfilled when Winston Churchill, leading a desperately embattled Great Britain against Nazi Europe in the darkest days of World War II, called upon "the new world to come to the rescue of the old." Moreover, Winthrop's theme is reiterated throughout our history: in Washington's Farewell Address, in Lincoln's Gettysburg Address, in John F. Kennedy's Inaugural Address, and in President Carter's campaign for human rights.

The Puritan notion that it was America's duty to serve as an ideal for all mankind was at once noble and audacious. It gave America a sense of historic destiny, but it was also subject to abuse, as, for example, in the more recent practice of sending in the CIA (an agency largely dominated, incidentally, by Harvard-trained men) to topple governments that the American government happened to dislike.

The Puritan tradition accounts for much that is best and worst in American culture; the early agitation against slavery, for example, was centered in New England, as was the movement for free public education. Along with it came a certain smug self-righteousness implicit in those who on the assumption that they are "the best and the brightest" presume to improve other people's morals.

The Puritan's intense sense of social responsibility was not shared by other Americans struggling to build homes and communities in the wilderness of the frontier. There an individualistic ethic seemed to evolve naturally out of the hard facts of life.

The Frontier Thesis

As the United States passed from the Revolutionary War period to continental expansion and conquest, it was clear that the ideas and doctrines of New England no longer described the actual experience of the American people, particularly that portion of our people who engaged in building railroads across a continent, who took California and Texas from Mexico by force, who were steadily pushing their way west, leaving a trail of murdered Indians and slaughtered buffalo.

As they created new farms, towns, and territories, the people of the West were also creating new heroes, new values, a new literature, and a new culture. Andy Jackson and Abe Lincoln redefined American democracy in terms of homespun rather than broadcloth. Davy Crockett became the first great popular hero of the new "coonskin democracy," to be followed later by a gaudy and colorful procession of western guides, gunslingers, and badmen such as Buffalo Bill, Wild Bill Hickok, and Jesse James. Mark Twain, hailed by the eminent New England critic William Dean Howells as the "Lincoln of Our Literature," became the definitive voice of this new America.

The frontier thesis found its most coherent and articulate spokesman in historian Frederick Jackson Turner,[5] who argued that "The existence of an area of free land, its continuous recession and the advance of American settlement westward, explain American development."

"[It is] to the frontier," Turner argued, "that the American intellect owes its striking characteristics. That coarseness and strength combined with acuteness and inquisitiveness; that practical, inventive turn of mind, quick to find expedients; that masterful grasp of material things, lacking in the artistic but powerful to effect great ends; that restless, nervous energy; that dominant individualism, working for good and for evil, and withal that buoyancy and exuberance which comes with freedom—these are traits of the frontier."

But if the frontier left us with a heritage of individualism and respect for the common man (and scorn for "the Elect of God"), it also helped accentuate certain other, less attractive traits. Waste, crime, and monumental contempt for the natural beauty and harmony of the physical environment, as well as the artistic deficiency noted by Turner, were also characteristic of frontier civilization. Van Wyck Brooks called the West "a gigantic, overturned garbage can." Vernon Louis Parrington noted that in the years between 1871 and 1875 a million head of buffalo a year were slain, "their skins ripped off and the carcasses left for coyotes and buzzards. . . . freedom," Parrington observed, "had become the inalienable right to preempt, to exploit, to squander." The freedom of the frontier, he said, was the freedom of buccaneers. The new America was "an anarchistic world of strong, capable men, selfish, unenlightened, amoral." [6]

Actually, many of the traits that Turner and others associated with the westward expansion of the United States had been noted by a French nobleman a century earlier when the eastern seaboard was still being settled. Jean de Crèvecoeur was enchanted by the dominant characteristics of the new American civilization. Like Turner, Crèvecoeur noted that the availability of cheap or free land inevitably meant a more fluid class structure and a more open society: "[The] land, descended from its great Creator, holds not its precarious tenure either from a supercilious prince or a proud lord . . . [the laws] are simple and natural. Tis all as free as the air." [7]

Impressed by American prosperity and freedom, Crèvecoeur nevertheless noted that the American was not truly civilized in the sense that he rarely

[5] Frederick Jackson Turner, "The Significance of the Frontier in American History," American Historical Association *Annual Reports* (1893), pp. 199–227.

[6] Vernon L. Parrington, *The Beginnings of Critical Realism in America: 1860–1920*, Vol. 3 of *Main Currents in American Thought* (New York: Harcourt, 1958), pp. 16–17.

[7] J. Hector St. John de Crèvecoeur, *Letters from an American Farmer* (New York: Dutton, 1957), Chapter 3, "What Is an American?"

understood the limits of individualism as opposed to the needs of society. While there was no caste system as in Europe, neither was there much concern for the poor and the unfortunate: "This [American] devoid of society learns more than ever to center every idea within his own welfare. . . . How should he be charitable? He has scarcely seen a poor man in his life."

Wealth, not family name or social position—least of all learning—brought power and prestige in this New World.

Implicit in the frontier thesis were many of the ideas and values most often cited by those, even today, who wish either to attack or to defend American culture and American character. When former Vice President Spiro Agnew attacked his critics in the press and on television, he labeled them part of the "effete eastern establishment," suggesting that it was the old story of the sissified East versus the manly West (although Agnew himself was from Maryland, about as far east as you can get in this country). Alabama Governor and frequent presidential candidate George Wallace has also been fond of assaulting the "pseudo-intellectual snobs." Two hundred years ago, Crèvecoeur found the frontiersman lacking respect for intelligence, learning, and wisdom. "Who" said the Frenchman, "can be wiser than himself in this half-cultivated country?" The debate continues over whether the frontier brought us individualism, manly self-reliance, and democracy, or crime, waste, and stupidity. The answer seems to be that it did both.

The Melting-Pot Thesis

In the late nineteenth century, Andrew Carnegie, having built one of the world's mightiest industrial and corporate empires and having acquired an immense personal fortune, turned to writing books. He set forth in plain English the philosophy that had made him rich and America great. "Fortunately for the American people, they are essentially British," he began one essay.[8] By watching and emulating their Anglo-Saxon superiors, argued Carnegie, the flood of Irishmen, Italians, and East Europeans pouring into the country (many of them to work in Carnegie's mills and factories) could learn to become true Americans and thus share in the nation's material abundance and spiritual grandeur. In this way, Carnegie affirmed, the immigrant's children would be as good as—even indistinguishable from—the *real* Americans.

This was an early and somewhat crude expression of the underlying idea that would eventually find expression in the melting-pot thesis. Although Anglo-Saxons were, numerically, a minority of the American people (blacks, for example, made up 11 percent of the population when Carnegie

[8] *Triumphant Democracy* (New York: Scribner, 1888).

wrote his essay), they embodied certain traits and values that contained the genius of Americanism. People of various races, nationalities, and cultures were welcome to come because their labor was needed for America's burgeoning farms and industries. But through education and assimilation they should be transformed from whatever they had been into true Americans. And if some "foreigners" were too old, lazy, or stubborn to effect such a transformation voluntarily, then it was the task of the public school system, the press, and popular culture to shame the "foreigners" into becoming true Yankees.

The symbol of this idea was the Statue of Liberty with its premise that the European migrants were "poor" and "wretched" while New York City was the "Golden Door." For millions of Europeans, this undoubtedly turned out to be the reality. For them, America became a "land of opportunity" offering education, personal and religious freedom, and a chance to work hard and thus earn a share of the world's greatest success story. For others, however, America meant sweatshops, bigotry, and new if more subtle forms of exploitation.

The melting-pot thesis underscored a certain definition of American character and culture. The "typical" American was middle-class and middle-minded, hard-working and democratic, practical and well intentioned, and optimistic about his own and his country's future. He was clear-eyed and clear-headed. He was the stuff Presidents and popular heroes were made of, in fiction as well as in fact. He was the Lone Ranger (but not Tonto), Huck Finn (but not Jim), Horatio Alger, Frank Merriwell, and, of course, Jack Armstrong, the "All-American Boy." On the screen he was Tom Mix and Gary Cooper and John Wayne. He was invariably white, male, and of Christian, Anglo-Saxon heritage.

Only within the last few decades have we begun to take seriously all the other Americans and Americas—the Tontos and Jims and Giovannis and Nathans—hitherto obliged to ride in the back of the cultural bus. With this new awareness, the popularity of the melting-pot thesis has declined. Today American scholars are more likely to use the salad as a metaphor for the variety of American cultures. Preserving rather than destroying the ancestral culture of the migrants is an increasingly recognized social and national goal. Black Americans, brought to the country unwillingly, had experienced a most brutal form of "assimilation." In the process of ensuring that black people would accept first slavery and later segregation, blacks were legally denied access to education. (In the nineteenth century, many southern states outlawed the teaching of reading and writing to slaves.) Black families were disorganized and scattered. Even after the Civil War, blacks were systematically denied the right to participate in the rewarding or prestigious occupations. (As late as World War II, when black men were hired to work in a Detroit auto-assembly line for the first time as the result of wartime labor shortages and the insistence of the federal government, bloody riots ensued.) Yet, despite this long and bitter repression, black Americans endured and some even prospered, adding new dimensions to American culture. Many critics believe, for example, that the most uniquely American contribution to the arts has come in the form of jazz music, a black creation.[9]

Similar if not quite so systematic and deliberate examples of repression and exploitation can be cited by virtually every other "minority" group coming to America. Children of the migrants were taunted and condemned, even by teachers, for "not speaking English" or for dressing, eating, or behaving in an unfamiliar way. For a period in the nation's history, "un-Americanism" was virtually equated with crime, and special committees of the House and the Senate and many state legislatures set out to investigate those whose patriotism was suspect.

Perhaps the failure of the melting pot to melt can best be measured by the prevailing fact that politics in America, particularly at the local level, is still very much concerned with voter blocs of various ethnic, religious, racial, and national origins. Even those who decry "bloc voting" often tend to practice it in reverse by appealing to the "middle-American" and the "silent majority."

Within a generation after Carnegie's essay was published, Randolph Bourne was calling America a "trans-national" nation, with "a color richer, and more exciting than our ideal has hitherto encompassed." [10] Bourne envisioned the United States as the first truly "international nation" in a world dreaming of internationalism. More recently, a number of critics and scholars have tended to see virtue in the fact that we have not become a single homogeneous people. The richness, diversity, and complexity of American life may pose some of our greatest problems, but it is also a source of much of our strength and vitality as a nation. "I hear America singing," wrote poet Walt Whitman in *Leaves of Grass,* "its *varied* carols I hear" (italics added). America, he wrote, "is not a nation but a teeming nation of nations. The United States themselves are essentially the greatest poem. It would be a poor sort of America where we all sang the same songs."

But what of the actual *behavior* of the American people? This may tell us as much or more about American culture than generalized theories.

Popular Culture and the American Character

First it should be noted that in popular mythology, at least, America is the country "where the common man is king." The tradition that "any

[9] See Marshall Stearns, *The Story of Jazz* (New York: New American Library, 1958).
[10] Randolph S. Bourne, "Trans-National American," *Atlantic Monthly,* **118** (1916).

boy can grow up to be President" clearly has some validity when one considers the obscure origins of most recent American Chief Executives, such as Richard Nixon, Harry Truman, Dwight Eisenhower, Gerald Ford, and Jimmy Carter. Following World War I, America created history's first consumer society, built around high wages for ordinary working men and women, mass production of goods, and high levels of consumption. At about the same time, Henry Ford was shocking the industrial world by paying his assembly-line auto workers the then-unheard-of wage of five dollars per day (on the shrewd premise that these workers would buy Ford's cars). What was then the world's tallest skyscraper, the F. W. Woolworth building, was erected as a symbol of America's new "five-and-ten-cent store" culture. Ordinary people could go into Woolworth's, or any of the five-and-dime chain stores, proliferating across the nation, and for the expenditure of a few dollars come out with a bag full of the wondrous new products of American industry: hairpins, dolls for the girls and tin soldiers for the boys, cheap perfume, fake jewelry, bubble bath, and photos of favorite film stars. The new movie business was discovering the tricks and themes guaranteed to draw huge new audiences all across the nation; these included stories about gangsters or cowboys and about "flappers" (usually society or college girls who wore short skirts, smoked cigarettes, and "petted" in the rumble seats of Ford roadsters and hence were called "fast"). William Randolph Hearst, Joseph Patterson, and Colonel Robert Rutherford McCormick had created a new kind of literature for the masses: tabloid newspapers that sold for a penny or two, and were designed to be read on the subway, featuring splashing headlines, copious photos of crime and sex, gossip about celebrities and the rich, advice to the lovelorn, the "funnies," and sports. The 1920s were a sports and show-business Golden Age. Jack Dempsey drew the first million-dollar gate for a single fight. Babe Ruth, Red Grange, and Bobby Jones became national idols, along with Clara Bow and Theda Bara. America, in short, was creating a new way of life, and Europeans began to grumble about the danger of becoming "Americanized." It was the first society in human history in which leading politicians, business tycoons, publishers, film producers, and radio executives found themselves diligently studying the tastes and wants of the common man.

In the process, Americans either created or brought to a new level of accuracy and refinement the arts of measuring and manipulating mass taste and mass opinion. The Hearst empire spread from newspapers to magazines to the movies. Denied the opportunity to become President himself because of personal idiosyncrasies, Hearst instead made and unmade Presidents. (His last-minute support was critical in securing the Democratic nomination for Franklin Delano Roosevelt in 1932. In 1898 he had boasted that he could start a war between the United States and Spain over Cuba, and the war came.)

With the invention and the proliferation of inexpensive radio sets, a new pop music, mostly the product of Broadway's "Tin Pan Alley," filled the air. Madison Avenue was becoming the worldwide headquarters for a new and strange industry, advertising. Intellectuals such as H. L. Mencken sneered at the new mass culture and claimed that the United States had created a new species of man, the "boobus Americanus" (the American boob), a new religion ("110 percent Americanism"), and a new class (the "boobocracy") made up of insurance salesmen, movie fans, chiropractors, "sob sisters," Bible-thumping clergymen, cow-college professors, stock swindlers, and politicians so ignorant, venal, and crooked that Mencken claimed to have trained himself to pull the lever on a voting machine with one hand while holding his nose with the other. Novelist Sinclair Lewis took up the theme and won a Nobel Prize for his satires of America's Main Street and the businessmen–Babbitts who presided over its affairs. (Others, like Ernest Hemingway and poet T. S. Eliot, simply left the country.) Asked why he did not follow the "expatriate" American artists and intellectuals who were flocking to Europe, Mencken insisted that he remained so that he could laugh himself to sleep every night watching the spectacle of American public life.[11]

Depending upon one's attitude or tastes, America's mass society and "pop" culture, which in the fifty years since it emerged in the 1920s has reached new heights of organization and technique are still viewed as either a fulfillment or a travesty of the American Dream.

We have noted that the mass media of the 1920s were quick to discover and seek to capitalize on the public's interest in two types that were soon to become mythical heroes of the mass society: the western cowboy and the eastern gangster. What these two characters had in common was a predilection for violence as the natural means of settling life's problems and the willingness to kill on the slightest pretext—in short, the gun. By the early twentieth century, the cowboys and the frontiersmen had all but vanished from America, to be replaced by a new breed of actors in the movies, the circus, and the rodeo. Like his forerunner, the medieval knight, the real cowboy was lost in the fanciful image of a hard-hitting straight-shooting hero of the plains. The gangsters, on the other hand, were just beginning to come into their own. In Chicago, the prototype of the hoodlum–hero, Al Capone, ruled a very tangible empire. At the height of his power, Capone liked to appear at massive public gatherings, like a Chicago Cubs baseball game. He would usually arrive late, surrounded by an entourage of hoodlums, and head for the box seat held in reserve for him. Upon Capone's appearance the action stopped, and the crowd would usually rise and applaud their appreciation of the honor bestowed upon them by this great man's presence.

[11] Frederick Lewis Allen, *Only Yesterday* (New York: Harper, 1931), Chapter 9.

Capone was credited with being a sort of Henry Ford of the underworld. He organized it and transformed random lawlessness into a major industry. *Organized* crime became a peculiarly American institution, mirroring a certain paradox that permeated much of American life. Order and organization, technique and technology somehow managed to go hand in hand with the most extreme forms of "rugged individualism." Superficially, America is a very orderly and certainly a highly organized society. Traffic flows with efficiency and smoothness. The great industries, supermarkets, and department stores of America have set a standard for the entire world. At the same time lawlessness has been and is one of the most distinctive of American traits. There are more murders committed each year in many American cities than occur in whole countries elsewhere in the world. Our Presidents have become popular targets for random assassins. Murder as a cause of death is so rare in much of Europe that it is statistically negligible. In the United States, it is the second highest cause of death among young men, exceeded only by auto accidents.

Certain features of popular culture in America clearly feed upon and perhaps nourish this penchant for murderous assault. It has been estimated that the average American child has witnessed at least twelve thousand television murders by the time he reaches maturity.[12] Crime shows, usually containing a murder or an aggravated assault every few minutes, are the staple of prime time TV. The movies become steadily more bloody, so that mindless brutality has become a universal trademark of the American film. Author Tom Wolfe has argued that the growing popularity of such "sports" as the demolition derby reflects the destructive impulses of the people. The symbolic meaning of the demolition derby, says Wolfe, is the violent annihilation of the extension of our person: the automobile.[13]

A recent poll claims that there are 90 million guns in private hands in America. In the early 1930s, only 3 percent of the American people listed crime as a major national problem. By the 1970s, crime had become a major issue in the nation. Many American cities were being abandoned, particularly at night, by middle-class families, often out of simple fear. There was serious discussion in the press as to whether or not it was safe for citizens to visit the nation's capital for bicentennial ceremonies. Certainly at least one cause of the financial crisis afflicting many large American cities could be found in ordinary street crime. New York alone had a reputed two hundred thousand heroin addicts, most of them presumably sustaining their habit through crime.

Just as street crime was profoundly if insiduously afflicting the nation's

---

[12] This estimate has been made by Nicholas Johnson, former Chairman of the Federal Communications Commission, based upon FCC studies of televised violence.
[13] Tom Wolfe, *The Kandy-Kolored Tangerine-Flake Streamline Baby* (New York: Farrar, 1965), Chapter 2, "Clean Fun at Riverhead."

American Political Process: '63 . . . '68 . . . '72 . . .

©1972 HERBLOCK

[American Political Process: '63 . . . '68 . . . '72
. . . —from *Herblock's State of the Union* (Simon
& Schuster, 1972).]

cities, so assassination attempts and threats seemed to be tranforming the
nature of American politics. At least one factor in Senator Ted Kennedy's
decision not to run for the Presidency appeared to be the steady stream
of murderous threats he regularly received in the United States mail. By
late 1975, President Gerald Ford reportedly was receiving an average of
thirty death threats a month; he was the victim of two assassination attempts and at least one other assassination plot that was aborted because
the plotters were jailed on an unrelated charge. Kennedy and Ford have
both said, in effect, "You just learn to live with it." But can democracy
live with it? Or will the mindless, murderous few finally succeed in forcing
the peaceably inclined majority to transform America into a police state?

A final word on this topic. The United States is not simply a victim of
violence. In 1975 the United States was exporting $10 billion worth of
arms to nations around the world, more than all other nations (including

the Soviet Union) combined. Our historic infatuation with weaponry has made this "peace-loving democracy" the world's leading arms merchant.

In fairness, it should be noted that not all Americans are addicted to the cult of violence. Pacifism and nonviolence have a long and distinguished history in the United States from colonial Quakers to Dr. Martin Luther King's leadership of the civil-rights struggle in the 1960s. It should also be noted that many of the ideas that inspired Gandhi to lead India to freedom through nonviolent resistance came from the Indian leader's study of the works of Henry David Thoreau, a nineteenth-century American writer and philosopher. Public opinion polls also have repeatedly indicated that most Americans disapprove of excessive violence on television and favor some restrictions on gun ownership. Whether this is a case of the majority's not practicing what it preaches or of a violence-prone minority's imposing its will upon a peaceably inclined majority is debatable.

Materialism

A commonplace criticism of American culture is its excessive preoccupation with material goods and corresponding neglect of the human spirit. Americans, it is alleged, worship only "the almighty dollar." We scramble to "keep up with the Joneses." The love affair between the typical American male and his automobile has been a continuing subject of derisive commentary by both foreign and domestic critics. Americans are said to live by a quantitative ethic. Bigger is better, whether in bombs or bosoms. The classical virtues of grace, harmony, and economy of both means and ends are lost upon most Americans. As a result, we are said to be swallowing up the world's supply of natural resources, which are irreplaceable. Americans constitute 6 percent of the world's population but consume 50 percent of the world's energy. These are now familiar complaints.

It should also be noted that although Americans do consume on a lavish scale, they also produce a disproportionate share of the world's goods, particularly with respect to food—the most basic of all commodities. And if it is true that Americans are consuming too much of the world's dwindling supply of oil, it is also true that American technology, industry, and capital discovered and developed much of that oil in the first place— and in the process made many once-impoverished lands rich.

In the late 1960s and early 1970s, many signs appeared that the Affluent Society was in trouble.[14] Some of the former recipients of America's material beneficence, such as Germany and Japan, began to compete seriously

[14] For a presentation of this point of view see Paul R. Ehrlich, *The End of Affluence* (New York: Ballantine, 1974).

39

Main Street, U.S.A. [Photo by Lorren Au, courtesy *The Daily Report,* Ontario, Calif.]

for the world's markets. The problem of inflation, always troublesome in an expanding economy, became a powerful and dangerous threat to stability. President Nixon was obliged to devalue the dollar twice. Chronic shortages of certain raw materials began to develop as other nations followed America's lead into the consumer society. The new science of ecology sounded dire warnings of the threats to the environment implicit in the new materialism. The smog in our air, the pollution of our waters, and the destruction of the landscape seemed to verify these warnings, and environmentalism became a major new force in American politics. Even bankers and businessmen who talked only of expansion and rising profits in the "go-go years" of the 1950s and 1960s began to concern themselves more with survival and soundness. Popular politicians, such as California's Governor Jerry Brown, preached economy and austerity and were rewarded with broad support from both conservatives and liberals.

In the winter of 1976–77 record-breaking cold in the East and drought in the West underscored the fact that essential sources of energy, oil, gas, and water, were becoming scarce at the same time that growing worldwide affluence was stimulating greater demand.

By the mid-1970s, it seemed that the days of the Affluent Society were numbered if not already ended. In the land often condemned as the most materialistic civilization since ancient Carthage, it is increasingly difficult to find anyone to speak a kind word for materialism.

Racism

Evidence of American racism is overwhelming. It reaches from the constitutional provision that counted black slaves as three fifths of a person to the inescapable fact that virtually every statistical measure, such as income, health, longevity, education, and housing, shows that blacks, Chicanos, and Indians (but not Jews or Asians) are at the bottom of American society. This dilemma has plagued American society from its beginnings. The issue was dodged by the Constitutional Convention (lest it split the nation before we became a nation) but emerged again during the Civil War and Reconstruction. Slavery was abolished at the price of a great national trauma, only to be replaced by a system of pseudo-slavery called segregation. Most of the nation's great cities are caught in the race-related grip of unemployment, crime, and poverty. Riots flared in virtually every major city in the nation in the late 1960s but seemed to change little or nothing. Every fall, Americans brace themselves to watch embattled adults attacking children and police on TV newscasts as the result of efforts to integrate the schools somewhere in the country. Racism unquestionably has been and remains one of our fundamental domestic problems.

Americans did not invent racism. Racist feelings and attitudes toward other ethnic groups have been and are common throughout much of the world. Also it should be noted that the United States has moved dramatically within the last decade to outlaw or restrain legal and institutional racism and to equalize opportunity for various disadvantaged groups. The United States will not be the last nation to eliminate racism from society. It may be the first. This hope was underscored by the overwhelming and positive response given the televised version of Alex Haley's book *Roots* in January of 1977.

The largest audience in television history, estimated by the American Broadcasting Company to have totaled approximately 133 million Americans, watched eight successive evenings of *Roots,* an unrelenting assault on

41

the brutality that white Americans inflicted on their black captives. If we are now willing to be honest in facing the facts of the human cost of slavery, rather than hiding behind the traditional stereotype of the "happy darky," some hope exists that a solution to the problem may finally be approaching.

Mobility

The history of America is, of course, a history of migration. From the Pilgrims landing in New England to the suburbanite carrying his television set into a new tract house, Americans have always been among the most mobile of the earth's people, in both a physical and a sociological sense. Europeans grow up in their grandfathers' houses. Americans move on the average of once every four or five years. Americans regard a neighborhood less as a community than as a place to move away, preferably up, from. The mobility of American life may contribute not only to social but also to personal instability. That many Americans have lost or abandoned their "roots" may have something to do with excesses of eccentric individualism on the one hand and bland conformity on the other, between H. R. "Bob" Haldeman's "zero defect system" and Jerry Rubin's "revolution for the hell of it."

Both academic sociologists such as David Reisman (*The Lonely Crowd*) and popular journalists like William Whyte (*The Organization Man*) have studied the paradox of American individualism and conformity seeming to exist side by side, often within the same individual. The prevailing image of American college students, for example, has passed from the "mindless conformity" of the "silent generation" of the 1950s to the wild radicalism that many believed characterized the student generation of the 1960s and back to a kind of numbing passivity in the 1970s. None of these images may be wholly accurate—average students probably do not really change very much year to year or generation to generation except perhaps for things like hair styles and skirt lengths—but they do reflect the most active and visible students at the most important and prestigous universities, like Harvard and Berkeley.

Another frequently noted paradox in America is that although ours is a mobile, urbanized, and industrialized society, most of our national myths and values are rooted in the rural past. We are a people who work in cities, live in suburbs, and dream of the countryside. From Jefferson's warnings to his countrymen to avoid the corrupting city, to Huck Finn's "lighting out for the territory" lest Aunt Sally "civilize" him, to President Ford's fulminations against the wicked ways of New York, a historic antipathy to the urban life and all of its works seems to permeate the American people, who, nevertheless, are among the most urban peoples on earth.

Our myths are of wagon trains pushing west, sturdy farmers conquering the plains, Presidents who were born in log cabins, lonesome cowboys and plantation belles, and "good ole boys." Until recently, when a number of black and Jewish American writers such as James Baldwin and Norman Mailer began writing about the urban experience, our literature was usually set in the country or in small towns, and the themes of writers like Faulkner, Hemingway, and Steinbeck were largely a celebration of the pastoral virtues as opposed to urban vices. Many of the political leaders of both parties play shrewdly to the American penchant for equating the countryside with honesty, simplicity, and "common sense." Indeed, of the four national candidates selected by the major parties in 1976, none were recognizably urban. Jimmy Carter was from Plains, Georgia and Walter Mondale from Afton, Minnesota. Gerald Ford was from Grand Rapids, Michigan and his vice presidential running mate, Senator Robert Dole, was from Russell, Kansas.

The Cult of Youth

Another important characteristic of American culture that is an unfailing source of both admiration and concern to foreign observers of the American scene is the extraordinary emphasis given to youth. Traditionally in European and Asian society, there have been only two kinds of people: children and adults. America invented the idea of adolescence and coined the term *teen-ager* to describe a status unique to American life. In Europe and Asia, the young typically leave school early and go to work, usually at menial and low-paying jobs. The young remain subject to parental control and discipline until they leave home, marry, and/or become self-supporting.

Perhaps because our affluence permits youth to enjoy a longer period relatively free from adult responsibilities; perhaps because we have always considered ourselves a young country; perhaps because Americans tend to look forward rather than backward; or because of all three, the young in America are the envy of their counterparts throughout much of the Western world. They have cars, money, and personal freedom to an extent unheard of in most cultures. When Frenchmen or Italians complain that their country is being "Americanized," they usually mean that their own young people are beginning to take on "airs" like the American young.

The young in America have become an important element in the economy of the nation. The pop recording industry, for example, caters largely to young girls between twelve and sixteen, who buy most of the records sold in this country. Advertisers quickly learned that the mature tend to follow the young, rather than the reverse, in matters of taste and style, particularly in industries like clothing, automobiles, and personal items like hair sprays. As a result, most Americans are bombarded with propaganda showing young, attractive people looking clean, radiant, and happy, while older folks worry about things like stopped-up drains and iron-deficiency anemia.

Traditionally, the American young have not been a very potent force politically. This changed, however, in the 1960s, when young people protested the Vietnam war and racism. Young people joined the "children's crusade" that helped Senator Eugene McCarthy become a major candidate for the Democratic nomination for the Presidency in 1968. In 1972 Senator George McGovern, relying largely upon a staff of people in their twenties, won the Democratic nomination. However, in the ensuing campaign against Richard Nixon, the young seemed to become disenchanted with McGovern and politics in general. Only about 20 percent of the newly enfranchised voters (under age twenty-one) bothered to go to the polls, and these tended to follow the rest of the population in giving most of their votes to Nixon.

In the late 1960s and early 1970s, there appeared a rash of books (Charles Reich's *The Greening of America,* Theodore Roszak's *The Making of a Counter Culture*) prophesying that American life was about to be transformed by a new, youthful "counterculture." By the mid-1970s, most of this talk seemed foolish. Moreover, the average age of Americans, which for the three decades after World War II was in the mid-twenties, will be, in 1980, right at thirty years of age and is expected to move higher as we approach the twenty-first century. With birth rates declining and life expectancy increasing, Americans, however symbolically young, are actually growing older.[15]

American Values

One can see running through American society a mixture of both idealism and pragmatism, the same traits that have been characteristic of our most quintessentially American political leaders: Franklin, Jefferson, Franklin D. Roosevelt, John F. Kennedy, and perhaps most importantly, Abraham Lincoln. These men had in common a shrewd and practical approach to politics as well as a certain idealism. They were all attacked for being both dreamers and hypocrites, and, in a certain sense, their detractors were right on both counts.

As we have noted, it is possible to dispute almost any claim that is made about "American culture" simply because the nation is so large and so various. And yet few if any other nations are quite so preoccupied with efforts to achieve self-identity. The phrase "the American way of life" appears constantly in political and ceremonial speeches. One does not

[15] *Newsweek* (Feb. 28, 1977), pp. 50–65.

hear or read about "the French way of life," "the German way of life," or "the Italian way of life" nearly so frequently, perhaps because in these older societies people know what their way of life is and hence have little need to discuss it.

It may be possible, however, to cite a few basic ideas and values that do underlie most political rhetoric in America and that are usually affirmed, at least verbally, by almost all Americans.

We believe these are

1. *Democracy.* This is a vague term but most Americans say they believe in it. It means, literally, rule by the people, (Which people is another matter.) Our democratic system requires that political power be vested in people chosen by a majority of those registered voters who use the franchise. The idea that any special group in society—the rich, the best educated, the military—have a right to rule on any other basis than election by the voters is foreign to America. There have been no military coups in America, and there is unlikely to be one so long as most people continue to believe in the electoral process, rather than force, as a means of resolving political and social differences. Groups such as the American Nazi party, which are frankly antidemocratic, get little support from the American people. Radical left-wing groups, which sometimes begin by preaching the necessity of armed revolution, often turn to electoral politics as they mature. (An example is the Black Panther party.) The fundamental problem of almost all totalitarian movements in America for the past century, left or right, has been the lack of anything remotely resembling popular support. The immense majority of the American people remain committed to ballots rather than bullets as a means of achieving social and political justice.

2. *Justice.* This is a more complicated idea than democracy. Justice is an ideal, like true love or perfect happiness, that is rarely if ever achieved but that nevertheless powerfully animates human behavior. The Ten Commandments, for example, are one expression of this ideal. Leon Jaworski, special prosecutor in the government's prosecution of the various high governmental officials involved in Watergate, has said that he came away from this experience convinced that the American people still strongly believe in the concept of equal justice. (Thus when President Ford pardoned Richard Nixon for his part in the affair, the polls reflected strong public disapproval.)

In America, justice has usually been associated with the belief in equal opportunity under the law, rather than equality of incomes, status, or power. The Supreme Court's "one man, one vote" decision was clearly a manifestation of our belief that the law should be no respecter of persons or status.[16] On the other hand, most people see nothing wrong or in-

[16] This was the landmark Supreme Court decision in *Baker v. Carr* (1962).

herently unjust about some people's amassing fortunes while others live in poverty. Nor are there many objections to the fact that popular athletes may earn hundreds of thousands of dollars a year while others—presumably doing work, such as teaching school, that is at least as useful socially —make a small fraction of that sum. In short, we believe in the equal right to become unequal.

On the other hand, it must be noted that even this concept of justice is difficult to achieve in practice. How could one argue, for example, that a child born to a black sharecropper in Alabama at the turn of the century had been endowed with opportunity equal to Nelson Rockefeller's?

3. *Freedom and individualism.* Most Americans appear to believe that personal freedom is the most important value of American life, the foundation upon which our society rests. Of course, we disagree as to what "freedom" means. (For example, there was vigorous opposition to those who demonstrated against the Vietnam war in the late 1960s and early 1970s, including documented efforts by the government to suppress and/or disorganize such demonstrations.)

At the same time, a good many of the anti-war protesters were themselves none too scrupulous about the rights of others. Still, most Americans appear to believe that people should be free to speak their minds, that the press should be free to criticize the government, and that individuals should be free to live their lives according to their own lights within the limits imposed by the law. Finally, the evidence is strong that most Americans believe in the private ownership of property. As Senator and former United Nations Ambassador Patrick Moynihan has pointed out, these are rights that are respected by a small and perhaps dwindling minority of the world's governments. Whether under a king, a dictator, or an all-powerful "party," much of the world throughout human history has regarded public order and "national unity" as more important than personal freedom. Even in America, maintaining the rights guaranteed to all Americans by the first ten amendments to the Constitution has been a continuing struggle. In the late 1960s, the editors of great newspapers, such as the *New York Times,* found themselves faced with the possibility of going to prison for defying a government order not to publish the *Pentagon Papers.* (The Supreme Court validated the paper's right to publish.) More recently, Americans were shocked by disclosures that organizations such as the FBI and the CIA were engaged in opening the mail and tapping the phones of law-abiding citizens. However, it is significant that such activities were usually conducted in clear violation of existing laws designed to protect individual privacy. Efforts to curb violence in America by restricting the sale of guns, for example, have usually foundered in the face of the belief that such a curb would represent a significant assault upon personal freedom. So too have many attempts at protecting the en-

46

vironment failed because the price of cleaner air, for example, involves some limitation upon the right to drive private automobiles.

Related to our belief in freedom is a belief that the individual has certain "inalienable rights." [17] The German philosopher Hegel assumed that the individual is subordinate to the state. Few Americans would agree. The state, we insist, exists to serve people. Again we do not always live by the ideal of freedom and individual dignity, but most of us believe in it and this belief has important consequences in daily life as well as in the practice of politics.

4. *Reason.*   From eighteenth-century thinkers like Jefferson we have evolved both a system of government and a life style founded upon compromise and conciliation rather than force or brute strength. We believe that most differences of opinion, most conflicts of interest, can be reconciled through reasoned discussion. Often reason and compromise fail us (the Civil War is an example). More often it does not. Our court system is based on the premise that a judge or a jury, upon hearing the best evidence from both sides, will be able to arrive at a just verdict through the use of reason. Most schools and other public institutions function through a committee system based on the idea that if responsible people meet and reason together, they will be able to solve their problems. Moreover, students are educated in courses like American history and government because state legislatures believe that taking such courses will make these students more knowledgeable about the nature of our government and hence better able to render a reasonable judgment as citizens.

5. *Progress?*   Had this book been written a decade ago, we probably would have felt constrained to include the idea of "progress" in this brief outline of basic American values. Today the necessity of its inclusion is not so clear. Continuing exposure to the realities and dangers of pollution resulting from unbridled economic development; a series of rude shocks to Americans' self-image as "winners" (outlined in Chapter One) including the "loss" of Vietnam; Watergate; frequent assassinations and assassination attempts; inflation; recession and an energy crisis—all have played a part in causing some to wonder whether bigger is really better and to question whether or not more might really mean less. Until fairly recently, most Americans believed that progress was built into the American system—that each new year must necessarily bring a somewhat higher level of abundance, an increase in American power and prestige, more opportunity for a better life for more people. All such notions are now being seriously reexamined.

---

[17] Americans' dedication to individual rights seems to be growing. A 1973 study by the National Opinion Research Center, University of Chicago, indicated a greater tolerance for individual rights among Americans than in the past.

America has celebrated its two hundredth birthday. No other major Western nation observes a "birthday." [18] Even should they wish to do so, most countries would not know which day to celebrate because most nations have evolved over hundreds, even thousands of years of wars, famine, migration of peoples, and many other factors only dimly known and even less well understood. The United States, on the other hand, was *willed* into existence. It was deliberately created by specific men at a specific time and place. Moreover it arrived, so to speak, with a silver spoon in its mouth: the culture of Europe. Finally, it was free to take what it wished from the accumulated experience of other peoples while being largely protected, as the result of sheer geographic luck, from having some of the less attractive aspects of the older civilizations, such as the rigid class system, imposed from without.

Given the task of writing the Declaration of Independence, thirty-two-year-old Thomas Jefferson, with the help of aging Ben Franklin, undertook to begin this document with a statement about the young nation's reason for being. He decided to borrow John Locke's phrase "life, liberty and property" as best describing the purpose of the new nation, but then he dropped the word *property* in favor of "pursuit of happiness." Two hundred years later, it may not be possible or even necessary to try to improve upon Jefferson's intuition. He obviously intended this admittedly vague phrase to include the activities of New England Puritans, Pennsylvania businessmen, and Virginia farmers. Jefferson's notion that the happiness of the individual is the purpose of government was and perhaps is America's unique contribution to political theory—and to human culture. Certainly traditional political thinkers such as Hegel would reject the idea. Indeed, "happiness" has never enjoyed much repute in the hierarchy of values praised by philosophers, poets, and prophets.

Plato disdained it [19] (although Aristotle wrote in its behalf). Neither Marx nor Adam Smith seem to have given the subject much thought. Milton, Byron, Nietzsche, Tolstoi, and Freud were preoccupied with nobler, more spiritual, and deeper human motives. The mundane pursuit of mere happiness is not the stuff of which heroes and saints are made. But it is the prime concern of a democratic culture. And in the pursuit thereof Americans have created the world's first and richest consumer economy; have undertaken to mass-produce education, entertainment, and culture on an unprecedented scale; and have sought to build a society in

[18] See Henry Fairlee, "Anti-Americanism at Home and Abroad," *Commentary* (Dec. 1975).

[19] Plato, *The Republic,* trans. Benjamin Jowett (New York: World, 1946). In Plato's ideal state, "The meaner desires of the many are held down by the virtuous desires and wisdom of the few," p. 146.

which most people would be free to follow the star of their own destiny in their own fashion. And if, in the process, we have become a restless, troubled, and sometimes divided people, perhaps that is a price that had to be paid for having shifted the focus of politics and culture from the grandeur of the few to the well-being of the many.

The Constitutional Framework

Origins
•
Principles
•
Federalism

How in the world did we get from the Federalist Papers to the Edited Transcripts?

Sheldon S. Wolin
"From Jamestown to San Clemente,"
New York Review of Books, Sept. 19, 1974

In the summer of 1787 fifty-five men gathered in the city of Philadelphia to draw up the Constitution of the United States of America.

The document they created begins with a memorable phrase, "We the people of the United States." The Convention thus undertook, for perhaps the first time in human history, to create a nation rooted in the supreme authority of "the people." But, of course, the fifty-five delegates were being somewhat presumptuous. While they assumed the right to speak for "the people" they in fact were representative of only a small, elite group within the total population. They were, for example, all male, white, upper-middle- or upper-class. Half of them were college graduates. Many, like Hamilton, Madison, and Franklin, were intellectuals. Could they really speak for black slaves, for women, for the illiterate poor—let alone the Indians, who, of course, had every right to affirm that *they* were really "the people"? The so-called three-fifths compromise, concluded July 16, 1787, dramatically illustrates the point. While proclaiming a social contract among all the people (and having all read the Declaration of Independence, which proclaimed, "All men are created equal"), the founders faced a particularly sticky issue. Were slaves equal? Did they have "inalienable rights"? Representation in the House of Representatives was to be apportioned to each state according to population. So, too, were taxes.[1] Clearly those states where slavery was practiced wished to count slaves as persons when calculations were made to determine how large their House delegations would be. Conversely, when taxes were levied (again according to population), these same states would prefer to consider slaves property rather than people. Nonslave states would, of course, have an opposite point of view. The dilemma was solved by the astounding technique of counting a slave as three-fifths of a person in both instances! In this fashion, the Constitution recognized slavery.[2]

In short, from the moment of its birth, America represented a paradox

---

[1] The Sixteenth Amendment, providing for an income tax, modified this provision.

[2] The word *slavery* was not used, but the distinction among "free persons," "Indians," and "three fifths of all other persons" made the intention clear. See Article 1, Section 2 of the Constitution.

between the stated ideals and principles about which the nation was to be organized and the practical realities of daily life. For, clearly, had the Founding Fathers chosen to include blacks, women, and Indians in their definition of "the people" by extending to them the full rights of citizenship, including the vote, the Constitution would never have been ratified and the United States would not have been created.

This conflict between ideals and practical reality remains with us today. Perhaps it will continue to trouble us as long as the United States of America exists as a political entity. For although the framers of the Constitution could claim to speak for "the people," Americans were not then and probably are not now *a people*—in quite the same sense that the French, the Italians, the English, or the Germans are a people.

In 1787 there were only thirteen states and 2.6 million people (according to the first census of 1790) who made up the United States. Today, fifty states and over 200 million people make the United States one of the largest and most heterogeneous nations in the world. From an agricultural, rural country, we have matured into a highly technical, industrial, urbanized society. Modes of communication were slow in the eighteenth century, and other places in the world were remote. Today we have virtual instant communication around the globe and military commitments in most geographic areas of the world, and Americans have walked on the moon. These developments, together with the mounting problems and concerns mentioned in Chapter One, force upon us the question of whether or not our Constitution is any longer viable.

Yet, despite whatever lack of prophetic power characterized those now sanctified Founding Fathers of 1787, they were concerned with certain fundamental issues of political society that still confound us today: How does a large, complex society maintain order and yet uphold individual freedom? How much individual freedom should be allowed? How much direct rule should be accorded to "the people" (whoever they are)? How much—and what kind of—power should be allotted to a central government? How can a Constitution assure that excessive, or even arbitrary, power not converge in a single individual (like the President) or a single group (like the oil companies)? What is excessive power? And so on. These are issues as familiar to the American student of the 1970s as they were to the American statesmen of the 1780s.

Origins

The Constitutional Convention capped a period in American history that can be described as revolutionary. In breaking from the British Empire, the United States became the first colonial possession to achieve independence from the mother country.[3] Separation from England created a technical problem with which later revolutionaries would have to deal. That is, once the break was made, what was now to be the legal basis for government? By what right would government govern? Prior to the Revolution, the source of political authority had rested in allegiance to the monarch in England. What now? This juridical dilemma was solved by the first large-scale use of what we call *constitutionalism*. The former colonies— in some instances simply revising their colonial charters slightly, in other instances making substantial changes—created written documents describing the functions and limitations of state governments. Such a practice had historical sanction in earlier "compacts" like the Mayflower Compact and the Fundamental Orders of Connecticut, in which the members of a community gathered together to agree on the rules that would govern them.

The first nationwide constitution was the Articles of Confederation, proclaimed in force on March 1, 1781. Designed to provide a loose political union of the thirteen independent states, the Articles described the United States "confederation" as a "league of friendship." The central government had limited authority, and there was only one national branch: the Congress. Among the most debilitating restrictions on the Congress were the inability to levy taxes (which could only be requested from the states) and the lack of authority to coin money and regulate commerce. Although some scholars have argued that under the Articles the new country was doing quite well,[4] there were problems. For example, Alexander Hamilton and others believed that the new nation needed a sounder and more sufficient currency, which could best be provided by a central government. Some people feared the consequences of trade wars among the states which could establish tariffs against one another. Substantial citizens in the East became alarmed in September 1786 when Daniel Shays led a rowdy group of western Massachusetts farmers to the capital at Springfield to protest various government policies. Although the militia crushed Shays' Rebellion, the event convinced an increasing number of people that a stronger central government might be needed to restrain this kind of civil disorder. Finally, the confederate nature of the United States caused serious difficulty in the conduct of foreign affairs. For example, was John Adams, American minister to London, to negotiate a trade agreement between England and the United States or between England and thirteen separate states?

In September 1786, five states sent delegates to the Annapolis Convention to discuss problems of commerce. On the initiative of Alexander

---

[3] It might be argued that the Dutch revolt against the Hapsburgs in the sixteenth and early seventeenth centuries represented such a struggle, but in context of our remarks, we may consider it an internal European political and religious struggle.
[4] Merrill Jensen, *The Articles of Confederation* (Madison: U. of Wisconsin, 1940).

Hamilton, this convention extended an invitation to all the states to convene the next year for the purpose of devising ways to make the Articles of Confederation "adequate to the exigencies of the Union." Congress, petitioned by the Annapolis delegates to call such a convention, sensed the danger to itself if such a meeting took place. After considerable debate, it recommended that the states appoint delegates to meet in Philadelphia the following spring, but only for the "sole and express purpose of revising the Articles of Confederation." This injunction was ignored, for between May 25 and September 17, 1787, in a Convention closed to public view, the delegates produced a brand new document of government: the Constitution of the United States.

It would be a mistake to assume that the Philadelphia delegates met only in an atmosphere of fear of social unrest, trade wars, and deficient diplomacy. These men, relatively young, well educated, and prosperous, represented, in the best sense, professional politicians. None among them believed that a perfect government was possible or that there could ever be unanimous agreement on any particular provision of the Constitution. Yet for such men this was an extraordinary opportunity to wipe the slate of history clean and draw up as fine an instrument of government as their instincts, wisdom, and experience could create.

Various influences conditioned their thoughts. For one thing, these were men of property and wealth. George Washington, chairman of the convention and owner of a large estate in Virginia, was reputed to be the richest man in America. This kind of information has led some historians to contend that the framers were not the virtuous patriots we learned of in grade school but were instead rich, elitist conservatives whose chief aim was to protect their economic interests and solidify their political power. Led by historian Charles Beard, who published his influential *An Economic Interpretation of the Constitution* in 1913,[5] this school of thought emphasizes that the founders opposed democracy. According to Beard, they held large amounts of Continental securities—pieces of debt paper circulated by the Continental government to pay soldiers and provide a circulating currency. These securities had depreciated in value, and the holders reasoned that a strong central government (with, presumably, a central bank) would redeem the securities at face value. Together with other conservatives who wanted a strong national government to check radicalism among poor farmers who owed them money, these men sought to establish a government designed to protect their elite status as well as their pocketbook. Since local, popular rule was, by this theory, the chief culprit, it was best to create a strong central government, to guarantee the rights of property, and to gain for the propertied class a dominant position in the new gov-

[5] New York: Macmillan, 1935, first published in 1913.

ernment. This antidemocratic elitism, scholars like Beard have maintained, meant that the Constitution of 1787 actually represented a counterrevolutionary conspiracy against the Declaration of Independence and the Revolution. In an age when wealthy and powerful oil companies, conglomerates like ITT, and enormously wealthy and influential persons like Nelson Rockefeller often play a dominant role in government, such a thesis has a certain credibility. But we must be cautious in imposing our present-day impressions (and/or prejudices) on the events of 1787. For one thing, the Industrial Revolution, which drastically altered American society and created some very rich and powerful people, was not even on the historical horizon in 1787. Additionally, if the founders had really wished to protect their propertied interests, why had they not included in the Constitution a property qualification for voting or even for holding public office? One might argue that they knew full well that the states would devise stiff property qualifications for political participation. But it was precisely those states, the conspiracy theorists suggest, that were too radical for the Philadelphia "conservatives." Moreover, as historian Robert Brown has shown in his severe criticism of Beard,[6] most men of the eighteenth century held enough property to meet any state's qualifications for voting. We should also note that by the 1820s most states had removed any property qualification at all. It is not legitimate to place a twentieth-century power-elite thesis on the events of 1787. Clearly, as we have noted, many "people" were left out of politics in those days. But, sometimes quickly, sometimes too gradually, the framework created by the Constitution absorbed more and different people into the political process. The relevant question for our day is not, Did we begin with an elitist *and repressive* society (it certainly was repressive to blacks); rather, the question is, What have we evolved to in the 1970s? And measuring where we are now with what was created in 1787 just might be a rewarding exercise.

More important influences on the founders are the following. First, these were men who had participated in a revolution. In this sense, certainly, they were not eighteenth-century conservatives.[7] They were literate, informed men, familiar with political thought dating from the ancient philosophers Aristotle and Polybius. Finally, they were men of the Enlightenment, a term that refers to the development of philosophical, political, and social thought in the eighteenth century. Impressed by the English physicist Isaac Newton, who had postulated a law of gravitation, thinkers in the eighteenth century believed that there were cosmic "natural" laws governing human society as well as the physical universe. Newton's theory implied that the universe was in rational order. Increasingly political thinkers believed that

[6] *Charles Beard and the Constitution* (Princeton, N.J.: Princeton U.P., 1956).
[7] An excellent short essay assessing the Founding Fathers is Stanley Elkins and Eric McKitrick's, *The Founding Fathers, Young Men of the Revolution* (Washington, D.C.: Service Center for Teachers of History, 1962).

by the use of reason, men could discover a rational order in politics as well. Some even spoke of God as the "Divine Mechanic." Enlightened human beings, they believed, could design a more perfect state and the result would be human progress, just as an engineer might design a machine to make human labor more efficient.

The leadership of the Enlightenment centered in France. Here the so-called *philosophes,* led by, among others, the satirist Voltaire and the political theorist Montesquieu, began to apply the test of reason and observation to existing social, political, and economic institutions, often finding these institutions (like schools, churches, and governments) in need of serious reform if not wholesale change.[8] The framers of the Constitution were well aware of the advanced thought of the Enlightenment. They were intellectuals as well as practical businessmen, politicians, and lawyers.

Other influences were also present at the convention. Delegates had as examples to consider the state governments, the practices established over a century and a half of colonial development, and finally, the influence of the English political tradition of which they had recently been a part, which included the ideas of representative government, supremacy of law, and liberty of the subject.[9]

Thus the Constitution they would ultimately draw up would be rooted in at least three major sources: the abstract ideas of the Enlightenment, the practical experience of the colonies and the states, and the traditions of English law and government.

With all of these forces at work, the delegates arrived at Philadelphia. Edmund Randolph, Governor of Virginia, introduced the first plan. Influenced by James Madison, this "Virginia" or "large-state" plan represented sweeping changes, and it became the basis of discussion for most of the convention. It provided for a central government with three branches: a legislature of two houses, a national executive (the position that ultimately became the Presidency), and a national judiciary. The legislature would choose the executive (or executives) and the members of the judiciary, and representation from the states in the legislature would be according to population. The smaller states sponsored an alternate plan, the "New Jersey" or "small-state" plan, introduced by William Paterson. Much closer in spirit to the Articles of Confederation, its key difference with Randolph's scheme was the basic assumption that all states were equal in the union and that sovereignty rested in the states individually rather than in the people as a whole. Consequently, Paterson recommended that each state have equal representation in the Congress.

The compromise of July 16 resolved these conflicting views. The states

[8] See Carl L. Becker, *The Heavenly City of the Eighteenth-Century Philosophers* (New Haven, Conn.: Yale U.P., 1932).
[9] Clinton Rossíter, *The First American Revolution* (New York: Harcourt, 1956), pp. 7–10.

57

gained an equal vote in the Senate, and representation in the House of Representatives was to be accorded by population. With this and some other disagreements settled, the delegates signed the Constitution and sent it to the states for ratification in special conventions.

Serious and long debates characterized many of these state meetings before the requisite nine states ratified the document to place it in effect. *The Federalist Papers,* written anonymously by Alexander Hamilton, James Madison, and John Jay, propagandized in favor of the new document. Circulated throughout the country, and widely read by state-convention delegates, *The Federalist Papers* not only aided the passage of the Constitution but also represented an important and scholarly discussion of constitutionalism. The new government commenced in early 1789, and by May 1790 all thirteen states had ratified.

Many Americans feared that the concentrated power of the national government would be manipulated to undermine individual rights. To prevent this from occurring, they insisted that a specific statement of the rights of individual Americans be included in the Constitution as the price of ratification. In 1791 James Madison, distilling several reservations and recommendations from various states, drew up the first ten amendments, which the states quickly adopted. Called the Bill of Rights, these amendments are usually considered part of the original document.

Principles

A constitution, by a definition deriving from 1787, is a written document that grants powers to and limits the authority of government, that defines the organs of government, and that explains the relationship between the government and the governed. One should read the United States Constitution. It is mercifully short and worthy of careful perusal. The essential principles contained in it are the following:

1. Rule by law.
2. Popular sovereignty.
3. Separation of powers.
4. Judicial review.
5. Civilian supremacy in military matters.
6. Protection of individual rights.
7. Possibility of change.
8. Federalism.

Let us examine these with some care.

   1. The principle of *rule by law* is an obvious extension of the definition of constitutionalism. Rather than having governmental actions take place at the whim and caprice of an individual or a special-interest group, we ex-

pect rule by law and proper procedure. For example, if we are arrested for committing a crime, we expect to have a trial, to have access to legal help, and not to be incarcerated until and unless we have been proved clearly guilty. Also, a law cannot be proclaimed in effect by a President, or a Congressman, or a milk producer. Rather, to become effective it must pass both houses of Congress and be approved by the President. It must then be obeyed by all unless the courts, following litigation, proclaim it unconstitutional.

A recent and dramatic instance of the application of this principle grew out of the Watergate crisis. When Judge John Sirica ordered President Nixon to turn over the celebrated White House tapes, the President refused to obey the judge's order, invoking the doctrine of executive privilege based upon the concept of separation of powers (discussed in point 3). The President's lawyers argued that if the courts could command a President to reveal the content of private White House conversations, the power of future Presidents would be irrevocably compromised. In a historic and unanimous decision, the Supreme Court disagreed. Acknowledging that under certain circumstances the doctrine of executive privilege might well prevail, the Court asserted that in a matter of the investigation of possible criminal conduct, the President would have to comply with Judge Sirica's order. That is, even a President is not above the law.

Another, and at times controversial, example of this principle has to do with the so-called exclusionary rule. The Supreme Court has ruled that evidence illegally obtained by the police cannot be introduced in a trial (that is, it must be *excluded*). Thus the police, the upholders of the law, must also obey the law. Then, too, in the course of the Senate Watergate investigations, which were televised nationally, Senator Sam Ervin, widely reputed to be among the foremost constitutional scholars in the Congress, rose at one point to challenge a claim by presidential assistant John Ehrlichman that he believed that the President had the power to order a secret break-in into the office of a Beverly Hills psychiatrist in the interests of "national security." Quoting an old English maxim, Ervin argued that even in the humblest dwelling of the poor, "The sun may enter, the wind may enter, but the King may not enter" without specific legal authority, that is, a warrant.

2. The principle of *popular sovereignty* is an integral part of the Constitution, yet it raises perplexing questions. The Constitution rests sovereignty in the "people," which is fundamental to the concept of democracy. Sovereignty means the greatest authority and power to command all others. Sovereignty resides somewhere in every stable national state. It may reside in a king (the "sovereign") or in a parliament. Under fascism, it rests in the state. Under the Articles of Confederation, it rested in thirteen states. But the Preamble of the Constitution declares: "We the people of the United States of America . . . do ordain and establish this Constitution for

59

the United States of America." Perhaps this language was fortuitous; no one knew in what order the states would ratify, so the Preamble could hardly say "We the states of Georgia, New York, Pennsylvania . . ." More importantly, the Founding Fathers had every intention of using this language. As we have already noted, the notion of a compact among the people of a community had developed historically in the American colonies. Moreover, the idea of a "social contract" among the members of a political society was a widespread and popular political theory in the eighteenth century. The most important social-contract theorist for Americans was the seventeenth-century Englishman John Locke. In his *Second Treatise on Government* (1690), Locke explained that, on balance, human beings were decent and good and that in an ideal state of nature they could live fairly happily. However, since virtually all people have certain needs that can only be met by organized society, some method must exist to bring about such a congregation. Earlier theorists, such as the Englishman Thomas Hobbes, had argued that for the sake of order, individuals should convene themselves under the control of a single monarch who would be the ultimate sovereign. Locke's social contract was considerably different. Reasoning that human beings were, by nature, free, equal, independent, and reasonable, he believed they came together by consent, retaining as much freedom as possible. Moreover, once this "contract" has established a society and a government, the latter could always be changed, preferably by majority rule but if necessary by revolution. The Founding Fathers, like Hobbes, certainly had grave doubts about the goodness of human beings, but in the aftermath of a war against a "sovereign" king, they found altogether practical the Lockean notion of resting sovereignty in the people.[10] (It should be noted that Locke suggested that the legislature would be the sovereign, whereas Hobbes implied that the executive would fill this role.)

Still, who are these "people" in whom sovereignty rests? Radical fringe groups in America, such as the SLA (Symbionese Liberation Army), often invoke the authority of "the people" as their justification for certain illegal acts, although these acts are disapproved of by the great majority of Americans. What, then, is meant by "the people"? Are they the people who can vote? If so, what of those who are not registered? And what of those who are registered but do not vote? Do "the people" include youths under eighteen? Black Americans before the voting rights acts of the 1960s? Women before their voting rights were obtained in 1920? Are there some people who are more sovereign than others? In simple words, *popular sovereignty* is an important but difficult term. At its best, we can hope that it means an ever-improving "democracy" that seeks to draw more and more of the citizenry into the bloodstream of political decision-making.

[10] Richard Hofstadter, *The American Political Tradition* (New York: Random, 1948), Chapter 1.

3. The doctrine of *separation of powers* derived from political theory as old as the classical Greeks. Recently it had gained further credence in Montesquieu's study *The Spirit of the Laws* (1748). It proved attractive to Americans who feared the concentration of power. Federalism, as we will see, was one mechanism to effect a scattering of power. So too was the separation of functions at the national level among a Congress, a President, and a court system. None of the three branches would be fully dependent on any of the others, yet there would always be some interdependence (for example, the President would appoint Supreme Court Justices with the consent of the Senate). Furthermore, in order to assure checks and balances and deprive any one class, interest, or faction of undue domination of the government, the personnel of each branch were to be chosen in different ways: the President by an independent Electoral College, judges by the President, members of the Senate by state legislatures, and members of the House of Representatives by popular vote. There have been some changes in these three branches, particularly in the methods by which their members are chosen. The President, though officially chosen by the Electoral College, is actually elected by popular vote. In effect, this means that we vote for electors pledged to a presidential candidate rather than having a separate set of electors mull over and finally choose a President, as the framers may have intended. And Senators too are now chosen by popular vote rather than by state legislators.

Despite these changes, the concern with curtailing excessive and concentrated power has continued to the present time. In recent history, this concern has focused on the Presidency. For example, when President Nixon impounded funds appropriated by Congress (that is neither signing nor vetoing legislation but refusing to spend monies authorized in bills duly passed by the House and the Senate), critics insisted that he had violated the separation of powers by unilaterally acting as the legislature.

A more celebrated example of this principle in action is contained in the articles of impeachment passed by the House Judiciary Committee in August 1974. The committee approved three articles of impeachment against Mr. Nixon. Each of these, but mainly the last two, charged the President with (among other things) overreaching his constitutionally constituted powers. Article 2 found him guilty of "impairing the due and proper administration of justice," a function of the judicial branch, and Article 3 charged him of failing to produce evidence needed by a committee of Congress (the Judiciary Committee) and of subverting the Constitution. That is, *at least* an implicit charge in the articles of impeachment was that the President had violated the separation-of-powers doctrine.

4. The Constitution does not directly mention but does imply *judicial review*. Judicial review means the right of the federal courts to determine whether or not a piece of law, whether state or national, is consonant with the Constitution. The power to review state laws is implied in Article 6,

Section 2: "This Constitution . . . shall be the supreme law of the land; and the Judges in every State shall be bound thereby, anything in the Constitution or laws of any State to the contrary notwithstanding." Thus from the beginning, federal courts could determine the legitimacy of state laws and constitutions. The right to review national laws was established in the landmark case *Marbury v. Madison* (1803), when the Supreme Court unanimously struck down a section of the Judiciary Act of 1789, finding that it violated a provision of the Constitution. Although the right of the Court to judge the constitutionality of federal law was thus established, it has continued to cause discord. Controversy reached a high point during the 1930s. Responding to the crisis of the Depression, the Congress passed several pieces of New Deal legislation, many of which were declared unconstitutional by the Supreme Court during the court session of 1935. A tremendous uproar ensued, and President Franklin Roosevelt even introduced legislation to force the resignation of older justices and to expand the number on the Court so that he could appoint more liberal members. The Court survived this presidential onslaught and so did judicial review, which, ironically, was used in the 1950s and the 1960s in rulings many old New Dealers applauded.

In the celebrated case of *Brown v. Board of Education,* the Supreme Court, led by Chief Justice Earl Warren, in effect ruled that state laws providing for segregated education on the basis of race were unconstitutional. This action provided the legal basis for numerous challenges to the prevailing practice of racial segregation throughout the United States and helped launch a civil-rights revolution (that is, efforts by American blacks and other minorities finally to achieve that "equality" implicitly proclaimed by the Declaration of Independence).

In our discussion of the system of justice we shall once again look at this principle of judicial review.

5. Deeply embedded in the Constitution is the principle of *civilian authority,* which means that military forces are subordinate to and separate from civilian administration. Military policy is to be directed by constitutionally constituted officials, not by the military establishment. Article 2, Section 2, grants the President broad authority. He (not a military person) is Commander in Chief of the Armed Forces. The most celebrated controversy regarding this principle arose in 1951, when President Truman, citing insubordination, dismissed General Douglas MacArthur when the latter openly demanded that the President's war policy in Korea be changed. More recently, Air Force General John LaValle was reprimanded for planning and conducting unauthorized air raids in Vietnam, and General Alexander Haig, in order to assume the duties of Chief of Staff for President Nixon, was required to give up his commission in the Army.

Of course Congress as well as the President has constitutional responsibilities in the conduct of military policy. According to Article 1, Section

8, not only must appropriations for military activity come from Congress, but only the Congress can declare war. This provision has led a number of critics, in and out of the legislature, to argue that American participation in the war in Indochina was unconstitutional.

Finally, the Constitution makers decided to limit the appropriation of funds for a standing army to a two-year period, thereby mitigating the danger posed by the growth of a professional military class, which many believed to be a menace to republican government.

6. Perhaps the most audacious and certainly one of the most important principles of the Constitution is the *protection of individual rights*. Based on the concept of the dignity of the individual, this principle reverses the common notion that the individual is subordinate to the state and declares the most important characteristic of a just society to be the recognition of individual worth.

The original Constitution (Article 1, Section 9) forbade bills of attainder (the conviction of a person of a crime by formal congressional declaration) and ex post facto laws (a criminal law whose effective date precedes its passage). But the Bill of Rights contains the most sweeping and substantive protections. Included, among other liberties, are the well-known rights to freedom of speech and of the press, the right to a recognizable procedure in criminal law, and the freedom of religion. Each of the rights outlined in the Constitution is worthy of a lengthy dissertation, but noting just one, the freedom of religion, accents how advanced the framers were. Until 1787, no major Western state had ever had the courage or the inclination to separate the institution of government from the practice of religion. By forbidding all religious tests for office holding and by separating church and state, the Constitution represented a significant milestone in the history of individual liberty.

Two relatively recent and hotly controversial applications of the principle of the protection of individual rights involved the career of the late Senator Joseph P. McCarthy and the publication of the *Pentagon Papers* by the *New York Times*.

In the case of Senator McCarthy, the Wisconsin legislator used his power as chairman of a powerful Senate subcommittee to issue subpoenas against dozens of Americans, many of them prominent in the arts, in government, and even in the military. Riding the crest of a wave of popular fear and hostility toward Communism and all those who might have had some association with Communists, the Senator made himself the most feared and controversial figure in Washington during the late 1940s and early 1950s. He became almost a fourth branch of government, using the power of investigation, exposure to maximum publicity, and inquisitorial "hearings" to drive prominent persons from public life. Many of McCarthy's victims sought refuge in various provisions of the Bill of Rights. For a while the term *Fifth-Amendment Communist* was widely used in the press to describe

63

many of McCarthy's "witnesses," that is, victims who sought refuge in the constitutional prohibition against being forced to testify against themselves.

Only after McCarthy's marauding investigations reached into the highest levels of the military command did President Eisenhower decide to challenge the Senator's power. The celebrated Army–McCarthy hearings, broadcast live on television, were widely understood to be a test of power between the executive branch and the Senator. They resulted in an erosion of the Senator's popular support around the nation and a consequent move shortly thereafter to censure him in the U.S. Senate. Only belatedly did the nation come to realize that the weapons McCarthy used to defame ordinary citizens could be and indeed were turned against the highest levels of authority, so that if the rights of citizens could be violated with impunity, so sooner or later would be the rights of Senators, generals, diplomats, and perhaps ultimately the President himself.

A second, more recent test of this principle came when Dr. Daniel Ellsberg, an employee of the Rand Corporation engaged in preparing a secret report on the origins of the United States government's decision to intervene militarily in the Vietnam war, took copies of this secret document to the *New York Times* for publication. The *Times* announced its intention to publish these papers despite the official label of government secrecy. The Nixon administration sought to prevent publication. In a historic decision, the Supreme Court decided that the federal government had no right to "prior restraint" under the terms of the constitutional amendment guaranteeing freedom of the press. That is, the government could not legally censor such publication. It could only wait until the offending material had been published and then take action against the newspaper, Dr. Ellsberg, or both. The *Times* published and the government proceeded to prosecute Dr. Ellsberg. However, the constitutional merits of the case were never finally resolved as the presiding judge dismissed all charges against Ellsberg because of various governmental improprieties.

7. As we have seen, sovereignty in our system theoretically rests in the people. It would follow that the people have a *right to change the Constitution*. Article 5 provides the mechanism to do just that. Still, changes have not come often. Indeed, following the approval of the first ten amendments, only sixteen others have become part of the Constitution. Since the Twenty-first Amendment revoked the Eighteenth (prohibition), there have been only fourteen permanent amendatory changes since 1791. The normal procedure is for the Congress, by a margin of two thirds of those voting in each house, to approve an amendment. It is then submitted to the state legislatures, three fourths of which must approve it (a majority vote being required in each legislature). It then becomes effective. The Equal Rights Amendment, supported by various women's organizations, has followed this path and at this printing was but a few states short of approval.

The Constitution provides two other methods for change. Congress may

In response to fears voiced by many that the federal government would prove oppressive, the Congress passed on September 25, 1789, twelve articles of amendment to the Constitution. Except for the first two, the articles were ratified by the required number of states by December 15, 1791. The remaining ten amendments have subsequently been known as the Bill of Rights. The original is on permanent display at the National Archives, Washington, D.C.   [Photo by Steven Ross.]

submit a proposal to special state conventions instead of legislatures (as was done in the case of the Constitution and the Twenty-first Amendment), or Congress, upon the demand of two thirds of the states, must call a convention to draw up amendments that would then be ratified by the states. The latter method has never been used.

Federalism

Federalism is a principle invented by the framers. Since in 1787 it was a unique form of government, and since it affects almost all the other principles, it requires more lengthy discussion. *Federalism* refers to a dual form of government in which there is a functional and territorial division of authority. We can understand federalism by contrasting it with other forms of political organization.

The most common form of political grouping we term *unitary*. Such a government has no autonomous units. Ultimate governmental authority rests in a central government. In such a situation, policies can be applied uniformly to the whole country. Most nations today are unitary. In fact, each state in the United States is, in theory, a unitary government. Note that unitary government in no way denies popular sovereignty. It merely means that there is *one level* of ultimate governmental authority: the central government.

An alternate form of political grouping is a *confederation* such as existed under the Articles of Confederation. The common central agency in a confederation may discuss policy and advise separate members, but it has no meaningful power. Each member unit (state, province, or whatever) retains ultimate governmental authority.

Federalism is a compromise between unitary and confederate political organization. In the United States, this means several things. First, there is a division of political authority (for example, the central government is responsible for coining money—the states cannot—whereas the states establish laws regulating marriage and divorce). Second, there are certain powers that both levels have, like the power to tax. Finally, the two levels can cooperate. The usual method by which this is done is through grants-in-aid, which are monies provided by the national government to the states to help finance a state program.

Although the Tenth Amendment leaves to the states "reserved" powers, these have never been adequately defined. Indeed, in explicit terms, the Constitution only limits state authority while granting no specific powers.

The Constitution would never have been adopted had not provisions for state sovereignty been retained. One could argue that the framers sought a compromise and came up with federalism virtually out of necessity. However, there is also evidence that the framers, particularly Madison, had thought carefully about how to unify a large and possibly expanding area with outlying territories and a variety of interests. The key problem, as the men of the eighteenth century saw it, was that a single faction or interest would almost certainly control the government. Consequently, as the widely read French political philosopher Montesquieu had suggested, a republic (a nonhereditary government reflecting the various interests in the state) could exist only in a city or a small territory. This reservation was based on the common assumption that nation states would be unitary. To solve this problem, Madison and the framers invented federalism which dispersed political sovereignty geographically as well as functionally.[11]

But which of the levels of the government—state or national—has *ulti-*

[11] Douglass Adair, " 'That Politics May Be Reduced to a Science': David Hume, James Madison, and the Tenth Federalist," *Huntington Library Quarterly,* **20:**343–360 (Aug. 1957).

mate sovereignty? Article 6 of the Constitution strongly implies that it is the national level. Most citizens, if asked, would probably agree. Many, in fact, might insist (perhaps unhappily) that the national government has over the years gained power at the expense of the states, some even contending that the states have lost power. Such is simply not the case. Since World War II, the fundamental trend has been for both levels of government to increase activity. Indeed, in terms of expenditures, state governments have actually increased activities more rapidly than the national government since the end of the war.[12]

There is no doubt, however, that the national government has grown in power since 1787 and in some instances at the expense of the states. There are many reasons for this. For one, the victory of the North in the Civil War determined clearly that the nation was one of people more than it was one of sovereign states. Thus no state, at its own whim, could leave the union (as, presumably, a member of the United Nations could leave that organization). Second, the doctrine of *implied powers* has given the national government authority not expressly stated in the Constitution. The Supreme Court's decision in *McCulloch v. Maryland* (1819) established this doctrine. In 1816 the Second Bank of the United States received a federal charter. It opened a branch office in Baltimore under the cashiership of one James W. McCulloch. The state of Maryland (along with other states) looked unfavorably upon the bank since the state wished to charter her own bank. The issue was complicated by the unsavory (though profitable) activities of Mr. McCulloch and certain directors of the branch office, whose practices one scholar has described as systematic "looting" of the bank.[13] Furthermore, there is evidence that opposition within the state of Maryland came chiefly from envious bankers there who wished to indulge in similar financially rewarding enterprises with state-chartered banks. In response to these latter interests, the state of Maryland enacted a law taxing the branch bank's bank notes—an attempt to drive it out of business. The imperturbable McCulloch simply refused to pay the tax and was in turn sued by the state, and the case went into the federal courts, arriving in 1819 before the Supreme Court. Now, Article 1, Section 8, of the Constitution accords no specific power to the Congress to charter a bank. Chief Justice John Marshall ruled, however, that since the United States government had a right to exist and a right to collect money (the Constitution does specify the authority to tax), it should have a place to put that money. That is, the Congress could reasonably determine that the establishment of a national bank was "necessary and proper" for carrying out its constitutional functions. Such a power was not specific in the Constitution but *im-*

[12] *Statistical Abstract of the U.S.* (Washington, D.C.: G.P.O., 1967).
[13] Bray Hammond, "The Bank Cases," in John A. Garraty (Ed.), *Quarrels That Have Shaped the Constitution* (New York: Harper, 1964).

67

plied. Moreover, the Court's unanimous decision went on to declare Maryland's tax on the bank notes unconstitutional because in a federal system a state (though of course having the right to tax) could not cripple the national government in carrying out its legitimate powers. Thus the national government, by implication, had more power than those specified in the Constitution and the states could not interfere with those powers.

"The government of the union, then," concluded Chief Justice Marshall, "is emphatically and truly a government of the people. In form and substance it emanates from them, its powers are granted by them, and are to be exercised directly on them, and for their benefit." [14] Of course, the Civil War physically confirmed this principle.

A third reason for the expansion of national governmental authority is the *interpretation* of express constitutional powers. For example, Congress can tax and thus supposedly spend money, even for reasons as vague as "to promote the general welfare." Congress can "regulate commerce among the several states." In *Gibbons v. Ogden* (1824), the Supreme Court ruled that such "commerce" included all forms of commercial intercourse.[15] Thus the national government has enacted laws fixing minimum wages and maximum hours and regulating child labor in any business involved in interstate "intercourse."

Finally, the national government's powers have expanded because of constitutional amendments. For example, the Sixteenth Amendment, passed in 1912, gives the national government the immense and specific authority to collect income taxes, The Fifteenth, Nineteenth, and Twenty-sixth Amendments establish national guidelines for voting requirements (a function initially accorded to the states) by providing the right to vote to blacks, women, and those eighteen years of age and older. Each of these amendments gives the Congress (that is, the national government) power of enforcement "by appropriate legislation."

Federalism seems to imply that each state will act independently from other states as well as independently from the national government. In fact, cooperation and coordination among the various levels have become characteristic of the system. The *interstate compact* has come to be used to effect such cooperation. These compacts are designed to handle problems affecting two or more states. The Port of New York Authority is perhaps the classic example of such a compact. It operates the harbor and coordinates the operation of airports in greater New York for the states of the area.

Cooperation between states and the national government is achieved mainly through "grants-in-aid." First used in the nineteenth century, a grant-in-aid is a grant of money to a state to help finance some state

[14] 4 Wheaton 316 (1819).
[15] 9 Wheaton 1 (1824).

activity, like building a highway or providing welfare payments. The normal practice has been for Washington to place conditions on these grants. That is, the money must be spent for a specific purpose, the state must meet certain federal standards (for example, money for education cannot be given to districts with segregated schools), and the state must match federal funds (for example, for every $9 the national government contributes to building a highway, the state must contribute $1). In recent years, both conservative and liberal critics have advocated an end to aid from the national government with strings attached, substituting instead direct grants with no federal government requirements at all. This scheme has been called *revenue sharing*. After considerable debate during the 1960s, federal legislation has at last provided for some revenue-sharing funds, resulting in the flow of large sums of money into states, to be used however those states wish. Although revenue sharing has grown increasingly popular, there are criticisms, some of which have resulted in the retention of certain federal guidelines. Critics point to the grants to states of money that the federal government has collected, thus separating the taxing and spending agents, which might lead to less responsible expenditure. Others say that the system rewards inefficient states, such as those that refuse to enact a state income tax, knowing they will receive large sums from Washington. Some city officials worry that state governments might not funnel enough of the money to urban areas. In response, the Congress has legislated that two thirds of the money must go to counties, cities, and towns. Civil-rights groups raised fears that the money might be used to support segregated facilities, and Congress responded by making adherence to the civil-rights laws a requirement of revenue sharing. Finally, some critics have suggested that the system is basically inefficient, that for every $3 the federal government collects for revenue sharing, only $2 makes its way back to the state. The remaining $1 goes to the bureaucracy collecting and then distributing the money. Despite these criticisms, revenue sharing remains popular. The federal government, mainly because of the income tax, can collect money from all citizens more easily than can individual states. Because the national government is the major source of money and because the states are in need of funds (and some cities are going broke), revenue sharing may be, proponents say, the most reasonable way to make federalism viable.

But does, or can, federalism really work as we approach the twenty-first century? Is tiny Rhode Island in any way similar or equal to Texas? Or is Alaska really comparable in any way to California, with her 20 million plus inhabitants? What kind of allegiance can we reasonably be expected to have to one state over any other? The major social aggregate most of us are familiar with is the city (or megalopolis), not the state. People live, work, and identify with Greater New York or Greater Los Angeles. In fact, some have said New York City is so different from the rest of New York that it should be a separate state. Also the city and its surrounding suburbs

69

pose such large and complex problems for America that they may perhaps be too complex for traditional states to handle. And what sense does it make to allow every state to have different laws regulating marriage, divorce, and a host of other things? Is it fair that a rich person can fly to Reno for a quickie divorce, whereas a poorer person wades through a lengthy litigation or simply gives up and lives unhappily ever after? Or is it fair for a person who lives in New Jersey to commute to work in New York, yet pay no taxes there?

Of course, such criticisms will be leveled at federalism as long as it exists. However, there may be advantages we do not wish to give up. Federalism offers a certain flexibility and possibility for experimentation not readily available in a unitary system. Most political and social reforms have begun in states and have later come to the national government. The direct, democratic election of U.S. Senators is an example. Several states set the precedent long before the Seventeenth Amendment was added to the Constitution. And Wyoming instituted women's suffrage many years prior to the passage of the Nineteenth Amendment. Furthermore, an individual state may provide valuable examples for other states. California's creation in the early 1960s of a master plan of higher education established a model that many other states subsequently followed.

Finally, in a large and complex society, the principle of there being a government (however complex) that is closer to the citizen than Washington, D.C. is still quite attractive. This, after all, is something Madison and the Founding Fathers knew. And that's why they invented federalism.

Here, then, are the core principles of the United States Constitution. Noting them does not explain all the essentials of the Constitution. The document is short and frequently ambiguous. Scholars and politicians can easily disagree as to its meaning. Many recent questions highlight this disagreement. What, for example, under our Constitution, constitutes an impeachable offense by a President? Are there any limitations on the authority of a presidential pardon? Is bussing a constitutional way to achieve racial integration in the schools? To these and many other questions the Constitution may not offer a universally agreed-upon answer, rather only a guide to action for our institutions of government.

Four final points should be made regarding the Constitution.

First, it is a genuinely national document. That is, in the dispute between "states' rights" and national power, the latter takes precedence. (Disagreement over this issue, of course, was a factor in precipitating the Civil War.) The history of the origins of the Constitution, briefly outlined here, underscores this point. So does Article 6, Section 2, which proclaims the Constitution and the laws made under it "the supreme law of the land."

Second, the Constitution was not completely satisfactory to anyone. In fact, Edmund Randolph, the sponsor of the Virginia plan, did not even sign the final draft. It was a compromise document, designed by well-informed, practical politicians who knew that much remained to be done in order to make the new government workable.

Third, the Constitution was revolutionary, both in technique and by its very nature. Its adoption was technically illegal because Congress had charged the Convention only with amending the Articles of Confederation and because this latter document required unanimous approval among the states for any changes (recall that the Constitution provided that nine states' approval would put it into effect). Also, as the first major written constitution, proclaiming the principles of the most advanced and in some cases the most radical thinkers of the age, it can reasonably be called a major document of what one scholar has called the "Age of the Democratic Revolution." [16]

Fourth, we should keep in mind that the Philadelphia delegates and the members of the first governments formed under the Constitution had a freedom of action unmatched in present-day revolutionary situations. Since World War II, any colonial possession that has successfully separated from a mother country, no matter what the nature of its constitution, almost automatically must look forward to some amount of "aid" or hindrance from other nations of the world. A striking example is the Congo (now called Zaire), which although gaining independence in 1960, experienced pressures and influence from Belgium (the former colonial possessor), the United States, the Soviet Union, and finally the United Nations, which stationed an international armed force there. Because of the long lines of communication and because Europe was soon (1789) to become absorbed in the French Revolution and subsequent wars, America was spared this kind of interference. Although a new state, born in revolution, she was able to develop independently. We can only speculate as to the positive effect this independence had upon the system of government outlined in the Constitution.

Finally, it should be noted that whatever its weaknesses (and we shall discuss some of these in ensuing chapters), the Constitution has accomplished its primary objective remarkably well. The country has held together for two hundred years under a single document. (France, in contrast, has had fourteen different constitutions in the intervening years.)

Social critic Edmund Wilson has noted that the United States is more a "society" than a "nation." (Alexis De Tocqueville had made the same point.) By this Wilson meant that the United States, unlike most of the world's countries, is made up of different races and nationalities and that it lacks many of the institutions that characterize most nations. There are no established religion, no hereditary aristocracy, and few ancient traditions

[16] R. R. Palmer, *The Age of the Democratic Revolution,* 2 vols. (Princeton, N.J.: Princeton U.P., 1959).

that are universally understood and honored. The Italian people, although achieving political unity relatively recently (1860), have a civilization that dates back twenty-five hundred years. Thus the Italians are often said to be indifferent to their government because they are bound together by religion, language, culture, and traditions that go far deeper than politics.

The United States in a sense is in the opposite condition. Divided by race, creed, and national origin, as well as by sheer physical size, Americans are dependent upon organized government to maintain national unity and social cohesion. The Constitution was designed to create a framework that would permit Americans to remain united while preventing any single faction, group, or class, from seizing absolute control. Whether it has done so or not remains a question of moment. However, that we can continue to seek a just society with a people so diverse is in no small measure due to the gift of the Founding Fathers.

Thus the Constitution has evolved over two centuries to become a secular version of "holy writ" for Americans. For as Mosaic Law provided the cement that bound the ancient Hebrews together, as the New Testament defines and unites Christianity, so the Constitution has become the definitive statement of American life and government.

The President as Superstar

It's not true that anyone can be President; most of us have better things to do.

> Gary Wills
> *"Hurrah for Politicians,"*
> *Harper's, Sept. 1975*

In primitive societies, much of what human beings do in the course of a normal day is permeated by magic. Normal activities such as work, hunting, eating, and making love are suffused by the world of spirits. Powerful if unseen gods and goddesses, embodied in age-old myths, ritual, and tradition, tell the farmer when and how to plant, why the seasons change, what must be done to overcome certain illnesses. "Sophisticated" people often describe primitives as "childlike" precisely because, like children, "natural" men or women live in a world that is dominated by magical spirits both good and bad, and hence their ordinary behavior tends to reflect emotional extremes of fear and dread on the one hand and a special kind of charm and happiness on the other.

Those who have grown up in scientific, technologically advanced cultures, on the other hand, tend to live in what Herbert Marcuse calls a "one dimensional world." [1] "A comfortable, smooth, reasonable, democratic *unfreedom* prevails in advanced industrial civilization," notes Marcuse. By "unfreedom" Marcuse means that the full range of human thought and feeling is somehow denied to most residents of what we call civilized states; that is the price of economic security, technical progress, and a secular rather than a spiritual view of the universe. But there is in the human mind something that refuses to be bound by the limits of reason and what is scientifically knowable. What Jean-Paul Sartre calls "a hunger for the absolute"—that is, a desire to transcend the mundane, physical limits of daily life—remains a powerful *political* impulse in human affairs. This impulse can be recognized most clearly in polls of political thought and behavior, in the appeal a "madman" like Adolph Hitler had for an advanced, scientific nation like Germany, and, more positively, in the spiritual qualities of leaders such as Gandhi or Dr. Martin Luther King, Jr. But it also exists as an important, perhaps a critical factor within the political mainstream.

Instead of gods and goddesses, ordinary people in secular societies have celebrities and "stars"—literally, objects of remote, mysterious, and

---

[1] *One-Dimensional Man* (Boston: Beacon, 1964).

illuminating power—whose marvel-filled lives, as recorded by the mass media, fill the hearts of people. The "magic" that once permeated the lives of ordinary folk has now been transferred to certain special and transcendent beings, entertainers such as Robert Redford or Elizabeth Taylor or Elton John, superathletes like O. J. Simpson, and political stars such as the Kennedys.

Eugène Ionesco has written a short play called *The Leader* that beautifully captures this phenomenon: the play begins with a radio announcer's proclaiming to an excited crowd the imminent arrival of The Great Man. The crowd is beside itself with anticipation. Shrewdly the announcer builds excitement by telling the people of the remarkable doings of their hero: "He brushes his teeth in the morning. He reads his newspaper and drinks his coffee. He puts on his pants. . . ."

The crowd is rapt with a truly religious ecstasy. Oh! The wonder of it all.

Anyone who has read a "gossip" column or listened to a broadcast interview of the charmed life of the annointed will grasp Ionesco's point. Ionesco's "Leader" is an ordinary person doing ordinary things. It is the crowd's need, not the deeds of its hero, that creates the aura of stardom. In this respect, much political gossip is not really very different from the stuff that fills the movie and TV fan magazines—some of it invented, much of it embellished to satisfy the demands of the market.

In a celebrity-worshiping society, the President of the United States is the Number One celebrity. He is invariably the most famous and usually the most admired person in the nation. Since the nation fell in love with the family of John Kennedy, this special status has been extended to most members of the President's immediate family as well. The question of whether or not Susan Ford should or should not tell her mother if she were planning to have an affair was, for many weeks, a profound *political* problem for the Ford administration and hence for the nation. That Jimmy Carter had sometimes looked upon women with lust in his heart was probably the most widely discussed single remark to emerge from the thousands of speeches and hundreds of interviews given by both major party candidates in the 1976 campaign, including three long, televised debates.

Of course, an American President must deal with far greater issues, matters of life-or-death concern to hundreds of millions of people. Why then do the media so often seem to fasten upon some trivial, purely personal, and apparently meaningless comment or eccentricity? Clearly it is because they believe that that is what the public wants to hear reported.

The President's real powers may be less significant than his symbolic role, which is to serve as a kind of physical embodiment of the whole nation.

Consider James Earl Carter's campaign for the Presidency in 1976.

He was first presented to the American people as "an outsider," not a professional politician but a farmer, a simple, good man with a loving family, a Sunday-school teacher, a softball player, a smiling, soft-spoken product of small-town America—a kind of adult Tom Sawyer. Millions of Americans rallied to him and carried Carter to victory in most Democratic party primaries. After winning his party's nomination, Jimmy Carter, the All-American Boy, was ahead of Gerald Ford by thirty-three percentage points in the national polls—the largest lead ever recorded by a candidate for the Presidency at that stage of the campaign.

In November 1976, Carter emerged with a narrow three-percentage-point victory over President Ford in the general election. And much of that support, according to most of the polls and pundits, came not because the voters were enamored of Carter personally but because he was a Democrat and people felt it was "time for a change." What happened to the Carter myth in the interval? For one thing, the media, which took him at face value as a "bright, new star" on the political horizon in the spring of 1976, began to examine Carter far more critically during the fall campaign. Clearly too, Carter made some mistakes, such as his highly publicized *Playboy* interview, which helped tarnish his halo. But we would suggest that what happened to Carter's astonishing summer lead was not his fault, or the media's fault, so much as it was the inevitable result of a certain natural process of familiarity. The public had discovered that James Earl Carter was not a vision in a television commercial (perhaps the smiling small-town grocer who recommends the toothpaste that keeps fighting cavities) but a mortal human being, a man who looks upon some women in the way most men look upon some women. Worse yet, he is a somewhat complicated man who reads books and thinks complex thoughts. Finally, he is a man who does not necessarily agree with every commonplace notion that is the stock-in-trade of high-school debaters, service-club luncheon orators, and unread editorial writers. Jimmy Carter was unmasked. The people discovered instead James Earl Carter, a complex, thoughtful, ambitious, imperfect human being.

Opposed to him, on the other hand, was Gerald Ford, widely perceived to be a simple, good-natured fellow—"a regular guy."

In the last two televised debates between the candidates, most polls and pundits suggested that Carter had "won" the debates; that is, he had appeared more knowledgeable and assured and seemed to have the more logical side of the argument. Nevertheless, Ford kept gaining in the polls. In the end, Carter was elected narrowly. Most experts agreed that his victory was due primarily to three factors: Ford's burden of Watergate and the Nixon pardon; the economic difficulties still besetting the nation; and the 2-to-1 registration edge Democrats had over Republicans. Few attributed Carter's victory to personal magnetism. The myth had simply dissolved.

76

Not the least among Carter's problems, upon assuming the Presidency, was the task of building a new, more enduring "superstar" image in the public mind.

Many of President Carter's most dramatic moves during his first months in the White House dealt more with the reconstruction of an image than with the substance of public affairs. His walking to the White House on Inauguration Day, deciding to enroll Amy in a public school, wearing a sweater while making his first televised "fireside" chat, taking phone calls from average people on a live, nationwide radio hookup, spending the night in the home of a New England family and appearing at a town meeting to answer questions from the audience—all of these actions helped erase the doubts many Americans had expressed about him in November. As usually happens with a newly-elected President in the early months of his tenure, Carter's popularity soared.

Once in office, he and his family became the focal point of an enormous industry that creates and sells celebrityhood to the American people. As we have argued, the existence of this industry is rooted, at least in part, in the emotional need of the people for larger-than-life figures who presumably live a charmed existence that the public can enjoy vicariously. This industry also exists because the people really do need leadership. The average person does not know, and knows he or she does not know, enough to solve all the complex problems of a large, powerful nation such as the United States. Does less unemployment necessarily mean more inflation? Even the most highly trained economists disagree on such matters, so how can the average person presume to know the answer? Is the B-1 bomber important to our defense or simply a disguised form of welfare for defense contractors? Again, experts disagree. Should we defend Israel at the risk of another oil embargo? Should we rely upon nuclear power to help meet the energy crisis, or is it inherently too dangerous? These and thousands of similar questions must be resolved. And people expect the President to have the answers.

Leadership

The question of leadership, therefore, is a critical question of politics. The leader normally makes decisions for the group. Should he fail to do so, he ceases to be the leader in fact if not always in form. (There is a familiar joke among students of politics about the leader during the French Revolution who, from inside his apartment window, saw a mob marching through the streets, grabbed his coat and rushed out the door. "Where are you going?" his wife asked. "To find out where the people are going so that I can lead them," replied the politician.)

What gives one man the right to make a decision that may shape the lives of hundreds of millions of his fellow citizens? Some people—anarchists, libertarians, even proponents of direct democracy—affirm that no one should have such a right. But in history, many groups have preferred or at least accepted an institution that—in one form or another—conferred the power to decide on a single individual. Attempts to rationalize the exercise of such power have revolved around what political scientists refer to as *legitimacy*. Among most primitive political groups, as well as among many of the most modern states, the authority that created and supported the power of the ruler was often thought to be divine. Moses was chosen by God to lead the children of Israel. Napoleon liked to tell his troops that he had extraordinary power to read their thoughts. He made it a point to expose himself to enemy fire in battle and had at least five horses shot out from under him but was never wounded. He did not discourage the soldiers' belief that this was because he was under some form of divine protection.

Despite their unhappy experience with George III, the creators of the American political system perceived the need for a single person to serve as both the symbol and the leader of the new nation. And so they created the Presidency. But because they feared that the President might assume kingly airs and powers, they limited his power. The right to declare war was reserved to the Congress, along with the right to levy taxes and authorize expenditures. The Congress had the right to override a presidential veto (an old Roman term meaning "I forbid"). Finally, the Congress could impeach the President for "high crimes and misdemeanors." Later, more constraints on the exercise of presidential power were added, such as the two-term limit for any President, and, more recently, Congress restricted the right of the President to sustain troop involvement in foreign lands without its sanction. And the Supreme Court gradually acquired the right to strike down both presidential and congressional acts in the name of the Constitution and the law. The Constitution, not the President's will, is the supreme law of the land.

Yet despite the clear intent of the Founding Fathers and the formidable barriers erected by Congress, the courts, and the Constitution, we have gradually developed what one scholar has called the "imperial Presidency." [2] The Presidency of the United States is often described as "the most powerful office on earth."

This power seems to have accrued to Presidents naturally and almost inevitably throughout the two centuries of the republic. Although most United States Presidents, and almost all candidates for the Presidency, have affirmed their personal and philosophical opposition to the concentration of power in the hands of one man, the office has grown in strength.

[2] See Arthur M. Schlesinger, Jr., *The Imperial Presidency* (Boston: Houghton, 1973).

A striking paradox was the Presidency of Richard Milhous Nixon, who campaigned on the basis of limiting government power. But it was during Nixon's administration that the debate among Americans as to the proper limits of presidential power reached its climax. (The issue had been raised at least as far back as Franklin D. Roosevelt's time.) Whether this debate and its fatal consequences for President Nixon's administration was simply a passing thing, an ephemeral response to a President who happened to rub too many people the wrong way, or whether it signifies a profound and permanent change in American politics remains to be seen. The question is not merely academic. For how it is answered will surely affect the fate of the nation.

The Nixon Presidency

August 8, 1974 was a remarkable day in our history. For the first time a President of the United States resigned. Richard Nixon, who less than two years earlier had won reelection to the Presidency by a remarkable landslide, left the office he had craved, planned for, and fought to possess for almost three decades. (Nixon first won election to the Vice Presidency in 1952 and appeared on his party's presidential ticket no less than five times, making him the most durable politician in our history, with the single exception of FDR, who was also a five-time candidate for the Presidency or Vice Presidency.)

As Nixon began his second term of office in the winter of 1973, his power seemed virtually unassailable. On his own authority he had authorized an invasion ("incursion") of Cambodia and the massive bombing of Laos. He had issued orders to the FBI, the CIA, and the Internal Revenue Bureau to use their vast police powers legally and illegally to reward his friends and punish his enemies. He impounded funds for various projects authorized by law and not vetoed. When Congress sought to investigate his actions, he cited "executive privilege" and issued orders to high officials in his administration not to cooperate with congressional committees seeking the information they needed to determine whether or not the President was acting properly and within the Constitution.

The President's disregard of the traditional American concept of a balance of power and his refusal to consult with, and in many cases, even talk to members of the Congress (even one of Nixon's strongest supporters, Senator Barry Goldwater, complained that he could not reach the President on the telephone) or to members of his own Cabinet, many of whom were effectively sealed off from the President by presidential aide H. R. "Bob" Haldeman's "zero-defect" system, were reminiscent of the doctrine of the divine right of kings; thus the term the *imperial Presidency*.

But the imperial Presidency was not always unpopular with the people. One month after he unilaterally ordered the carpet bombing of Vietnam, in December 1972, public opinion polls showed Mr. Nixon's popularity at an all-time high.

However, the American constitutional system, facing an unprecedented challenge by an administration all but oblivious to the dangers of one-man rule, received some unanticipated support. In 1973 and 1974, the country began to feel the effects of both an unprecedented inflation and a sharp business downturn, which tended to erode Nixon's popularity.

The second, critical, factor that began to undermine the Nixon Presidency was the continuing Watergate scandal. Beginning as a simple investigation of what the Nixon administration had dismissed as a "fifth-rate burglary"—the break-in to the Democratic National Committee Headquarters at the Watergate Hotel in June 1972—the developing scandal soon went far beyond this and *Watergate* became synonymous with a growing perception of the Nixon administration as lawless, arrogant, and arbitrary. Neither the Constitution nor the people called for a weak Presidency. On the contrary, both seemed to require a strong Chief Executive who, together with his family, would serve as a symbol of the nation and whose voice would be decisive in national affairs. But neither the Constitution nor the people envisioned a President who, acting without consultation or formal authorization, would launch wars, order illegal acts, and seek to suppress public criticism of his actions.

By the summer of 1974, actions by both the Congress and the courts had severely checked the President. On July 24, the Supreme Court (containing four justices appointed by Mr. Nixon) unanimously rejected the President's contention that he could withhold 64 tapes subpoenaed by special prosecutor Leon Jaworski. Then by the end of July, after the Judiciary Committee of the House of Representatives had agreed on three articles of impeachment, it became certain that the President would be impeached by the House and convicted by the Senate. Under the gathering storm, Mr. Nixon had little choice but to leave. Even under these extreme circumstances, with little or no important support left, there were fears that Mr. Nixon might resort to an unconstitutional seizure of power to maintain his Presidency. A Nixon-appointed Cabinet member, Defense Secretary James Schlesinger, sent secret orders to the armed forces designed to prevent a possible presidential coup.[3]

The end of the Nixon Presidency highlighted a perplexing set of questions that had developed over the preceding decades: Henceforth, what should be the nature of presidential leadership? Should Congress now take a larger role in initiating policy? Did the President really have too much power? Or, paradoxically, did he have too little, particularly in

[3] See New York Times, *The End of a Presidency* (New York: Bantam, 1974).

domestic affairs? Had the imperial Presidency (which some say began with FDR) finally come to an end?

In trying to answer these questions, the country turned to the new President, Gerald Ford. In style, President Ford was unlike his predecessor. He was a friendly, outgoing man, willing to listen. Much was made of his personal humility: the President was shown picking up his own newspaper in the morning and cooking his own breakfast. Mr. Ford had not even been elected Vice President, but had been appointed to the office by the now-deposed Mr. Nixon less than a year earlier in order to replace Spiro T. Agnew, who had been forced to resign when evidence emerged that he had taken illegal payoffs while Vice President! A more dramatic change in the Presidency could hardly be invented by the most imaginative mind.

Overnight we had deposed a famous leader known for his toughness, his passion for privacy, and his record as a bruising political in-fighter, in favor of a man largely unknown to the American people but with a reputation among his colleagues and Washington commentators for being "a nice guy" in a profession in which "nice guys finish last."

So here was Gerald Ford, President by choice of Mr. Nixon, with no election and certainly no mandate, no normally understood sanction for action—in short, no "legitimacy" aside from a series of bizarre historical accidents. Was the Presidency at its nadir? Were we to repeat the history of the late nineteenth century, when, following the assassination of a very strong President (Lincoln), the Congress became the leading branch of the national government? Was the imperial Presidency dead?

Then, but days after assuming office, the new President announced to a shocked TV audience that he had personally pardoned the former President for any crimes Nixon *may have committed*. The public outcry was immense. The legal questions were confusing (how can someone be pardoned for crimes he has not been charged with, much less convicted of?). But perhaps more significant was the manner by which Mr. Ford reached his decision. He did not consult Congress nor the courts. There is evidence that he did not even consult most of his close advisers. That is, he consulted no constitutional officials. In this initial important decision, Mr. Ford consulted God. His decision may or may not have been good, well, and right. But it was an action of an imperial President, as imperial as those actions of kings who believed in divine right. For if God spoke to Gerald Ford, who dared dispute His word? [4]

It was for this reason that many liberal Democrats were reluctant to support Jimmy Carter in the 1976 campaign. The fear was that Carter's much publicized religious commitment might lead him to divinely inspired acts not authorized by the Constitution. For it is the nature of

[4] "The Theology of Forgiveness," *Time* (Sept. 23, 1974).

the Presidency that it does wondrous and awesome things to and for people, both those who are President and those who are not. It is the most interesting political office in the world.

What Is the Presidency?

The modern Presidency has three basic components. First, it is defined in and has developed from Article 2 of the Constitution. Second, it is a product of historical forces. Finally, it is a reflection of the people who have held the office and the precedents they have established.

The Constitution defines the Presidency in the following manner.

The Presidency exists as a separate branch of government, unlike the parliamentary system currently favored in most European democracies. A Prime Minister is, in a sense, the leader of his party in Parliament; he is "first among equals." A President, on the other hand, has no formal, binding relationship to his party. In this sense, he is free to act with greater autonomy.

Thus the President can be only one person (as Lyndon Johnson was fond of reminding his opponents, "I'm the only President we have"), and his election is not tied to election of the legislature. The President serves for a fixed term, four years, and could, until adoption of the Twenty-second Amendment, be reelected indefinitely. The President's powers were specifically detailed by the Constitution, and these were different from those given to the Congress. Some authorities claim that the phrase "the Executive power shall be vested in the President of the United States of America" is much broader than the specific powers allocated to the President. (See the section entitled "Roles, Power, and the President.") Furthermore there was no "council of revision" with the power to overrule the President, although this was a common feature of state governments at that time and some members of the Constitutional Convention advocated that it be included. Finally, the President or any member of his administration was precluded from serving in either house of Congress. This again tended to reinforce the "separateness" of the Presidency.[5]

Clearly, these decisions, imbedded in the Constitution, created a Presidency of considerable strength. Certain historical forces added to that strength.

First, the economic developments that changed the United States from an agrarian, rural society into a highly industrial, technological, and urban society have influenced the Presidency. Independent farmers had less need of strong leaders than urban populations. And particularly in the twentieth century there have been increasing demands on government

---

[5] Clinton Rossiter, *The American Presidency* (New York: Mentor, 1956), pp. 56–59.

to control and/or ameliorate the problems associated with industrialization and urbanization. This growing reliance on government has resulted in legislation that has hastened the expanding power of the federal government, and particularly the President. Think, for example, of the growing bureaucracy designed to deal with such problems: the Departments of Labor; Agriculture; Health, Education and Welfare; and Housing and Urban Development; the Federal Energy Office; and much more. This elaborate bureaucracy is under the direction and command of the President.

A second historical force affecting the President has been the growing involvement of the United States in international affairs and foreign wars. As late as 1938, America belonged to no military alliance, had no troops stationed in any foreign country, and had an army of less than two hundred thousand with a budget of less than $500 million. At the peak of the Vietnam war, on the other hand, the United States had 1.5 million soldiers and sailors stationed in over one hundred countries, military alliances with forty-eight nations, and a defense budget of about $80 billion.[6] This whole diplomatic and military operation is presided over by the President, in some instances directed solely by him.

A third historical factor affecting the Presidency has been the rapid growth of the country in terms of both its geography and its population. It has devolved upon the President to be the national representative of this large area. There are Congressmen, mayors, governors, and state legislators; but the personage around which controversy swirls is the President. We can all focus on him. Harry Truman's famous remark that "the buck stops here" is a simple explanation of the truism that when the most important and fundamental decisions are made, they are made by the President. That fact suggests enormous responsibility. It also suggests enormous power.

Also, the Presidency is a highly democratic office. That is, the President is the only person chosen from the electorate of the entire nation. The extension of the suffrage to women, minority groups, and eighteen-year-olds has created the largest and perhaps the most unwieldy political constituency in history. It is, nevertheless, solely the President's.

Precedents

Certain men who have held the office have, by initiative and innovation, created an image of what the office is. Recent Presidents have been more inclined to justify their actions by pointing to the precedents of their predecessors than they have by pointing to the Constitution.

[6] Stephen E. Ambrose, *Rise to Globalism* (Baltimore: Penguin, 1971), p. 11.

On April 30, 1789, George Washington, was inaugurated as the first President of the United States. Although not required to deliver an inaugural address, Washington chose to do so to assure the people and the nation that he would govern with restraint and would respect the rights of all. The custom of delivering an inaugural address has continued to this day. Illustrated, the first page of Washington's inaugural. [Photo by Steven Ross.]

Important individuals who have affected the office are George Washington because he was first and because his precedents (such as the origin of the Cabinet and the traditional two-term limit) have the most sanctity; Thomas Jefferson because he was Thomas Jefferson and also because he was the first President to become a political leader of a political party; Andrew Jackson, who ostensibly proved that a commoner could be President, because he considered himself the "voice of the people" and who showed what could be done with the veto (he used it more times than all previous Presidents combined); and Abraham Lincoln because he led the country through its most trying crisis (and because he is the closest thing to a religious/mythical figure we have).

But two twentieth-century Presidents have influenced the office most spectacularly. Woodrow Wilson (whom Nixon regarded as the greatest President of the twentieth century) was very influential. Using his expertise as a Ph.D in history and political science and a Democratically controlled Congress, he effected a greater body of domestic legislation than any President before him. More importantly, Wilson led us into our first European war *with allies* and then told us and the world that we were morally superior to those allies and sought a different and better peace settlement. His vision of international order, with a world government on the lines of American democracy, and led by the United States, has affected America's perception of her place in the world from that time forward. Wilson was a strong, religious, charismatic, and sometimes unbending man. His notions of international affairs were at first rebuffed in the United States, but by the end of World War II, they had become sacrosanct principles of our foreign policy. The strong image he implanted on the executive office cannot be underestimated.

Even more important than Wilson was Franklin Delano Roosevelt, who led the country through the Great Depression and World War II, in the process breaking the two-term tradition and serving as President longer than anyone. A master of politics, he also proved himself adroit with the new technological device of radio. The enormous bureaucracy that is our government today began under FDR in order to fight the Depression and the Nazis. (For a fuller discussion of the bureaucracy, see the discussion in Chapter Eight.) Some people during and even after his lengthy term associated the Presidency and Roosevelt interchangeably. Political scientist Thomas E. Cronin has even argued that in the aftermath of Roosevelt, the notion of a "textbook President" developed, overemphasizing the beneficence, competence, and near omnipotence of the office.[7]

Thus the modern Presidency is a combination of Article 2 of the Constitution, historical forces, and precedents established by individual Presidents. All of these have led to a certain general perception of the President's role in American life.

Roles, Power, and the President

Each of us assumes certain roles at different times in our lives, sometimes at different times in the same day. At times we are a son or a daughter,

[7] "Making the Presidency Safe for Democracy," *The Center Magazine* (Sept.–Oct. 1973).

at times a student, a teacher, a wife or a husband, a boss, a lover, a best friend, and many more. These roles carry with them expected behavior. For example, someone's expected actions as a student in a classroom differ from the same person's expected actions as a lover. The combination of all roles a person plays is his or her total behavior.

Any individual who becomes President assumes unique roles that make up the total behavior of the Presidency as an institution. Many of these roles are mandated by constitutional law and by historical precedent. Moreover in virtually every instance, these roles represent power, rarely if ever a position of subservience.

The constitutional roles of the President are the following:

He is *head of state*. That is, he is ceremonial head of the government, just as a king or a queen would be. He grants pardons, receives ambassadors, and holds state dinners. In this function, President Ford received heads of state like Japanese Emperor Hirohito and also celebrities like soccer star Pelé, Miss America, Beatle George Harrison, and others. Presidents have frequently complained about the amount of time such ceremonial functions take away from other duties. And yet, as *Newsweek* magazine has noted, "ceremony is essential to the magisterial awe that surrounds the nation's highest public office, and a powerful weapon in any Chief Executive's political arsenal." [8]

Second, the President is charged by the Constitution to be *Chief Executive* of the United States. According to the first line of Article 2, the executive power is vested in the President. He is responsible for taking care "that the laws be faithfully executed." As a consequence, the President, explicitly or implicitly, has the powers of appointment and removal, and as the administrative head of government, he directs the federal bureaucracy.

The President is *chief diplomat*. Authority over the State Department, negotiation of treaties and executive agreements, recognition of governments, and appointment of diplomatic personnel are some of the responsibilities of the President as chief minister of foreign affairs. Presidential power has increased enormously during the twentieth century as a consequence of this authority. [9] Moreover, despite considerable controversy regarding the conduct of foreign policy during the last months of Nixon's tenure, and despite large Democratic majorities in both houses of Congress, the White House still evinced great power in the field of diplomacy. The conclusion of an important Egyptian–Israeli agreement in 1975 under the guidance of Secretary of State Henry Kissinger was indicative of this. Indeed, the Congress even agreed to the sending of American civilians

[8] "King or Country," *Newsweek* (Sept. 8, 1975), p. 65.
[9] Aaron Wildavsky, "The Two Presidents," *Trans-Action* (Dec. 1966).

to operate surveillance posts in the Sinai. Clearly the President is still expected to be chief diplomat.

The Constitution designates the President as *Commander in Chief of the Armed Forces*. During wartime, as was the case in the Civil War, this power expands tremendously. Today the President, as Commander in Chief, has at his command the Defense Department, the Joint Chiefs of Staff, the National Security Council, the Central Intelligence Agency, an enormous army, the most powerful navy and air force in history, commitments all over the globe, vast nuclear power, and a little red box containing a telephone ready to alert the whole defense establishment to a nuclear war. Simply in technological terms, this is enormous power. And even with the debacle in Indochina and the apparent challenge of Congress to restrict such awesome unilaterial authority, significantly President Ford's defense budget for 1975 was accepted virtually in toto and without a whimper by the Democratically dominated Ninety-fourth Congress.

The President holds the position of *chief legislator*. From the constitutional mandate to "from time to time give to the Congress information of the state of the union, and recommend to their consideration such measures as he shall judge necessary and expedient" (Article 2, Section 3), the President has become chief lawmaker. Importantly, he is responsible for presenting the annual budget to Congress, and he is expected to introduce and seek the passage of a legislative program. Of course, Congress can (and perhaps sometimes should) be successfully hostile to the President. At any rate, the President is expected to initiate a great deal of legislation.

There are other roles, not precisely mandated by the Constitution, that the President has assumed. He is, for example, *head of his political party*. He is nominated by a party and elected largely on the efforts of that party. He chooses his own Vice President, he selects the chairman of his political party, he campaigns for members of his party, and (especially when his party is a majority in Congress) he works with the party to pass his legislative program.

Some observers have called the President the *tribune of the people* or the spokesman for the country. In a society of such political divergence as ours, this is a difficult task, but certainly no one else can speak for the whole nation. When the country found itself all but prostrated by the Great Depression, newly elected President Franklin D. Roosevelt seemed to accept personal responsibility for leading the people back to prosperity. His efforts were not altogether successful or always wise, but the people responded to his evident concern for their welfare by electing him to an unprecedented four terms. John F. Kennedy, an attractive and charming man, used television as FDR had used the radio—to establish a personal rapport with millions of Americans who admired the man whether or not they agreed with his policies. President Dwight D. Eisenhower likewise seemed to enjoy an abiding sense of the people's faith in his good judgment throughout his administration, so that even when his opponents opposed his policies or programs, they were careful to avoid criticizing him personally.

Other responsibilities of the President might include *maintaining domestic order*. Lincoln's suppression of the southern rebellion and Eisenhower's sending of troops to Little Rock in 1957 to enforce court-ordered integration are examples of this.

Finally, the President, especially since the 1930s, has been held *responsible for the economic health of the country*. The Employment Act of 1946, which virtually makes it illegal to have another depression, established the Council of Economic Advisers to be used by the President to preserve the economic well-being of the country.

Emerging concerns in the area of the environment and energy have placed other responsibilities on the President. President Carter has apparently accepted the new roles of *protector of the environment* and *administrator of energy*. Carter's support of a cabinet-level energy department and his comprehensive energy proposals are indicative of this.

These roles represent a vast reservoir of power. In fact, given the economic, technological, and war-making strength of the United States, it is clear that today's President is the most powerful person in the history of the world. Alexander the Great, Napoleon, and Hitler would surely envy such power.

Are there any restraints on the President? Or does this vast array of power actually represent a form of despotism that would frighten our Founding Fathers?

Checks, Real or Imagined

There are constitutional and institutional checks on the President. Constitutional limitations include the four-year term, qualifications on the power of the veto, and the ban on the third term.

There are also institutional checks. Congress is the most important of these. Intended as a coequal branch with the executive, the Congress has the important power of appropriating or not appropriating whatever money the national government needs or whatever the President wants. Congress must approve all new agencies of the bureaucracy; Congress, after all, makes the laws the President will carry out. Congress can investigate presidential actions and can impeach and remove the President from office. Congress can override a presidential veto by a two-thirds vote of both houses. The Senate must approve appointments by the President and all treaties (by a two-thirds vote). And, theoretically, only Congress

88

has the right to declare war. Of course, Presidents can circumvent these checks. Mr. Nixon, for example, authorized the invasion of Cambodia in 1970 without congressional sanction; he impounded funds duly authorized by the Congress; and his very closest advisers—H. R. Haldeman, John Ehrlichman, Ron Ziegler, and (before becoming Secretary of State) Henry Kissinger—were all chosen as aides by the President without congressional approval. On the other hand, Congress was on the verge of impeaching the President at the time of his resignation.

Another institutional check is the judicial branch. However, the courts rarely hamper presidential power. Exceptions to this rule are the Steel Seizure Case in 1952 (*Youngstown Sheet and Tube Company v. Sawyer*), which denied President Truman the power to take control of a steel plant during the Korean War, and *U.S. v. Richard M. Nixon* (1974), when the court denied Mr. Nixon's claim of executive privilege in withholding tapes.

Other potential checks include periodic elections, which, however, might increase a President's power by giving him an apparent mandate (like the presidential elections in 1964 and 1972) as well as check him by increasing the strength of the opposition party (as in the 1974 off-year elections.) Rarely do elections remove a President who wishes to remain in office. In the twentieth century, this has happened only three times, always under unusual circumstances: in 1912, when Taft was defeated because a popular former President, Theodore Roosevelt, ran as a third-party candidate; in 1932, when Hoover lost reelection in the midst of the Great Depression; and in 1976, when Ford, an unelected President, was narrowly defeated by Carter.

The federal bureaucracy represents a restraint of sorts simply because of its enormous size and sometime inertia. This is particularly true for active Presidents, such as John Kennedy, who found himself frustrated by the executive bureaucracy.

The political system itself may represent a check. The "out" political party keeps up a fairly constant criticism of the administration, and even in his own party the President sometimes must make concessions to achieve harmony.

The press represents another, very important check on the power of the Presidency. As the Vietnam war dragged on, one version of that war was presented to the American people by the Johnson and Nixon administrations and quite another by newspaper and television reporters who were covering the day-by-day events. The government's story was that we were successfully helping a gallant ally defend itself against a cruel foreign invader. Certain sections of the press more and more told the people that we had involved ourselves in a civil war between factions and that the side we were supporting was weak, corrupt, and often unwilling to fight. More importantly, they told us that the war was simply not being won. Ultimately the people had to choose between believing the "official" presidential view of the war or the picture presented by the press. In this struggle, the press, not Presidents Johnson or Nixon, ultimately proved correct.

Even more dramatic was the confrontation between the press and President Nixon. Mr. Nixon, never a favorite of the media (although, ironically, he was invariably supported by the great majority of newspapers in all of his bids for public office), developed an intense dislike for the press. He clashed openly with reporters on television. The press certainly played an instrumental role in forcing the nation to deal with Watergate as a serious national scandal. (See Chapter Nine.)

Finally, public opinion may represent a check, but the nature and depth of this restraint are difficult to analyze. The President has enormous manipulative powers over public opinion. He is always front-page news. He can call a presidential press conference or make a public speech whenever he wishes and command a large audience. Yet, as the late Harold J. Laski has noted, even the most active President cannot lead the people outside the realm of common expectation.[10] This may explain why FDR was unable to pack the Supreme Court in 1937 and why Richard Nixon encountered so much hostility in the last year of his Presidency.

The Milieu of the President

Powers and restraints are not the whole story. There are important conditions that make up the milieu of the modern President and that influence the effectiveness of presidential leadership. Think, for example, of the awesome structure of the Presidency. It includes eleven Cabinet departments; the White House staff, including special assistants, aides, and the press secretary; the National Security Council; the Council of Economic Advisers; the Office of Management and Budget; and many more.

It is estimated that the President is personally involved in the selection of perhaps the top two hundred officials in the executive branch. These are "the President's men," sometimes shadowy figures, little known to the public but nevertheless wielding great power, sometimes flamboyant "stars," such as former Secretary of State Kissinger. Because the nature of the Presidency tends to isolate the President from access to the kind of easy give-and-take of opinion that many Americans are exposed to in the course of their work, school, or social lives, members of the President's "inner circle" often have enormous power simply because they can and do control the flow of information and people that go into the Oval

[10] *The American Presidency* (New York: Grosset, 1940), Chapter 1.

THE STRUCTURE OF THE PRESIDENCY

The President's Cabinet

Department	Date Established	Current Administrator
State	1789	Cyrus R. Vance
Treasury	1789	W. Michael Blumenthal
Interior	1849	Cecil D. Andrus
Agriculture	1862	Bob Bergland
Justice	1870	Griffin B. Bell
Commerce	1903	Juanita M. Kreps
Labor	1913	F. Ray Marshall
Defense (replaced War Department)	1947	Harold Brown
Health, Education and Welfare	1953	Joseph Califano
Housing and Urban Development	1965	Patricia Roberts Harris
Transportation	1966	Brock Adams
Energy	1977	James Schlesinger

Important Members of the Executive Office of the President

Office of Management and Budget	James McIntyre, Acting Director
National Security Council	Zbigniew Brzezinski, National Security Adviser
Council of Economic Advisers	Charles Schultz, Chairman

Important Members of the White House Staff

Walter Mondale, Vice President and Special Adviser to the President
Jody Powell, Press Secretary
Hamilton Jordan, Assistant to the President for Administration
Tim Kraft, Appointments Secretary
Margaret Costanza, Office of Public Liaison
Robert J. Lipshutz, Counsel to the President
Stuart Eizenstat, Assistant to the President for Domestic Affairs and Policy
Frank Moore, Assistant to the President for Liaison with Congress
Jack H. Watson, Assistant to the President for International Relations

Office. An extreme but interesting example of this is detailed in Woodward and Bernstein's book *The Final Days*.[11] The authors relate how, in the closing days of the Nixon administration, the President's lawyers and closest advisers had concluded that he would be impeached by the House and that conviction in the Senate was certain. They then set about devising a strategy to convince Nixon that he must resign. Most of the last third of the book is given over to detailing how this strategy unfolded

[11] New York: Simon & Schuster, 1976.

91

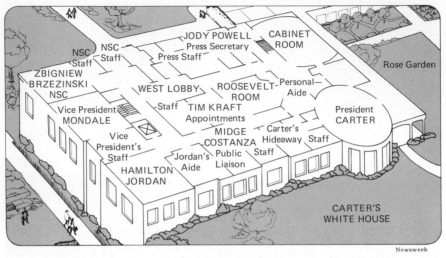

Who sits where: At the President's headquarters, location can mean as much as title

and how the President was ultimately convinced that resignation was the best course available to him.

A second condition in the environment of the modern President has to do with the technological advances in communications. The age of radio, TV, and instant news means that the President's image can be projected instantaneously before millions of people. This may give him great manipulative power. It also means that his image may become more important than the substance of his acts. It is important that he appear resolute, firm, dominant, and responsible, never soft or uncertain. Recognizing this, President Carter chose to revive the FDR tradition of the "fireside chats" early in his administration. He spoke to the nation in a manner, and against a carefully arranged backdrop, designed to project an image of calm strength and confidence.

The world is much more complex today than ever before. Nuclear weaponry, rising nationalism, economic interdependence, and energy problems around the globe all affect America. The President's environment, unlike that of the rest of us, is the whole world. He must live in it and be aware of it every day.

At the same time, American society has grown more, not less, complex. The President's constituencies are many and vociferous, as can be seen in the rising demands of women, minorities, youth, labor, environmentalists, and others. All of this, too, surrounds the President.

Dealing with his environment has become more difficult because of the development of what has come to be called a credibility gap. Excesses and secretive actions during the war in Vietnam and the cover-up of Watergate activities have created in the public mind a deep cynicism

Official photograph of President Carter preparing to deliver his first "fire-side chat." [Official photograph, the White House, Washington, D.C.]

93

regarding any statement emanating from the White House. All future Presidents will have to deal with this. President Ford, obviously aware of public suspicions of presidential deception and overstatement, removed the normal hyperbole from the 1975 State of the Union Address. "I must say," he told Congress, ". . . that the state of the union is not good." He had bad news, he said, "and I don't expect much if any applause." Such humility helped gradually restore faith and credibility to the White House during Ford's two years in office.

George E. Reedy, Press Secretary to Lyndon Johnson, believes that Presidents are becoming increasingly remote from the real world. How, he wonders, can a President accurately assess a problem and reach a solution when he is surrounded by sycophants and when those who disagree with him are excluded from his councils.[12] As a candidate, President Carter expressed concern that once elected he would soon find himself isolated from the people. As a consequence, he has organized his immediate staff in such a way as to encourage diverse opinions coming before the President. Thus, instead of having a single chief of staff who funnels all information to the President (as H. R. Haldeman did to Nixon) Carter has established several coequal aides.

Another condition that has come to be part of the President's daily life is the threat of assassination. President Ford's brushes with death in California in September 1975 only highlight the striking fact that in less than one hundred years four Presidents were assassinated (Lincoln, Garfield, McKinley, and Kennedy), many others were shot at, and candidates for the office are in constant danger. Within the political consciousness of readers of this book are the political assassinations of John F. Kennedy, Robert F. Kennedy, and Martin Luther King, Jr. and the attempts on the lives of George Wallace and President Ford. Moreover, Gerald M. Kaplan, Director of the National Institute of Law Enforcement and Criminal Justice, says that the number of potential presidential assassins is on the increase.[13]

The issue of assassination raises the further question of stability in the Presidency. In fact, stability and order may be mythical, and the real condition may be impermanence. Consider, for example, the Presidents of the twentieth century. Only *one,* Dwight Eisenhower, served an actual, normal two terms. Theodore Roosevelt assumed the Presidency upon the assassination of McKinley, and although he won his own election in 1904, he retired in 1908 and then was unsuccessful in a try for reelection in 1912. William Howard Taft served one term and was defeated in 1912. Wilson was elected twice but was totally disabled by a stroke midway through his

---

[12] *The Twilight of the Presidency* (New York: World, 1970).
[13] Robert J. Donovan, "Alone in the Crowd . . . with a Gun and a Goal," *Los Angeles Times* (Sept. 11, 1975), Part 2, p. 7.

94

second term. Harding died in office. Coolidge, who succeeded him, won election in 1924 but was snubbed by his party in 1928. Hoover was defeated for reelection in 1932. Franklin D. Roosevelt broke all precedents by winning four terms, then died in office. Truman, who succeeded him in 1945, won election in 1948 but was very unpopular in 1952. John F. Kennedy was assassinated. Lyndon Johnson carried the country with a landslide in 1964 but was almost politically impotent by 1968 and unable to run for reelection. Nixon resigned during his second term. Ford was defeated. Thus, contrary to popular conception, there is no stable, normal tradition for the Presidency.

Finally, as regards the milieu of the President, his term is a time when he is expected to lead, not only to act. This may explain why in 1976 Carter, who promised to "lead the country once again," was ultimately successful in defeating Mr. Ford, who frankly promised mainly to check the excesses of the Congress rather than to lead the country. Nevertheless, where and how the President leads are points of controversy.

What's Wrong?

What's wrong with the Presidency and what, if anything, can be done about it? Is the structure of the office acceptable, does it need to be changed, or do we simply need to find the right person for it?

The process of nominating and electing a President has often been cited as a problem. What makes a successful candidate in modern American politics may not always make a good President. More and more of the process of "selling" a presidential candidate to tens of millions of Americans has become a matter of "sell the sizzle instead of the steak." That is, sell the "image" of the man you think most people will approve of rather than the real human being with both his virtues and his shortcomings. Most Americans were shocked to discover the disparity between the real President Nixon, as revealed by the publication of the contents of taped presidential conversations (even after the more colorful epithets were deleted), and the carefully contrived public image of the President. President Lyndon B. Johnson, according to the testimony of those who served him, was a vain, crude, domineering, colorful, and earthy man who, among other things, loved to collect and tell stories about the sexual improprieties of famous politicians. The public image he sought to project was of a wise, tolerant, experienced, and selfless leader. The real Lyndon B. Johnson may have been a more interesting and a greater man than the public LBJ. But most of us never really knew much about him until after his death.

Reference has already been made to President Carter's "image" problem in the 1976 campaign.

In all probability, the sort of man the public seems to want its President to be—a sort of super Boy Scout leader, YMCA secretary, and pillar of rectitude—would not dream of running for the Presidency in the first place and could not possibly be elected if he did.

Presidents are not supposed to be human. It is not permissible for them to have an eye for pretty women, as JFK and FDR certainly did, or like to swear, as LBJ and Nixon did. Harry Truman was a skilled pianist who liked classical music. But in public he had to keep playing "The Missouri Waltz," which he privately disliked. And even Eleanor Roosevelt objected when her husband showed a strong interest in good food. She thought a President should have more important things to think about.

The practice of manufacturing presidential images is not new and certainly was not invented by Madison Avenue. As long ago as the presidential campaign of 1840, millionaire banker Nicholas Biddle gave the following "advice" to the managers of presidential candidate William Henry Harrison: "Let him say not a single word about his principles. . . . Let him say nothing. . . . Let no Convention, no town meeting ever extract from him a single word about what he thinks now, or will do hereafter. Let the use of pen and ink be wholly forbidden." [14] Harrison followed Biddle's advice and became President of the United States. Some of President Carter's closest advisers have suggested, only half jokingly, that Carter might have kept more of his huge summer lead over President Ford had he not campaigned, not granted interviews, and not debated President Ford.

Certain critics find that a major defect in the Presidency rests in the President's relations with Congress. The built-in constitutional hostility between the two branches often precludes any significant governmental action, particularly when the Congress is of one party and the White House of another. The late presidential scholar Edward S. Corwin once suggested a constitutional amendment to allow the President to choose part of his Cabinet from leading members of Congress.[15] Others have simply said that the President ought to pay more attention to Congress.

Other suggestions have to do with making the Presidency more efficient. Congressman Henry Reuss, for example, has proposed an amendment to the Constitution that would create a separate office of "Chief of Staff," thus leaving more time to the President to carry out his other functions.[16] There are motives other than efficiency in Representative Reuss's proposal. He wishes also to remove some of the trappings of majesty that so enhance presidential power.

Thus we return to a fundamental question. Does the President have too

[14] Arthur M. Schlesinger, Jr., *The Age of Jackson* (Boston: Little, Brown, 1945), p. 211.
[15] Edward S. Corwin, *The President* (New York: New York U.P., 1957), p. 297.
[16] "A Federal Master of Ceremonies," *Newsweek* (Sept. 8, 1975), p. 65.

much power? Various contemporary critics answer yes. Pulitzer Prize-winning historian Barbara Tuchman has even suggested the radical solution of abolishing the Presidency as we know it and replacing the single executive with a cabinet of six people. This directorate of six would be nominated as a slate for a single six-year term with a rotating chairman. She notes that such cabinet governments have worked well in some other countries.[17] Others believe the President actually has too little power. Liberal journalist Robert Sherrill, although conceding that the President has overgrown his bounds in foreign affairs, believes that he is too weak in domestic affairs.[18]

The common argument for a stronger President has been that in an age of rapid change and constant crisis, we need someone who could act instantaneously and before it was too late. This would be particularly true in matters of foreign affairs and defense policy where hesitation and the normal deliberative process of gaining congressional sanction might well prove dangerous if not fatal for the nation. Thus Presidents, elected, after all, by the whole body of voters and with as much information as possible, are really in the best position to make judgments regarding war and diplomacy.

But is this assumption correct? In light of recent history, have we been better off since Presidents have bypassed Congress and unilaterally decided upon diplomatic and war-making actions? Several examples would suggest that the answer is no. Think of all the ill-advised and at times disastrous interventions just since 1960: the Bay of Pigs (1961); the Dominican Republic (1965); Vietnam, Cambodia, and Laos (1960s and 1970s); and Chile (1970s). It is conceivable that in each of these instances the long-run interests of the nation would have been better served by the normal constitutional processes of debate, discussion, and consultation.[19]

Yet the question penetrates deeper than the issue of power or no power. On the one hand, we must distinguish between power misused or abused and power used constitutionally, and on the other hand, we must consider the nature and the necessity of "leadership" in the modern world. It is unlikely that we will divest the Presidency of the power it has. But how can it be controlled so that we retain a constitutional government and avoid despotism? The Greek philosophers thought that that was almost impossible, and Imperial Rome proved them accurate. And how can we use that power to attack the problems that confront contemporary society? In an age of environmental decay, erosion of energy sources, urban blight

[17] "Should We Abolish the Presidency?" *New York Times* (Feb. 13, 1973).
[18] *Why They Call It Politics,* 2nd ed. (New York: Harcourt, 1974), Chapters 1 and 3.
[19] This argument is made by Henry Steele Commager, "The Misuse of Power," *New Republic* (Apr. 17, 1971).

and financial ruin, and rising expectations of a heterogeneous people, we can ill afford a succession of weak Presidents.

There is a distinction between acting and leading. The former requires competence in order to be successful and the latter requires charisma (at least in a democratic society). Herbert Hoover was a very competent man. He was also very much disliked. Adolf Hitler was a very charismatic person. He was also not always competent, and he led Germany to defeat and disaster. Does the unique American institution of the Presidency provide us with the possibility of finding a competent, charismatic, and yet constitutional figure to assume the most important, interesting, and powerful position in the world?

Democracy and the President

Shortly after the second unsuccessful attempt upon the life of President Gerald Ford, an anonymous woman called a local radio talk show in Los Angeles to observe: "President Ford cannot walk the streets safely and neither can I." This comment highlights a curious notion: somehow the fate of 215 million Americans and the fate of the President of the United States are inextricably bound together. In the minds of most people, the tragedy of the Civil War and the fate of President Lincoln can never be separated. On the other hand, the triumph of America in World War II and the leadership of Franklin Roosevelt are no less a unity.

The American people grow up idealizing Presidents as naturally and inevitably as a Catholic grows up idealizing the Popes. Most elementary-school classrooms contain pictures of Presidents. Most of us learn our history largely in terms of presidential personalities. George Washington embodied the Revolutionary War as Lincoln embodied the Civil War, as FDR has come to embody America during the Great Depression, and as Eisenhower seemed to personify the 1950s and JFK the early 1960s.

A kind of fear, similar to that which might afflict us if someone had tried to kill a member of our immediate family, grips the whole nation when an attempt is made upon the life of the President. Except for a tiny and irrational minority, it matters not whether we approve or disapprove of a given President's policies or person; we react with horror to threat of violence against him.

President Nixon, despite his evident abuses of power, had, and perhaps still has, a substantial following among the people who felt that, regardless of what he may have done or not done, driving a President from office represented an almost unthinkable indignity, not for one man but for the country.

Under the terms of the Constitution, Americans do not and cannot have a state religion. But the need to believe in a kind of god–king, an

98

all-wise and all-good father, not only in heaven but in Washington as well, remains a powerful impulse in the people.

Yet as Lyndon Johnson used to point out, there are "President haters," people who take an unreasoning, automatically negative view of anything a President does. He did not add that there are also President lovers, people for whom the President can virtually do no wrong.

Both the Constitution and common sense tell us that the President is a mere mortal. But in a secular and democratic society, there is clearly a need for spiritual as well as political leadership, and the President is virtually the only person in the nation who is in a position to provide that leadership to the great majority of the people. It is not enough that he be an efficient administrator and an honest servant of the people. If there is to be some sense of national direction or purpose, only the President can provide it. The nation may exist to serve the well-being and support the freedom of the individual. But the individual is unlikely to find either freedom or well-being except within the context of a sound and healthy nation. The President's task is to keep the nation sound and healthy, not, of course, all by himself, but in cooperation with the Congress, the courts, and the people. As Harry Truman once said, "My job is to get people to do what they ought to do anyway." That is why the quadrennial selection of a President is the nation's most important business.

Congress and Its Critics

T here is no distinctly native American criminal class except Congress.

Mark Twain
Pudd'nhead Wilson

It is almost impossible to imagine a democracy without a popularly elected legislature. Cetrainly none has ever existed. For democracy implies a system under which, in one form or another, people choose other people to represent them, and these representatives come together to make the laws that will govern society. (The only conceivable alternative to this might be a system of direct democracy, in which the people themselves voted on every item of legislation, obviously a practical impossibility in a nation of 215 million persons.)

Other democracies have chosen their chief executives by means other than by the vote of the people and have given those executives different kinds of power and responsibility; other democracies have no institution quite like our Supreme Court; but all democracies have a popularly elected law-making body. Hence one might assume that the most universal and indispensable element of a democratic government is the legislative branch. And yet a poll commissioned by the Ninety-fifth Congress in February 1977 found the following:

1. The public does not think very highly of members of Congress, ranking them toward the bottom of all groups of American leaders but slightly ahead of business executives and labor leaders.

2. At the same time, most Americans think their own individual representatives in Congress are doing a pretty good job. (Although most could not name their Congressman or Senators, and fewer still knew whether their representatives were Democrats or Republicans.)

To compound the problem, pollster Louis Harris found that members of Congress defined their job much differently than did the general public. Congressmen and Senators told Harris that they thought their most important job was to legislate, presumably for the whole nation. Voters, on the other hand, felt that the most important responsibility of a member of Congress was to act as a sort of bird dog for the people of his district, that is, to secure lucrative contracts that help the district's economy, to help smooth the way for people who were having problems with the federal bureaucracy, and to perform similar chores.

Thus there appears to be some confusion in most people's minds about both the function and the effectiveness of the Congress.

102

"To live is to choose," said French existentialist Jean Paul Sartre.[1] A government, if it is to govern, must decide. There are two ways decisions can be made: (1) a group of people, usually representing various interests and points of view, can decide collectively by voting; (2) the decision must be made by a single individual. There is no known third alternative except to do nothing at all.

The group or committee system for making decisions is easily derided ("A camel is a horse designed by a committee"). Its decisions will usually come as the result of compromise and consensus, neither of which seems very heroic. The individual decision-maker, on the other hand, does strike people as dramatic and is a more satisfying figure. (Someone must be willing, says Dostoevski's revolutionary hero Raskolnikov in *Crime and Punishment,* "to take the suffering on himself and act for all the trembling ant heap.") And yet experience, particularly recent experience here in America, suggests that decisions made by large, inefficient, and sometimes unimpressive groups may be less catastrophic than those made by heroic individuals.

Remembering a visit to the Austrian parliament of his youth, Adolph Hitler once delivered a kind of classic condemnation of representative bodies:

> There is no principle which, objectively considered, is as false as parliamentarianism. A wild gesticulating mass screaming all at once in every different key, presided over by a good natured old uncle. . . . The majority can never replace the man.
>
> *Adolph Hitler*
> *Mein Kampf*

Critics of representative government in America also point to the American Congress as prima facie evidence of a weakness of democracy. Among the more common criticisms of the U.S. Congress are the following:

1. The Congress is dominated by an "old boy" (seniority) system that virtually guarantees that the leaders will be aged mediocrities whose principal interest is political survival and personal power rather than public policy. In the words of the late Speaker of the House Sam Rayburn, "You have to go along to get along."

2. The Congress represents so many diverse interests, regions, and loyalties that it is hopelessly inefficient. The late President Kennedy once observed that if any private corporation were as inefficient and clumsy as the Congress, it would be bankrupt within a year. President Truman made the "do-nothing Eightieth Congress" the target of his successful race for the

[1] See *Existentialism,* trans. Bernard Frectman (New York: Philosophical Library, 1947).

Presidency in 1948. Virtually all Presidents since have attacked the Congress, usually with little or no fear of arousing public anger.

3. Congressmen and Senators are often third-rate political hacks whose primary concern is with serving the parochial interests of "the folks back home" and who have little knowledge of or interest in broader national concerns.

4. Congress is irresponsible. It spends money wantonly. It cannot be trusted to guard vital secrets (as in the recent furor surrounding congressional investigations of the FBI and the CIA).

5. The congressional power to conduct investigations for the purpose of legislation can be abused, so that congressional hearings often turn into headline-grabbing "circuses" intended to gain the national spotlight for ambitious individuals rather than gathering needed information. (Such criticisms were heard from the left during the era of Senator Joseph McCarthy and the House Un-American Activities Committee and from conservatives more recently.)

6. Since the Congress, as a body, is clearly incapable of controlling and conducting foreign policy, its efforts to meddle in the process often produce division at home and the appearance of weakness abroad.

7. Congressmen are more frequently involved in corrupt practices and sex scandals than in making laws. For example, recent accusations suggest that some congressmen may have been bribed by South Korean lobbyists.

Two of the most important leaders of the Ninety-fourth Congress, Wayne Hays of Ohio and Wilbur Mills of Arkansas (both Democrats), were involved in headline-grabbing sex scandals that, apart from any questions of private morality, showed a lamentable lack of common sense or ordinary prudence and clear evidence of "the arrogance of power" on the part of these men. As juicy revelations followed one after another, complete with the frequent appearances of the former Mills and Hays mistresses on television and as the authors of best-selling books, the question that emerged was not really about the personal peccadilloes of these two men but whether or not Congress should even be taken seriously.

8. Finally, the point is often made that the Congress is not truly a representative body, since its members are usually older, richer, and better educated than the average American. Clearly the Congress does not represent women, minority groups, and the young in anything like their proportion of the population. The credence one gives such arguments would seem to turn on whether or not one believes in a quota system to some degree and on how one defines *representative*. In one sense of the word, a representative should be a reasonable facsimile of those he represents; in another a representative acts as an "agent" for others just as an attorney may represent a client who is a great deal poorer or less educated than the average lawyer.

104

highly respected governor. Samish liked to boast about his power. Once he posed for a picture for *Collier's* magazine with a dummy on his lap. The dummy was labeled "the California legislature." The California liquor industry levied what in effect was a tax of five cents upon its members for every case of beer or bottle of liquor sold in the state. This money was turned over to Samish to be used at his discretion to promote the industry's interests and protect it from competition. (To this day it is illegal to sell liquor in California at cut-rate prices.) An example of how this money was used is cited by Samish himself in his book *The Secret Boss of California.*

A member of the State Assembly, Clair Woolwine, aroused Samish's anger by voting contrary to Samish's wishes. Samish was determined to defeat Woolwine when he next faced reelection. The district Woolwine represented included an old section of downtown Los Angeles where derelicts congregated, known as "skid row." Seeking an opponent for Woolwine who lived in the district, Samish visited one of the downtown "soup kitchens" where free meals were handed out and selected one of the derelicts as his personal candidate. The man was equipped with a hotel room, a new suit, and some spending money and was instructed to have a bath and a shave. Samish did the rest. That November his candidate was elected over the incumbent Woolwine. Unhappily Samish's man died in office, thereby prematurely ending what might have been a brilliant political career.

Samish later defended his actions by pointing out that as many of the people in that district were derelicts, why shouldn't they be represented by one of their own? His logic was similar to that of a U.S. Senator, Roman Hruska (R. Neb.), who, on being informed that one of President Nixon's nominees for the Supreme Court was a mediocre lawyer, responded that he would vote for Nixon's man anyway since the nation's mediocrities had a right to representation on the Supreme Court. These are examples of the "mirror theory" of representation. The representative mirrors his constituency.

In one sense, a Congressman or a Senator is a literal spokesman for the people of his state or district. In the same way that a person or a company might hire an attorney to represent him—that is, to defend his interests and present his view—in court, they collectively elect someone to speak for them in the Congress. That seems simple enough, but in practice the matter is more complex. For example, what if a given Congressman disagrees with the views held by a majority of his constituents? Is he bound to vote as they wish him to vote, or should he be guided by his own conscience? This dilemma is not an uncommon one for members of the Congress. A legislator may believe that strict economy is necessary to control inflation. What then should he do about a controversial but popular defense project (such as the B-1 bomber) that would cost a great deal but could well mean thousands of jobs for his constituents? Or he might feel that bussing is essential to achieve an integrated society, whereas a majority of his constituents see the matter quite differently. Does Senator Edward Kennedy's view of the Constitution take precedence over his obligation to the voters of Massachusetts? It is not for nothing that legislators are sometimes called "Solons," after a very wise man and lawgiver of ancient Greece. For it often requires the wisdom of a Solon to resolve successfully the commonplace problems of a conscientious lawmaker.

In the United States, members of the House of Representatives are elected to represent districts and Senators to represent states, so that each is the national spokesman for a given number of people and a certain geographical area. But collectively the Congress acts not only for 435 separate districts and 50 states but also for the whole nation. When local interests and concerns conflict with the national welfare, what is a legislator's duty? He is pledged to act and speak for his people and his area. He is also pledged to uphold the Constitution and serve the nation.

A reflection of this dichotomy is found in the fact that a Congress member must often occupy two homes (in an extreme case, Congressman Leggett, Democrat from California, even had two families), one in or near Washington, another in his home district. The divided residence may symbolize a certain divided loyalty. Let us cite a hypothetical example:

Young Congressman Smith, having just seen the film *Mr. Smith Goes to Washington* on late-night TV (a film about a young idealist who successfully battles the corrupt Washington congressional establishment) is elected to the House of Representatives. He goes to Washington determined to be honest, faithful, reverent, and true. Let us further postulate that the people in his home district badly need or want some federal assistance, such as defense contracts, a new dam, or help with a proposal to create a rapid-transit system. Naturally Congressman Smith will do his utmost to get one or more of these good things approved by his colleagues. Upon arriving in Washington, Congressman Smith is shocked to discover that several key leaders of the Congress are corrupt, alcoholic, or otherwise unsuited to their roles, which they have acquired largely as the result of seniority. Other, like-minded young Congressmen ask Smith to join them in battling the leadership and exposing its unfitness. The leaders, on the other hand, approach Congressman Smith and give him a bit of helpful advice. If Congressman Smith expects the House leaders to look favorably on his bills to help his district, he had best not associate himself with the "radicals" who want to change a system that has been worked out over two hundred years. Further, if Congressman Smith, who has a certain amount of personal ambition, would like to be appointed to important committees, committees that will help keep him in the public eye and benefit the folks back home, he had better learn to cooperate. Finally, his work as a young Congressman will be made less burdensome, and his way smoother, if he happens to be assigned to an attractive office, near the parking lot and with a nice view.

Our idealistic hero must make a hard decision: to fight the system and consign himself to the outer limits of the congressional club, thus rendering himself ineffective in terms of his ability to serve the people who elected him, or to become part of the very thing he came to Washington to try to change.

What do the folks back home want and expect him to do? If the question were put as we have put it, most would probably encourage him to choose the harder but apparently more moral course. But in practice the voters frequently seem to make quite a different kind of choice. Congressman Hays, for example, easily won his party's renomination *after* the disclosures about his alleged payroll-padding in 1976. (Hays subsequently decided not to run for reelection.) Congressman Wilbur Mills was also reelected by the people of his district after his celebrated difficulties. Other, less well-publicized instances could be cited. In most cases, the voters seemed to believe that a powerful, well-connected Congressman brings many benefits to his constituents, and as long as the representative can "deliver the goods" for the folks back home, many are not really concerned about his public ethics or private morality.

A "well-respected," easily reelected member of Congress is apt to be someone like the late Representative L. Mendel Rivers of the First Congressional District of South Carolina, who remained unbeatable as long as he lived, which just might have had something to do with the fact that some 35 percent of the payrolls in his district are alleged to have come about largely because of Rivers's power as Chairman of the key House Armed Services Committee, which passes on a $100-billion defense budget annually.

Finally, there is another aspect of a Congressman's job that is important but not very well understood by the public. That is what might be called customer service. An average of a third of a typical Congressman's time may be spent servicing the personal and private needs of his constituents.[3] Some of this service is providing help to innocent tourists and to visiting constituents, meeting school children who want an autographed picture, and so on. But the bulk of his efforts in this area go into trying to meet the demands of various individuals for special favors of one kind or another. People who want their children appointed to a military academy, veterans who think they should be getting a better pension from the Veterans Administration, businessmen with tax problems or those seeking a piece of the

[3] Donald G. Tacheron and Morris K. Udall, *The Job of the Congressman,* 2nd ed. (New York: Bobbs, 1970), pp. 303–304.

Much of a Congressman's work involves servicing the personal and business needs of his constituents. Here Congressman Glenn M. Anderson (D. Calif.) chats with representatives of a major employer of the people in his district. [Reprinted with permission.]

federal action, corporate officials looking for laws that will inhibit foreign competitors, people accused of crimes who want a letter on their behalf to the judge, even schoolchildren who want the Congressman or Senator to do their homework; all look to their representative in Washington.

Many members of Congress spend decades in Washington without ever pushing very hard or conspicuously for or against nationally important and well-publicized legislation and still remain popular with voters simply because they are diligent about handling these personal requests. Again, a legislator must often choose between devoting his limited time and attention to studying complex legislative matters or "taking care of the folks back home."

But even this is an oversimplification. For the "folks back home" may mean in practice about 1 or 2 percent of his constituents. Most Americans rarely if ever write to their representative in Congress. Fewer still would dream of seeking congressional help for the resolution of a personal problem. Most people would be surprised to discover how far their Congressmen will go to help them if they take the time to visit his office personally.

110

That is true because only a handful of the half-million or so people that a Congressman represents ever go anywhere near his office.

Thus the mundane and practical realities of a Congress member's job may be somewhat removed from the vision of the "people's champion" and spokesperson inherent in the theory of representative government. The work of the elected representative is important, indeed indispensable, to the maintenance of a free government and hence a free society. But it is sometimes difficult to extrapolate that truth from the daily routine of a working member of Congress. Like the people who bring us water or electricity, we tend to think about members of Congress only when they fail.

Thus, despite the all-too-frequent sex and financial scandals surrounding the Congress in recent years, and although Congress as an institution normally ranks very near the bottom in polls of public regard for major American institutions, it can be reasonably argued that the Congress serves the American people at least as well as, and perhaps a great deal better than, other branches of government.

The Achievements of Congress

For decades the mass media (newspaper cartoons, films, and TV comedians) have pictured a U.S. Congressman or Senator as a figure of comedy or corruption, whereas the other two branches of government, the Presidency and the Supreme Court, are normally treated with respect if not reverence.

And yet consider the relative position of the Congress, the Presidency, and the courts on some of the most important issues to face the United States during the past decade.

1. It was the Congress that led official opposition to the Vietnam war. Whereas recent American Presidents insisted upon pushing that struggle to its dismal conclusion, men like Senator J. William Fulbright, Chairman of the Senate Foreign Relations Committee, were, for years, critics of the war. Largely as the result of specific laws passed by the Congress, American forces were withdrawn from Indochina. At the same time, the Supreme Court consistently refused to rule on the critical question of whether or not this undeclared war was constitutional.

2. It was the Congress, acting with what many observers have described as great skill, prudence, and patience, that brought the Watergate scandal to a decisive and yet peaceful conclusion, culminating in the resignation of President Nixon to avoid certain impeachment and conviction.

3. It was the Congress, acting through its power to investigate, that brought to light the scandalous and dangerous abuse of power by the CIA and the FBI, which, unchecked, might well have constituted a threat to the personal freedom of every American citizen.

111

4. Although Presidents like to appear frugal and conservative in fiscal matters and frequently accuse the Congress of wasteful expenditures for political purposes, the fact is that the executive, not the congressional branch, has most consistently sought larger and larger appropriations for what is certainly the most expensive and probably the most wasteful single element in the national budget, military expenditures. Furthermore, it was the executive branch that decided to fight the Vietnam war on credit, which was an important element in undermining world confidence in the dollar and setting off a serious inflation.

5. Finally, it is the Congress, not the Presidency, that in recent years has been most responsive to the domestic needs of Americans: proposing and passing programs designed to provide jobs for the unemployed or lower interest rates for the purchase of homes, many of which have not been enacted into law because of potential or actual presidential vetoes.

The Congress is, of course, the most representative element in the structure of representative government. Supreme Court judges are appointed for life and are thus shielded against changes in public mood, at least insofar as tenure of office is concerned. The nature of the Presidency also creates a certain barrier between the people and the man who occupies the Oval Office. Even the most well intentioned and democratic of Presidents must find it difficult if not downright dangerous to do more than "press the flesh" of the ordinary citizen. Presidents may appear before the people and speak to the people. But they can rarely find a practical means of listening to the average citizen, even if they so desired. A Congressman or a Senator, on the other hand, *must* listen to the people if he is to survive in office.

Finally, history indicates that the Congress does indeed reflect the national mood far more reliably than other branches of government. For example, when the American people were generally supportive of the Vietnam war, the Senate responded with an overwhelming endorsement of the Tonkin Gulf Resolution, which in effect authorized President Johnson to escalate the war. (Interestingly, the only two Senators to vote against the resolution, Ernest Gruening of Alaska and Wayne Morse of Oregon, were defeated in their next bid for reelection, evidence of what sometimes happens to legislators who vote their conscience rather than public-opinion polls.)

By 1975 most Americans had turned against further direct involvement in that war, and in the spring of that year the Congress refused President Ford's request for supplemental financial appropriations designed to make it possible to continue the struggle. The Presidency, clearly, has superior means to shape and lead public opinion. But once that opinion forms and settles on a clearly discernible path, the Congress is usually responsive.

Thus the notion that the Presidency is the embodiment of our democratic way of life is to some extent misleading. For it is the Congress, rather than the Presidency, that most nearly embodies the ideal of self-government in a pluralistic society.[4] The President, being one man, is limited on matters of public policy. The Congress, being many men and women, comes far closer to reflecting the scope of American society with all its divergent interests and outlooks.

And yet it is probably inevitable that the image of hundreds of people, arguing, compromising, bargaining, striving to reach a consensus acceptable to the majority, is less dramatic and less aesthetically satisfying than the image of a single man struggling to make a decision upon weighty matters—knowing all the while that the lives of millions, perhaps even billions, of people will be affected by what he alone has the power to decide. For although it is not so in practice, it usually appears to the general public that the Congress can propose but only the President can dispose. From the standpoint of drama, all Presidents are continually playing Hamlet—the tragic, lonely, soul-searching individual—while the Congress plays the crowd. The President is the star. The Congress is the supporting cast, whose names flicker quickly by on the screen *after* the drama is done.

What and how we think about the Congress is normally a reflection of our estimate of the man who occupies the Presidency because the Congress is, in the nature of our constitutional system, a countervailing force to the White House. Even when the Congress is dominated by members of the President's own party, it is frequently perceived by the public as an antagonist to the President's role as protagonist. Thus admirers of Franklin Roosevelt and John Kennedy tended to be critical of Congress for not being willing to enact all the legislation that these two liberal Presidents proposed. On the other hand, conservatives saw the heavily Democratic Congress elected in the immediate post-Watergate era as a profligate foe of President Ford's efforts to control federal deficits and hence inflation. Democratic President Harry Truman deliberately made the Republican-controlled Eightieth Congress the foil of his campaign to win reelection in 1948, apparently with some success. Liberals chastised Congress for its reluctance to follow Franklin D. Roosevelt's leadership in mobilizing the nation prior to America's entry into World War II. Most of the same people praised Congress for the restraints it imposed upon President Nixon during the Vietnam war.

Privately, many Congressmen and Senators complain that theirs is the least understood and appreciated branch of American government. Lawmakers receive numerous letters of complaint, few of praise. (Again, this is the opposite of the case of the President—most of whose mail is normally laudatory.) As we have seen, among the great bulk of the American people who rarely or never write letters, Congress is held in low esteem.[5] Only

[4] For a discussion of pluralism, see Chapter Eight.
[5] Louis Harris, "Congress Gets Poor Ratings," *Washington Post* (March 1, 1971), p. A13.

113

about half of the people know who their Congressman is and even fewer know which party controls Congress.[6] Congressmen may try to close the gap that separates them from the public but without much success. A Congressman elected from California, for example, may fly home twenty or thirty weekends a year and accept virtually any and all speaking engagements or opportunities to meet the public. Still, at the end of his term (two years), he will have had personal contact with only a fraction of the constituents he represents.

With respect to coverage by the major media, the lawmaker is clearly at a disadvantage. Most Americans now rely on television for daily news, and except in rare instances, a single Senator, let alone a Congressman, is simply not important enough to warrant much attention by television, the important metropolitan newspapers, or the weekly national news magazines. The most notable exceptions occur when a Congressman or a Senator is heading a spectacularly interesting investigation, such as the Senate Watergate committee, or when a lawmaker is engaged in an all-out assault upon the executive branch of government. Thus the late Senator Joseph McCarthy became almost overnight the nation's most feared and powerful legislator when he stood up on the floor of the Senate and charged that he had in his hand a list of hundreds of Communist agents at work in the State Department. The press rushed to cover the story, not bothering to find out that what the Senator actually had in hand was a stage prop—a blank sheet of paper—and that he was unable to furnish the name of a single Communist agent then at work in the State Department. With a single, headline-grabbing "gimmick" the Senator became a celebrity, a major power in the nation. Within the next few years, McCarthy was to repeat essentially the same trick over and over again, with the press invariably printing his charges in bold headlines and burying the mundane truth—which turned out to be that there was little or nothing to support the Senator's charges—days later in small type. By exploiting an inherent weakness of the press—its love of combat and noise—McCarthy made his name a synonym for an era in American history, an era that most Americans now look upon as disgraceful.[7]

On the other hand, Congressmen and Senators with little taste for engaging in personal epithets and baseless charges against prominent fellow citizens, who prefer hard and conscientious work on the nation's real problems, are rewarded with almost total anonymity. For example, Senator Sam Ervin had spent much of his life in the Congress and had achieved a reputation among his fellow legislators and a handful of knowledgeable

[6] Donald E. Stokes and Warren E. Miller, "Party Government and the Saliency of Congress," *Public Opinion Quarterly* 2:531–546 (Winter 1962).
[7] See Eric F. Goldman, *The Crucial Decade—and After: America, 1945–1960* (New York: Vintage, 1960), pp. 137–145.

observers as a wise and witty man, a serious constitutional scholar, and an able legislator. But he remained unknown to the nation at large until he was named to head a Senate committee to investigate the Watergate scandal, whereupon he became a national idol.

Apart from becoming embroiled in a nationally televised combat with the President or his top staff members, about the only sure way to national attention for most members of Congress is through scandal. Thus Congressman Wilbur Mills became one of the few nationally known members of Congress not because as Chairman of the powerful House Ways and Means Committee he had played a critical role in making the nation's tax policy, which directly affected the economic well-being of virtually every American, but because his mistress leaped into a shallow creek after the two were stopped by Washington police following a minor traffic incident. Before this incident, few Americans knew or cared anything about Wilbur Mills, although he was certainly one of the most powerful men in the Congress and in the nation.

Members of Congress are customarily treated more respectfully by local, "hometown" newspapers across the nation than by the major media. However this too may be a mixed blessing because there is strong evidence that most people do not read home-town papers seeking enlightenment on national affairs.

Finally, if a member of the Congress were to receive "equal time" with the President, a rarity, how could he presume to speak for 535 members?

The Functions of Congress

Whatever we think about Congress, what it does is important and affects all of us, because its essential function, accorded to it by the Constitution, is to make laws. The Congress is bicameral, made up of a House of Representatives of 435 members, each representing an approximately equal number of constituents, and a Senate of 100 members, 2 from each state. Congressmen and Senators earn $57,500 a year, not a paltry sum, but not as much as some could earn in law practice or in a business firm. Representatives serve two-year terms and all 435 run for reelection every even numbered year. Senators serve six years. One third of that body is elected every two years.

Both houses must agree on the exact wording of a bill before it is passed and sent to the President for signature. Other than its most important function of making laws, the Congress has other duties, provided by the Constitution:

1. Congress can, by a two-thirds vote, propose amendments to the Constitution.

2. The House has the power to impeach (by majority vote), and the

115

Senate the power to try, any civil officer of the United States. If the Senate upholds the impeachment charges by a two-thirds vote, the officer is removed.

3. The Congress has powers of investigation. For example, the Senate Select Committee on Intelligence, chaired by Senator Frank Church, has investigated activities of the CIA and FBI pursuant to recommending legislation. Investigations such as those of the Church committee frequently cause public controversy, with opponents charging that they represent witch hunts and blemish the reputation of civil servants with allegations unproved in court. Supporters of congressional investigations argue that they are necessary at times to help Congress draw up legislation (as on campaign financing, watchdog control over the CIA, and so on) and that they properly expose excessive and at times unconstitutional activities within the executive branch of government.

4. Congress also has the authority to establish its own rules, that is, the procedures it will follow in all of its functions.

5. Finally, the Senate has some functions that the House does not. The Senate advises and consents to treaties by two-thirds vote. In practice this has come to mean approving treaties negotiated by the executive branch. The Senate also confirms most presidential nominations (to the Cabinet, the federal courts, and diplomatic posts). Such confirmations require only a majority vote.

Committees and More Committees

If you were to visit Washington, D.C. and attend a formal session in one of the houses of Congress, you might be astounded at how few Congressmen are on the floor. The reason for this is that most of the work of legislators is done in committees or in subcommittees. Given the large membership in both houses, it is not difficult to understand why the Congress has divided itself into smaller, more manageable components to deal with legislation in certain categories. There are four kinds of committees in Congress: standing, special (or select), joint, and conference.

Standing committees are permanent and the best known of congressional committees. The House has twenty-two such committees, which include committees of Appropriations, Ways and Means, Rules, and so on. The Senate has fifteen standing committees, including Foreign Relations, Judiciary, and others. Standing committees are bipartisan. The majority of the members are from the majority party. The chairman of the committee is also from the majority party and normally chosen by seniority. That is, the majority party member of a committee who has had the longest continuous service on that committee is its chairman. (The absolute rule of

116

seniority was significantly challenged by the Ninety-fourth Congress. We will discuss this challenge later. Suffice it to say at this point that seniority is the normal manner of determining chairmanships.)

Committees may hold hearings that are either open or closed. Decisions are made by majority vote. The chairman of a committee has considerable power. He appoints subcommittees, calls meetings, and determines the agenda.

In the House, Republicans are placed on committees by a Committee on Committees. Democrats are chosen by the Democrats on the Steering and Policy Committee, elected by the Democratic caucus. In the Senate, the Democratic Steering Committee appoints Democrats to standing committees, and Republicans have a counterpart Committee on Committees.

Special or *select* committees are temporary committees instituted for specific purposes. Recent examples of select committees in the Senate include the Select Committee on Watergate, chaired by Sam Ervin, and the Select Committee on Intelligence, chaired by Frank Church. In the House, Otis Pike has chaired a recent select-committee investigation of the intelligence agencies.

Joint committees are usually permanent and are composed of members from both houses. The Joint Committee on Atomic Energy, formed after World War II, was an example.

Finally, *conference* committees are, technically, special joint committees. That is, they are nonpermanent and contain membership from both houses. Their purpose is to discuss and reach agreement on legislation when there are disagreements between the versions passed by the two houses. Thus these committees have great power because they decide what will be in the law.

In 1977 the Senate, for the first time in thirty years, reorganized its committee system by a vote of 89 to 1. The chief sponsor of the reorganization was Adlai Stevenson III (D. Ill.), who argued that the reorganization would help make the Senate a more democratic body and cut back on multiple and overlapping committees. Stevenson also stressed that the new structure would enable the Senate to work more smoothly with the Carter administration's efforts to reorganize the government.

The plan reduced the number of standing Senate committees, and it sought to eliminate overlapping hearings and legislative work. It created a new Energy and Natural Resources Committee, limited the number of committees on which a Senator may serve, and restricted the number of committees a Senator may chair.

In addition to committees, each house has a hierarchy of leadership, which, among other things, appoints members to select, joint, and conference committees. Leaders in both houses are elected by their party. In the House, the majority party elects the Speaker, who is the presiding officer.

The Speaker is currently Thomas "Tip" O'Neill of Massachusetts. Next in line is the Majority Leader, James Wright (Texas), who frequently succeeds the Speaker upon the latter's retirement or death.

The minority party elects its leadership as well. The current minority leader in the House is John Rhoades of Arizona. He succeeded Gerald Ford, and should the Republicans win a majority of seats in the House, he would become Speaker.

In the Senate, the majority party elects the President pro Tempore, a position more of honor than of power, and the Majority Leader. The Majority Leader is currently Robert Byrd of West Virginia, who succeeded Mike Mansfield of Montana. The Minority Leader is Howard Baker of Tennessee. He would become Majority Leader, should the Republicans gain control of the Senate.

What's Wrong with Congress?

The organization of the Congress suggests some of the criticisms of it. A key complaint has been that the rule of seniority gives too much power to older, more conservative representatives from states where there is little political competition. In the one-party South, for example, once a Democratic candidate is victorious in a primary, his chances are great of remaining in Washington and moving up the seniority ladder. This process accounts for the disproportionate number of Southerners (normally more conservative) in positions of power in the Congress. Interestingly, the rule of seniority was developed in 1911 as a reform tactic designed to take excessive power away from the Speaker of the House, who, until then, had appointed the chairmen of committees. This arrangement had created a one-man rule in the House, and younger, reform-minded legislators actually promoted the rule of seniority in order to modify the authority of the leadership and to give more independence to the committees. More recently, seniority itself has come to represent a problem in many people's minds. During the 1960s, a liberal bloc of reform-minded Democrats, known as the Democratic Study Group, began to agitate for changes in the House of Representatives. When the Ninety-fourth Congress convened in January 1975, these liberals found themselves in control of the Democratic caucus, and they effected some of the most dramatic changes since 1911. Among other things, they dislodged four powerful southern chairmen from important committees, despite their seniority. W. R. Poage (D. Tex.) was replaced as Chairman of the House Agriculture Committee by Thomas Foley of Washington; crusty old Louisianan F. Edward Hebert was shocked when displaced as Chairman of the Armed Services Committee by Melvin Price of Illinois; Henry S. Reuss of Wisconsin took over the Banking and Currency Committee from Wright Patman, at eighty-one, the oldest member

118

THE ORGANIZATION OF CONGRESS

Congressional Leadership

Senate

President—Walter F. Mondale
President Pro Tempore—James O. Eastland (Miss.)
Majority Leader—Robert C. Byrd (W. Va.)
Majority Whip—Alan Cranston (Calif.)
Minority Leader—Howard Baker (Tenn.)
Minority Whip—Ted Stevens (Alaska)

House

The Speaker—Thomas P. O'Neill (Mass.)
Majority Leader—Jim Wright (Tex.)
Majority Whip—John Brademas (Ind.)
Minority Leader—John J. Rhodes (Ariz.)
Minority Whip—Robert H. Michel (Ill.)

Senate Standing Committees

Agriculture, Nutrition and Forestry, Herman E. Talmadge (Ga.), Chairman
Appropriations, John L. McClellan (Ark.), Chairman
Armed Services, John C. Stennis (Miss.), Chairman
Banking, Housing and Urban Affairs, William Proxmire (Wis.), Chairman
Budget, Edmund S. Muskie (Maine), Chairman
Commerce, Science and Transportation, Warren G. Magnuson (Wash.), Chairman
Energy and Natural Resources, Henry M. Jackson (Wash.), Chairman
Environment and Public Works, Jennings Randolph (W.Va.), Chairman
Finance, Russell B. Long (La.), Chairman
Foreign Relations, John Sparkman (Ala.), Chairman
Governmental Affairs, Abraham A. Ribicoff (Conn.), Chairman
Human Resources, Harrison A. Williams, Jr., (N.J.), Chairman
Judiciary, James O. Eastland (Miss.), Chairman
Rules and Administration, Howard W. Cannon (Nev.), Chairman
Small Business, Gaylord Nelson (Wis.), Chairman
Veterans' Affairs, Alan Cranston (Calif.), Chairman

House Standing Committees

Agriculture, Thomas S. Foley (Wash.), Chairman
Appropriations, George H. Mahon (Tex.), Chairman
Armed Services, Melvin Price (Ill.), Chairman
Banking, Finance and Urban Affairs, Henry S. Reuss (Wis.), Chairman
Budget, Robert N. Giaimo (Conn.), Chairman
District of Columbia, Charles C. Diggs, Jr., (Mich.), Chairman
Education and Labor, Carl D. Perkins (Ky.), Chairman
Government Operations, Jack Brooks (Tex.), Chairman
House of Administration, Frank Thompson, Jr., (N.J.), Chairman
Interior and Insular Affairs, Morris K. Udall (Ariz.), Chairman
International Relations, Clement J. Zablocki (Wis.), Chairman
Interstate and Foreign Commerce, Harley O. Staggers (W.Va.), Chairman
Judiciary, Peter W. Rodino, Jr., (N.J.), Chairman
Merchant Marine and Fisheries, John M. Murphy (N.Y.), Chairman
Post Office and Civil Service, Robert N. C. Nix (Pa.), Chairman
Public Works and Transportation, Harold T. Johnson (Calif.), Chairman
Rules, James J. Delaney (N.Y.), Chairman
Science and Technology, Olin E. Teague (Tex.), Chairman
Small Business, Neal Smith (Iowa), Chairman
Standards of Official Conduct, John J. Flynt, Jr., (Ga.), Chairman
Veterans' Affairs, Ray Roberts (Tex.), Chairman
Ways and Means, Al Ullman (Oreg.), Chairman

of Congress; and earlier, powerful Wilbur Mills of Arkansas had given up his chairmanship of the Ways and Means Committee to Al Ullman of Oregon. These changes, according to Maurice Rosenblatt, founder of the National Committee for an Effective Congress, meant that Congress would "never be the same again, for it will be far more responsive than in the past to majority opinion." [8]

Another, and related, charge against the Congress, particularly the House of Representatives, has been that it disproportionately represents rural over urban interests. Journalist and critic Robert Sherrill has pointed out that most important chairmen are from small, rural towns and can hardly appreciate the problems and needs of the majority of Americans who live in urban/suburban clusters.[9] This circumstance is due in part to a combination of the seniority system and the nature of representation characteristic of the Congress until recently. We must keep in mind that Congressmen to the national House of Representatives are chosen from districts within states. How many districts a state has depends on its population. Every ten years there is a national census, and the 435 seats in the House are awarded to states on the basis of the census findings. Some states gain seats, some lose them. After 1970, for example, California received the largest number of seats (forty-three) because it had the largest population (bypassing New York). Traditionally it was the *state* legislature that every ten years was responsible for drawing up these *national* congressional districts within its state. Since state legislatures were usually disproportionately dominated by rural interests (until recently Los Angeles County had the same number of state senators—one—as did counties with much smaller populations), they tended to carve up congressional districts to the advantage of the less populated rural areas. This practice changed with certain dramatic decisions by the Supreme Court in the 1960s. In 1962, in the case of *Baker v. Carr,* the Court ruled that under the equal-protection-of-the-law clause of the Fourteenth Amendment, all citizens of each state should have equal representation in state legislatures. This was the so-called one-man, one-vote rule. By the early 1970s, after considerable haggling and finally court intervention, most state legislatures were thus apportioned. This meant that as state legislatures came to represent more substantial urban interests, so would the national Congress. To assure this, the Supreme Court extended the one-man, one-vote rule to national congressional districts in the 1964 decision *Wesberry v. Sanders.* Thus the courts have reformed Congress, and ultimately we should feel the impact of these decisions in a more urban-oriented legislature than in the past.

Other criticisms of the Congress include the charge that it is made up

[8] "Weakening of the Seniority System Will Strengthen Hand of Congress," *Los Angeles Times* (Jan. 26, 1975), Part 5, p. 1.
[9] *Why They Call It Politics,* 2nd. ed. (New York: Harcourt, 1974), pp. 114–116.

MAKEUP OF THE NINETY-FIFTH CONGRESS

House		Senate
	Party	
292	Democrats	61
143	Republicans	38
0	Independent	1
	Sex	
418	Men	100
17	Women	0
	Age	
27	Youngest	34
77	Oldest	80
48	Average	54
	Religion	
255	Protestants	69
107	Catholics	12
18	Jews	5
4	Mormons	3
51	Others	11
	Profession	
215	Lawyers	65
81	Businessmen and Bankers	13
45	Educators	6
14	Farmers and ranchers	6
22	Career government officials	0
24	Journalists and communications executives	4
2	Physicians	0
0	Veterinarians	1
0	Geologists	2
6	Workers and skilled tradesmen	0
25	Others	3
	Ethnic Minority	
17	Blacks	1
2	Orientals	3
4	Spanish	0

Source: *Newsweek* (Jan. 10, 1977).

largely of business people, lawyers, men, old people, and conservatives. Certainly it is made up mainly of businessmen and lawyers. These are types that seem to go into politics. Although there have been some important political victories recently for women, the Senate has one hundred men (Margaret Chase Smith retired in 1972), and the proportion of women in

121

the House of Representatives in no way approximates the percentage of women in the national population. On the other hand, *Science* magazine reported that in January 1975, most of the departing Congressmen (those defeated or retiring) were conservative, to be replaced predominately by young liberals.[10] The 1974 Senate election in normally conservative Colorado was indicative of the changes suggested by *Science*. Here Republican Peter Dominick was defeated by young liberal Gary Hart, who had served in 1972 as George McGovern's campaign director. And the Ninety-fourth Congress did not act conservatively. During the spring of 1975, it refused further aid to South Vietnam despite President Ford's demands, and in an astonishing move, it completely wiped out the oil-depletion allowance, for years one of the major tax incentives for a large and powerful corporate interest.

Critics also charge that the Congress is more responsive to "special interests" than to "the people." [11] This, of course, takes us back to the discussion of who the people are. Most of the "people" are at least tangentially associated with one or more interest groups. Large corporations lobby Congressmen. So do environmentalists. Common Cause, Ralph Nader and friends, welfare-rights organizations, labor groups, the National Rifle Association, and others *are* special interests. Congress can hardly ignore these groups, nor can any other level or branch of government.

The charge of corruption is often leveled at Congress, and in the case of maladroit and even illegal uses of campaign funds, it is a justified criticism. However, it is hardly of the magnitude of campaign corruption that has been revealed regarding the Presidency in the early 1970s. A more complicated problem has to do with conflicts of interests. For example, how disinterested can a Congressman's vote on a tax bill be if that bill contains provisions that might financially affect a company in which he owns stock? There has never been a satisfactory answer to this problem. Recently, suggestions for exposure of some or all of the assets of Congressmen have gained ground.[12]

For years Congress has been criticized as being ineffective and obstructive. In the House, the Rules Committee, which must usually issue a rule to bring a bill on the floor, has frequently been cited as a hindrance to progress in the legislature. And in the Senate, the most famous (or infamous) of obstructionist tactics has been the filibuster, the allowing of unlimited debate, which provides opponents of a bill the opportunity to talk continuously until a bill is removed from consideration. Here again, there have been some changes. For the first time in recent memory, a northern liberal,

[10] Nov. 1974, p. 717.
[11] See, for example, Mark J. Green, James M. Fallows, and David R. Zwick, *Who Runs Congress?* (New York: Bantam, 1972), pp. 29–52.
[12] Interview with Congressman Glenn Anderson (D. Calif.), Aug. 1975.

Ray Madden of Indiana, is Chairman of the House Rules Committee. In 1961, under pressure from President Kennedy, the Rules Committee was enlarged from twelve to fifteen, and it has become more responsive to progressive legislation since then. The most direct way to get a bill by the Rules Committee (or out of any committee that has refused to act on it) is through what is called a discharge petition. This is difficult but can be effected if, after the bill has been in committee for twenty days, such a petition is signed by 218 representatives (one-half the total). In that case, the bill must come to the full House.

To stop a filibuster in the Senate is at least as difficult. Traditionally two methods have been used. First, the majority can keep the Senate in continuous session and hope that the speaker will give up, and second, supporters of the bill can try to gain *cloture*. Until 1975, cloture required that sixteen Senators sign a petition to discontinue debate; two days later a vote was taken; if two thirds voted to discontinue debate, no Senator would be allowed to speak more than one hour, after which the bill would be brought to a vote. In March 1975, the Senate liberalized the rule to require only a three-fifths vote (sixty votes as a minimum) rather than the two thirds to close off debate.[13] The new rule will be more effective in curtailing filibusters only if there is a large attendance in the Senate, because under the *old* rule, two thirds of *those present and voting* could close debate; under the new rule three fifths of the whole Senate (one hundred members) is required.

Making Law

Ultimately, however, it is the whole labyrinthine procedure that a bill must go through that confuses and frustrates many Americans. Briefly, this is the procedure:

1. A bill is introduced. Anyone can draw up a bill—a Congressman, the President, or a student. Many major bills are either conceived or written elsewhere. Thus members of Congress spend considerable time processing what has been invented outside the Congress. However, official introduction of a bill can come only from a Representative or a Senator. In the House, a member puts the bill into a box called a hopper or gives it to the clerk. A Senator orally introduces a bill to the floor.

2. The bill is referred to committee by the leadership in that particular house.

3. The committee takes action (or, usually, no action). If the committee approves the bill, it is reported to the full House. In the House of Repre-

[13] *Los Angeles Times* (March 8, 1975), Part 1, p. 1.

sentatives, the Rules Committee issues a rule or resolution to bring it to the floor.

4. The bill then goes on a calendar, which is a traffic-regulating device. In the House, there are five calendars: the union calendar for revenue and appropriations bills, the House calendar for all other public bills, the consent calendar for items having no opposition, the private calendar dealing with private matters such as a veteran's pension, and the discharge calendar for bills brought out of committee by discharge petition. In the Senate, there are two calendars, one legislative and one "executive," which contains treaties and nominations.

5. The bill goes to the floor (usually in its order on the calendar, although the Senate, by majority vote, and the House, by a special rule from the Rules Committee or a two-thirds vote, can bring up a pressing matter out of order). In the House, the bill will probably go to the committee of the whole, which is all of the House in informal session, usually under the rules of debate established by the Rules Committee. The House then resolves itself into formal session and votes. The smaller Senate maintains formal sessions, where, as we have seen, debate is unlimited.

6. After a bill is passed by one house, it goes to the other, where frequently a similar bill has been considered, although the bill could be ignored or rejected.

7. If there are similar bills from both houses, a conference committee meets to resolve differences.

8. Once the exact wording is agreed upon by both houses, the bill goes to the President for his approval or veto.

The Lawmaker

One current member of the Congress, Glenn M. Anderson (D. Calif.), believes the low opinion that most polls show people have of the Congress may be misleading. He points out that while it is true that people generally are critical of the Congress, most seem to think their own particular Congressman is doing a good job. (Only about 5 percent of the members of Congress that seek reelection are defeated in a normal election.) Furthermore, he believes the poor collective view of the Congress may be based upon a widespread misunderstanding of the congressional role in our form of government. The Congress, he points out, is a legislative body. It was never intended to be a group that actually runs the nation. Under the Constitution, the Congress passes laws and reviews executive actions and proposals. It is not and cannot be an alternative to a strong and popular executive. Typically, he points out, it takes at least a year for a congressional proposal to work its way through complex committee hearings and find its way to the point where it will be approved or repudiated by the members.

The leaders of the Congress, men like Thomas O'Neill and Robert Byrd, are chosen because they are moderates, respected by their colleagues for their fair-mindedness. They are rarely hard-driving executives chosen because they have provided outstanding leadership on important issues.

Finally, in the facedown between heads of congressional committees and representatives of the executive department, Congress is almost always at a disadvantage. Cabinet officers and other executive department heads are usually well-known men, often distinguished authorities in their fields. A Congressman who happens to head a committee on taxation or foreign affairs or transportation may have been trained and educated in some other, entirely unrelated field. He got his job through seniority and by making himself agreeable to voters and fellow Congressmen and party leaders. He understandably feels a certain insecurity at being asked to cross swords with a Dr. Kissinger on foreign policy or the former head of a giant industry or corporation on matters of economics or a four-star general on defense policy. (This is particularly true in view of the limited staff support available. Congressional staff are frequently hired for their political skills, not policy expertise.)

It might be possible for Congress to take a much more aggressive role and to reorganize itself so that it could more effectively compete with the President in providing an alternative national leadership, Anderson acknowledges. But he believes it could not do so without departing from the clear intent of the Constitution and perhaps becoming a less representative and a more dictatorial body. In short, he argues that the Congress is functioning well, along the lines intended by the framers of the Constitution and traditionally approved by the American people.[14]

Still, there is a pervasive sense that Congress does not serve the nation as well as might reasonably be expected. Maurice Rosenblatt, founder of the National Committee for an Effective Congress, although generally defending the work of the Ninety-fourth Congress, acknowledges that "there is an anti-parliamentarian mood in the country." He argues that Congress is reflecting the "emotional malaise and intellectual indecision" of the nation. "History may call this [the Ninety-fourth Congress] 'the transitional Congress' for it stands with one foot firmly planted in the past while the other foot is groping for a toehold in the 21st Century."[15]

Since Congress is the most representative agency of government, disaffection with it may to some degree reflect underlying uncertainties about

---

[14] Some information here and elsewhere in this chapter is based on interviews conducted in August 1975 with California Congressmen Glenn Anderson and Jim Lloyd and members of their staffs.

[15] *Los Angeles Times* (Feb. 1, 1976), Part 8, p. 3.

125

the future of self-government itself. In the spring of 1976, for example, polls indicated that the three problems troubling most Americans were unemployment, inflation, and crime. No one could honestly pretend that the government was moving effectively to deal with any of these. Nor was there much evidence of specific and concrete progress on the more chronic and perhaps deeper problems, such as race relations, inadequate public transportation, protection of the environment, and energy depletion.

As we have said, the Congress's supreme and indispensible function is to enact legislation. But in the wake of the failures or the limited successes achieved by Lyndon Johnson's Great Society at home, the Vietnam debacle, and Watergate, there appeared to exist a widespread disbelief in the efficacy and wisdom of passing laws and spending tax dollars to solve specific social ills and achieve certain goals. The government has passed laws and appropriated tremendous sums to eliminate poverty, but the poor we still have with us. The government has sought to achieve racial integration, but America remains a largely segregated society. Perhaps the "21st Century Congress" that Rosenblatt alludes to will indeed have to redefine itself and its role under our federal system if it is not to suffer the fate of the Roman senate, which became less and less effective as Rome changed from a republic to an empire. The culmination of the senate's loss of power and prestige came when a Roman emperor appointed his horse a member of that once-august body. References to the Congress, both as individuals and as a group, made by the inner circle of the Nixon administration and revealed by publication of the contents of the White House tapes, are hardly less disparaging to the dignity of the U.S. Senate.

The Ninety-fourth Congress made a start toward reversing a historic decline in congressional influence and power by severely limiting the President's ability to conduct foreign policy unilaterally, by demanding increased accountability from and authority over such powerful agencies as the FBI and the CIA, and by creating a joint Senate–House Budget Office designed to give the Congress more control over federal expenditures. In the Ninety-fifth Congress, the House of Representatives adopted more stringent rules regarding the ethical behavior of its members. And the Senate, as we have seen, streamlined its committee structure. Such steps may be the harbingers of a stronger and more effective Congress acting in concert with the President to find new solutions to chronic problems. Many sincerely hope so, for as history demonstrates, a vibrant, active Congress is simply indispensable to the survival of this or any republic.

The Courts:
The Search for the
Just Society

Fishes and beasts and the fowls of the air devour one another. But to man, the gods have given justice.

Homer
The Iliad

Like love, justice is praised more than it is practiced. Virtually all governments—dictatorships no less than democracies—claim to be just. For all attempt to *justify* their acts. Hitler believed that the systematic murder of millions of Jews was just. Stalin would not have agreed, but on the other hand he found little to quarrel with in the mass imprisonment and murder of those who aroused his wrath. The CIA apparently thought the assassination of unfriendly foreign leaders was justifiable. Most people praise justice but define it according to their tastes.

Justice is only a word. But the word reflects an idea and an ideal that probably predate recorded history. Wealth, power, and brute force have always played a critical role in human relationships and in attempts to establish and maintain government among men and women. But few if any have attempted to govern—that is, to control the behavior of other human beings—without appealing to some notion of justice, however primitive. In one sense, all government may be viewed as a struggle for power. In another, government is also a struggle to achieve justice. When the two are somehow reconciled and brought into harmony, a state may be called just.

Some would argue with this statement. An anarchist, for example, presumably believes that all forms of power are inherently unjust because power, by definition, implies coercion—the right to make others behave as one wishes them to behave through force, actual or implied. Right-wingers and libertarians base much of their political philosophy upon the premise that virtually all forms of governmental power carry at least the possibility of abuse and hence political "bureaucrats" are unjust by definition. (For example, many believe that compulsory income-tax laws represent an unjust theft of one man's property by the government for the purpose of bestowing it upon others.) Leftists, on the other hand, approach private wealth (that is, private power) with much the same built-in hostility. "All property is theft," said the nineteenth-century Socialist Proudhon. Thus the private acquisition of wealth is inherently unjust and the rich are the eternal and inevitable enemies of a just society.

As people clearly do not, and perhaps never will, agree upon what justice is, why bother about the word or the concept at all? Well, for one thing there seems to be no way to exclude the idea from human affairs. In every relationship involving two or more persons, there will inevitably be some discussion, from mild disagreement to murderous hostility, about what is "fair" or "right"—that is, what is just. Husbands and wives, parents and children, teachers and students, no less than governments and citizens, or governments and other governments, will disagree, each insisting that its own point of view is right. If human beings could live without morals, ethics, or abstract intelligence, they would have no need for a definition of justice.

Governments may be instituted among men to ensure peace and order, to provide for the common defense, and to protect lives and property. They are also created to achieve justice. In the Old Testament, the state of Israel is created by God and His first act is to give the Law, the Ten Commandments, to Moses. By living in accordance with God's laws, Israel will be a just state and the Israelites a chosen people. The Israelites were not the first nor the last to profess that their laws carried divine sanction. When Jefferson asserted that "all men are created equal," he too, in a sense, was proclaiming that the fundamental principle of the United States government was in harmony with the nature of creation.

The Just Society

An ancient and classic study of the relationship between justice and government was written by the Greek philosopher Plato. In *The Republic,* Plato wrote that the search for justice was the foundation of all civil society. *The Republic* began and ended with an attempt to define the nature of the just society. Clearly Plato did not settle the argument, for statesmen, philosophers, politicians, and ordinary people (whether they knew it or not) have been debating the same questions ever since.

Plato attempted to destroy two notions of justice popular in his own time, as in ours, among people not inclined to think deeply about such matters. Justice, he affirmed, cannot simply be a matter of giving a person what he wants or thinks he wants. Suppose a friend were to give you a sum of money with instructions to safeguard it for him. A little while later, this friend reappears, obviously drunk and not in control of himself, and demands the return of his money. Would it be just to give it back to him under those circumstances? No, Plato argued, there are times when it is just to do not what is wanted but what is best in the long run. Should a physician treat every patient according to that patient's wishes, even when he knows that the patient's desires will do harm rather than good?

Plato's second common definition of justice was offered by the young and impetuous character Thrasymachus, who argued, simply, that "justice is the interest of the strong." That is, might makes right. Stated this baldly

129

most people would disapprove of the definition, and yet Thrasymachus attempted to prove that, in fact, this is what we really mean by justice. We may disapprove and call unjust an act of force, such as a robber stealing money at the point of a gun, when it occurs—so to speak—on the retail level, as the private act of a private person. But when it happens wholesale, as when the ruling class passes laws that ordain that they shall pay little or no taxes while middle-income people bear the cost of government, we accept it and some even defend it as "just." (For example, in practice, the very rich in America often pay a much smaller percentage of their total income in taxes than does the middle-class worker.) Or we accept it as "right" that strong and populous nations, such as the Soviet Union or the United States, should have far more influence in world affairs than small and weak countries.

Plato refuted this argument with the assertion that the purpose of any art, such as medicine or farming or government, is or should be the well-being of others. A physician is a healer of the sick, not just "a maker of money." A teacher must impart knowledge to his students. Hence a ruler should be guided by "the interest of his subjects." This idea is admittedly idealistic, but remember that justice itself is an *idea*. It exists, if at all, in the minds of men.

Both the ideal and the system—that is, the machinery of justice—that exist in the United States are the product of centuries of such philosophizing by men wise and unwise. They are also the product of human experience. In an attempt to resolve disputes between human beings peacefully and justly, rather than through sheer force (which would obviously make civil life impossible), we have developed a system of laws and courts. The police and, when needed, the military support and enforce the edicts of the courts. Only the government, except in rare instances, usually involving self-defense, has the right to resort to force to settle a question of right or wrong. If two drivers approach the same intersection on a collison course, it is the law, not who is strongest or bravest or who has the biggest car, that is supposed to determine the question of who will stop and wait for the other. There are times when the law itself may be unjust. (For example, the segregation laws that existed in most southern states prior to the 1960s were thought to be unjust by Dr. Martin Luther King, Jr., who proceeded to organize mass violations of these laws that ultimately succeeded in having the laws changed or abolished.) On the other hand, in most instances the professed aim of the law is to provide equity and justice for all.

The system of laws and courts that exists in the United States today is the product of history and culture. We have borrowed from the ancient Greeks and Romans, from English common law, and from the Old and the New Testaments in creating our judicial system. Both the system and the laws are subject to continual change and evolution. At one point in our history, the system of segregation under the doctrine of "separate but

130

equal" was upheld by our courts. At a later time, this doctrine was ruled unconstitutional—that is, illegal—because "separate was and is inherently unequal." [1] The people of Little Rock, Arkansas, physically sought to prevent the enforcement of a court order integrating their high schools in the 1950s. They felt that such an order was unjust and a violation of their rights. A conservative President, Dwight Eisenhower, who may have shared their distaste for compulsory integration, nevertheless felt constrained to enforce the court's order with the use of federal troops. Even California's former Governor Ronald Reagan, in many ways the most conservative figure on the national scene in the mid-1970s, has acknowledged that he would feel constrained to enforce the protection of civil-rights laws "at the point of a bayonet if necessary." More recently, the citizens of Boston, Massachusetts, who probably approved the integration of Little Rock's high schools in the 1950s, have gone into the streets protesting court ordered bussing for the purpose of achieving integration in South Boston. Still, the courts have maintained the necessity of integration.

People who favor capital punishment sometimes cite the Bible as an authority for the death penalty for certain crimes. The Bible proves, they argue, that the death penalty is in accord with God's will and hence is just. Biblical scholars opposed to the death penalty argue that on the contrary, specific punishments for specific crimes were included in the Bible because the death penalty was then a popular form of punishment for virtually *all* crimes, including some that we today would consider trivial or nonexistent (such as witchcraft.) Hence the effect of the prescribed death penalty for certain offenses and no others was to bring a more humane and enlightened concept of crime and punishment to the people of that era. We should live, it is argued, by the spirit, not the letter of the law. For the letter killeth, quite literally.

In the same way, many persons have argued that because "swift and sure punishment" is the best, if not the only, deterrent to crime, legislatures should prescribe fixed and severe punishments for crimes of violence, thus removing from judges discretionary powers to grant probation, to accept plea bargaining, and to use other devices that some believe have made the administration of justice more humane and flexible but that opponents believe have resulted in "coddling criminals" and thus encouraging crime.

Most Americans were shocked when President Ford granted Richard Nixon a full pardon for any and all criminal acts he may have been involved in with regard to the Watergate scandal. Dozens of Nixon's subordinates went to prison, whereas Nixon was granted immunity. Many Americans believed that the pardon violated the concept of "equal justice under the law." It seemed unjust that the President's men should go to prison for carrying out the President's instructions while he lived graciously in a

[1] This was the landmark case *Brown v. Board of Education, Topeka* (1954).

131

palatial home in San Clemente, enjoying a substantial government pension and other privileges associated with his role as a former President. Moreover, since the pardon was issued before any conviction, it precluded the possibility of the nation's learning all the details of Watergate during a trial of the former President.

Did President Ford believe that his act was just? ("Nixon has suffered enough.") Or was there some other factor, more important than simple justice, that determined his action? Those defending Mr. Ford's act have pointed to Nixon's poor health at the time of the pardon, arguing that Ford acted in the belief that he might be saving Nixon's life. Critics have alleged that there was "an understanding" in effect at the time of Ford's appointment to the Vice Presidency; Ford would get the job contingent upon an implied promise to pardon Nixon, should Nixon be forced to step down.

The struggle over civil rights, the conflict between labor and management over who gets what, the complaints of students about the fairness of grades, disputes between buyer and seller—these are all predicated upon varying definitions of what is and is not just. Because what we deem to be "right" and "fair" is to a large extent determined by what we have become accustomed to in our upbringing, nations like the United States, with a large and various population and many different kinds of cultures, are likely to experience more and deeper disagreements than relatively homogeneous populations. All Catholics do not agree about everything. But most do agree about some things, for example, that the Pope should be obeyed in matters of religious doctrine. This agreement helps to eliminate some grounds for potential conflict.

The Supreme Court

For this reason, Alistair Cooke, author and narrator of a popular television series on the history of America, has concluded like some other observers that the true strength of American society lies in a uniquely American invention: the Supreme Court.[2] For given the profound divisions among our people, there is need for a body that has the power to decide, once and for all, what is or is not constitutional.[3] In the one instance in which the Court failed to find a solution to a great national issue acceptable to the entire nation, the result was civil war, Cooke argues. Thus when the Court fails, the only alternative, he suggests, may lie in armed conflict. "Liberty and justice for all" may be more of an ideal than a reality in the United States, even today. But the Court exists to sustain the ideal and the society that rests upon this premise.

[2] *America* (New York: Knopf, 1974), pp. 144–147.
[3] What is constitutional—that is, what is "the supreme law of the land"—is not necessarily synonymous with what is "just."

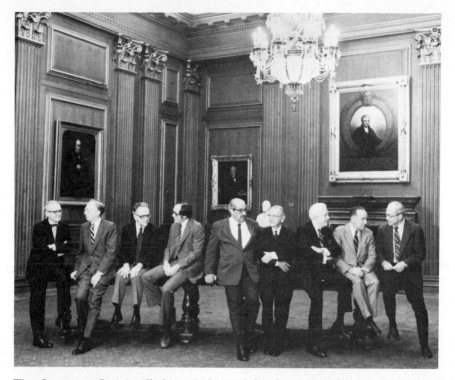

The Supreme Court, off duty. *Left to right:* **Associate Justices John Paul Stevens, Lewis F. Powell, Jr., Harry A. Blackmun, William H. Rehnquist, Thurgood Marshall, William J. Brennan, Jr.; Chief Justice Warren E. Burger; Associate Justices Potter Stewart and Byron R. White.** [Photo by Yoichi Okamoto, Photo Researchers, Inc.]

Justices of the Supreme Court are appointed by the President, with the approval of the Senate, for life. By giving the justices lifetime tenure of office, the authors of the Constitution hoped to create a body of learned men who would be insulated from personal ambition and political pressure, thus providing the republic with a certain stability. By and large, the Court probably has been a more stable element in the American system of government than either of its two counterparts, the Presidency or the Congress. At the same time, the Court has played from time to time an innovative and sometimes even a revolutionary role in American life.

Since the Justices appointed by a given President normally outlast the tenure of that President and the Congress that appointed them, the Supreme Court may reflect a somewhat different political philosophy than the existing President or Congress. In the heyday of the New Deal, the Court acted as a brake upon Franklin D. Roosevelt. During the conservative Eisenhower era, the Warren Court become an instrument of great social change.

133

The conservative majority appointed to the Court by Richard Nixon and Gerald Ford may well be in command of the Court for much of the remainder of the twentieth century, whether or not more liberal Presidents and Congressmen come to office.

When the United States was in the grip of anti-Communist hysteria during the Truman and Eisenhower eras, it was the Supreme Court that ultimately upheld and proved the surest defender of the right of political dissent. It was the Warren Court, of course, that opened the path to the civil-rights movement with the *Brown v. Board of Education* decision. The Court that helped to bring the Watergate crisis to a peaceful resolution by insisting unanimously that President Nixon must cooperate with the prosecution included several jurists and a Chief Justice who were Nixon appointees, thus vindicating the wisdom of the Constitution in insulating the Justices from politics. On the other hand, the Court has sometimes failed to meet its responsibility to act as a counter to the passions of the moment. For example, it failed to take exception to the enforced and blatantly unconstitutional internment of Japanese-Americans during World War II on no other grounds than a general fear of and distaste for all Japanese following the attack on Pearl Harbor. Ironically it was Earl Warren, then Attorney General of California, who was a leader in the clearly unconstitutional detention of thousands of American citizens of Japanese ancestry. That Warren later became the Chief Justice of perhaps the most liberal and civil-rights–oriented Court in the nation's history may suggest that the Court, like the Presidency, often seems to improve the character and extend the range of the men who join it. Another example of this process was the tenure of Justice Hugo Black, a member of the Klu Klux Klan in his youth, later to become one of the most distinguished defenders of equality and civil liberty in the Court's history.

"In a nation with no monarchy and no established church," according to *Newsweek* magazine, "the Supreme Court of the United States approaches the level of a sacred institution." [4] If the Supreme Court is sacred, it is also controversial. Our history is strewn with frequently vitriolic attacks on the Court.[5] While Chief Justice John Marshall, who served from 1801 to 1836, presided over some of the most important decisions in our history, he also feuded openly with two of our most powerful Presidents: Jefferson on matters of presidential appointments and Andrew Jackson on the issue of the national bank. One can hardly imagine a more explosive court decision than the case of Dred Scott in 1857, in which the Court of Chief Justice Roger Taney declared slavery to be legally binding on all states and maintained that even free blacks could not expect to be treated as citizens

---

[4] Nov. 1, 1971, p. 16.
[5] See Robert G. McCloskey, *The American Supreme Court* (Chicago: U. of Chicago, 1960).

134

under the Constitution. The Dred Scott controversy fueled the Republican party, and in criticizing it, Illinois lawyer Abe Lincoln established a national reputation. In the 1930s, the "nine old men" of the Court angered another powerful president, FDR, by striking down New Deal legislation. Roosevelt attempted to push through Congress legislation that would set up a mandatory retirement age for judges and expand the number on the Supreme Court so as to allow him to install justices more favorable to his views. Roosevelt failed in this attempt.

Finally, there are still weathered highway signs in the West demanding the impeachment of Earl Warren, who has been gone from the bench since 1969 and died in 1974. The popular hostility against the Warren Court (1953–1969) has been the most recent reflection of how controversial the Court can and has become.

But the Court has held up against assault. And many liberals who believe the Warren Court's decisions to have been prudent and protective of fundamental rights probably are pleased that FDR was unsuccessful in attempting to establish a precedent for popularly elected officials' meddling with the judicial branch.

There is, however, a certain irony about the present (Burger) Court that must not go unnoticed. As we have seen, very powerful and popular Chief Executives have been checked in their desire to control or unduly influence the Court. As for the present Court, one man (and a politically discredited man at that) has had more influence on it than anyone since George Washington appointed the original Court. Richard Nixon, who as we have seen would have been impeached had he not resigned, was responsible for the appointment of five Justices (a majority) on the current Court. Four were appointed directly by him: Warren Earl Burger (Chief Justice); Harry A. Blackmun; Lewis F. Powell, Jr.; and William H. Rehnquist, And the fifth—John Paul Stevens—was chosen by Mr. Nixon's hand-picked successor, Gerald Ford. Since it might be expected that these Justices would reflect Nixonian ideology, Nixon's views on jurisprudence could dominate the Court well into the next century. Thus, despite Mr. Nixon's unprecedented resignation, his influence on American government may be heavy for many years.

This possibility, of course, raises the interesting point of the nature of judicial appointments. Earl Warren was a three-term Republican governor of California and thus represented a partisan political appointment. Mr. Nixon's appointments were less representative of political partisanship than of ideological "conservatism." During the third presidential debate of 1976, Jimmy Carter maintained that he would base his Court appointments upon a careful screening process so as to find the most competent jurists. Yet, when pressed further, Mr. Carter conceded that if several potential appointees were of the same level of competence, he would pick the one most compatible with his own views.

THE CURRENT SUPREME COURT		
	Appointed by	Date
Chief Justice:		
Warren E. Burger	Nixon	1969
Associate Justices:		
William J. Brennan, Jr.	Eisenhower	1956
Potter Stewart	Eisenhower	1958
Byron R. White	Kennedy	1962
Thurgood Marshall	Johnson	1967
Harry A. Blackmun	Nixon	1970
Lewis F. Powell, Jr.	Nixon	1972
William H. Rehnquist	Nixon	1972
John Paul Stevens	Ford	1975

Nevertheless, the student must keep in mind that many Supreme Courts have proved surprisingly independent of the views of the Presidents who appointed them. For example, Earl Warren, appointed by President Eisenhower, proved liberal and activist, which surprised most observers, including Mr. Eisenhower.

The National Court Structure

Article 3 of the Constitution only vaguely defines the organization of a court system, calling simply for a Supreme Court, with inferior courts to be created by Congress. In the Judiciary Act of 1789, the First Congress divided the nation into districts. This essential principle of division continues today. The current structure, from bottom to top, includes district courts, courts of appeals, and one Supreme Court.

There are currently ninety *district courts*. Each state has at least one district court, and there is one in the District of Columbia and one in Puerto Rico. Larger states have more than one. This is the level at which most national court work is done. There may be one or more judges at each district court. There are currently a total of 368 district judgeships, all filled by the President with the consent of the Senate. All district judges hold office for life (of course, they can be impeached). District courts are courts of original jurisdiction. That is, if you violate a federal law, you will be charged in and go to court before a district court. These are the only national courts that use *grand juries* (indicting juries) and *petit juries* (trial juries). Various district courts and district-court judges have become well known in the mass media in recent years, particularly District Judge John J. Sirica, who served in the district court in Washington, D.C. and presided over the Watergate break-in case.

If a case is successfully appealed, it will normally go to a *U.S. court of*

136

appeals in one of eleven judicial circuits in the country (including one in the District of Columbia). These courts have only appellate jurisdiction. They do not use juries, and they consist of from one to nine judges, all appointed for life by the President with the consent of the Senate.

Next, and at the top of the hierarchy, is the *Supreme Court,* whose jurisdiction is both original (this original jurisdiction is severely limited in Article 3, Section 2 of the Constitution) and appellate. The Court spends most of its time on cases on appeal. It is the Court of last resort, with the last word on matters falling within the jurisdiction of the Constitution.

Now, two cautionary notes must be emphasized: (1) the national court structure outlined above is different from but related to *state* court systems, and (2) the *prosecution* of law violators is different from but related to the court system.

Most states also have a hierarchical system ranging from lower courts to a state supreme court. These courts try civil (such as divorce) and criminal (such as murder) cases in which state laws are violated (there are some areas of concurrent jurisdiction). As a general rule, the only national court that can review a state court decision is the Supreme Court—and this only after all appeals at the state level have been exhausted (that is, the case has gone all the way through the state supreme court).

Judges, whether in national or state courts, decide cases; they do not prosecute people. At the national level, government prosecution is the responsibility of the Justice Department, part of the President's Cabinet. The Justice Department is directed by the Attorney General and aided by the Solicitor General (who argues cases for the government before the Supreme Court). The department uses U.S. Attorneys throughout the country. These attorneys are appointed for four-year terms to the district courts by the President with the consent of the Senate. Assisted by the FBI, which is housed within the Justice Department, these attorneys commence criminal and civil proceedings for the government in district courts.

Note that when members of the executive branch of government were being investigated during the Watergate matter, serious confusion arose. In effect, members of the Nixon administration (in the Justice Department) were investigating (preliminary to prosecution) their own administration (two former Attorneys General, for example—John Mitchell and Richard Kliendienst—were directly or tangentially touched by the scandal). This is why Congress maintained the right to create a "special" prosecutor, distinct from but active in the Justice Department. When Archibald Cox, the first special prosecutor, became untenable for Mr. Nixon, the President fired him in October 1973 (as he would fire any member of his Cabinet). Neither the Attorney General at the time, Elliott Richardson, nor the Deputy Attorney General, William Ruckelshaus, was willing to carry out the firing because they believed it was an action of bad faith vis-à-vis the Congress. Solicitor General Robert Bork was thus temporarily elevated to

Attorney General, whereupon he officially fired Cox. The ensuing public outcry became so intense, however, that Mr. Nixon had to agree to another special prosecutor, Leon Jaworski, who ultimately unraveled so much of the scandal that the President left office.

The Venerable Court

Ultimately it is the Supreme Court that makes history, but it does so selectively, for although it takes cases on appeal from both state courts and lower national courts, it takes only a few, and these few are usually of national importance.

In order for a case to come before the Supreme Court from a *state* court, a national question must be involved (for example, a constitutional question or a question involving a national law or treaty), and the litigant must have exhausted his appeals at the state level. Even then, the odds are against the case's being presented to the Supreme Court. The Court also uses extreme discretion in deciding which appealed cases from lower national courts it will review.

In either case, a disappointed litigant must petition the Court. If at least four justices find the case worthy, the Court issues a *writ of certiorari* (Latin for "make more certain") to the lower court, ordering it to send up all records of the case.

Thus the Court essentially performs two functions. First, it determines what cases it will hear (a small minority of the total appealed to it); and second, it hears and issues judgments on those cases. The Court is in session from October through June in the palatial and dignified Supreme Court building in Washington, D.C. The Justices hear cases in the courtroom there and discuss cases among themselves in a private chamber. Decisions are made by a majority vote, and the Court almost always announces reasons for each decision. These can come in an *opinion for the Court,* which is the majority opinion, written by one of majority; a *concuring opinion,* again written by a member of the majority, but one who wishes to emphasize different views; and, of course, *dissenting opinions,* written by those who voted in the minority, explaining their reasoning.

Judicial Review

The Supreme Court has maintained an awesome authority, in part because of the right of *judicial review*. This term needs careful clarification. *Judicial review* refers *first* to the national Court's power to decide whether or not a *state* law or provision of a *state* constitution is or is not consonant with the U.S. Constitution. This authority is based upon the statement in Article 6 of the Constitution that the Constitution is "the supreme law of the land . . . anything in the constitution or laws of any state to the contrary notwithstanding." The Judiciary Act passed by Congress in 1789 confirmed this power of the Court.

Judicial review refers *second* to the national Court's right to declare whether or not a piece of statutory legislation passed by the *national* Congress or a presidential action is or is not consonant with the Constitution. Precedent for this latter authority was established in the landmark case *Marbury v. Madison* (1803). Briefly, here is the essence of the case. In the election of 1800, Thomas Jefferson defeated incumbent John Adams for the Presidency. Moreover, followers of Jefferson won control of the Congress from Adams's Federalist party. However, as the newly elected administration was not scheduled to assume office until March 4, 1801, lame-duck President Adams, with his lame-duck Federalist Congress, determined to place Federalists in the national Court system. Congress accordingly created several new judicial posts, and Adams hastened to fill them. In the late rush, not all of the commissions were delivered. Interestingly, Adams's Secretary of State, who was responsible for delivering the commissions, was a Virginia Federalist, John Marshall, whom Adams had appointed Chief Justice of the Supreme Court. Marbury had been appointed to a judgeship in the District of Columbia, but had not received his commission, and after March 4, 1801, the new Secretary of State, James Madison, under orders from Jefferson, refused to deliver it. Marbury then appealed to the Supreme Court for a writ of *mandamus*. According to Section 3 of the Judiciary Act of 1789, the Supreme Court was authorized to issue such writs to persons holding United States office.

Chief Justice Marshall spoke for a unanimous Court. He said first that Marbury was entitled to his commission, but second, and surprisingly, he said that the Supreme Court could not issue such a writ of *mandamus,* because Article 13 of the Judiciary Act of 1789 was contrary to Article 3, Section 2 of the Constitution, which accorded the Supreme Court *original* jurisdiction *only* in cases affecting ambassadors or foreign ministers or in cases in which a state is a party. Marbury fitted none of these definitions! Thus Article 13 of the Judiciary Act of 1789 was invalid. Although in this particular case Marshall limited the power of the Court by effecting judicial review of national legislation, he provided the Court with immense power.[6]

---

[6] An excellent essay regarding this case is by John A. Garraty, "The Case of the Missing Commissions," in John A. Garraty (Ed.), *Quarrels That Have Shaped the Constitution* (New York: Harper, 1964).

The Warren Court

Since World War II, Supreme Court review of state laws and actions has created the most public controversy. One reason for the increased activity of the Court during Warren's term was the Court's insistence that the provisions of the Bill of Rights protecting individual rights against the national government also apply to state governments. This position is based on the Court's reading of the Fourteenth Amendment, passed during the Reconstruction period after the Civil War.[7] Let us look at Section 1 of this amendment, which contains four important ingredients: first, a definition of United States citizenship: "All persons born or naturalized in the United States, and subject to the jurisdiction thereof, are citizens of the United States and of the State wherein they reside"; second, restrictions on states, protecting individual rights: "No State shall make or enforce any law which shall abridge the privileges or immunities of citizens of the United States"; third, a statement restricting states with respect to *just* procedure: "nor shall any state deprive any person of life, liberty, or property, without due process of law" (due process of law means, basically, that justice demands a knowable procedure for someone accused of a crime; thus there must be a law before there can be a violation, and there must be a formal accusation, a show of cause for detention, a right to counsel, a formal plea, and a trial); a final restriction on states is that they may not "deny to any person within [their] jurisdiction the equal protection of the laws."

This short sentence of the Constitution has provided the fodder from which a judicial revolution of sorts developed during the 1950s and 1960s. For it was during these years that the Warren Court came to be concerned about and active in supporting substantive individual rights. It was in this regard that the Court was both condemned and praised for its "judicial activism." The Nixon nominees have openly criticized such activism. When Mr. Nixon ran for election in 1968, one of his main promises was to bring the Court into line by appointing "strict constructionists" to replace the "loose constructionists" then on the Court. And Gerald Ford, while he was in Congress, led a movement to impeach one of the most liberal of the judges—William O. Douglas.

Why was the Warren Court so controversial? And has the Burger Court substantially reversed the impact of its predecessor or will it do so?

As to the first of these questions, the Court was probably controversial because of the subject matter of the cases and the people involved. That is, the Court was concerned with civil rights and individual rights for ethnic minorities, the economically underprivileged, and the politically unpopular

[7] Many of the landmark decisions of the Warren Court years, outlined here, were based upon the extension of rights in the First, Fifth, and Sixth Amendments to states as well as the federal government. See Charles H. Sheldon, *The Supreme Court: Politicians in Robes* (Beverly Hills, Calif.: Glencoe, 1970).

(atheists and Communists, for example). In each instance, however, the Court firmly contended that it was upholding the Constitution, particularly the First, Fourth, Fifth, Sixth, and Fourteenth Amendments. Indeed, Hugo Black, who joined the majority in most of the controversial issues, argued persuasively that he was in fact a "strict constructionist."

Let us look at the most important cases of the Warren Court:

1. First, we must consider the category of *racial integration* of public schools. In 1954, the Court issued its famous decision in *Brown v. Board of Education, Topeka, Kansas.* For fifty-eight years the Court had consistently held that separate public facilities could be considered equal and therefore constitutional. The question before the Court was whether segregation deprived black children of equal educational opportunities and thus of the equal protection of the law (see the Fourteenth Amendment). The Court, in a unanimous decision, answered yes, holding that separation was inherently unequal, thus reversing the separate-but-equal doctrine of *Plessy v. Ferguson* (1896). As we have seen, there was considerable resistance to this decision.

2. In the category of *freedom of political expression,* the Court in *Yates v. U.S.* (1957) overturned the conviction of some second-string Communists on the basis of free speech, no matter how unpopular the issue. In other cases the Court upheld the right of freedom of expression.[8]

3. *Separation of church and state.* In *Engel v. Vitale* (1962), the issue before the Court dealt with a New York State Board of Regents' requirement of an opening-day prayer at all schools. Ten parents had brought suit against the requirement. The Court ruled that this state-mandated prayer violated the First Amendment as applied to the states by the Fourteenth Amendment. Thus the New York law violated the constitutional wall of separation of church and state. As Jefferson would have certainly agreed, government, according to the Court, should neither deprive you of your religious freedom nor further any particular religious beliefs. Unpopular among many Americans, this decision underscored the secularity of our political society, which had been a unique contribution of our Revolutionary era.

4. *Voting rights and democracy.* We have discussed these in our chapter on the Congress. To recapitulate, in *Baker v. Carr* (1962), the Court ruled that, under the equal-protection-of-the-law requirement of the Fourteenth Amendment, state legislative districts must represent people equally on a one-person, one-vote basis. The principle was extended to national Congressional districts in *Wesberry v. Sanders* (1964). The decision clearly implemented democracy and gave more political weight to urban areas, crowded with ethnically diverse peoples.

[8] See Robert L. Cord, *Protest, Dissent and the Supreme Court* (Cambridge, Mass.: Winthrop, 1971).

5. *Rights of the accused.* The key decision in this category was *Miranda v. Arizona* (1966). The Court said that when a person is deprived of his freedom (in this case by state officials), that person has certain rights consonant with the principle of due process (see the earlier discussion of the Fourteenth Amendment). In reviewing this case, the Court discovered that certain police interrogation methods violated the right against involuntary self-incrimination. The essence of the ruling was that the arresting and investigative unit (the police) must inform you of your rights the moment you have been detained. Under the *Miranda* formula, you would (a) be told that you may remain silent, (b) be told that anything you say can be held against you, (c) have a right to counsel prior to and during questioning, and (d) if indigent, have a right to have counsel appointed for you. That is, the decision clarified the rights of an accused person (not a convicted criminal).

The Burger Court

These are the important areas in which the Warren Court made controversial decisions. A comparison of these decisions with later judgments by the Burger Court should reveal how dramatically the new Court has reversed (or not reversed) its predecessor's actions. In making this comparison, we should keep in mind that the five more conservative justices appointed by Nixon and Ford have not all been serving together since 1969 (John Paul Stevens replaced William O. Douglas in December 1975). Nevertheless, we should be able to gain insight into the direction in which the new Court is moving.

First, under the category of *school integration,* the Burger Court has actually implemented earlier decisions (contrary to President Nixon's wishes), even going so far as to condone bussing in order to achieve racial balance. Mr. Nixon's first appointee, Chief Justice Burger, has written that "all things are not equal in a system that has been deliberately constricted and maintained to enforce racial segregation. . . . Desegregation plans cannot be limited to the walk-in school"; bus transportation, he said, is "one tool" for desegregation. The Court has stuck by this judgment.[9]

In terms of *freedom of political expression,* the Court has maintained the Warren tradition.[10] In one of the most dramatic expressions, the Court let stand California court rulings that black activist Angela Davis could not constitutionally be fired from the UCLA faculty because she was a member of the Communist party.

[9] *Los Angeles Times* (Feb. 27, 1972), Section G., p. 2; (Oct. 25, 1972), Part 1, p. 3.
[10] For an interesting discussion of the history and importance of First Amendment decisions, see Alexander M. Bickel, "The 'Uninhibited, Robust, and Wide-Open' First Amendment," *Commentary* (Nov. 1972).

For the most part, the Court has also maintained support of the doctrine of *separation of church and state,* most particularly by holding unconstitutional any state laws that directly or indirectly represent government sponsorship of religious activity. Thus, despite the support of both President Nixon and President Ford for government aid to private and parochial schools, the Court has denied or struck down any laws that would provide such aid. However, in recent decisions the Court has altered this position somewhat by condoning public aid to church-related private colleges. The majority of the Court still opposed such aid to elementary and secondary schools but decided that institutions of higher learning spend little time on religious teaching and are rarely influenced by church authorities.[11]

The Court has likewise maintained the "one-man, one-vote" principle in reapportionment cases.

The Burger Court has even entered some controversial areas never, or only slightly, touched by the Warren Court. For example, the new Court has ruled that women have a constitutional right to an abortion in the first six months of pregnancy. This 1973 decision struck down antiabortion laws across the country.

In the apparent conflict between freedom of expression and freedom from "obscenity," the Court has taken some actions, but the results remain ambiguous. Within the past few years Americans have witnessed considerable change in standards of public morality. The result has been more open acceptance of sex in literature, art, and motion pictures. Thus there is today an increasing number of profit-making "skin" magazines, underground sex newspapers, and explicit X-rated movies. Some private individuals and government officials have tried to suppress such material, only to be opposed by those who say that the First Amendment prohibits actions against freedom of expression. The Warren Court attempted to define and limit "obscenity" by ruling that material "utterly without redeeming social importance" was not protected by the Constitution.[12] But application of the principle proved ineffective in checking the increase in alleged obscene material that contained even the slightest "social value." In 1973 the Burger Court ruled in effect that local communities could set their own standards as to what was or was not tolerable in works dealing with sexual conduct.[13] Thus, although state legislatures can apparently pass laws giving local communities more control over such matters, the money-making explosion in "pornography" continues.

The one category in which the new Court has substantially altered (and may undermine) precedents established by the Warren Court, is in the

---

[11] This was the 1976 case *Roemer v. Maryland Public Works Board.* The decision was by the barest of margins, 5 to 4.
[12] *Roth v. U.S.* (1957).
[13] *Miller v. California* (1973).

["That's to take care of obscenity cases"—*copyright 1977 by Herblock in The Washington Post.*]

area of due process and the rights of the accused. For example, the Court has made more flexible the rules requiring police to obtain court warrants for search and seizure, even deciding that many persons detained on minor charges (like traffic violations) may be searched for evidence of more serious but unrelated offenses. Moreover, the Court has (1) permitted prose-

144

cutors to introduce into court statements made by a defendant before his being told of his right to counsel, (2) allowed testimony by witnesses whose identity was determined during illegal interrogations, (3) authorized the introduction in court of a confession after a subject had asked for an attorney, and (4) allowed police to proceed with interrogation even after a suspect has invoked the right of silence. These decisions have led dissenting Justice William J. Brennan to worry that the current Court will entirely overthrow the *Miranda* decision.[14] But Miranda remains partially intact. In *Brewer v. Williams* (March 1977), the Court in a 5–4 decision, ruled invalid a confession made by a suspected murderer in the absence of counsel.

Justice: Where Do We Stand?

Implicit in the idea and the practice of judicial review is the notion that government rests upon a "social contract." The individual must obey the law, but in return the law must not trample upon the rights of the individual. Judicial review suggests that there are some things that even the most popular President or the most powerful Congress cannot and must not do.

If the judicial system has been concerned, at least in part, with maintaining public order and political stability while sustaining the freedom of individuals, it has had some success in achieving both objectives. The Constitution has remained alive for two hundred years, and despite monumental problems, the United States government remains among the most stable on earth. Our elections are settled with ballots, not guns. There has never even been a serious attempt at a military coup in our entire history—something very few nations can boast.

On the other hand, if Americans are not necessarily the "freest people on earth," as her politicians are wont to claim, clearly they continue to enjoy a degree of personal freedom that can be matched by only a handful of the world's population.

When Nikita Khrushchev prepared to make his bid for power among a group of men who were leaders of the Soviet Union, he tells us, he found it prudent to carry a pistol with him into the meeting of the men who ruled the Soviet Union. He had to be prepared to arrest or, if necessary, shoot the head of the Soviet secret police before the secret police arrested or shot him. This is not an ideal way to select the leader of one of the most powerful and technologically advanced nations on earth. The judicial system has succeeded in preventing anyone from taking power in America

[14] *Los Angeles Times* (Dec. 22, 1975), Part 2, p. 6.

145

except by lawful means and, as in the case of President Nixon, played its part in removing from office an administration that abused that power.

In most nations on earth, even today, men and women who openly attack and defy the policies of their government, particularly in time of war or national crisis, face deportation, prison, or execution. Large numbers of Americans did attack and defy the policy of their government during the Vietnam war. When the government attempted to jail some of the most prominent dissident leaders, as in the trial of the Chicago Seven, the effort failed. Most of the antiwar leaders are free men today; many hold prominent positions, including positions within the government; and at least one, Tom Hayden, was a primary candidate for the U.S. Senate in California in 1976. Although there unquestionably was some repression of the rights of antiwar leaders, such as illegal opening of their mail, wire taps, and other forms of harassment, on the whole the government was prevented by the judicial system from crushing resistance to the Vietnam war, despite evidence that the Nixon administration, at least, would very much like to have done precisely that.[15]

When a novelist such as Aleksandr Solzhenitsyn wrote books critical of the Soviet Union's political leaders, his works were suppressed in the Soviet Union and he was deported. This would be more-or-less normal response of many governments to criticism from a popular artist or a leading intellectual. American writers can and do write the most defamatory things about our political leaders and customarily can expect to receive nothing but substantial royalty checks by way of reprisal. They are protected by the law.

When the *New York Times* decided to publish the secret *Pentagon Papers,* which revealed some embarrassing truths about the nature of our gradual involvement in the Vietnam war, in direct defiance of a governmental order not to do so, the Supreme Court defended the *Times*'s right to publish without submitting to government censorship. Later, when the man who brought the *Pentagon Papers* to the *Times,* Daniel Ellsberg, was tried for stealing these documents, the judge threw the case out of court because the government had acted improperly. This action prevented a clear-cut decision on the substance of the case itself. But a subsequent poll of the jurors indicated that most were prepared to acquit Ellsberg.

Americans who run afoul of the law in some foreign countries, even in such nearby states as Mexico, are astonished to discover that they can be arrested and held for months, even years, without trial and that instead of a presumption of innocence, they are presumed guilty unless they can prove they are innocent, under the theory that the police would not have arrested anyone who was not doing something wrong. They find corruption

[15] For a variety of views on the extent to which political protest should be allowed, see Marvin Summers, *Free Speech and Political Protest* (Boston: Heath, 1967).

and bribery rampant in the judicial system, so that some prisoners have said that théy do not even have the "right" to lie down on a cement floor in their prison cells without first "renting" the space from their jailors.[16] Such things may sometimes happen in America. But they are rare exceptions.

Finally, most Americans do not live in fear of sudden and mysterious arrest should they happen to criticize the authorities or back the losing side in an election. Freedom in the United States is far from perfect. But on the whole it need not fear comparison with any other nation.

On the other hand, the judicial system has failed to extend "equal justice under the law" in a number of important respects.

Although few Americans fear arbitrary and unreasonable arrest, many do fear to walk the streets of their communities, particularly after dark. And although they do not live in dread of a midnight raid by the secret police, many do fear that the sanctity of their homes will be invaded by armed hoodlums. Older people, many of whom are forced by limited incomes to live in high-crime areas of the major cities, are too often virtual prisoners in their own shabby apartments. Old people living alone are frequently the prime targets of cruel young hoodlums, not only at home, but when walking the streets or even when riding public streetcars or subways. It is cold comfort not to be repressed by the police if one's fellow citizens behave like wolf packs.

As we have previously noted, the United States is probably the most crime-ridden society in the Western world. Efforts by conservatives to curb crime by "getting tough" and "law-and-order" campaigns have not helped very much. Neither have efforts to apply humanitarian principles—counseling services and greater welfare benefits and educational opportunities. A few decades ago most enlightened people believed that crime was an unnatural course of behavior usually brought about by extreme poverty, lack of educational opportunity, and family or societal neglect. But increased educational opportunity and greatly increased efforts on the part of society to deal with criminals, particularly young criminals, with understanding and compassion have resulted in rising, not falling, crime rates. Perhaps we might have been even worse off without such efforts. Perhaps there would be less crime if the "do-gooders" would abandon the field to the police. Perhaps what we have been doing is totally irrelevant, like some of the "cures" for certain deadly epidemics that swept the world in the past ages. No one can say for sure because we simply do not know what causes some people to prey upon others.

But the fact remains that "equal justice under the law" depends upon people's being willing to respect each other's rights as much as it does upon

[16] See *Los Angeles Times* (Jan. 12, 1976), Section 2, p. 1; (Jan. 14, 1976), Section 1, p. 2; (Jan. 16, 1976), Section 2, p. 1; (February 3, 1976), Section 2, p. 5.

official actions. And many Americans feel that the government, particularly the courts, has failed them in this respect.

A second serious concern with America's legal system was dramatized by the Watergate case. Most of the principal culprits in this tawdry series of events, including the President and the Attorney General, were lawyers, presumably men trained to respect and enforce law, who used their special knowledge and training to break the law. (It is, of course, true that most of those who prosecuted the Watergate defendants were also lawyers.) Thus John Dean makes clear in his book, *Blind Ambition,* that many of his early assignments in the Nixon White House, even prior to his involvement with Watergate (for which he went to prison), required him to use his special legal skill to plan and/or to cover up plans for blatantly illegal acts, such as a proposal to burn down the Brookings Institution. The President, himself a lawyer, needed another lawyer to help him break the law, an approach not confined to politicians. Some corporation executives, labor leaders, and gangsters retain counsel for the same reason. It is as if a large-scale plot were discovered among the nation's most eminent doctors not to cure but to make their patients sicker. As a result of Watergate, more and more Americans have begun to wonder if there is not some serious flaw in the very nature of the legal system or in the training and education of lawyers. For the national attention focused on the legal profession by Watergate simply highlighted a widespread popular impression that the special skills of lawyers are too often used to obstruct justice and cheat the individual of his rights rather than the reverse.

In this respect, the legal profession is unique among the learned professions in the degree to which the benefits of its knowledge are disproportionately commanded by the rich and the powerful and denied to the ordinary citizen. Many American families are able to secure at least a reasonable degree of medical care through either governmental or private health-insurance programs. Access to education, including higher education, although not ideal, is widely available, and although the rich can still afford the most exclusive private colleges and the middle class cannot, in many areas of the nation the best schools and universities are public, tax-supported institutions open to all at relatively modest fees.

Only the legal profession remains largely what it has always been—primarily a tool of the affluent, of the wealthy corporation or the labor union or the governmental bureaucracy. The very poor can get free legal services, but no one believes that such services are in any way comparable to the kind of legal power that a great corporation can muster or that a wealthy individual such as Patty Hearst has at her disposal. Litigation is expensive, far too expensive for the ordinary family to contemplate except under the most extreme circumstances. As a result, it is often alleged that "90 percent of the lawyers work for 10 percent of the people."

Additionally, according to a growing number of critics the court system simply has become too overcrowded. Between 1970 and 1975 the average number of cases pending before a federal district judge increased from 285 to 355, and in state courts crowding is even worse.[17] For those in jail awaiting trial but without sufficient funds to afford bail, the system seems hardly just.

If "equal justice" is to become more than rhetoric, clearly some fundamental reforms are needed. Legal services must be made more widely and cheaply available, or the laws must be simplified so that the average person can go into court without an attorney, and/or lawyers must be made responsible to human rights rather than legal hairsplitting.

In a society grown complex and bureaucratic, the legal profession has increasingly come to resemble the scribes of ancient Egypt or the priesthood of the Middle Ages, a self-serving elite in possession of enormous power because they alone can translate the mysterious and often arbitrary rules that govern everyone's life.

Finally, an investigation of the Federal Bureau of Investigation in 1975 by a congressional subcommittee headed by Representative Otis G. Pike (D. N.Y.) revealed that during the administration of the late Director J. Edgar Hoover, the agency was used to harass persons such as the late civil-rights leader Dr. Martin Luther King, Jr. on no other grounds than that Hoover happened to dislike and disapprove of Dr. King's politics. It was also revealed that for decades Hoover had run the agency like a feudal lord, rewarding and punishing agents largely on the basis of loyalty to the director, using its vast police power to spy on and harass reporters and politicians who were critical of the director, and gathering secret dossiers on the private lives of prominent persons, specifically on their sexual activities, so that many Congressmen, Senators, and perhaps even Presidents of the United States feared exposure by the director and were thus hesitant to curb his power. That such power could be concentrated in the hands of one man, despite the aforementioned constitutional guarantees and Supreme Court decisions intended to protect the rights of Americans, is evidence that the formal, legal structure, however liberal, is never adequate in and of itself to preserve personal freedom from powerful and ruthless bureaucrats. The finest system in the world can be subverted by determined and ambitious individuals who choose to ignore the law, particularly if they happen to be the very people responsible for enforcing those laws.

Perhaps even more alarming are statements attributed to Hoover's successor, Clarence Kelley, defending the right of his agency to use illegal and unconstitutional means in the investigation of crime.

Interestingly, although the FBI under Hoover was preoccupied with the pursuit of Americans engaged in political advocacy displeasing to the director, the Mafia established itself as an underworld government in the

---

[17] "Too Much Law," *Newsweek* (Jan. 10, 1977), p. 43.

United States with apparent immunity from, and at times outright collaboration with, the legal government.

What happened to the FBI under Hoover suggests that the Constitution and the court system cannot by themselves secure the liberties of the American people if and when the people grow careless about their freedom and loath to exercise the rights guaranteed to them by the law.

And although, on balance, the judicial system of the United States has served the nation and the people well—perhaps better than most systems yet devised by mortals—Plato's ideal of the just republic remains a lovely, remote, and obscure goal.

The Art of Politics:
Parties and Elections

Politics is the art of creating wonder out of emptiness.

Aristotle

Politics has been defined as a business, a profession, a sport, a calling, a science, and a racket. It is also an art. For like literature, painting, or music, it contains an element of unpredictability, mystery, and creative intuition. Like the artist, the successful politician somehow appeals to fundamental human emotions and stirs the passions of people. Often he speaks in a language that transcends logic or reason. The talented politician may use his gifts for noble or ignoble ends. He may rouse what is worst in man or what is best. Among the most successful politicians of the twentieth century have been men as dissimilar as Adolph Hitler and Benito Mussolini; Mao Tse-tung and Franklin D. Roosevelt; and Winston Churchill and John F. Kennedy. They were vastly different kinds of human beings, with varied, often directly antithetical political philosophies. What they had in common was the ability to move men and women.

In the early 1930s, the United States and Germany—both heavily industrialized nations, both republics, each possessed of a well-educated and technically competent population, each believing itself to be a civilized and moral nation—found themselves plunged into an economic depression. The German people responded to the Depression by electing a spellbinding orator, Adolph Hitler, to lead their country. The Americans responded by electing another gifted speechmaker, Franklin D. Roosevelt, to lead them. Hitler took his country down a path that led to dictatorship, genocide, war, and perhaps the most evil orgy of hate the world has ever witnessed. Franklin D. Roosevelt led his country into domestic and economic reform, culminating in prosperity and leadership of the Western world. Hitler came to power at a time when many Germans hated the Jews who lived among them. He exploited this bigotry and used it to establish his control of the German state. Roosevelt came to power at a time when many Americans were prejudiced toward black people. He began a long, slow, and still not altogether successful process of raising the status and economic well-being of blacks in American life. Despite his lack of dramatic success in these attempts, FDR won the love (and the votes) of most black Americans and the enmity of most white racists for his efforts.

What kept the American people from turning to a Hitler as the solution to our depression, and what kept the Germans from finding an FDR to solve theirs? Luck? The character and culture of the peoples concerned? The nature of the political system extant in Germany and in the USA?

A politician once remarked, "God looks after drunkards, children, and the United States of America," which is another way of saying that historically we have been a relatively "lucky" nation. The United States has suffered no dictators, famines, or devasting plagues. No American city has been devasted by bombardment; the country has not been invaded by a foreign army since 1812. Is this, indeed, "luck" or have other factors been responsible for the durability and relative success of the American political system?

For most people, life must be lived on two levels. There is private life: the life we share with friends and family, the life of schools, work, and play. And then there is public life: the role as a citizen, a member of a larger community whether that community be city, state, nation, or the world. Politics is largely, but not exclusively, concerned with the latter aspects of human existence. It concerns itself with such matters as how people live together; it establishes the ground rules for the buying and selling of labor and goods in the marketplace; it attempts to guide and control the social behavior of people.

Politics and People

People who say they "take no interest in politics" imply that they are absorbed in their own private lives; they lack the time, interest, or imagination to concern themselves with the problems or the destiny of the society in which they live. A man who lives in, say, the city of Los Angeles might follow the fortunes of the city's athletic teams, such as the Dodgers or the Rams, with passionate intensity. He is knowledgeable about the players, their performance, even their salaries. He will argue vehemently for or against a given strategy, the wisdom or folly of trading this or that player or using this or that play. But he may barely know the name of the mayor of his city and probably will not be able to recall the names of most of its councilmen.

There are good reasons for this contrast. Sporting events are relatively simple, focusing on direct physical conflict. Politics, on the other hand, is complex, involving subtle, abstract, half-hidden conflicts of ideas, social and economic interests, and issues. The irony is that the athletic fan so often seems unaware that although sports may give him pleasure and touch his imagination, politics controls his life. The wages or salary we earn for our labor, the profits we reap on our investments, and the amount we are permitted to retain after taxes for either or both are largely determined by politics. The quality of the air we breathe and the food we eat, the nature of the courses taught in school, and the determination of who shall be allowed to teach and/or study them, how we drive our cars and whether or not we are allowed to drive at all, how much we pay for these cars and

153

for the fuel that powers them—that is, virtually everything touching our lives as members of a social group—are ultimately shaped by politics. Thus, as Pericles noted of his fellow Athenians twenty-five hundred years ago, "We regard the man who takes no interest in politics not as harmless, but as useless." The uninvolved nonvoter is the fifth wheel of democracy. He asks society to nourish and protect him and offers nothing in return but an occasional platitude: "It's all politics," "They're all a bunch of crooks." Or as the lady polled by a CBS news team as to how she had voted in a recent election replied, "I never vote. It only encourages 'em." [1]

But since government goes on whether the ordinary citizen knows or cares about it or not, the actual day-by-day practice of politics has tended to become the special preserve of the professional politician and a handful of courtiers, aides, and small groups (such as political-science students or teachers or members of the press) and lobbyists for various special interests whose economic stake in government warrants serious attention, time, and expense. Most of these people have a strong personal and often an economic interest in influencing, controlling, and holding public office—because people who hold public office have power.

Politics is often described as the art of determining "who gets the cookies." [2] That is, it can be viewed as simply another phase of the economic struggle among individuals, groups, interests, classes, states, or nations. Most people, it is said, "vote their pocketbooks." We find such an explanation somewhat too simple. For although economics obviously plays a fundamental, perhaps even the most fundamental, role in politics, other concerns can and sometimes do compete with or even transcend purely economic issues. For example, opposition to the Vietnam war in the late 1960s and early 1970s cut across social and economic classes and seemed to be rooted in a general perception of the war as essentially immoral. Prominent conservatives, normally found in the camp of major corporate and banking interests on most issues, nevertheless objected violently to some phases of America's detente with Russia, which involved economic trade between such pillars of big business as the Rockefeller-owned Chase Manhattan Bank and the Soviets. In the late 1960s, too, President Nixon and Vice President Agnew campaigned strongly and were perhaps elected by the "social issue," that is, by people who were voting against "hippies," "black militants," antiwar protesters, and "permissive" government. Many of those who voted for Nixon and Agnew on this basis stood to gain little direct economic benefit from a conservative administration. They voted their anger and fear rather than their pocketbooks. And in 1976, noneconomic issues, such as "trust in government" and how one felt about

[1] For a discussion of voting behavior see Chapter Eight.
[2] See Harold D. Lasswell, *Politics: Who Gets What, When, How* (New York: McGraw-Hill, 1958).

154

President Ford's pardon of Richard Nixon, played a role in the outcome. Many people believed, for example, that Richard Nixon was a dominant, if largely unspoken "issue" in the 1976 presidential campaign.

If it is not possible to reduce all of the complex behavior we call politics to a single motive—self-interest—it may be more defensible to stipulate a single objective, at least among the dominant leaders of the two major parties that constitute the mainstream of American politics—and that goal is winning elections.

To paraphrase an aphorism of the sports world, "Winning isn't the most important thing in American politics—it is everything." In Europe, where political parties are organized around class and ideological factions, politicians may lose elections while retaining influence, prestige, and real power. (For example, Italy's and France's Communist parties have never achieved enough votes to win control of the government in either country, but they remain a potent political force. In America, a party that had not achieved power in over a quarter century would almost surely have disappeared or been reduced to impotence.) Under the parliamentary system, a losing candidate for prime minister becomes the leader in parliament and in the nation of "the loyal opposition." In America, a man may be a major-party candidate for President one day and, within a few weeks after defeat, be reduced to relative obscurity. (Such was the fate of Alf Landon and Thomas E. Dewey.) For once beaten badly enough to make another bid for the Presidency unlikely, an erstwhile presidential candidate has no clear role to play either in his party or in the nation (unless he manages to gain or hold another high office). Hence he is unlikely to have ready access to the mass media, which quickly lose interest in even the most eminent politicians once they are out of office. Harold Stassen's fate, going from a leading candidate for the Presidency to a perennially unsuccessful also-ran, haunts many politicians. An example of how quickly a man can be shifted from the center of national affairs to virtual anonymity is the case of Senator William Fulbright of Arkansas, who as chairman of the Senate Foreign Relations Committee led the battle against the Vietnam war for almost a decade. After losing his Senate seat in 1974, Fulbright has ceased to play a major role in public debate, much less policy formulation. On the other hand, political stakes are even higher in totalitarian countries, where loss of power is sometimes quickly followed by arrest, prison, or death, as was apparently the case in China with Madame Mao Tse-tung following her husband's death.

It follows that to the professional, the art of politics is almost synonymous with winning elections. If a scientific formula for winning elections existed, and if it could be tested objectively and used under varying circumstances and conditions to obtain success, politics could accurately be called a science. As no such formula exists, politics remains an art.

Of course, a certain degree of prediction and control—which is the essence of science—does exist within the American political system. Polls usually can predict the outcome of elections with a high degree of accuracy. Incumbents can, by and large, expect to be reelected. In most cases, the candidate who spends money lavishly will defeat a candidate who does not or cannot. On the other hand, surprises do occur. Senator McGovern was given only a remote chance of winning the Democratic nomination at the beginning of his campaign in 1972. Everyone talks about Harry Truman's stunning upset victory over Thomas Dewey in 1948 ("Truman is the short-enders deity; they invariably invoke him," observed A. J. Liebling in his book, *The Press*). And, of course, President Ford, regarded as hopelessly behind Jimmy Carter at the outset of the 1976 campaign, came very close to repeating Truman's upset. Jimmy Carter's drive from relative obscurity to the Presidency was itself largely unforeseen by most political experts. As Meg Greenfield noted in *Newsweek* magazine, "Who really foresaw Watts or Tet or OPEC . . . or Martha Mitchell? Yet they all confounded planning and changed history." [3]

Politics and Issues

A few weeks before the presidential election of November 1976, the *Wall Street Journal,* noting a widespread negative reaction to the first two Ford–Carter television debates, the apparent lack of voter interest in the campaign, and the high percentage of "undecided" voters remaining at that rather late stage of the campaign, decided to give the candidates a bit of advice: "Whichever of the two, President Ford or Governor Carter, is willing to speak out clearly and forcefully on the issues before the country will probably swing the undecided voters to his cause and win the election." [4]

This suggestion would seem plausible enough. But there is evidence that the exact opposite may be true. At least in the recent past, candidates, particularly presidential candidates, who have spoken out clearly and forcefully on issues have been defeated, often overwhelmingly. The best examples of issue-oriented candidates to go down to defeat were Senators Goldwater and McGovern, both by overwhelming margins. In the 1950s, most voters preferred President Eisenhower, who was rather fuzzy about most issues before the nation, to Adlai Stevenson, who was more eloquent and precise. The overriding "issue" in the John Kennedy–Richard Nixon debates was the question of what the United States would do to defend the tiny islands of Quemoy and Matsu should they be attacked by mainland

[3] Nov. 22, 1976.
[4] Oct. 14, 1976, p. 22.

China. The differences between the candidates were never really clarified, and few would argue that Kennedy's victory could be attributed to his stance on a given issue rather than personal magnetism. Richard Nixon captured the Presidency in 1968 while virtually refusing to discuss the most burning issue of the day: the Vietnam war. He won again in 1972 largely by avoiding strenuous personal campaigning and using "surrogates" to attack Senator McGovern's record. Perhaps the most issue-oriented presidential candidate in 1976 was Ronald Reagan, who was denied the nomination, although he had considerable support among conservative Republican voters because of his stands on issues. And even Reagan recognized that he would have to soften his strong conservative stance (by naming Senator Schweiker, perhaps the most liberal Republican in the Senate, as his running mate) if he was to keep alive his hopes for winning nomination.

Professional politicians are sensitive to the danger inherent in taking hard-and-fast positions on highly emotional and controversial issues. They know that the vote, gesture, or statement that makes a man look like a hero to a given group today may make him appear villainous to the self-same people tomorrow. "Politics makes strange bedfellows" is not just a joke. It is a description of what usually happens as issues, events, and roles change, requiring that former friends become enemies and vice versa. This is one reason that politics appears to many people to be "dirty" and politicians seem unprincipled. For while seeming to be "tough-minded" and "decisive" to the average voter, the politicians must in fact be subtle, always mindful of the need for compromise, conciliation, and shifting alliances. A year after naming Nelson Rockefeller to the Vice Presidency, President Ford allowed Rockefeller to remove himself from contention for renomination to that office with hardly an expression of regret. What had changed in the interim was that Ronald Reagan had mounted a strong bid to take the Republican presidential nomination from Ford. And Rockefeller was anathema to conservative western Republicans.

Jimmy Carter was constantly criticized for "waffling" on issues in 1976. But when Carter spoke out plainly—for example, in pointing out that President Johnson had lied to the people about Vietnam (which was true) —he was roundly condemned, particularly in Texas.

It was presumed that liberals would take heart from the election of Jimmy Carter and the Democratic sweep in congressional and Senate races in 1976. (We will discuss the meaning of the term *liberal* and *conservative* a bit later in this chapter.) But a careful reading of the election returns might suggest that many other factors may have been at work. Jimmy Carter supported some form of gun control. But voters in Massachusetts, where Carter won, at the same time defeated proposed gun-control legislation overwhelmingly. Carter sided with the critics of nuclear-energy proposals. But the voters across the nation approved several such proposals. While electing Carter and the Democrats, voters in many states turned

157

down bond issues and tax overrides for such things as schools and other public programs of the sort that Democrats normally support.

In short, if the voters were "sending a message to Washington," that message was not altogether clear. As is often the case in American elections, the issues sometimes were less important than other factors, such as the personalities of the candidates, the traditional voting habits of the people, and such imponderables as what effect the Nixon pardon had on the electorate.

Parties and Politics

The public has a stake in the game of party politics. One of the great, albeit unwritten, functions of politics is the elimination of violence and the solution of conflict between contending elements of society. Through much of human history, and in many nations even today, differences of opinion about public policy are settled with guns, not votes. The strong have their way simply because they are the strongest. In *The Revolt of the Masses,* Ortega y Gasset argued that the common man, having been born perfect, sees toleration of dissent as "unnatural" and "acrobatic." Why should error be tolerated when the means exist to eliminate it? In the face of this widespread belief, political parties that legally and openly contend for public favor have emerged slowly and with some difficulty. Even in the Western world they are relatively recent innovations.

The Founding Fathers of the United States distrusted party politics and hoped that the nation could be governed without recourse to "faction." There is no reference to political parties in the Constitution. The first political parties took shape in the United States by 1800, when supporters of Thomas Jefferson (eventually called the Democrats) banded together to oppose the ruling Federalists. It is ironic that Jefferson, among the founders of the nation who warned Americans against the dangers inherent in "faction," was responsible for the formation of the nation's oldest and strongest political party.

Why has the two-party system become so dominant in American politics? Why not many parties, as in most European nations, or one, as in much of the rest of the world? The *Los Angeles Times* has suggested that, "There will always be a two-party system in the United States simply because it works well to get two names on the ballot for every office." [5] Some Americans look upon the quadrennial presidential battle between two major candidates as a kind of sporting event, a political version of the Superbowl or the World Series. If politics is about winning and losing, then there is an obvious aesthetic tidiness to having one big winner and one big loser.

[5] Oct. 28, 1974, Part 2, p. 6.

Students of the American political system have suggested other reasons for the curious persistance of the two-party system. One is that we elect people from single-member districts so that there is only one winner. (There is no proportional representation by which, for example, a party receiving 10 percent of the votes would get 10 percent of the seats.) Thus it is difficult for smaller parties to sustain long-term support. Also, Americans generally do not tend to seek out a candidate who champions a given political philosophy or view of public policy; they seem to prefer a more pragmatic approach. They do not ask, "Which candidate will best reflect my political philosophy?" but rather, "Which candidate will best serve my interests and those of the nation?" or even, "Which candidate seems to be the nicest guy?" And most minor parties depend on ideological commitment for long-range support. Finally, the federal system, with its dispersal of power, makes one-party rule difficult to achieve and a multiparty system difficult to sustain because patronage and money, "the mothers' milk of politics," are hard for minor parties to come by. Even when a strong regional third party emerges, such as Robert La Follette's Progressive Party in 1924 or George Wallace's American Independent Party in 1968, it is usually unable to build a national base. Wallace, for example, moved back into the Democratic party's ranks in 1972. Governor Reagan, often mentioned as a conservative-party candidate in 1976, chose instead to seek the Republican party nomination and announced his intention of staying within that party regardless of the outcome of his bid for the party's presidential nomination. Serious professional politicians, who seek to win elections rather than simply to raise issues, invariably elect to stay within the two-party system.

Even when one of the two major parties collapses, as happened to the Whigs and the Federalists, it is simply replaced by another party incorporating elements of the old party and some new elements. From the time the Jeffersonians formed the Democratic party until the 1850s, the Democrats dominated American politics. By the 1850s, a new party, the Republicans, had emerged, organized around the issue of slavery. The new party was antislavery. It was also probusiness, favoring land grants to railroads, a new banking system and protective tariffs, and a homestead law to provide cheap land for farmers in the West. After the Civil War, black voters joined the businessman–farmer coalition, and the Republicans became the dominant party until the 1930s. Although the numerical strength of the two parties, Democratic and Republican, as reflected by registration figures, was about even, the Republicans in fact dominated American politics during most of the last half of the nineteenth and the first third of the twentieth centuries. During this period, the Democrats elected only two Presidents— Grover Cleveland and Woodrow Wilson—in each case as the result of a split among Republicans. GOP dominance came about because the party had led the country successfully through the Civil War and had become identified (outside of the South) in the mind of most voters with the "respectable" elements of American society: the businessman and the independent farmer, the older and hence better-establishd WASP families, the growing financial and corporate elite, the solid citizens and "100 percent Americans." The Democrats, on the other hand, were characterized by one GOP critic as the party of "Rum, Romanism, and Rebellion." It was, of course, a partisan overstatement, but it contained an element of truth. For with the Republicans representing the nation's established and successful people and institutions, the Democrats moved to organize the poor and the excluded. They built a curious alliance made up of southern businessmen and landlords, impoverished southern sharecroppers, and the Jewish, Italian, and Irish immigrants who were being herded into ghettos in the large eastern cities. New York's Tammany Hall became the prototype of the big-city political machine. And the big-city political "boss" emerged as a distinctive new American political type. The bosses weren't interested in ideology or political rhetoric; they were interested in votes, which could be translated into money and power. Massive, flagrant, and barely concealed corruption became a fixture of American political life.

But while enriching themselves and providing high-paying, easy jobs for their relatives, cronies, and sycophants, the men who ran the big-city machines maintained their power by providing indispensable services to the millions of immigrants pouring into America. They met the immigrants almost as they stepped off the boats, usually arriving poor and frightened, speaking little or no English, and coming from lands racked by famine, war, and oppression. Organizations like Tammany Hall helped people find jobs, houses, and relatives and even acted as marriage brokers for young migrants seeking spouses. They provided loans and a friend at city hall in times of trouble. In short, they acted as a sort of unofficial welfare agency, run by local politicians called "ward heelers" (because they were usually walking the streets of the ward, or local political district), rather than welfare workers. It is debatable whether the largely uneducated ward heelers may not have done a better job at less ultimate cost to the taxpayers than today's welfare workers trained in sociology, counseling, and psychology.

During the Great Depression of the 1930s, the American business and political establishment was shaken. Hundreds of millions of dollars in paper wealth disappeared as the stock market sank to record lows. Thousands of banks failed and, at a time when there was no federal deposit insurance, took the life savings of millions of people with them. Of the American working force, 25 percent were unemployed. Bread lines appeared in the streets of every American city. Even members of the solid middle class—doctors, lawyers, druggists, businessmen—lost their homes and businesses and in many cases were reduced to becoming itinerant laborers; the "tramp" who once was a business tycoon became part of the folklore of American life and the song "Brother, Can You Spare a Dime?" almost the national anthem.

The Republican party, which was supposed to have been managing the nation's affairs, was held responsible for the calamity of the Depression. Franklin D. Roosevelt was swept into office in 1932 with vague promises of a "new deal" for the American people.

While setting in motion a host of measures designed to provide immediate relief from the most paralyzing effects of the Depression, Roosevelt also began to forge a new political coalition which would result in the Democrats, rather than the Republicans, becoming the dominant American political party for the next four decades. It included the traditionally Democratic South and added the urban workers, who, under the Wagner Labor Relations Act of 1935, formed labor unions, which became a new source of power in American political and economic life. Many farmers and small businessmen, ruined or at least badly frightened by the Depression, threw their support to FDR. So too did millions of black people, who had traditionally voted Republican largely because of memories of Lincoln's role in emancipation. Blacks, the first to be fired and the last to be hired in American business, were particularly hard hit by the Depression and therefore were among the most important beneficiaries of New Deal relief efforts. Also, they sensed a friend in FDR and particularly in Mrs. Roosevelt, who outraged many white people by her public concern for blacks, including young black men who had been sentenced to long prison terms on what she felt were unjust or baseless charges. Another important element in the new Democratic coalition was the intellectual community. The nation's artists, writers, teachers and professors, journalists, and the growing army of welfare workers and planners shifted toward liberalism and the Democrats. They did so partly because the Democrats, rather than the Republicans, increasingly reflected their own economic and social interests and because they came to believe that the Democrats were the party of progressivism, whereas the Republicans were portrayed as the party of business and narrow conservatism. Not until the 1960s—when men like William F. Buckley, a literate, intelligent, and urbane spokesman for the new conservatism, and economist and Nobel Prize winner Milton Friedman began to emerge—were conservative Republicans able to mount a serious intellectual challenge to the dominant New Deal ideology.

Although the Republicans managed to elect two Presidents, Dwight D. Eisenhower and Richard Nixon, during the four decades of Democratic dominance of the electorate, neither was able to make a significant shift in the balance of power in American political life in the way that Roosevelt had. Both faced predominantly Democratic legislatures during all or most of their terms in office. Eisenhower, a popular war hero, had a personal disdain for party politics and left party affairs largely to his subordinates.

Nixon was a partisan, and members of the Nixon administration talked vaguely about "our revolution," meaning a fundamental shift in the American balance of political forces in favor of the Republicans, which they hoped would take place during Nixon's second term. However realistic or not these plans may have been, the Watergate scandal effectively wrecked any chance of accomplishing them, so that in the congressional elections of 1974, the Democrats emerged with sweeping new gains approaching the political majorities they enjoyed during the early days of the New Deal. And the 1976 results simply reinforced those Democratic gains.

By 1975, polls indicated that only about one American voter in five, just over 20 percent of the people, was willing to call himself or herself a Republican, whereas 44 percent labeled themselves Democrat and 35 percent preferred to call themselves independent, thus indicating at least some degree of displeasure with both of the major parties.[6] These figures suggested to some observers that America was indeed ripe for a new political shift of forces, similar to those that occurred after the Civil War and during the Great Depression. But a shift toward what and whom remained in doubt.

What Parties Do

Historically, what do parties do? There are several functions we may attribute to the two-party system:

1. Parties offer choices and simplify issues, which makes the voter's job easier. The parties sift through all the issues to find the most popular, and via a variety of techniques, they sift through all the candidates and, in each case, offer us alternatives.

2. The selection of candidates is a job in itself. Initially, parties chose candidates in meetings called *caucuses,* which were closed meetings of party leaders. Later, beginning in the 1830s, the party convention was adopted and is still used by the national party to nominate presidential and vice-presidential candidates, as well as to debate, draw up, and adopt a platform. During the early twentieth century, various states began to adopt the direct primary as a means of nominating candidates. The direct primary allows every voter of the party a chance to participate in choosing the nominee. In many states, candidates for all offices—local and statewide—are chosen in this manner, and some states use a primary election for determining the choice for President among that state's party members.

3. In the general election itself, parties play a crucial role. They raise money for their candidates, campaign for the candidate, provide poll watchers, mobilize volunteers, and even become involved professionally in

[6] More recent surveys indicate that Republicans have failed to raise their percentage of registered voters much above these 1975 figures. While Democrats continue to lead in registration, independents remain more numerous than Republicans.

162

It is unlikely that any future presidential candidate will be nominated without a string of victories in the primaries. [Reprinted with permission from *Intellect,* Feb. 1977.]

politics. There is, needless to say, plenty of work for volunteers, and almost anyone interested in party work will be welcomed. In this way, of course, the rank-and-file party members can influence their party. For example, conservative activitists at the GOP convention of 1976 forced President Ford to accept a platform critical—at least by implication—of his Secretary of State, Henry Kissinger.

5. Parties, some believe, help shape public opinion. Each of the major parties has a national committee with publicity divisions constantly propagandizing in the party's favor. Perhaps more than offering worthwhile information, the parties simply stimulate interest.

6. The party in power is expected to develop policies and govern. This is particularly true when the executive and legislative branches of government (whether at the state or at the national level) are controlled by the same party.

8. Some scholars maintain that the two-party system helps to keep the country unified, because in seeking to win elections, especially presidential elections, the party must appeal to as many geographic and ideological areas as possible. Thus the parties tend to keep politics in America moderate because both parties seek to be middle-of-the-road in order to win elections.

Third Parties

What role, then, do third parties have? By definition, a third party is a party outside the two major parties that is unable to mobilize a majority of votes in elections.

1. Their major function, it has been argued, is to bring attention to controversial issues that the major parties often ignore or seek to compromise on. In 1968, the American Independent Party under George Wallace, for example, was segregationist in domestic politics and hawkish in foreign policy, whereas the two major parties straddled those issues or were not identified with them.[7]

2. Third parties can allow an expression of political discontent. The AIP and the Peace and Freedom parties in 1968 are examples of this.

3. A third party's candidate for President might influence national politics by gaining so many votes in the Electoral College that no one candidate receives a majority. Thus the election would be thrown into the House of Representatives. The third-party candidate, using the electoral votes of the states he had won, could bargain with the two candidates of the majority parties. Perhaps the third-party candidate could receive a Cabinet post or a promise by one of the two major candidates to follow a certain

[7] Daniel A. Mazmanian, "Hopes Are Slim for a Third Party," *Los Angeles Times* (Sept. 21, 1975), Part 7, pp. 1, 4.

policy. Governor Wallace may have hoped to do this in 1968. (This eventuality has not yet occurred.)

4. Third parties might have an effect on subsequent political programs. For example, Wallace's large showing in 1968 may have influenced President Nixon's so-called Southern strategy. That is, partly in order to attract more Wallace-like southern votes to the Republican party, Mr. Nixon nominated Clement Haynesworth and G. Harold Carswell, both southern conservatives, to the Supreme Court. (As it happens, however, the two nominees were not confirmed by the Senate.)

5. Some third parties seek to counter third parties of the opposite ideological persuasion. For example, the leftist Peace and Freedom party argued in 1968 that it needed to gain official sanction in order to counterbalance the more right-wing AIP party. Otherwise, the Peace and Freedom people maintained, the whole political spectrum would move to the right.

6. Finally, some third parties, not hoping to win elections, have worked to educate the electorate. Norman Thomas, who last ran as the Socialist candidate for President in 1932, had this goal in mind: to present voters with clear programs that might eventually be accepted by the major parties. Former Senator Eugene McCarthy's 1976 campaign was largely motivated, he claimed, by an effort to "open up" the American political system to new ideas. McCarthy, for example, advocated a four-day work week as a solution to the unemployment problem. We should add that the proposals initially advanced by a third-party candidate that seem too "far out" and radical to one generation sometimes become accepted national policy in the next. Norman Thomas used to point out that many of the ideas he advocated in his perennially unsuccessful bids for the Presidency as a Socialist gradually became the law of the land. (The eight-hour workday is one example.)

But no third-party candidate has ever won the Presidency. Although Republicans emerged in the 1850s as a new party, they quickly displaced the Whigs, so that by the time of the 1860 election they were part of the two-party system. Indeed, for a third-party candidate even to make a good showing, certain conditions seemingly must be met: there must be an intense feeling and disagreement over fundamental issues like peace or war, integration or segregation. The two major parties must avoid taking a stand on these issues or alienate a minority by their stands. And there must be a personality with some following to lead the new party. All of these conditions need not arise at once. Apparently the most important is the last, the strong political personality. For example, in 1912, Theodore Roosevelt, running on the Progressive ticket, actually came in second to Woodrow Wilson. And in 1924, Robert La Follette garnered millions of votes running on a third-party ticket. But the 1968 election, which we have already noted, presents a classic case. Not only was there a noteworthy third-party candidate (Wallace), but there were intense feelings and disagreements on basic issues (race and war), and the two major parties avoided or rejected segregation in domestic affairs and at the same time promised (however vaguely) to end America's prosecution of the Vietnam war. Thus those who favored segregation and a hawkish position on the war could vote for Wallace–LeMay, and some 13 percent did.[8]

Are the conditions necessary for a successful third party present today? Will they be in the near future? And what chance, if any, does a new party have of displacing one of the older parties? We will return to these questions later when we discuss the concept of a "critical election."

The System Changes

The parties have changed over the years. For example, although there remain a few urban political machines (notably in Chicago), most tightly run machines have disappeared. Nationally regulated welfare programs, initiated during the New Deal period, replaced the kind of aid local ward heelers gave to prospective voters. Civil service jobs at the city and county level have removed the tool of patronage by which political parties rewarded party workers. And some cities, especially in the West, have legally made local elections nonpartisan, thus attempting to remove party influence altogether.

Another change has been the emergence of a two-party system where there used to be only one. In some southern and border states, like Oklahoma, Texas, and South Carolina, Republicans now offer a challenge and not infrequently win elections where the Democrats formerly had almost complete success. Moreover, in some northeastern states Democrats are much more powerful than they were a few years ago. Maine, for example, has traditionally been solidly Republican yet now has a strong Democratic party led by Senator Edmund Muskie.

Finally, there is much less political loyalty among American voters than in the past. Recent research has suggested that voters increasingly, and sometimes calculatedly, cross party lines, believing that opposition parties in the executive and legislative branches represent a healthy balance.[9]

What's Wrong with the Two-Party System?

1. *The parties are just alike.* A major complaint about the two parties is that they are really not very different. Both try to appeal to the moderate,

---

[8] Ibid.

[9] Nelson W. Polsby, "What Do the Voters Want?" *Newsweek* (Oct. 20, 1975), p. 15. Also see Gerald M. Pomper, "The Decline of the Party in American Elections," *Political Science Quarterly,* **92:**21–41 (Spring 1977).

middle-of-the-road voter, and each party includes both liberals and conservatives. For example, liberal Jacob Javits, Republican Senator from
New York, is ideologically far removed from conservative Senator Barry
Goldwater, and the Democratic party has such diverse personalities as
former New York Congresswoman Bella Abzug and crusty conservative
Congressman F. Edward Hebert (La.). What kind of sense does this make?
European critics have long marveled at America's "absurd" system and
regularly predict a fundamental realignment of American parties. Yet there
are, clearly, ideological differences. Democrats, as a rule, tend to be more
liberal and Republicans more conservative. Many of the major political
figures in each party underscore this assessment: Jimmy Carter, Walter
Mondale, George McGovern, Hubert Humphrey, and Edward Kennedy
are considered liberals; Gerald Ford, Robert Dole, and Ronald Reagan are
conservatives. Moreover, increasing numbers of Americans are becoming
aware of the ideological differences of the parties.[10] Thus an intriguing
question is raised. If voters are more aware of ideological differences, and
if, as the Gallup Poll suggests, most Americans call themselves "conservatives," why are there so many more registered Democrats than Republicans?
Probably the answer is that the simple terms *liberal* and *conservative* are
inadequate to explain an individual's understanding and perception of
politics. That is, it might be more informative to ask what a person's view
is regarding environmental, energy, tax, and foreign policies, or what he or
she thinks about Watergate, the CIA, congressional reform, and defense
spending. Did the overwhelming success of Democrats in the 1974 and
1976 congressional elections suggest that voters, at least at the time, favored
liberal, Democratic positions on these issues? [11] Pundits wondered whether
this success was a reaction to Watergate. But the fact that the "Watergate
Class of 1974" was reelected in 1976 suggested that the change might prove
permanent. Part of the reason may lie in the differences between the major
parties. Such differences can be found in the kinds of people who normally
support the parties with both their votes and their money, in the historical
experience of the two parties, and in their stance on the issues. We must
keep in mind, however, that when we are talking about groups of tens of
millions of persons, there are bound to be many exceptions to the general
rules.

Generally the Democrats attract people who are not white-skinned or
whose ethnic background often places them psychologically outside the
American "mainstream," such as Jews and to a lesser extent many Catholics. Most labor unions and hence most union members support Democrats.

[10] Ibid., and Gerald M. Pomper, "From Confusion to Clarity: Issues and American
Voters, 1956–1969," *American Political Science Review,* **66:**415–428 (June 1972).
[11] See "Congress: A Seismic Shift Toward the Young and Liberal," *Science* (Nov.
22, 1974), p. 717.

Democrats usually carry the big cities of the country. Younger voters tend to be Democratic. Artists and intellectuals and people active in the communications industries, such as journalism, also lean toward the Democrats.

On the other hand, white business and professional people are more often Republicans. So are older voters, wealthy people, suburbanites, and Protestants (particularly if they are both suburban *and* Protestant). People in the West, where there are more suburbanites and residents of wide-open spaces than in the densely crowded Northeast, have been voting Republican more often than not in recent national elections.

Ideologically the Democratic party nationally is normally liberal, whereas the Republican party nationally is usually conservative. But do these terms have any useful meaning today?

Partly they arise from historical experience, particularly in Europe. Traditionally the conservatives represented the hereditary land-owning aristocracy of Europe. They enjoyed positions of great power, wealth, and prestige; hence they were interested in preserving the existing rules of society. Liberals, on the other hand, represented the rising business and industrial class, which was challenging the traditional prerogatives of the nobility; hence they stood for change and social innovation. At the far left stood the radicals, such as the Communists, who demanded nothing less than the complete overthrow of existing social institutions with the end of establishing perfect equality among all persons. At the far right were the fascists, urging social violence as a means of crushing any dissident forces. Fascists raise traditional aristocratic values such as war and blood superiority to a kind of political religion.

Such designations fit uneasily into the American social and political scheme because here there is no land-owning class of aristocrats. Instead there are large corporations, run by boards of businessmen, who generally have become the dominant conservative force in American life. Here wealth and race, and more recently age, tend to differentiate conservatives and liberals, rather than class. (Although some argue that wealth and race frequently amount to class.)

The terms *left* and *right* in politics, corresponding roughly to *liberal* and *conservative,* originated in the seating arrangements in the first French assembly following the successful revolution again Louis XVI. Generally the more radical members sat on the left side of the hall, the more conservative on the right. The terms have somehow stuck.

With respect to issues, liberals (hence normally Democrats) stress full employment, as Governor Carter did in 1976, as a matter of national concern. Republicans give first priority to controlling inflation, as President Ford did. Thus liberals prefer economic and monetary policies favoring expansion of the economy, whereas Republicans worry about the growing national debt and the printing of "paper money." Liberals condemn "tax loopholes," which conservatives often defend as "tax incentives" necessary to stimulate private investment. In a straight business–labor confrontation, liberals usually tilt toward labor, conservatives toward management.

Liberals tend to support government spending on social programs; conservatives look more kindly on spending money on national defense and on such things as highway building, which is a kind of subsidy to the auto industry. Liberals usually argue that ethnic and religious minorities have been discriminated against and that the government has a responsibility to help such people overcome unfair handicaps. Conservatives are more inclined to believe that the government should not interfere much in telling people who they may or may not hire or associate with and that although inequalities may exist, they can be overcome by individuals who are willing to work hard and "lift themselves up by their own bootstraps."

Liberals tend to stress individual liberty. Conservatives talk about the need for social order and stability.

In foreign policy, it is more difficult to tell the two apart because the nation has had, by and large, a bipartisan foreign policy since the end of World War II. Generally the *rhetoric* of foreign policy debate, which is not always the same thing as the actions of those in power, indicates that liberals are more disposed to talk and conservatives more disposed to exercise a military option. (An example is Ronald Reagan's "tough" posture on the Panama Canal and South African issues.) On the other hand, Lyndon Johnson and Jack Kennedy were certainly not doves, whereas Richard Nixon astonished many people, after a lifetime of "tough" rhetoric, with his opening up of negotiations with China and Russia.

Finally, conservatives tend to see themselves as the "real Americans"— true descendents of the Founding Fathers in appearance, values, and style. Liberals see America as a very complex and diverse nation and doubt that (except perhaps for Indians) members of any group qualify as the "real Americans."

2. *Parties are run by an elite.* Another criticism of the parties is that they are responsive not to their members but to party hacks and large contributors. Because most Americans take no part in party activity, pay no dues, and, at best, simply register in that party, it would not be surprising if the average voter had no input into party decisions. Yet the charge is not altogether fair. Recent state and federal campaign laws have tried to restrain some of the influence of large monied interests, the parties use political polls to get an impression of grass-roots attitudes, and finally, many states use the direct primary, in which all members of a party may vote, to nominate candidates. Moreover, there has been a dramatic change in the past few years in the method of nominating presidential candidates. In 1976, more rank-and-file party members than ever in history voted in presidential primaries (thirty states held such primaries).

3. *Parties obscure issues.* A constant charge against political parties is that they oversimplify issues and do not take clear stands. Vague and insub-

stantial party platforms and rambling, unspecific speeches by politicians leave us scratching our heads as to what the party and its candidate really intend to do. This, of course, is the characteristic practice of a party more interested in winning than in logic. For what good is logic if you have no power? And, as we have seen, parties and candidates who take clear-cut positions on the issues often do not win.

But despite the relative rarity of clear-cut divisions on specific issues that characterizes most American elections, some party differences do exist and are probably perceived by most voters.[12]

In 1976, for example, the GOP platform stressed "the integrity of our money" and the need to put an end to deficit spending. The Democratic platform pledged legislation that would reduce unemployment to 3 percent within four years. The GOP platform pledged tax reduction; the Democratic platform pledged tax reform. The GOP opposed the breakup of oil companies; the Democrats favored it. The Republican platform opposed federalizing the welfare system and a guaranteed annual wage; the Democrats advocated both. The Republican platform supported efforts to secure a constitutional amendment banning abortion; the Democrats did not. The Republicans called for a stronger national defense; the Democrats proposed a cut in defense spending. The Republicans took a hard line on the Panama Canal; the Democrats felt that there should be a new treaty. The Republicans were against compulsory national health insurance; the Democrats were for it.[13]

These differences may not be as fundamental as those that separate the traditionally capitalist and the traditionally socialist parties in Europe, but they are not inconsequential.

Party platforms, of course, are not binding upon anyone. They usually represent a compromise of the views and interests of the dominant party factions and individuals. Party platforms are not solemn pledges to be enacted to the letter by whichever party wins the election. But neither are they wholly meaningless. They simply tell the voter what the party would like to accomplish and what the leaders think the people would like to see accomplished.

Finally, the nation has tended to turn to the Democrats as the party of change and innovation when it felt the need for leadership in active and energetic new directions. (JFK's slogan, "Let's get the country moving again," although largely rhetorical, was probably perceived by most people as an alternative to the somewhat staid Eisenhower years.) On the other hand, when what was wanted was a firm, fiscally conservative, no-nonsense President, the people turned to Republicans Eisenhower and Nixon.

[12] Pomper, "From Confusion to Clarity," pp. 416–420.
[13] Newsweek (Aug. 30, 1976).

170

John F. Kennedy's election in 1960 seemed to spark action and changes in American society—the civil-rights movement, for example, and later the youth movement—whereas Nixon's election eight years later signified to many people that the nation had tired of years of tumult and social experimentation and wanted to return to traditional values and forms of behavior.

Thus, although the substantive differences between the parties on any given issue may not seem very wide, in fact, they often have a symbolic meaning that may unleash or hold in check forces far greater than they themselves intend or are willing to acknowledge publicly.

Comparison of the symbolic postures of the two parties, or at least of the parties' best-known leaders, may help to explain the decline of the Republican party over the last four decades. Whereas the Democrats have seemed inclined to attract the new forces that have emerged in American social and economic life, the Republicans often have seemed to give a chilly reception to cries for fundamental change in America's social structure. Thus, in the last few decades, as blacks fought for an end to segregation, they found Democratic leaders such as Lyndon Johnson and John F. Kennedy often supporting at least their more moderate objectives. Famous Republican leaders, such as Gerald Ford and Barry Goldwater, were not so receptive. As a member of the United States Senate and the likely presidential candidate of the Republican party in 1964, Goldwater voted against the Civil Rights Act of 1964. Ford spoke out frequently and vigorously against bussing both while a member of Congress and as President.

Two decades earlier the GOP was no less cool to the emergence of organized labor as a power in American economic life, as we have previously noted.

In the 1970s the women's movement emerged as a growing new force in America. Governor Carter campaigned actively in support of the movement's primary goal—passage of the Equal Rights Amendment (E.R.A.), a constitutional amendment guaranteeing equal rights to women. Both President Ford and Governor Reagan were in opposition to passage of the E.R.A. Whether or not the amendment ultimately becomes part of the Constitution, the Democrats are likely to emerge from this contest with a net political gain in the support of women voters, particularly of young, educated women who have been the E.R.A.'s most vigorous supporters.

As a political party the GOP suffered a striking defeat in 1976 when it not only lost the White House (albeit narrowly) but also experienced an even further erosion of its already dangerously weak position in the Congress and in the state governorships and legislatures across the nation. Talk of creating a new party based upon the idea of a coalition of conservatives in both the Republican and Democratic parties was revived. Governor Reagan suggested that perhaps the party might do better if it were to adopt

171

a new name. But the history of the last four decades seemed to suggest something far more fundamental would be necessary if the Republicans were to achieve anything like numerical parity with the Democrats, let alone recapture the dominance they enjoyed during the long era between the Civil War and the election of Franklin D. Roosevelt. Clearly the Republicans needed to find leaders and policies that could speak for and to the American people, few of whom belong to country clubs or serve on corporation boards of directors.

At a meeting of Republican state leaders held in Los Angeles, both Ford and Reagan spoke to this issue.[14] Although himself a lifelong conservative, Ford acknowledged that "the old slogans of Republicanism will not attract the American people. . . . Too many people see our party as tired, old, wedded to the past . . . as a tool of big business, indifferent to minorities, unfeeling toward the poor and unemployed, an enemy of progress." Ford added that he thought the image unfair but warned that as long as it existed, "the party faces the danger of oblivion."

Reagan, on the other hand, raised the idea of a conservative majority (see comments by and on William Rusher in the section that follows). He complained that Washington-based Republicans too often "pay too much attention to liberal pressures and forget that we conservatives are in fact a majority not only of the our party but of the nation."

In short, the nation's two most eminent Republican leaders seemed to be calling for directly opposite approaches to restoring the party's favor with the people, perhaps laying the groundwork for another Ford–Reagan battle for the GOP presidential nomination in 1980.

In the meantime, the Democrats, after years of bitter division caused by disagreement over the Vietnam war, seemed disposed to unite around their newly elected President. However there is more than a remote possibility that Carter might well be facing a challenge from the left wing of his own party by 1980, particularly if detente falters and/or unemployment is not cut substantially.

A Theory of Critical Elections

Although candidates usually avoid discussion or debate about substantive issues, there periodically arises in American politics an issue or a crisis so overwhelming (such as slavery or the Great Depression) as to force a realignment of political parties based on new coalitions of groups demanding a response to the crisis. Such a coalition formed the basis of the Republican party in the 1850s, as we have noted, and led to a fundamental change in the Democratic party in the 1930s.

[14] *Los Angeles Times* (Apr. 17, 1977), Part 2, p. 1.

Some scholars refer to the election of 1860 (won by Lincoln) and the election of 1932 (won by Franklin Roosevelt) as *critical elections*.[15]

What Are the Characteristics of a Critical Election?

First and foremost, a critical election responds to a profound, revolutionary change in the nation's way of life and in the balance of political forces. Republicans after 1860 ended slavery, successfully led the nation through the Civil War, and went on to preside over the transformation of the nation from a "prairie democracy" into an industrial giant.

Second, a critical election draws together a new coalition, resulting in a new balance of political power. Thus the Republicans became dominant after 1860 and the Democrats after 1932 because they were able to draw new and substantial support from new combinations of elements in the population. The Republicans combined businessmen, western farmers, and virtually anybody opposed to slavery. During the 1930s, the Democrats brought together a diverse coalition, including southern whites, blacks, labor, farmers, urban ethnic groups, and intellectuals. Many of these were new voters.[16]

Third, a critical election is characterized by the importance attached to an issue or a group of related issues. This does not mean that either Lincoln or FDR ran issue-oriented campaigns. What it does mean is that using historical hindsight, we can see that the election of these men signaled a decisive new turn of events. As we have said, politics under normal circumstances is largely if not exclusively devoted to winning elections. By and large, the surest way to win an election is to appeal to the values of the voters. Most voters acquire their basic values when they are young. Thus there is normally a certain element of nostalgia in any political campaign. Politicians do not "tell it like it is"; they much prefer to tell it like it was. For example, the campaign of 1964 gave the voters an opportunity to redecide the issues that had been settled when the New Deal took power in 1932, thirty-two years earlier. President Johnson ran as a disciple of FDR. (He even cultivated a certain physical resemblance to FDR). His Great Society was in part an extension of Roosevelt's New Deal. Senator Goldwater, on the other hand, seemed to be campaigning against FDR: Should we continue with welfare and Social Security? Should the TVA be sold to private business? The election was fought out on these issues and the New Deal won still another resounding victory. But the reality of American life had to do with much different issues. What would happen in Vietnam? What did the candidates propose to do about racism, urban decay, inflation? Could the Affluent Society go on as it had been going without ruining the environment or running out of energy? These issues

[15] Walter Dean Burnham, *Critical Elections* (New York, Norton, 1970).
[16] Ibid., pp. 92, 97–134.

were on the horizon in 1964. But the major-party candidates felt, probably correctly, that most voters were not interested or would much prefer to hear still another campaign on the now-familiar topic of whether or not the New Deal revolution had wrecked or saved the nation.

One could cite evidence of issue-dodging in other major recent political campaigns. As we have noted, the famed Nixon–Kennedy presidential debates of 1960 turned, in the last few encounters, on the burning question of what America was going to do about the islands of Quemoy and Matsu. In 1968 candidate Nixon ran for the Presidency in the midst of a raging war in Vietnam, promising to "end the war and win the peace" but refusing to say how or when. Questioned about this, Nixon insisted that his plans must be kept secret. Thus one might say that it is normal for political rhetoric to concern itself with the burning issues of three or four decades earlier, while ignoring the realities of the moment.

Finally, the new coalition created by a critical election must be enduring. For example, the coalition that carried Eisenhower to two terms in the White House collapsed when he left office, whereas FDR's coalition transformed the Democrats from the minority to the majority party. In 1969, many Republicans, such as Kevin Phillips, columnist and GOP strategist, believed that the Nixon victory in 1968 would lead to a new and decisive shift in the power balance of the two major parties.[17] These Republicans urged a "southern strategy" that would, in essence, add to the normal Republican vote those whites—largely but not exclusively in the South—who supported Governor Wallace, in order to create a "new majority" of predominantly conservative voters. The possibility of such a coalition may have existed, but if it did, the Nixon administration obviously failed to unify it.

More recently, William A. Rusher, editor of the conservative journal *The National Review,* has been arguing for a new conservative party.[18] Noting that the polls show that a majority of Americans identify themselves as "conservative," Rusher calls for a party that would be much more aggressively anti-Communist in foreign policy, by junking detente, for example, or by giving more support to Nationalist China (Taiwan) and showing less friendliness to mainland China. On domestic policy, conservatives attack the welfare state. Rusher wants to see a new party formed around the "producers" in America, mainly working people and businessmen, as opposed to the "consumers": welfare recipients, civil servants, and bureaucrats.

In a sense, Rusher's proposals are logical. But his logic cannot prevail

---

17 *The Emerging Republican Majority* (New Rochelle, N.Y.: Arlington, 1969).
18 "A New Party: Eventually, Why Not Now?" *National Review* (May 23, 1975), pp. 550–555.

In the late sixties and early seventies American college students became a major political force in the nation. But as the war in Vietnam declined, so did student involvement in politics. [Photo by Dean Immenschuh, Upland, Calif.]

over the simple realities of American political life. The man he had targeted to lead his new party, former California Governor Ronald Reagan, chose instead to run for the Republican party presidential nomination in 1976 and did so with an announcement that he would pledge his support to whomever the party chose as its nominee. And he abided by his pledge when President Ford defeated him for the Republican nomination.

On the liberal side, there has also been much talk of a new coalition.

175

Senator McGovern's strategists in 1972 believed that the Senator would be carried to victory on the impetus of the votes of 15 million young people, believed to be overwhelmingly liberal, who would vote for the first time as the result of a constitutional amendment lowering the voting age to eighteen. But the young people did not vote in great numbers, and those who did seemed only slightly more partial to McGovern than their elders.

Was the campaign of 1976 a "critical election"? Clearly it is too soon for the Carter administration to have met the test of our fourth and perhaps most important criteria, the test of time. Almost every new administration sweeps into office believing that it is about to embark upon a historic and wondrous adventure. Even the staid and conservative Eisenhower regime pictured itself as a "crusade for freedom." John Kennedy spoke of conquering the "New Frontier." Lyndon Johnson sought to create a "Great Society." Richard Nixon's supporters believed that his election signaled the emergence of a "new majority." Although there is an element of mere electioneering rhetoric in all such claims, the rhetoric probably reflects the hope that each new administration represents a kind of "new dawn" in American life rather than simply a change in party, personnel, and/or policy. Each new administration hopes, and its strongest supporters believe, that it will indeed prove "critical," just as most human beings believe their own lives will have importance.

Events, rather than the character and the policies of a given administration, play a role in whether or not such expectations are fulfilled. If there had been no Civil War, Lincoln's administration might not now be regarded as quite so important. The Great Depression and World War II provided the context for the unfolding of FDR's New Deal.

One cannot presume to know what opportunities and obstacles history will place in the path of the Carter administration. Still, it seems that at least in some respects the 1976 election may fit our description of a critical election.

First of all, the manner by which Carter won his party's nomination does represent a change. Carter was the first successful presidential candidate in our history to rely almost solely upon public, contested primaries to achieve his goal. The only other President to have been nominated by his party largely because of success in the primaries was John Kennedy. But Kennedy fought and won in only a few, carefully selected primary campaigns. He appeared before the Democratic National Convention in Los Angeles in 1960 not simply as a primary winner but also as the scion of a wealthy and politically powerful family and as a U.S. Senator. Kennedy had come within an eyelash of winning his party's vice-presidential nomination only four years before. Carter, on the other hand, was a virtual unknown outside of the South, and his party's professional hierarchy did not take him seriously at the onset of the primaries. He had no firm base in Washington and no support from any nationally potent interest group. He could never have

176

won the nomination except by doing what he did, entering thirty primaries (more than have ever been held in our history) and winning enough of these to make certain that the convention could not refuse him the nomination without inviting scandal and probable defeat.

The Democratic party had lost the Presidency to Richard Nixon in 1968 at least in part because it could neither contain nor satisfy the demands for fundamental changes voiced by militants within its own ranks, particularly among students and intellectuals. These changes included:

1. An end to the war in Vietnam and, perhaps more important in the long run, an end to the Cold War mentality on the part of government leaders.
2. A major assault by the government upon the racism that permeates much of American life.
3. An opening up of the political and economic systems to young people, minorities, women, and the poor.

The champion and symbol of those within the Democratic party who opposed all of these changes was Alabama Governor George Wallace. Wallace proved in 1968 and in 1972 that he had broad support in the South and a substantial following in the rest of the country as well. He existed as a major threat on the right flank of any Democratic presidential candidate, like George McGovern, who seemed to go too far leftward in embracing these changes. At the same time, there were elements in the Wallace movement that were genuinely populist, particularly his appeal to those who resented the arbitrary rule of "the best and the brightest," that is, the Democratic party's Washington establishment.

By defeating Wallace in the Florida primary of 1976, Carter removed the Wallace threat and signaled that he might be the means of reconciling the conservative South with the liberal northern Democratic party. Interestingly, Carter was elected by the South and the Northeast, which he carried by 53 percent and 55 percent, respectively. Carter carried the South primarily because he received the overwhelming support of black voters in that region. In short, his election would not have been possible except for the Voting Rights Acts of the 1960s, which enfranchised southern blacks. Ironically, on election night, as viewers watched the televised returns, it was Mississippi that finally gave Carter the last few electoral votes he needed to win the election, and it was in Mississippi that three young civil-rights activists, "freedom riders" as they were then called, were murdered in 1963 trying to register blacks. This act shocked the nation and helped bring about the reforms that made it possible for Carter to win in 1976.

Another important difference between the Carter candidacy and those immediately preceding it was that Jimmy Carter—and most of his closest

177

associates—first entered seriously into politics in the turbulent 1960s. Virtually all of the other major figures on the national scene during the last generation—Ford, Nixon, Hubert Humphrey, John Kennedy, Lyndon Johnson—were products of the post-World War II Cold War era. That is, their political socialization took place during a time when the Cold War ideology permeated the nation. They were in positions of great power at a time when secret break-ins, assassination plots against foreign leaders, and domestic spying were accepted by many governmental insiders, usually in the name of "national security." On the other hand, Carter first ran—unsuccessfully—for the governorship of Georgia in 1966, in the midst of a civil-rights social revolution in his native South. He was elected governor in 1970. In a sense, he is a product of contemporary American politics rather than of the Cold War era.

Finally, although personally a model of middle-class conservatism, with his heavy stress upon such values as home, church, the small town, and moderation, Carter embraces politically progressive values. This position may be in harmony with the general sense of where the American people are going. Surveys suggest that a majority of Americans favor more serious actions to protect the environment, to curb pollution, to integrate our society, to cease interfering in the internal affairs of other countries, to help the poor, and so on.[19] Moreover, there is strong evidence that Americans are growing rapidly and increasingly tolerant—of ethnic minorities (in 1971, 69 percent said that they would vote for a black for President; in 1958 only 38 percent said this), of the women's movement (in 1949, only 48 percent of Americans said that they would vote for a woman for President; in 1971, 66 percent said so),[20] and of those basic rights that we have traditionally ignored (recent surveys show that increasingly Americans are supportive of substantive protection of individual rights, whereas in the past we only gave lip service to such rights as freedom of speech and the rights of the accused).[21] Carter understands and may represent these views. For example, during the 1976 campaign he got the highest marks of any candidate from environmentalist groups; activists in the women's movement supported him; he received, as we have seen, overwhelming support from blacks; he talked of ending the policy of intervening in the internal affairs of other countries (he is the first President since the end of World War II to promise this explicitly); he wants to reduce international arms sales, simplify the tax structure and make it more progressive, cut the defense budget, and develop solar power so that we do not need to rely so much on petroleum; he favors a national health-care program, revenue

[19] Louis Harris Poll, January 10, 1971, in Robert Sherrill, *Why They Call It Politics,* 2nd ed. (New York: Harcourt, 1974), p. 323.
[20] See Gallup Opinion Index, August 1971 and November 1971.
[21] National Opinion Research Center, University of Chicago, 1973.

178

sharing that would directly aid the cities; and on and on. These programs are not necessarily liberal or conservative. However, they do seem current, especially in comparison with the 1964 campaign, which we discussed earlier, during which the combatants (LBJ and Barry Goldwater) debated the issues of the 1930s and the New Deal rather than issues of more immediacy.

Thus it would appear that the Carter Presidency has a chance to satisfy the demands of the militants of the 1960s (ending the Cold War mentality, opening up American society to hitherto excluded minorities, and reducing racial injustice and conflict) in substance, while satisfying their staunchest critics—the former supporters of George Wallace—in style. The Carter administration appears to be intent upon resolving the great social divisions that emerged in America in the 1960s.

On the other hand, those who believed Carter's election might pressage a new era in American life and government could draw only cold comfort from the record of that administration in its first few months in office. In the first place, most of Carter's top appointees, unlike FDR's "brain-trust" or Kennedy's "whiz kids," were fairly old-style establishment figures. (See Chapter 8, "Who Rules America?") There were of course some exceptions, such as Andrew Young, the new ambassador to the United Nations. It is normal for a President, particularly after a close election, to seek to unify the country and reassure his opposition by appointing key officials who will seem nonthreatening to the defeated factions. But Carter appeared to be going much farther along this path than most of his recent predecessors. His first major legislative proposal, to stimulate the economy by giving every tax-payer a $50 refund, was withdrawn after it ran into strong criticism from conservative economists and the business community. His most unorthodox and imaginative appointment, the nomination of Theodore Sorenson, John Kennedy's former speech writer and close advisor and a widely respected liberal, to head the CIA, was also withdrawn, somewhat abjectly, after strong opposition developed from hawkish senators and the CIA itself. After Carter's first three months in office, journalist Robert Samuelson could find little or no real difference between Carter's economic program and that of his predecessor, Gerald Ford, whom Carter had lambasted during the campaign for being far too conservative in economic policy and lacking in compassion for the unemployed.[22]

That President Carter may not be successful is clear to anyone who remembers the early hope and promise of the Lyndon Johnson and Richard Nixon administrations. Johnson promised a "Great Society." Nixon vowed to "bring us together." Today few would call America under Lyndon Johnson "great," and fewer still would argue that Richard Nixon helped to unite America.

[22] *Los Angeles Times,* (Apr. 17, 1977), Part 2, p. 2.

Carter's essential strategy seems to embody an almost "pop" psychology ("I'm O.K., you're O.K.") in moving the nation from a preoccupation with guilt to a more positive kind of hope for the future. To accomplish this there will have to be substantive as well as rhetorical changes in American life and in our role as a world leader. Success or failure may be determined by events beyond his or any individual's control, but it will also be influenced by whether or not he can refashion the Democratic party—now more than ever the party of the majority—into a creative and positive force.

Finally, it may be true that politics is often a dreary and sometimes dirty business (although probably no drearier or dirtier than most other businesses). Too often politics in America comes down to a matter of ambitious and unprincipled individuals' seeking power or an easy life at the expense of the taxpayers. Much that passes for political action is simply artfully and often deceitfully manipulating the many while pandering to the wealthy and powerful few.

On the other hand, one should consider the millions of individuals who have thrown themselves wholeheartedly and unselfishly into the political campaigns of such diverse figures as Adlai Stevenson, John and Robert Kennedy, Eugene McCarthy, Martin Luther King, Jr., Barry Goldwater, and Ronald Reagan—to name but a few recent leaders with an extraordinary ability to arouse great energy and loyalty on behalf of their ideas and ideals. The people who marched with Dr. King or rang doorbells for Ronald Reagan were not all fools, nor were they saints or martyrs. They were simply individuals who had found an exhilarating cause, something that helped to give their lives meaning and purpose. They were also patriots, in the best sense of that much abused term, for they were prepared to sacrifice time, energy, and money and to set aside purely personal indulgences and ambitions in order to join with other, like-minded citizens and go out and do battle for their vision of the future of this republic. Whether they won or lost the battle, whether their champion prevailed or not, they shared in one of the richest and most deeply satisfying experiences available to free and civilized men and women. For Hamlet-like, political man is always and forever ambiguous, doomed to crawl in the dust, and yet how like an angel in his apprehension of a better world.

180

Who Rules America?
The Elite, the Interests,
the Bureaucracy,
and the Voter

Democracy: Rule by the People
•
Pluralism: Rule by Interest Groups
•
Elitism: Rule by the Powerful
•
Bureaucracy: Rule by Administrators
•
Voting
•
Political Socialization
•
Apathy and Anger
•
The Attentive Public

What's good for General Motors is good for the country.
Charles Wilson
Former president of General Motors,
Former Secretary of Defense

There can be no question as to who is supposed to rule the United States of America. The premise of Abraham Lincoln's Gettysburg Address—that this is a "government of the people, by the people, for the people"—is the foundation of virtually all official political rhetoric. The *only* source of legitimate power in the United States is the people. As C. Wright Mills has pointed out rhetorically, "No American runs for office in order to rule or even govern, but only to serve." [1]

The late Supreme Court Chief Justice Earl Warren believed that the most important judgment handed down by the Court in his tempestuous era was the *Baker v. Carr* decision of 1962. In this decision, the court established the principle of "one-person, one-vote." So, too, President Lyndon Johnson believed that the decisive weapon in the struggle of black people to gain equality was the passage of the Voting Rights Act of 1965. Given the right to vote, Johnson argued, the blacks would use their political power to gradually overcome any economic, social, or educational disadvantages.

Democracy: Rule by the People

Again the assumption of both these judgments is that America is ultimately ruled by decisions made at the ballot box. This is an appealing idea and part of every American child's most elementary education in citizenship. But is it true? Many think not. California Governor Edmund G. Brown, Jr. has noted, "I don't think the President runs the country, nor do I think the Governor runs the state." [2] Novelist Gore Vidal—author of *Burr* and *1876,* both presenting a somewhat jaundiced look at American history and American society—thinks that it does not matter whether a Democrat or a Republican is elected President or which Democrat or Republican happens to win his party's nomination, because the President will end up serving the interests of the wealthy in any event. At the other end of the political spectrum are many conservatives who believe

---

[1] *The Power Elite* (New York: Oxford U.P., 1956), p. 17.
[2] See interview in *Playboy,* (Apr. 1976).

TABLE OF ORGANIZATION

THE GOVERNMENT OF THE UNITED STATES

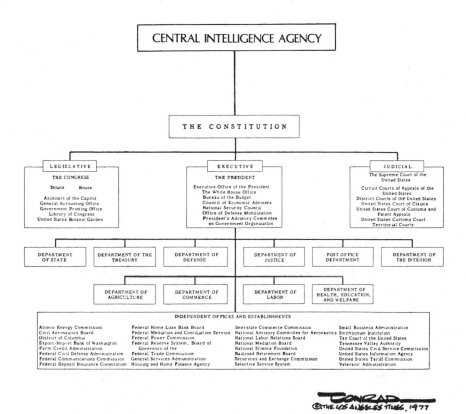

[Editorial cartoon by Paul Conrad. Copyright © 1977, Los Angeles Times. Reprinted with permission.]

that it has become virtually impossible for a President to defy the will of the liberal-establishment media (such as the *Washington Post,* the *New York Times,* and the major TV networks), and they point to the destruction of the Nixon–Agnew administration as proof that the media rule no matter how the election may turn out.

In politics, as in many human endeavors, there is often a difference between image and substance, between theory and reality, between what is said and what is done. There is evidence that millions, perhaps tens of millions, of Americans, ranging from Marxists on the left to the John Birch Society on the right, simply do not believe that ours is a government of, by, and for the people. Perhaps never before in our history have so many been willing to believe that they are being misled by so few. New candidates for the role of the "real rulers" or the "secret government" of America seem to arise almost weekly. Among those most frequently mentioned are the eastern establishment (sometimes personified as "The Rockefellers"), the military–industrial complex, big labor, the Mafia, the Jews, the Kennedys, the WASPs, Wall Street, the Council on Foreign Relations, the media, the CIA, "America's sixty families," the oil cartel— one could go on almost indefinitely. There is hardly a group of Americans so poor and so powerless that someone is not willing to accuse them of being "the secret rulers of America."

In the search for these hidden masters, some have even delved into feudal lore, tracing conspiracies back to such arcane (or nonexistent) groups as the *illuminati*—a group of exceptionally tall people who supposedly came from another planet to rule the world. (Lyndon B. Johnson was very tall, so was Charles De Gaulle—obviously they were part of a conspiracy by the tall to dominate the rest of us.)

It is easy, almost too easy, to dismiss all such notions of a conspiratorial secret government as part of the prevailing paranoia. But where there is that much smoke, might one not expect to find some fire? The very fact that so many people refuse to believe that the American political system works the way it is supposed to work suggests that the question of who has power in America is worth considering.

First of all, let us define power simply as the ability to decide how the resources of the nation, the energy of the people, and the apparatus of the government shall be used. Second, we should consider *for whom* power is being exercised. Let us appraise the problem in a historical context, as it is easier to judge policies and events that can be seen in a perspective of time and with some knowledge of their consequences.

Pluralism: Rule by Interest Groups

As was discussed in Chapter Three, the American Revolution was not a result of a spontaneous uprising of the great majority of the people who lived in the thirteen colonies. It is impossible to know just what percentage of the colonists supported rebellion and independence, but historians have variously estimated the number, some as being as low as 10 percent and few placing it higher than one third of the total population. (Perhaps another third opposed the Revolution, and the rest of the people apparently preferred not to get involved.) In fact, the Revolution was largely the work of a group of political activists, mostly young and many of them lawyers, who took it upon themselves to act in the name of the people. Moreover, strictly speaking, the Constitutional Convention of 1787 was of dubious legality and had no clear mandate from the majority to establish a national government. Thus it can be said that power in America at the very beginning of the nation's history was wielded largely by an elite—men like Jefferson, Washington, Madison, Franklin, and the Adamses.

By the time of the Civil War, two groups had emerged to compete as arbiters of power in America: the planter aristocracy of the South and the businessmen–politicians of the North. The Civil War settled the issue in favor of the northern businessmen and politicians. From the Civil War until the Great Depression brought Franklin Roosevelt's New Deal to power, the businessman, now usually referred to by somewhat grander titles in keeping with his exalted status—such as "industrialist," "tycoon," "corporate magnate," and "robber baron"—had things pretty much his own way.

As William Randolph Hearst, himself a tycoon of no mean proportions, pointed out in a letter to Arthur Brisbane written in 1906:

> We still maintain the republican form of government, but who has control of the primaries that nominate the candidate? The corporations have. Who controls the conventions? The corporations. Who count the votes to suit themselves? The corporations. Who own the bosses and the elected officials? Are they representatives of the people or the corporations? Let any fair-minded man answer this question truthfully.
>
> If the corporations do all this—and they surely do—can we maintain that this is any longer a government by the people?[3]

By the 1920s, perhaps the high point of unchallenged business power in America, President Coolidge could observe, with little fear of contradiction, "The business of America is business." [4]

The worldwide capitalist crisis of the Great Depression of the 1930s brought an end to this era in America. In totalitarian states such as the Soviet Union, Nazi Germany, and Fascist Italy, political functionaries became the prime decision-makers and true rulers, even though in the fascist states the businessman continued to own his property and often enjoyed great personal wealth. The real power to set production schedules and to determine prices and wages and other fundamental prerogatives of ownership were in effect usurped by party bureaucrats.

In America, Franklin Roosevelt created another means of redistributing the power and prestige lost by the business classes in the wake of the Depression. Economist John Kenneth Galbraith has described this as a system of "countervailing power." [5] Labor unions, for example, were

[3] Oliver Carlson, *Hearst, Lord of San Simeon* (New York: Viking, 1936), p. 140.
[4] Speech to the Society of American Newspaper Editors, Jan. 17, 1925.
[5] *American Capitalism* (Boston: Houghton, 1956), Chapter 9.

185

deliberately encouraged and strengthened as a counterforce to the power of the great corporations. Government bureaucrats also acquired new powers to limit, control, and direct economic activity.

By and large, the Roosevelt innovations were created pragmatically as specific responses to specific problems and injustices rather than as the result of an ideology, as was the case in the totalitarian states. Only after the fact did a philosophy arise that attempted to explain and justify the Roosevelt revolution. The doctrine has come to be known as *democratic pluralism*. Pluralism insists that power in America is shared by various interest groups, each attempting to influence government and direct the nation's affairs in a manner congenial to themselves. Such groups are usually perceived to be competing with one another for power, and this competition is considered healthy because it is consistent with both our capitalistic and our democratic traditions.[6] Typical of such interest groups are labor unions, business and manufacturer's associations, and ethnic blocs such as the NAACP. *Special-interest groups* are normally defined as organizations, formal or informal, with a particular concern, such as the National Rifle Association (guns) or Common Cause (political reform).

These groups may play a critical role in elections, contributing money and work to their chosen candidates. Once they have elected their candidate, they expect to receive his loyalty and support for their concerns, sometimes despite the wishes of a majority of the people that the politician is supposed to represent. For example, polls have indicated that for many years most Americans have favored some form of a national health-insurance program run by the federal government. (The cost of medical care for the average American family reached about 10 percent of family income in 1976, far higher than in any other Western nation.[7]) But the American Medical Association opposes such legislation and many physicians are substantial political donors. Their view has prevailed. The same point could be made about labor organizations, such as the Teamsters Union, which though engaging in practices that many people think should be regulated usually has sufficient political muscle to block hostile legislation.

In addition to indirect influence over legislators and sometimes over members of the executive branch (the Secretary of Agriculture, for instance, is unlikely to propose policies disliked by most farmers), interest groups often hire lobbyists directly.

According to the legal definition of the Federal Regulation of Lobbying Act of 1946, a lobbyist at the national level is any person who solicits money or anything of value to be used to influence the defeat or success

---

[6] See Robert A. Dahl, *Pluralist Democracy in the United States: Conflict and Consent* (Chicago: Rand McNally, 1967).
[7] *Los Angeles Times* (Apr. 24, 1976), p. 1.

186

of legislation in the Congress. Most important American organizations have lobbyists in Washington, from the American Medical Association to Ralph Nader's groups.

Lobbyists can use a variety of techniques to affect government. They can try to influence legislators through personal contact; they can provide campaign contributions and other favors such as expense-free vacations at plush resorts; they can encourage the membership of their group to write and call legislators; and they can testify before congressional committees.

How effective lobbyists can be depends on many factors, not the least of which is the intensity of feeling a group has about a particular matter. For example, although public opinion polls have for some time shown that the majority of Americans favor gun-control legislation, the National Rifle Association has thus far been successful in thwarting substantive control laws. This success can be explained in part because the NRA is more intensely interested in the issue and more active than other groups and thus has an impact disproportionate to its total numbers. That is, the NRA effectively uses its lobbyists and at the same time mobilizes its membership to flood lawmakers with calls and letters. On the other hand, members of the NRA may have an opinion but little interest in a labor law, whereas the AFL–CIO will be very interested and may affect such a law's defeat or passage.

Some Americans believe that lobbyists are a threat to democracy. Others believe that they are indispensible. If you are president of General Motors and you influence the government to establish a tariff making it more expensive for Americans to buy foreign automobiles, you may argue that that's good for America because it will result in more jobs in domestic car manufacture. If you are a member of a consumer-advocacy group you may believe the General Motors lobbyist to be antithetical to the interests of the typical middle-class American. However, if your advocacy group influences the government to lower tariffs on foreign automobiles so that you pay less for whatever car you choose to buy, you might reason that your lobbyist has acted in the best interests of the country. The point is that groups normally have more power than individuals. You agree with the aims of some groups and disagree with others.

Pluralism maintains that interest groups are beneficial. It is to be expected that organizations will develop to protect specific interests in public policy. If certain organizations gain too much power (like corporations), others will emerge (like labor unions and consumer groups) to counterbalance that power. According to pluralism, we are all, in a sense, somehow connected with interest groups, and our relationship to politics is very much influenced by the relationship of our interest group to government. For example, we may be students; thus our interests frequently coincide with those of other students, and we probably would oppose a tuition increase of 100 percent. We may be members of a labor union; thus we, along with other labor-union members, might be keenly interested in a piece of labor legislation. The same might be said about those of us who are home owners, taxpayers, and so on. Those interest groups that best represent us and have the most power are the ones that are best organized. These would include such groups as the National Association of Manufacturers, the AFL–CIO, the Sierra Club, the American Civil Liberties Union, Common Cause, the National Organization of Women, and the NAACP. Because each of us can identify with an interest group, each of us can be represented. Thus power in America rests neither in individuals nor in a single monolithic hierarchy. Rather, according to pluralism, there are "multiple centers of power, none of which is wholly sovereign," which will check excessive power, secure common consent to government policies, and provide the possibility for settling conflicts peacefully.[8]

Elitism: Rule by the Powerful

If power in America was substantially diffused during the early years of the New Deal, the onset of World War II required that it quickly be concentrated again in the process of mobilizing the nation for war. The industrialist, scorned by Roosevelt in the early New Deal days as an "economic royalist" and a "malefactor of great wealth," was courted once again. Invited to come to Washington as "dollar-a-year men," many of the nation's foremost businessmen found themselves working with the visionary New Dealers they had regarded as enemies a few years earlier. By the time America emerged victorious from the war, the public had largely forgotten the bitterness against business that followed the 1929 crash, and America's leading corporations trumpeted their war record in full-page newspaper and magazine ads proclaiming that "free enterprise won the war." But if the businessman had successfully returned to the center of American life and power, he now found himself in mixed and— from his standpoint—often dubious company. The politicians' and bureaucrats' power had also swollen enormously, and they found the change agreeable. Organized labor, too, had played a key role in the war years, holding down strikes and excessive wage demands. The triumvirate of "big business, big labor, and big government" became a common catch phrase in the writings of those who chronicled the shifting balances of American power in the immediate postwar years.

But there was still another element of American society that emerged from the war with far greater power and prestige and income than would

[8] Dahl, p. 24.

have seemed imaginable a decade earlier: the military–industrial complex, often referred to currently simply as the MIC. This term refers to an ostensible alliance between the military establishment and certain large corporations (such as Douglas, Northrop, and Lockheed) whose business is sustained by contracts from the government to produce goods for military use (planes, rockets, and so on). President Eisenhower shocked many of his conservative and military supporters by including in his farewell address to the nation a warning against the growing power of the MIC.

Traditionally Americans liked to think of the United States as a peace-loving democracy. In theory, the common people had the most to lose and the least to gain from war. Therefore it was assumed that a democracy would naturally be antimilitary. Wars, it was argued, were started by ambitious generals, greedy munitions makers, and arrogant kings and dictators. For most of the nations of the world throughout history up to and including the modern age, an essay on who rules would be an exercise in elaborating the obvious. The military—that is, the people who have the most efficient and destructive weapons and the men to use them—rule.

The Founding Fathers were aware of this and debated long and hard about how to prevent military preeminence in the United States. Some suggested that the only safe course was to abolish the professional military class altogether; the new country would do without a standing army or navy and rely upon the patriotism of the people to defend it. Ultimately it was decided that a military force was essential, but the authors of the Constitution took the precaution of making the President the Commander in Chief, an unusual arrangement (because most Presidents obviously would not be professional soldiers), as a means of ensuring that the military would remain subordinate to the civilian government.

Thus John Adams wrote that Americans

> believing that in the long run interest, not violence, would rule the world, and the United States must depend for safety and success on the interests they could create, were tempted to look upon war and preparation for war as the worst of blunders; for they were sure that every dollar capitalized in industry was a means of overthrowing their enemies more effective than a thousand dollars spent upon frigates or standing armies.
>
> *John Adams*
> *American Ideals*

Through most of our first century and a half of national life, this principle was rarely challenged. Avoidance of foreign wars and the maintenance of a relatively small and weak standing army and navy was thought to be one of the secrets of prosperity in America, especially when she was compared with European states, which, in the American view,

189

were almost perpetually recovering from the last war or preparing for the next one, with the result that the people were impoverished by a rapacious military establishment.

Pearl Harbor brought an end to majority support for this idea. Within the next three decades, the United States became the strongest military power on earth and fought three bloody wars, plus engaging in numerous "minor" military actions, such as the landing of American troops in Lebanon during the Eisenhower regime. In fact, American troops were stationed more-or-less permanently in forty to forty-five countries, and the nation spent well over $1,000 billion on weapons during the Cold War era. As a result, the MIC became a critical new power center in American life, controlling millions of jobs and many of the nation's largest businesses.

The growth of the MIC required a radical reassessment of who has power in American life, and the seminal work in this field was done by sociologist C. Wright Mills.[9] Mills began by affirming what has become the common complaint of many people. Ordinary citizens have little real impact on decision making in the government or in the larger society. (Who decided to go to war in Vietnam? What role did the average citizen play in Watergate? Did the people choose to have a recession in 1975?) Rather, Mills argued, the people are in fact manipulated by forces they can neither understand nor control. Mills called these forces "the power elite" and argued that a relatively tiny handful of persons in the government (largely the upper echelon of the executive branch—the Congress he considered irrelevant), the leadership of the large corporations, and the top brass of the military, in fact, run the country. Moreover, he suggested that these three hierarchies frequently interlock so that the same people or groups float among the general staff, the corporate boards of directors, and the command positions in the White House and the President's Cabinet. He went on to argue that the men (and they are virtually all men) who rule America are not usually "the best and the brightest" but more often the most ruthless, the most selfish, and in a certain sense among the least enlightened of our citizens:

> In so far as the elite flourishes as a social class or a set of men at the command posts, it will select and form certain types and reject others. The kind of moral and psychological beings men become is in large part determined by the values they experience and the institutional roles they are allowed to play. . . .
>
> The men of the higher circles are not representative men; their high position is not a result of moral virtue, their fabulous success is not firmly connected with meritorious ability. Those who sit in the seats of the high and the mighty are selected and formed by the means of power, the

[9] See *The Power Elite.*

190

sources of wealth, the mechanics of celebrity. . . . Commanders of power unequalled in human history, they have succeeded within the American system of organized irresponsibility.[10]

Later theorists have elaborated upon Mills's beginnings. Thomas R. Dye has extended the hierarchies to include other important institutions such as the "newsmakers" (those corporations whose concentrated power

Two men whose names invariably appear on lists of the most powerful living Americans, President Carter and Walter Cronkite, as they prepared for the nation's first presidential radio "talk show." [Official photograph, the White House, Washington, D.C.]

[10] Ibid., p. 15.

is in the mass media), the "superlawyers" (like Clark Clifford, who has worked in the executive branch of the federal government off and on since World War II and whose clients are among the largest corporations in the world), the foundations (such as the Ford and Lilly Foundations), and the presidents and trustees of the top private universities in the country such as Harvard, Yale, and the University of Chicago.[11]

An interesting addition to the elite theory has been made by G. William Domhoff, who has studied the social backgrounds of these powerful men. He has discovered that they attend the same universities, belong to the same clubs, are directors in the same corporations, and tend to vacation at the same resorts.[12]

Domhoff's studies suggest further the interlocking nature of this elite. It appears that a few men circulate among and serve in most of the hierarchies referred to. Two examples may suffice:

1. C. Douglas Dillon is chairman of the board of Dillon, Reed and Company; a member of the New York Stock Exchange; a director of Chase Manhattan Bank, the Rockefeller Foundation, the Metropolitan Museum of Art, the Brookings Institution, and the American Assembly; and a trustee of Harvard University. He is a large political contributor and has served as Secretary of the Treasury and Undersecretary of State.

2. The current Secretary of State, Cyrus R. Vance, has been a senior partner of Simpson, Thacher and Bartlett law firm and a director of Pan American World Airlines, Aetna life insurance company, IBM, the Council on Foreign Relations, the American Red Cross, and the Rockefeller Foundation. He is also a trustee of the University of Chicago and was chief United States negotiator at the Paris peace talks on Vietnam under President Johnson.[13]

Although the theory of the power elite was originally developed by a Marxist professor, it proved attractive and popular enough to be quickly expropriated in somewhat altered form by the right wing of American politics. But instead of seeing an unholy alliance of business, the military, and government as the true rulers of America, conservatives pointed to the "eastern liberal establishment" as the new power elite. They professed to see an alliance of left-leaning intellectuals and liberals, government bureaucrats, labor leaders, and the media as the focus of American power. They pointed to the power of the great foundations, the television networks, and such chummy groups as the Council on Foreign Relations as the true manipulators of American life, acting as "fronts" for the aforementioned groups.

[11] See Thomas R. Dye, *Who's Running America? Institutional Leadership in the United States* (Englewood Cliffs, N.J.: Prentice-Hall, 1976).
[12] See *Who Rules America?* (Englewood Cliffs, N.J.: Prentice-Hall, 1967). Also see the same author's *The Higher Circles* (New York: Vintage, 1971).
[13] Dye, pp. 131–132.

By 1964, Senator Barry Goldwater had become the Republican candidate for President in a campaign whose central theme was a demand that the liberal establishment be turned out of power. His principal opponent in the Republican primaries was Nelson Rockefeller. When Rockefeller rose at the Republican Convention in San Francisco to attack Goldwater's ideas, he was roundly booed and prevented from speaking for many minutes. This proved to be the beginning of the end of Goldwater's hopes for attracting broad mainstream support for his campaign, and Rockefeller has ever since been regarded by the Republican right wing as the very embodiment of the eastern liberal establishment that they believe is systematically undermining traditional American values in favor of the "Rockefeller interests" and world government.

In 1972, Democratic candidate George McGovern, although not embracing the power-elite thesis in so many words, sounded very much like someone who had read and agreed with Mills when he promised to cut the military budget by 50 percent and transfer both income and power from the rich and privileged to the poor, the young, and the powerless. He was beaten even more decisively than Goldwater.

Thus both major political parties have put forth a candidate who embraced some form of the power-elite thesis and failed to win election. Yet it remains a popular point of view, particularly among intellectuals. And although the average American has probably never heard of C. Wright Mills, he apparently agrees that somehow, some way "the people" are no longer in control (if they ever were) and that most of the nation's large and powerful corporations, unions, and the government itself have become enemies of the common man and the commonweal.

"The ancient authorities" wrote Walter Lippman, "were blended with ancient landmarks, with fields and vineyards and patriarchal trees . . . with old men who knew wise sayings . . . modern man is an emigrant." This sense of being an "emigrant" or a stranger in one's own country, called *alienation* by sociologists, has become a steadily more important and widely discussed issue in American politics, perhaps culminating in the 1976 presidential campaign, when, for example, a Harris Poll conducted after the Democratic primary campaign and published June 17, 1976 disclosed that the most attractive quality of Democratic nominee Jimmy Carter was that he was not part of the Washington establishment. Other polls showed that Ronald Reagan's unexpected strength in the GOP primaries was due to the same basic reason.

There was a growing sentiment that the government was now a foe rather than a friend to the aspirations of the common American. This sense of alienation grew precisely when the nation's leaders began focusing their resources—and perhaps even more importantly, their attention—on the relatively spectacular problems of global military and diplomatic

193

strategy, while relegating purely domestic concerns to a role of secondary importance. This preoccupation with foreign affairs reached its high point during the Presidency of Richard Nixon, who turned over much of the responsibility for running the nation's day-to-day affairs to his aides, H. R. Haldeman and John Ehrlichman, while concentrating his attention on working out global diplomacy with Henry Kissinger. By the end of the decade of the 1970s, an unemployed teen-ager in California might well feel that his government was less concerned about whether or not he could find work than it was in playing power politics in Latin America, Asia, or Europe.

Shortly after taking office under historically unique circumstances, President Gerald R. Ford found himself facing a serious economic crisis. Double-digit inflation was raging, and the nation's economy was sliding downhill at a rate that many found reminiscent of the early days of the Great Depression. The stock market was diving. Unemployment had gone to the highest level since the Depression and was still climbing. Faced with these problems, the President hit upon a novel idea. He called for the formation of a committee. But not just an ordinary committee. A super-committee. He summoned to Washington for a widely heralded economic summit conference many of the nation's leading economists, industrialists, financiers, and labor leaders representing both conservative and liberal thought. He asked these eminent men and women to meet and confer and submit to the President their best collective judgment on how the nation should deal with the crisis. Many of the sessions were covered live on network television. Out of this came two presidential actions. The President asked the Congress for a 5-percent tax increase. The Congress ignored him, which was fortunate because a few months later the President reversed himself and asked for an even larger tax *decrease.* (This time the Congress agreed.) The President's second bold stroke was to go on television and speak to the American people, urging them to wear "WIN buttons" in their lapels to manifest their determination to triumph over the crisis.

As it happened, the nation did indeed begin to recover economically in the fall of that year, but no one would seriously claim that this came about as the result of the tax increase that did not occur or of the wearing of WIN buttons, which also, by and large, did not occur. Somehow the economy began to right itself (although unemployment remained very high through 1976). Assuming that this did not happen by divine intervention, somewhere, somehow, decisions were made that proved helpful. What were those decisions? How and why were they made and by whom? Not one American in ten thousand could even begin to guess. And yet there is hardly a man, woman, or child in the nation whose life was not influenced by whatever the government and the banks and the corporations and the labor unions did or did not do to meet the crisis of 1975.

194

Bureaucracy: Rule by Administrators

Between 1969 and 1973, the Federal Bureau of Investigation, using female informers, spied on women's liberation groups throughout the United States. In response to a Freedom of Information Act request in 1977, the FBI made public fully 1,377 pages of information obtained in such covert activities. This federal agency compiled data on the political beliefs and the sexual habits of individual women and learned that most of them wore faded blue jeans.[14] It remains a mystery what possible usefulness such data could have had in combating crime, which is the FBI's mission. In fact, it appears that this spying on American citizens was carried out on the unilateral order of FBI Director J. Edgar Hoover. Of course, there are other agencies of the federal government—an important one is the Internal Revenue Service—that compile all kinds of information on Americans. And we have been told that there are enormous data banks that know everything about us.

But who is in charge of all this information? What is it used for? Such questions have led some observers to argue that America is not run by elites, interests, or the people but by administrators (like Hoover) in the government bureaucracy, responsible to no one in particular, and without any general idea of where the government is going or what it should do. Peter Drucker, a student of administration, has said that "Government agencies are all becoming autonomous ends in themselves" and that because of "administrative incompetence," "modern government has become ungovernable." [15] More simply, Hannah Arendt has called bureaucracy "rule by Nobody." [16]

Such comments will come as no surprise to many Americans. We deal on almost a daily basis with state or federal government bureaucracy, from the mailing of a letter to the renewal of an automobile license and the paying of taxes. And we frequently find that bureaucracy difficult to understand, irritating, and unhelpful. But it is large and it is important. About one fifth of our national income is taken in taxes by the federal government to provide us with certain goods and services. This money is used to defend the country (indeed, about 40 per cent of the full-time civilian employees of the federal government work for the Defense Department), deliver the mail, operate parks, finance research into malnutrition, pay farmers not to grow crops, and a host of other things. The agencies that administer these activities are part of the bureaucracy, and although the term *bureaucracy* has taken on a negative connotation, it is a necessary fact of life.

---

[14] *Los Angeles Times* (Feb. 6, 1977), Part 1, pp. 1, 8.
[15] *The Age of Discontinuity* (New York: Harper, 1969), p. 200.
[16] *Crises of the Republic* (New York: Harcourt, 1972), p. 137.

All large organizations are "bureaucratic," which means, simply, that they must be administered. Most bureaucracies have certain fundamental characteristics. A university gives example to these. First, a university, like most organizations, is *hierarchical*. That is, it has a president, a vice president, academic deans, department chairpersons, faculty members, and students. Each person more-or-less knows who his or her "boss" is and what responsibilities he or she has. Second, there is a *division of labor*. Individual jobs require certain tasks, no matter who holds the position: the president calls deans' meetings, the dean's office is responsible for class scheduling, the faculty are responsible for meeting classes and advising students, and so on. Third, as in most bureaucracies, in the university there is the assurance of *tenure*. That is, after holding the job for a certain amount of time and demonstrating competence, a faculty member can be fired only for some serious reason.

At the federal-government level, there are currently over 3 million employees in the bureaucracy working in various kinds of agencies. These include the organizations that work within each of the twelve *Cabinet departments* (see Chapter Four), which are directly responsible to the President.

Other agencies are also part of the federal bureaucracy. Independent *executive agencies* also report to the President but are not part of the traditional Cabinet departments. Examples of such agencies are the National Aeronautics and Space Administration, the U.S. Arms Control and Disarmament Agency, the Central Intelligence Agency, and the Veterans Administration. Independent *regulatory agencies* are not in the chain of command leading to the President. They regulate private businesses and activities, thus representing a compromise between "socialism" and unregulated—sometimes cut-throat—competition. Although the President appoints the members of regulatory agencies, once they are in office they serve for a set term and are independent of control from the traditional branches of government. Some of the more important of these agencies can be seen in the accompanying illustration.

Finally, there are some *government-owned and -operated corporations* that are under presidential control. The latest of these is the U.S. Postal Service, and other examples are the Federal Deposit Insurance Corporation, established in 1933, which guarantees bank deposits, and the Tennessee Valley Authority, also created in 1933, which generates hydroelectric power.

Although presidential appointments fill some of the important posts in this giant bureaucracy, most jobs are filled by civil servants. Individuals gain employment by taking scheduled civil-service exams and are then appointed on the basis of merit. The merit system is supervised by the U.S. Civil Service Commission and has been in effect since the passage of the

IMPORTANT REGULATORY AGENCIES

Agency	Date Established	Functions
Interstate Commerce Commission	1887	Regulates railroads, oil pipelines, bus lines, and so on.
Federal Trade Commission	1914	Prevents unfair competition, price fixing, false advertising, and so on.
Federal Power Commission	1930	Regulates interstate utilities and energy businesses.
Federal Communications Commission	1934	Licenses and regulates TV and radio stations.
Securities and Exchange Commission	1934	Regulates stock exchanges.
Civil Aeronautics Board	1938	Regulates airlines.

Civil Service Act in 1883. This act considerably modified the patronage system by which federal jobs were given as political favors.

In 1970, the Office of Management and Budget was created to serve as a coordinating staff to connect the President with the numerous agencies of the administrative branch of government. The OMB is now part of the Executive Office and is presided over by James McIntyre, acting director upon the resignation of Bertrum Lance, who with some sixty budget examiners will try to tighten up the management of the federal government.

Nevertheless, most Americans remain suspicious of the federal bureaucracy specifically and of all bureaucracies in general. (For example, the Academy Award-winning film *One Flew over the Cuckoo's Nest,* based on Ken Kesey's novel of the same name, was a devastating portrait of a medical bureaucracy that seemed more intent on keeping patients submissive than on effecting cures.) A popular and satirical assault on the bureaucratic mind has been embodied in "Parkinson's law": "Work expands to fill the time available for its completion." [17]

In his campaign for the Presidency, Jimmy Carter asserted he would reorganize the federal bureaucracy to make it more humane and efficient. But other Presidents have promised the same. Whether Carter will succeed or not remains to be seen. One step the President did take early in his administration was the introduction of a novel technique for talking to the American people directly by taking phone calls for a stipulated time period. Whether or not this experiment worked, most regarded it as an indication of the President's determination to make the government more directly responsive to the people, thus blunting the criticism of insensitive rule by the bureaucracy.

[17] C. Northcote Parkinson, *Parkinson's Law* (Boston: Houghton, 1957), p. 2.

We have considered four reputed sources of power in American society: the people, pluralism, the power elite, and the bureaucrats. A plausible case can be made for each. The will of the people does count for *something* in America. (For example, when public opinion turned against the Vietnam war, the politicians and the generals began to search for a way out.) President Nixon may have believed himself to be a "sovereign" after his sweeping victory in the 1972 presidential election, but he soon found himself under siege by the press, then the courts, and finally the Congress, and his resignation would seem to reaffirm the premise of pluralism, that power is shared by many competing groups in America under our federal system. Nevertheless, the power-elite thesis does seem to present a coherent and reasonable explanation of our foreign policy, which does not really change very much regardless of who wins the elections.

How one feels about this question is probably related to how one judges American society and one's role within that society. Those who view America as "a noble experiment" will probably hold to the notion that the people, after all, do rule. Those who see America as having abandoned its stated ideals will tend to embrace one form or another of the elitist theory. And although it is beyond the purview of this book to attempt to convince the reader of the correctness or falseness of any of these viewpoints, the fact is that regardless of who ultimately rules, power in America can be legitimized only through the ballot box. If we are being manipulated, the manipulators must somehow affect our decisions as voters. Thus how and why we vote as we do, and whether or not we bother to vote at all, is important.

Voting

The 1976 presidential primaries would offer scant consolation to the power-elite theorists. At the onset of the campaign, most experienced observers would have postulated that President Gerald Ford would easily handle the challenge of former California Governor Ronald Reagan for the GOP presidential nomination because Ford enjoyed the solid backing of the Republican party establishment plus all the advantages of incumbency in a year of peace and a generally improving economy. On the Democratic side, it was anticipated that one of the party's stalwarts, such as Hubert Humphrey, Morris Udall, Birch Bayh, or Henry "Scoop" Jackson, would emerge as the nominee, although it was expected that Alabama Governor George Wallace might well prove disturbingly popular with the rank-and-file voters as he had in the previous two presidential campaigns.

Instead, Ronald Reagan came on to very nearly destroy Ford's renomination hopes, and an almost complete outsider, Georgia's former governor Jimmy Carter, emerged as the strongest candidate in the primaries and

198

won the Democratic nomination. Clearly neither Carter nor Reagan would qualify as party-establishment choices. (However, it was possible that once in office, either would be expected to fall into general agreement with the dominant views of their respective party establishments. In fact, Carter's choice of such establishment Democrats as Secretary of State Cyrus Vance convinced some observers that that is exactly what happened.)

The same pattern existed in the 1972 Democratic campaign, when George McGovern took his party's nomination despite implacable opposition from traditional Democratic leaders who much preferred either Senator Muskie or Senator Humphrey as their candidate.

In these examples, the voters in the primaries insisted upon voting as if their choices mattered, more often than not simply refusing to follow the advice of their party leaders.

The most direct, clear, and understandable way that most individuals can influence the acts of their government is by voting. Voting is the fundamental political act in a democratic nation. Only the vote of the people can bestow legitimacy and legality upon government. People who consistently refuse to exercise their franchise, either because they "can't be bothered" or because "it doesn't matter who I vote for, they're all a bunch of politicians and crooks," have in effect abandoned the idea of self-government. This attitude is most prevalent among young people, the great majority of whom did not bother to vote after the Twenty-sixth Amendment lowered the voting age to eighteen in 1971.

To speak of voting is to speak of the individual citizen. When the country was founded, there were many who doubted the ability of ordinary Americans to choose their own leaders through the ballot box. In response to a Jeffersonian plea to trust the people, Alexander Hamilton reportedly said, "The people, Sir, are a great beast." Few would dare echo this sentiment today, at least not in these words, but there are some who still agree with Hamilton's fundamental premise: the average citizen is too ignorant, self-centered, and irrational to be trusted to chose his or her own leaders. One such voice was that of H. L. Mencken, who for three decades wrote a newspaper column for the *Baltimore Sun* containing some of the most caustic criticisms of American society as well as some of the best political reportage ever published:

> Of the two candidates that one wins who least arouses the suspicions and distrusts of the great masses of simple people. Well, what are more likely to arouse those suspicions and distrust than ideas, convictions, principles? The plain people are not hostile to shysterism save it be gross and unsuccessful . . . but they shy instantly and inevitably from the man who comes before them with notions that they cannot immediately translate into terms of their everyday delusions; they fear the novel idea, and particularly the revolutionary idea, as they fear the devil. . . . This

fear of ideas is a peculiarly democratic phenomenon, and is nowhere so horribly apparent as in the United States.[18]

The same notion was expressed four decades later by Peter Gruenstein, Director of the Capitol Hill News Service, in commenting upon the 1976 presidential primary campaign:

> In fact, no recent *successful* candidate for the Presidency has come forward with any significant new ideas during his campaign . . . it is no accident that what passes for debate during our presidential campaigns consists of little more than conventional political pieties and gobs of self-serving posturing.[19]

Conservative columnist George F. Will has put a positive face on the same observation. Granting that voters were uninterested in and uninformed about the issues, Will said, "Voters do not decide issues, they decide who will decide issues." In short, they vote for "the person," not the program.[20] But in voting for the person, they often, in fact, wind up voting for an image that has been carefully manufactured and artfully sold.

Partially because of such doubts about the ability or the inclination of the voters to choose wisely, the authors of the Constitution left to the states the question of establishing qualification for voting. But gradually a series of constitutional amendments and statutory acts has eliminated most restrictions on the franchise:

1. By the late 1820s, most states had eliminated property qualifications for white males.
2. In 1870, the Fifteenth Amendment to the Constitution forbade states to deny the right to vote because of "race, religion or previous condition of servitude."
3. Women gained the right to vote with the Nineteenth Amendment in 1920.
4. In 1964, the Twenty-fourth Amendment prohibited states from requiring a poll tax in order to vote.
5. The Voting Rights Act, passed by Congress and signed by President Johnson in 1965, provided for the replacement of local election officials by federal registrars in areas in the South where the denial of the right to vote to blacks was widely practiced.
6. The Twenty-sixth Amendment in 1971 forbade states to deny the vote to any citizen eighteen years of age or older.

[18] Malcolm Moos, ed., *On Politics: A Carnival of Buncumbe* (New York: Vintage, 1960.)
[19] *Los Angeles Times* (March 23, 1976), Part 2, p. 5.
[20] *Newsweek* (March 8, 1976).

Consequently, in the almost two hundred years our Constitution has been in effect, the franchise has expanded to include virtually everyone over seventeen years of age.

But, as we have seen, not everyone who is eligible votes. The Gallup Poll discovered after the 1972 election that fully 62 million Americans qualified to vote did not do so (78 million—about 55 percent—did vote). Of these, 24 million did not register.[21]

Who then does vote? Two important factors answering this question are education and occupation. The higher a person's educational level, the more likely he or she is to vote. Moreover, the higher the status and income of the person's job, the higher the likelihood is that he or she will vote.

Although these are the key factors, other influences may be important. For example, a person may be more likely to vote if he thinks the election will be close, because he believes his vote will be more important. That is, he may be more likely to vote if he believes he can be effective.[22] Finally, those most interested and informed are more likely to vote.

This is not to suggest that the American voter is rational. Although we might expect the citizen to arrive at a voting decision by thoughtful judgment, almost all studies of voter behavior belie this expectation. Indeed, an eminent group of scholars has suggested that America has "an electorate almost wholly without detailed information about decision making in government . . . almost completely unable to judge the rationality of government actions." [23] Rather than reasoned decision-making, voters seem to act out of sentiment, mood, and disposition.[24]

Thus, for example, a poll of Jimmy Carter's supporters for the presidential nomination in the spring of 1976 revealed that 50 percent of those supporting Carter simply had no idea of where their candidate stood on a

---

[21] *Gallup Opinion Index,* Report No. 90, (Dec. 1972), p. 11. In the 1976 election only 81 million of 146 million potential voters bothered to go to the polls. This was about the same proportion (55 percent) as in 1972. In order to encourage more widespread voting President Carter presented to Congress in the spring of 1977 election reform proposals that would include provisions to allow voters to register on election day rather than having states require earlier registration.

[22] Angus Campbell, Philip E. Converse, Warren E. Miller, and Donald E. Stokes, *The American Voter* (New York: Wiley, 1960), Chapter 5. This last generalization does not always apply. For example, in 1948, the presidential election was close, with Harry Truman edging challenging Republican Thomas E. Dewey. There were also two other candidates: Henry Wallace, a liberal progressive, and Strom Thurmond, a states-rights "Dixiecrat." Yet despite the variety of views in the campaign, the intense rhetoric, and, ultimately, the closeness of the outcome, the voting turnout was the lowest for a presidential election in the last half century (51.5 percent).

[23] Ibid., p. 543.

[24] See Bernard R. Berelson, Paul F. Lazarfeld, and William N. McPhee, *Voting* (Chicago: U. of Chicago, 1954), Chapter 14.

THE PURSUIT OF HAPPINESS

group of important issues before the nation, 25 percent had the wrong idea, and only one Carter supporter in four could correctly identify their candidate's stand on the issues. (On the other hand, supporters of a more ideologically based candidate, such as Ronald Reagan, were able to identify his positions on the issues much more precisely.)[25]

Although fuzzy about a given candidate's specific stand on specific issues, voters often seem to be drawn toward candidates whose *values* reflect their own, particularly in primaries. Given a choice, a farmer will vote for another farmer more often than not. Catholics who deserted the Democratic party in droves to vote for Eisenhower returned to vote for Kennedy, a Catholic. Jerry Brown, the youngest of the presidential candidates in 1976, had the greatest appeal for young voters. Jimmy Carter, a "born-again" Christian, scored most heavily among rural Protestants. (Although he also drew strong support from black voters.) Two-time presidential candidate Adlai Stevenson, considered an intellectual, drew strong support from academics. To some extent, voters seem to ask themselves, consciously or unconsciously, "Which candidate is most like *me?*" and vote accordingly. However, this theory would seem to be contradicted by the success of Ronald Reagan, who is a former movie star and a fairly wealthy person. But Reagan's appeal may lie precisely in the extent to which he has successfully portrayed, in film *and* in politics, the part of an average, concerned citizen.

Political Socialization

The factors that influence the way we vote normally have little to do with rationality. To a large extent, we are *socialized* into voting behavior, like other human behavior.[26]

The first agent of socialization affecting virtually all of us is the *family*. Some sociologists maintain that the family is still the most important influence on our behavior, which would be true of voting behavior and political-party identification. On the whole, people tend to identify with the political party of their parents.[27]

[25] *Los Angeles Times* (June 4, 1976).
[26] There is a growing body of literature on political socialization. Two useful and stimulating studies are Richard E. Dawson and Kenneth Prewitt, *Political Socialization* (Boston: Little, Brown, 1969), and Anne E. Freedman and P. E. Freedman, *The Psychology of Political Control* (New York: St. Martin's, 1975), Chapter 4, "The Socialization of the 'Good Citizen.'"
[27] See M. Kent Jennings and Richard G. Niemi, "The Transmission of Political Values from Parent to Child," *American Political Science Review,* **62** (March 1968). For a revisionist view of the impact of the family see R. W. Connell, "Political Socialization in the American Family, the Evidence Re-examined," *Public Opinion Quarterly,* **36** (Fall 1972).

By the time a growing child reaches adolescence, he begins to be influenced by his *peer group,* an influence that will continue throughout life. In the United States, children seem to be spending increasing amounts of time with their peers, as much as twice the time as with their family. The impact of this development on political behavior is as yet uncertain, for young people tend to be uninterested in politics.[28]

School is also of some importance in socialization. School, of course, is where the young child usually first encounters peer groups outside his family. Moreover, some scholars see the school as a primary instrument of political learning, using flag salutes, national-holiday celebrations, and the hierarchical and authoritarian organization of the school to foster conformity and obedience.[29] Other scholars discount such an influence on the part of the schools, and still others point out that at the college level of education, students may actually experience a significant and lasting shift in political attitudes, usually from conservative to more liberal.[30]

Finally, the impact of the *mass media* as a political socializer may be important, but it is difficult to assess. We will return to a discussion of the media in a later chapter. At this point, suffice it to say that politicians *believe* that the media have an affect on voting behavior, at least as measured by the enormous sums of money spent on political advertising. Also, when politicians speak of *image* and *momentum,* they are usually referring to how their campaigns are being presented to the voter through the media. For example, in the 1964 campaign, political strategists presented President Johnson in the image of a warm-hearted, humane man and a masterful politician—in the tradition of FDR—while his opponent, Senator Barry Goldwater, was widely perceived as a rather headstrong, reckless man. Johnson won overwhelmingly. Eight years later, the Democratic nominee, Senator McGovern, developed an image as a well-meaning but inept and unrealistic man, whereas the incumbent, Richard Nixon, was portrayed as a practical statesman. In this case, Nixon won overwhelmingly. In retrospect, most people would now be willing to acknowledge that these oversimplified "images" of all four men were distortions.

In the 1976 primary campaign for the Presidency, the term *image* began to yield to a new word: *momentum.* That is, the candidates who won the early primaries were quickly labeled "front runners" by the media, and a certain mystique began to develop around them, with the result that their opponents quickly found funds, support, and media attention difficult to come by. Jimmy Carter clearly had momentum going

[28] Freedman, pp. 103–104.
[29] See Robert Hess and Judith V. Torney, *The Development of Political Attitudes in Children* (Chicago: Aldine, 1967), pp. 93–115.
[30] Kenneth Reich, "Students Cast Liberal Votes Survey Shows," *Los Angeles Times* (Jan. 22, 1973), Part 1, p. 21.

for him in the early primaries. So did President Ford until he met with a series of surprising defeats by Ronald Reagan in the South and the West.

This glance at factors influencing our socialization suggests those people and events that teach us about politics. As youngsters, we learn about politics from those in authority over us—our parents and our teachers. Later we learn from those in positions of equality to us—our age peers, our friends, and still later, and importantly, our work associates.[31] We also learn about politics from the media.

Finally, we might learn from and slightly change our attitudes because of political experiences themselves.[32] For example, we know that there were significant shifts in political loyalties and attitudes toward government as a consequence of the Great Depression; a larger number of people came to believe that government had more responsibility to regulate the economy than had so believed before. Many people came to consider themselves as Democrats rather than as Republicans. So, although political ideas, and thus political behavior, are usually passed on from one generation to another, significant alterations in political attitude may occur as a consequence of experiences. In part, this happens because the real political world rarely operates in as perfect a way as the young citizen expects. Some disillusionment sets in and some alteration of political attitudes takes place. When the young person then becomes an adult, this slightly altered political belief is transferred to the next generation.[33] in this way the impact of the Vietnam war, the Watergate scandal, and revelations about the FBI and the CIA may well influence a significant shifting of political attitudes, causing larger numbers to oppose policies and promises of foreign adventurism and to support those political figures who promise more open government.

Apathy and Anger

Despite all, the basic characteristic of the American voting population seems to be apathy. It is well known that a lesser percentage of eligible voters vote in the United States than in any other industrialized, democratic nation. What causes this political apathy?

For one thing, political activity is somewhat threatening.[34] Many of us, wanting to be well liked, abide by the famous dictum to avoid discussions of politics and religion so as not to endanger our relations with our friends. Moreover, we may fear that we will reveal our ignorance if we launch too seriously into a political debate or activity. And finally,

[31] Dawson and Prewitt, pp. 203–215.
[32] Campbell et al., p. 17.
[33] Dawson and Prewitt, pp. 203–215.
[34] See Morris Rosenberg, "Some Determinants of Political Apathy," *Public Opinion Quarterly,* **18:**349–366 (1954).

sometimes we feel that political activity might threaten our occupational success.

Another factor causing apathy is the feeling that political activity is futile.[35] Study after study has demonstrated the widespread feeling of political powerlessness on the part of large numbers of Americans.[36] Why get involved in or be concerned with politics when politicians do not really care about us, when political decisions are in the hands of powerful, anonymous forces, and when government has grown too complicated to understand anyway? [37] Moreover, there seems to have been in recent years a loss of confidence on the part of Americans that government can really accomplish anything worthwhile and a feeling that it in fact is basically corrupt and unworthy of concern.[38]

Political scientist Morris Rosenberg has suggested that there are simply too few influences or stimuli to get people involved in politics.[39] Political institutions deal with the total society, thus they seem abstract and impersonal, if not dull and remote. Political activity yields little in the way of immediate satisfaction and politics does not seem to meet our daily concerns; for example, who will I go out with this weekend, can I get my car serviced in time, and should I study for the mid-term exam? Even those people who might be interested in political activity are too frequently not contacted by friends, activists, or party organizations. Finally, a number of Americans insist that they are simply not interested in politics.[40]

Lastly, we should note that some potential voters may refuse to exercise the franchise merely as a way of protesting against the government and a political process they believe is beyond their control.[41]

On the other hand, political apathy in the United States might reflect a basic satisfaction with things as they are. Moreover, if increased numbers of voters became agitated and excited about politics, would that not mean that an increasing number of ill-informed voters would be going to the polls and making irrational judgments? Indeed, political scientist Angus Campbell has shown that when a smaller percentage of voters vote, it is usually the best informed who do vote and that a large turnout usually means an increase in uninformed voters.[42] This finding would seem to

[35] Ibid.
[36] See Robert S. Gilman and Robert B. Lamb, *Political Alienation in Contemporary America* (New York: St. Martin's, 1975), pp. 14–18.
[37] Ibid., p. 18.
[38] See Donald W. Harward, Ed., *Crisis in Confidence, The Impact of Watergate* (Boston: Little, Brown, 1974).
[39] Rosenberg, p. 361.
[40] Gilman and Lamb, p. 96.
[41] Michael Parenti, "The Harvesting of Votes," in *Democracy for the Few* (New York: St. Martin's, 1974).
[42] Angus Campbell, "Voters and Elections: Past and Present," *The Journal of Politics,* 26:745–757 (Nov. 1964).

suggest the wisdom of *limiting* the number who can vote! Such a policy would be based on the traditional arguments that historically have kept large groups from participating in government. The British cited "virtual representation" to deny American colonists representation in the Parliament, insisting that the views of the Americans were always presented in London. Such arguments have been used to exclude blacks, women, and young people from voting. Yet our history has gone in the opposite direction, opening ever wider the opportunity to vote. And recent evidence suggests that we may have to deal with a larger and heightened interest in politics on the part of Americans. If one's educational level is a determinant of his political interest, then the increasing percentage of Americans going to college should result in less political apathy. In fact, a recent study suggests that although the American voter has indeed grown more dissatisfied and disillusioned with politics, he is nevertheless increasingly less apathetic and less passive than formerly believed. Rather, the voter is more aware of and sensitive to political issues and more likely to cross party lines than in the past.[43]

Moreover, in 1976, a Gallup Poll showed some surprising trends. In answer to the question "Are you more or less interested in politics than you were in 1972?" 42 percent said more interested, 29 percent said less, and 28 percent said the same. Of the respondents, 77 percent said that they believed that voting in the elections was still the most important way for Americans to influence government.[44]

Surely this was a hopeful sign in the year of our bicentennial. Our dedication to democracy demands a great deal of us as individuals. It demands that we be part of an informed, enlightened, and active body politic. How much power over us elites or anonymous forces have probably depends upon how informed, enlightened, and active we are.

The Attentive Public

One should note that "the power elite," if it in fact exists, is probably dynamic rather than static. Few observers of the American scene would have listed the military establishment as a decisive element in the power structure during the 1920s or 1930s. Organized labor, certainly not part of the power structure before the 1930s, might have to be included today. Even the most celebrated newspaper and radio commentators and reporters prior to World War II probably had nothing like the influence they wield today. Intellectuals, too, would appear to have much more voice in the affairs of state these days, if only because there are so many

[43] Norman H. Nie, Sidney Verba, and John R. Petrocik, *The Changing American Voter* (Cambridge: Harvard U.P., 1976).
[44] *Newsweek* (Apr. 12, 1976), pp. 30–31.

more of them and because they speak with and for an infinitely larger clientele. Certainly one of the dominant themes of politics in the past decade in America has been a determined challenge by men and women whose roots are in the intellectual and/or protest communities, such as Ralph Nader and John Gardner, rather than the more traditional businessmen–politicians who normally decide things in this country.

Summing up the national scene with one of those gaudy, sweeping generalizations he was so fond of, H. L. Mencken concluded that American life "is in three layers—the plutocracy on top, a vast mass of undifferentiated human blanks bossed by demagogues at the bottom, and forlorn *intelligentsia* gasping out a precarious life between." [45]

What Mencken called the "forlorn intelligentsia," political scientists— preferring a more discreet style—sometimes call "the attentive public." [46] These are the people who read the news magazines, the political columns, and even the editorials in the press; watch the public-affairs shows regularly on television; and even read nonfiction books dealing with current events. If we take the circulation of the news magazines or the number of people who watch serious public-affairs programs on television regularly as a guide, we can probably estimate their total number as no more than 5 percent of the population. And yet, despite their relative smallness in number, these people may play an important and at times critical role in politics.

First of all, although a President may require the votes of tens of millions of what Mencken called "undifferentiated human blanks" to get elected, in the day-by-day operation of his office he deals with a much different and more sophisticated audience. The Washington press corps, students and teachers of politics in and out of the academy throughout the nation, plus well-informed professional politicians and party activists weigh the President's words and judge his deeds against their own, often sophisticated knowledge of events and issues.

The attentive public can also prove decisive in a more positive role. Students, teachers, and political activists transformed Senator Eugene McCarthy from a lonely crusader to a major candidate for the Presidency in 1968. They played an important part in bringing Senator McGovern from the point where he was favored by 1 or 2 percent of the Democratic voters in the national polls early in 1972 to his party's nomination that summer. Lord Keynes observed many years ago that abstract theories written in little-read journals and books by economists of one generation become the slogans of the man in the street in the next generation. Ideas that the average man takes for granted today—the right of working

[45] See H. L. Mencken, "The National Literature," *Yale Review*, **9**:804–817 (July 1920).
[46] See Gabriel Almond and Sidney Verba, *The Civic Culture* (Princeton: Princeton U.P., 1963).

people to form unions, the right to public education, medical insurance, social security, the forty-hour work week—were all proposed by theorists at one time or another and only gradually permeated the thinking of ordinary citizens to the point where they became politically popular and feasible.

The same principle may often be seen at work in foreign affairs as well. For several decades following the victory of the Communists in China, discussion of a possible detente between the leaders of mainland China and the United States was limited almost exclusively to a small circle of liberal intellectuals, most of them involved professionally in education and/or communications. This remained the case until President Nixon, once the nation's foremost critic of those who preached any sort of accommodation with China, deemed the time right to go to Peking. The general public, which had supported the anti-China policy of the government for decades, now did a quick about-face and supported the new policy.

Who, in fact, was responsible for the change in America's policy toward China? Henry Kissinger, who made the initial diplomatic overtures? Richard Nixon, who made the actual decision? The professors who had been agitating for just such a change for decades? The military–industrial complex, which saw China as a potential ally in the continuing struggle against Russia and as an enormous potential market for American goods? The American people, who voted Richard Nixon into office at least partially on the basis of his "secret plan" to "end the war and win the peace" in Vietnam?

Perhaps a whole series of events—such as the need to find a negotiated settlement to the Vietnam war, President Nixon's desire to make the theme of "a generation of peace" the keystone of his 1972 campaign for reelection, and recognition by Cold War strategists of the increasing possibility of playing China off against Russia—combined to make a change in policy diplomatically desirable and politically possible. Failure to deal realistically with mainland China was at least partially responsible for America's becoming embroiled in two wars in Asia in the past two generations. A new and different policy held out at least the hope for less tragic and bloody consequences. Finally, the people themselves, both the apathetic and the attentive alike, seemed to be ready for a change in our policy toward China, and they endorsed the new policy with votes for Nixon in 1972 and high marks in the polls for his Secretary of State.

Moreover, if the new policy succeeded, the American people would benefit from expanding trade and friendship with one of the world's oldest and greatest civilizations. They would also pay the price if it failed. That remains the one compelling and unanswerable argument in favor of the democratic principle of one person, one vote. For regardless of who

208

makes the decisions, it is the people who will either be its beneficiaries or bear its consequences.

Can the question posed by the title of this chapter be answered then, even tentatively? As we have noted, President Carter's path to the Presidency would suggest that the people do indeed rule.

But if one examines the Carter administration, as opposed to the Carter candidacy, the answer is not quite so clear. For in selecting the top officials of his administration the President confounded many of his supporters by turning to the same kinds of people—in many cases the same individuals—whom Mills had described as "the power elite." For three of his most important and sensitive appointments, that is, for Secretaries of State, of Defense, and of Health, Education and Welfare, Carter chose three familiar faces from the Johnson years—Cyrus R. Vance, Harold Brown, and Joseph Califano, respectively. For Secretary of the Treasury he chose Michael Blumenthal, the head of a large corporation. For his principal adviser on energy policy he chose James Schlesinger, a top official in the Nixon and Ford administrations. For Director of the Office of Management and Budget he picked Bertrum Lance, a prominent Georgia banker. Indeed, at one point, one of Carter's appointees, Cecil D. Andrus, felt constrained to make a little joke of the fact that, unlike most of his fellow cabinet members, he had not graduated from an Ivy League university and was not a banker or a Wall Street lawyer.

If Jimmy Carter had intended to confirm the Mills thesis that, regardless of who wins elections, essentially the same self-perpetuating group of elitists will actually run the country, he could hardly have done a more convincing job.

But the question of who rules America is not necessarily answerable only by Jimmy Carter. Because a person is elected to the highest office in a nation does not mean that, from the moment of election, he is the sole determiner of its destiny. Such may be the case in a monarchical or totalitarian state. In a republic the responsibilities of individual citizenship are much more demanding. Dedicated individuals, working separately and in groups, may influence the direction of political events. Preservation of the democratic system requires that they try.

Media, the Shadow Government: Power and the Press

The duty of the press is to print the truth and raise hell.
Mark Twain

Education is civil defense against media fall out.
Marshall McLuhan

When asked to account for the enduring success of *The Reader's Digest* (which for three decades has been the world's largest selling magazine), editor Dewitt Wallace responded, "We sell hope." It was Wallace's way of pointing out that his magazine is not simply in the business of publishing stories and word games; rather it brings to its tens of millions of readers throughout the world a certain view of life. Typical, standard *Digest* fare includes such titles as "How One Town Solved Its Juvenile Delinquency Problem," "Ten Ways to Increase Your Word Power," "What America Means to Me," and "The Joys of Sexual Renewal." What all of these seemingly disparate subjects have in common is that they tell a story of ordinary people triumphing over life's problems by the use of common sense and traditional values, all told in simple sentences and short words.

So, too, almost any successful magazine, newspaper, or television or radio program brings to its audience not only information and entertainment but a version of reality.

There was a time when most people depended upon experience with life itself, careful observation of nature, and myth makers and religious and political leaders to define and create the world around them. Increasingly, the mass media have assumed this function. The myths of our day deal with celebrities, not demigods. Celebrities are created by the media. People once tried to estimate tomorrow's weather by looking at the sky; now they watch a TV weatherman. In much the same way, the media have replaced the prophet, the priest, and the prince as the arbiters of moral and political truth.

As Theodore White has pointed out,

> The power of the press in America is a primordial one. It sets the agenda of public discussion. Today, more than ever, the press challenges the Executive President, who, traditionally, believes his is the right to set the agenda of nation's action.
>
> *Theodore White*
> *The Making of the President, 1972*

212

What Is News?

The function of the mass media (a term usually used to describe the press, television, radio, and the major magazines) is to bring the world and all of its infinite variety to the attention of the average citizen. A war in Southeast Asia, a famine in Africa, an election in Italy, a scandal in Washington, a coup in Latin America, a new film in Scandinavia, a new style in Rome, the price of meat in supermarkets, or the rate of exchange between the dollar and the mark—these are the commonplaces of the media. It is impossible to compress everything unusual or important that happens anywhere in the world into a thirty-minute TV news broadcast, a daily newspaper, a magazine, or all three combined. Thus the media, in a sense, have a Herculean responsibility, which they can never really hope to fulfill. They can only try. This means they can only select from the almost limitless number of happenings—some important, some trivial —those that they believe to be of interest to their audience.

There have been many attempts to define "news." Perhaps the most satisfactory is an old bromide of the city room: "News is whatever the editor thinks it is." The consequences of that editor's decision go beyond whether or not the reader's or viewer's interest is aroused or satisfied. The power to decide what is news is the power to define reality for many people.

A distinction should be made between "hard news" and opinion or commentary. In theory, hard news is an objective report of factual events —what Walter Cronkite does on the six o'clock news. Opinion is reserved for the editorial pages and columnists in the print media. On television it is the prerogative of commentators such as Eric Sevareid or Howard K. Smith. Although most working members of the press believe in and try to conform to this difference, in practice it is virtually impossible to do so. For one thing, as we have noted, there is an inescapable element of subjectivity in the mere selection of what is or is not news. In the early months of the 1976 presidential campaign, for example, much media attention was given, usually good-naturedly, to President Ford's frequent mishaps, both with respect to physical and mental lapses. This helped create an impression of Ford as a not-too-bright and hence not very effective leader, which unquestionably damaged Ford greatly. The press might have chosen to ignore Ford's mishaps, just as it ignored the fact that Franklin D. Roosevelt had been crippled by polio. Ford bumping his head was news because reporters and editors subjectively believed it was an important key to the man's performance as President. Roosevelt's polio was ignored because most reporters and editors deemed it irrelevant.

By deciding what is news and what is not, the media inevitably project a certain view of the world which cannot help but reflect their own values and biases.

A young man who is told by newspapers, TV, and radio that the United States is engaged in an honorable and unselfish struggle in Southeast Asia to help a brave people defend freedom against totalitarian aggressors is not likely to resist when and if his government calls upon him to help in that struggle. But what if the young man is subjected to a conflicting version of the truth? What if his government tells him that this war is just and necessary but the media tell him that it is in fact a useless and unwarranted effort to prop up with American lives and money a corrupt regime disliked by its own people? If he is at all reflective, the young man will experience a personal crisis. Who should he believe? His response to a draft call will probably be considerably less positive than in the first example. That, of course, is what happened during the Vietnam war. In the beginning, only a handful of journals opposed American intervention in Vietnam. But as the years went by, one by one many of the nation's most influential media gradually brought reports to their readers and viewers that were in conflict with the government's version of events. Newspapers like the *Wall Street Journal* and the *Los Angeles Times,* traditional bastions of establishment opinion, opposed continuing the war. Finally, Walter Cronkite of CBS television joined the ranks of the war's critics. (It is, of course, unthinkable that Cronkite could have made so important a change in his public position on the war without at least the tacit approval of CBS.) When that happened, President Lyndon Johnson is reported to have concluded that all hope of uniting the people behind his Vietnam policy was gone. The President had conceded that he could not make his view prevail against that of the media, particularly against a powerful television network.[1]

This example illustrates the enormous power of the media: the power to define reality for and hence to direct the opinions and behavior of the people. It is not a power that the media, by and large, covet, as we shall attempt to make clear. But it is a consequence of the conditions of modern life.

The Mass Audience

Studies have shown that as many as 54 percent of the American people are "unable or only marginally able to cope with basic reading tasks, *regardless of level of formal education completed.*" [2] Thus over half the population is dependent upon mass media, particularly the electronic media

---

[1] David Halberstam, "CBS: The Power and the Profits," *Atlantic Monthly* (Feb. 1976).

[2] Coleman McCarthy in the *Washington Post* (June 19, 1976).

214

(which of course do not require reading skills), for information about the world they live in. (*Mass media* may be defined as a TV station, magazine, or newspaper that attempts to serve most or all of the people in its potential market. Commercial radio and TV stations are mass media. Most public radio or TV stations, which usually seek a selected audience, are not. *People* is a mass magazine. The *New Republic* is not.) And although it is true that these people can select from among competing media, the fact is that on any given evening, almost all daily newspapers across the United States choose to headline much the same story or stories, and the thousands of radio and television stations follow suit.

Traditionally, we consider indispensable in a democratic society the ability to read the written word and hence to root out information and opinion for oneself. If, as many studies indicate, both the ability and the inclination to read and ferret out the truth for oneself are in decline, the prospects for democracy are not good.

It should be noted, however, that there are different audiences for the mass media, and for television particularly. There is the general public, which, as a rule, is ill informed about public affairs. And there is what we have called "the attentive public" (see the discussion of this topic in Chapter Seven). For many Americans, TV and radio news broadcasts, with perhaps an occasional glance at the day's headlines in the news-papers (almost half of American families no longer take a daily newspaper), represent the only source of information and opinion about the government and its leaders.

For the fully literate minority, however, there are a great many other sources. First of all, these people usually have some knowledge of history, so that they can judge current happenings in context rather than as in-explicable events. Second, the attentive public read books and serious magazines on current affairs, which offer various and frequently conflicting points of view. Third, they watch public-affairs programs on television and often listen to both radio and TV talk shows. Finally, many are active themselves in political affairs and hence have personal and specialized knowledge.

The mass media seem to have a different effect on these two audiences, which can be illustrated by the responses to one of the most stirring and exciting media events in recent history, the riots that erupted at the Demo-cratic National Convention in Chicago in 1968. The TV viewer saw swarms of young people, most of them looking rather illkempt and disreputable, fighting the Chicago police in the streets outside of the convention and the principal hotels where the official delegates were staying. The public re-sponded with strong condemnation of the behavior of the young protestors and support for Mayor Daley's police. More-informed persons, on the other hand, who knew something about the background of these riots and the nature of the issue between the young people and the official delegates were more likely to criticize Mayor Daley and the police for what the investigative Walker Commission later described as "a police riot."

The point is that the "attentive public" may gain more information from media news and may respond with more understanding of events than those people who rely strictly on the mass media for their information.

Presidents and the Media

Both Lyndon Johnson and Richard Nixon believed that their right to govern the country after having been elected President was, in part, subverted by the press. Johnson stated repeatedly that his Texas accent and style, particularly following John Kennedy's high Harvard glitter, doomed his Presidency. Describing his doubts about running for a full term in 1964, after having succeeded the assassinated Kennedy a year earlier, Johnson expressed his belief that the nation could not be united around a southern President. "I was convinced," said Johnson, "that the metropolitan press would never permit it." Subsequent events persuaded Johnson that he had been right all along. Mr. Nixon carried on a lifelong battle with the press. Columnist Jack Anderson has said that, "Nixon came to power with the conviction that he had gotten there by circumventing the press and could govern successfully only so long as he continued to do so." [3]

In a sense, both Johnson and Nixon were right. They began their political careers and achieved great power and prominence when the press had had a different and more modest role in national affairs than it assumed during their Presidencies. What happened in the interim was the brief era when John Kennedy was President. Kennedy changed the relationship between the government and the media in a way that neither Johnson nor Nixon fully understood or accepted.

Kennedy, of course, was not the first President to manipulate the media to achieve both personal and political goals. Franklin Roosevelt made masterful use of the radio. President Eisenhower led a charmed life insofar as criticism of the man or even of his administration was concerned. Fulminations against the Presidency seemed tasteless and ill mannered during the eight years of Eisenhower's regime. On the other hand, Eisenhower's opponent in two campaigns, Adlai Stevenson, a charming, witty, and eloquent man who today would surely be a great favorite of the media, was sometimes treated like a pariah for presuming to run against the great war hero. Questions put to President Eisenhower during his press conferences were respectful and usually intended to be helpful. Stevenson, on the other hand, was sometimes greeted with hostility and often downright rudeness, to the point where he noted, more in sorrow than in anger, that the press

[3] *The Anderson Papers* (New York: Ballantine, 1973), p. 19.

216

seemed to react to a Democratic presidential candidate the way dogs react to cats: "They invariably want to chase us down an alley." [4]

What was unique about the Kennedy administration was not that Kennedy enjoyed a largely favorable press (Eisenhower's was perhaps more adoring) or that he used television to charm the voters (FDR used the radio even more skillfully) but that he deliberately attempted to make the press a vital part of his administration, and in the process, he gave it a kind of legitimacy and power it had never before enjoyed. That is, Kennedy elevated the press to a fourth branch of government, equal and in some ways superior to the Presidency, the Congress, and the judiciary. Neither of Kennedy's two immediate successors could or would accept the new status of the press as an accomplished fact.

To understand the impact of the Kennedy administration upon the role of the mass media, it is necessary to touch upon the history of the press just prior to 1961, when JFK took office.[5] American journalism evolved out of two impulses: the need to advertise goods and services, which is why the front page of most early American newspapers contained advertising exclusively, and the desire to educate or propagandize (depending on your point of view) the people. Thus, Ben Franklin began his *Almanac* (which later became one of the nation's first mass magazines, the *Saturday Evening Post*) with the statement that he had become a publisher not so much to spread wisdom and enlightenment but because "my wife needs new pots." The shrewd Franklin understood that the hardheaded farmers who were to be his audience might not respond favorably to a publication presuming to improve their minds, but that they preferred a sound commercial motive.

The Media Business

Unlike Europe, where many newspapers and magazines were subsidized by political factions and religious, social, and artistic movements, the American press was first and foremost a business, like any other business, that existed to sell advertising. (Although the press does obtain revenue from circulation, this is usually an expense rather than a profit to the publisher. Paid circulation is important because it offers the most convincing proof to advertisers that a publication is being read.)

Through most of America's history, the business community has been conservative politically, and the press, with few exceptions, has followed suit. One exception occurred briefly during the early days of the Great Depression, when something akin to panic seized American business lead-

[4] Labeling candidate Stevenson "an egghead," *Time* went on to define the term as "an intellectual educated beyond his intelligence."
[5] For an illuminating discussion of the American press prior to 1960, see A. J. Liebling, *The Press* (New York: Ballantine, 1961).

ers, causing many businessmen and some newspapers (such as the then-influential Hearst press) to desert the Republican party and support Franklin D. Roosevelt. By 1936, however, the panic had eased sufficiently to find both business and the overwhelming majority of American newspapers and magazines solidly behind the Republican candidate, Alf Landon, who, nonetheless, was buried in the election.

Another important exception to the general rule of a largely conservative and compliant press occurred during the early part of this century, when a few audacious publishers, such as William Randolph Hearst and Joseph Pulitzer, engaged in "yellow journalism." That is, they created newspapers, usually tabloid-sized, designed to be sold for a penny or two to subway-riding working people. The success of such newspapers depended upon creating an aura of excitement and crusading zeal, together with the stock ingredients of big, splashy photos and plenty of sex, violence, and gossip. Occasionally these papers would engage in a struggle on behalf of the "common man" against the interests, such as private utilities, great trusts, and corrupt political machines. In the end, however, the successful tabloids, once firmly established, settled down to a cozy relationship with their advertisers and used their editorial crusades to champion the businessman beleaguered by "bureaucrats" and tax collectors.

As Joseph Patterson, publisher of America's largest-selling newspaper, the *New York Daily News,* noted, "Newspapers start when their owners are poor, and take the part of the people and so they build a large circulation, and, as a result, advertising. That makes them rich and the publishers naturally begin to associate with other rich men . . . then they forget all about the people." [6]

By World War II, the United States, unlike most European nations, had developed a press with an almost exclusively regional base. The nation's two most politically influential national publications were *Time* and *Life* magazines, owned by Henry R. Luce. Luce, the son of an American missionary, grew up in China and developed two ideas that were to have a profound influence on his magazines and, through them, on the nation. One was his unshakable belief that America's destiny was to spread Christianity and capitalism (which were virtually inseparable in his eyes) around the world. The other was a morbid hatred of communism.

Luce saw journalism not merely as a means of amassing wealth or as a vehicle for giving information to the American people but as an instrument for spreading the gospel of Americanism. As he once observed in a letter to senior editors at *Time* magazine who had complained about the magazine's lack of objectivity, "Within our company there is some confusion on this score. For example, there is a persistent urge to say that *Time* is 'unbiased,' and to claim for it complete objectivity. This, of course, is non-

[6] Liebling, p. 19.

sense. The owners make no such fantastic claim." Later Luce added, "Our great job at *Time* magazine is not to create power, but to use it." [7]

By 1940, Luce believed that America would soon enter World War II and foresaw the probability that the United States would emerge from that conflict as the dominant power of the non-Communist world. In a widely discussed editorial entitled "The American Century" (which Luce paid to have published in many leading American newspapers as well as in his own magazines), Luce argued, "The complete opportunity of leadership is *ours.*" He urged that in the postwar years America undertake to feed and care for all friendly peoples and governments but "take a very tough attitude toward all hostile governments." America must become the world's greatest economic and military power and pursue a policy of unrelenting opposition to any who dared defy that power. Although Luce's views drew a varied response at that time, ranging from support from business and conservative interests to strong attack from liberals (including a speech by Vice President Henry A. Wallace entitled "The Century of the Common Man"), in fact he had outlined the essential elements of what would become America's postwar foreign policy under both Democratic and Republican leadership.

Luce was a tireless foe of both Franklin D. Roosevelt and Harry S. Truman. Roosevelt was able to go to the people directly via radio, over Luce's head as it were. (He once "awarded" Luce a Nazi Iron Cross for giving "aid and comfort to the enemy.") But Truman, a poor radio and television speaker, was effectively portrayed as "a little man" and a political hack—an impression that dominated the public image of Harry Truman until his reputation experienced a recent revival to the point where he has become something of a folk hero in the 1970s. John C. Merrill has written a classic study of how *Time* successfully stereotyped Truman by comparing its coverage of HST with that afforded Dwight Eisenhower, a Luce favorite. For example, according to *Time,* Eisenhower was,

> A smiling warm-hearted, sincere leader. . . . A patient and peaceful man, who wanted to keep his campaign promises. A president who moved quietly . . . who loved children, who was forgiving and religious . . . who was cautious, warm, charitable, modest, happy, amiable, firm, cordial, effective, serene, frank, calm, skillful and earnest . . . who spoke "warmly" and chatted "amiably."

On the other hand, Truman was

> a bouncy man, sarcastic and shallow; very unpopular, a "little man" . . . a President who condoned "shabby politicking" . . . a man who practiced "government by crony." A petulant, stubborn man with "shoddy friends."

[7] W. A. Swanberg, *Luce and His Empire* (New York: Scribner, 1972), p. 246.

219

Eisenhower "said with a happy grin," Truman "barked." Eisenhower, "paused to gather thought," Truman "grinned slyly and avoided answering." Eisenhower folded his "long and reflective fingers." Truman's fingers were "blunt." [8]

When John Kennedy was nominated as the Democratic candidate for President in the summer of 1960, his father, Joseph P. Kennedy, was watching the event on television with Henry Luce at the Luce suite in the Waldorf hotel in New York City. The elder Kennedy, a long-time friend of Luce (dating back to the time when both had briefly admired the Nazis for resistance to communism prior to the war), sought to win Luce's favor for his son's cause by affirming, "Henry, you know goddam well that no son of mine could ever be a goddam liberal." Luce demurred, pointing out that JFK would inevitably have to court the traditional Democratic liberal vote on domestic policy. That, Luce went on, was not really serious. "But if Jack shows any sign of going soft on communism [in foreign policy] then we would clobber him." [9]

There is evidence that JFK was mindful of the Luce threat and took it very seriously indeed. For example, with respect to China, he confided to foreign policy advisers Adlai Stevenson, Ambassador to the United Nations under Kennedy, and Chester Bowles, Undersecretary of State, that he agreed with them that United States policy toward China (that is, pretending that the Chiang Kai-shek government-in-exile on Taiwan was the representative of China) was "moonshine." [10] Sooner or later United States policy toward China would have to be changed. But, Kennedy added, "if Red China comes into the U.N. during our first year in town, they'll run us both out." By "they" Kennedy principally meant the *Time–Life–Fortune* Luce empire.

Kennedy and the Media

There is evidence that John Kennedy deliberately set out to shift the balance of media opinion from Republican to Democratic, conservative to liberal, and specifically to create a countervailing power to the influence of the Luce magazines. Kennedy did this with no more of a congressional or constitutional mandate than Lincoln had for freeing the slaves or Wilson had for attempting to draw a blueprint for world peace after World War I. He did it by making reporters, columnists, and editors part of his administration and by deliberately cultivating close personal friendships with im-

[8] John C. Merrill, *Journalism Quarterly* (Autumn 1965).
[9] Swanberg, p. 576.
[10] Ibid., p. 581.

portant figures in the major media. He used these men and women as both advisers and sounding boards. Often sympathetic reporters, editors, and media executives played a more important role in his policy decisions than members of his official Cabinet. Members of the press knew this was happening, and despite some misgivings about where their loyalties were supposed to lie, they loved it and in time came to accept it as perfectly natural. When the doors to the Oval Office, which had been open to the press during the Kennedy years, closed during the Johnson and Nixon eras, the press reacted with predictable hostility.

The Kennedy administration invented the term *news management.* This meant using the powers and prerogatives of the Presidency to control the flow of information and commentary going to the American people through newspapers, radio, and television on a day-by-day and even an hour-by-hour basis.

Kennedy accomplished this control not simply by being a charming fellow and making himself available for interviews, or by issuing judicious invitations to Jacqueline Kennedy's dazzling White House parties, but to a considerable degree by becoming a student of American media. Thus someone like Benjamin Bradlee, then *Newsweek's* White House correspondent and now managing editor of the *Washington Post,* found to his astonishment that Kennedy knew more about the Washington press corps— who the correspondents were, what publications or broadcasting stations they represented, and what the circulation, financial, and political problems of those publications and stations were—than Bradlee himself knew.[11] According to Bradlee, Kennedy genuinely liked reporters, had once been one himself, and planned to enter journalism when he retired from the Presidency.

More importantly, Kennedy not only knew the personalities and the day-to-day problems of the working press, he also understood the inherent limitations of the mass media.

As Bradlee wrote:

> Kennedy worried out loud about the widening gap between the people who can discuss the complicated issues of today with intelligence and knowledge, and those he later referred to as "the conservative community" . . . the great majority who just don't understand these issues and hide their lack of understanding behind the old cliches.

Kennedy sometimes complained that the major media were compelled to please their audiences by oversimplification and "entertainment values." He made this the theme of a major address at Yale University.

[11] *Conversations with Kennedy* (New York: Norton, 1975).

No American President, before or since, has thought through the role of the media in a mass society as carefully. No American President, before or since, *read* as many newspapers or magazines. (Lyndon Johnson was fond of watching all three TV network newscasts at once. Richard Nixon publically claimed to be indifferent to what the networks said or the press printed about him. He would confess only to watching Washington Redskin football games.) Kennedy (like Carter) was one of the few Presidents of this century who appears to have read nonfiction for pleasure and whose public comments were liberally sprinkled with allusions or ideas that he had gleaned from a wide reading of the best contemporary journalism.

Two important examples can be cited. Perhaps the most celebrated came during the Cuban missile crisis, when the President was under considerable pressure from most members of the National Security Council, particularly the representatives of the military, to take direct military action against Cuba and/or the Soviet Union. Although never closing the military option, Kennedy delayed, hoping for the diplomatic triumph that ultimately materialized. In doing so, he referred on several occasions to a book he had recently read, *The Guns of August* by historian Barbara Tuchman. Tuchman's work traced the outbreak of World War I in a manner that left the reader with the impression that this war and all its attendant agonies happened largely because of the stupidity, the rigidity, and the incompetence of the leaders of the European powers. Kennedy told his closest advisers that if World War III were to happen as the result of the impasse between Russia and America over Cuba, he did not want some future Tuchman to lay the responsibility at his door.[12]

The Kennedy administration also credited a book, Michael Harrington's *Poverty in America,* with having provided the initial impetus for what Lyndon Johnson would later call the War on Poverty.

Thus two of the most important decisions made during JFK's brief tenure in office were influenced by writers rather than generals, economists, bankers, labor leaders, or politicians—whose views are customarily sought by Presidents regarding important policy decisions.

In the early days of the Vietnam war, Idaho Senator Frank Church spoke out against the policy of his President and party leader, Lyndon Johnson. One evening at a Washington party, President Johnson collared Church and asked him why he had taken this position. Church replied that he had read an article by newspaper columnist Walter Lippman that convinced him that the President's Vietnam policy was a mistake. To which the President replied, "The next time you want a dam built in Idaho, ask Walter Lippman for it." [13] It was Lyndon Johnson's way of reminding the Senator

---

[12] Robert F. Kennedy, *Thirteen Days* (New York: Norton, 1968), p. 40.
[13] For Johnson's relationship with Church, see David Halberstam, *The Best and the Brightest* (New York: Vintage, 1972), pp. 742–743.

that there was a real world occupied by real men with power and a paper world of mere words.

Kennedy would probably have understood that the opposition of Walter Lippman, then the acknowledged dean of American newspaper columnists, was a major obstacle to waging war successfully. Lyndon Johnson, on the other hand, would never have been so indiscreet as to say, "My father told me that all businessmen were sons of bitches, and he was right" (a remark made after an altercation with the United States Steel Corporation). For just as Johnson understood the power of business and sought, with considerable success, to use it to achieve certain personal and political ends, so Kennedy understood the power of the media and sought to use *them* for much the same purposes.

Kennedy cultivated the friendship of the moderately liberal publishers of the *Washington Post* and *Newsweek* magazine, Phillip and Katharine Graham. When JFK took office, the *Post* was simply a good Washington newspaper. *Newsweek* was a poor and distant second to *Time* in the field of weekly news magazines, rumored to be facing imminent sale or suspension. By the end of the decade, the *Post* was a serious rival of the *New York Times* for the role of the nation's most influential newspaper. And *Newsweek* caught *Time* in prestige and advertising. This development was certainly helped by the friendship of Kennedy, Bradlee, and the Grahams.[14]

Another, less direct example of this impact on a major American newspaper was the transformation of the *Los Angeles Times* from a solidly Republican, strongly conservative newspaper to a position much closer to the center of the American political spectrum, which occured about the same time. The *Times*—for decades the all-powerful spokesman for the most conservative elements in California, the richest newspaper in the country, and arbiter of the Republican party in California—suddenly began a series of changes in both personnel and political philosophy. It brought into *Times* management and top editorial positions several people known in the profession as "Kennedy men," such as Robert Donovan, who became the *Times*'s chief writer on national affairs, replacing Robert Hartman, a conservative who later became an adviser to President Ford. The *Times* also entered into a loose editorial agreement with the liberal *Washington Post*—something that would have been impossible a few years earlier —whereby the two newspapers traded certain services and had the right to print each other's columnists.

The *New York Times,* although nominally a Democratic newspaper for many decades, met the challenge of the *Post* and the *Los Angeles Times* by moving significantly to the left. The *New York Times* became an early and powerful opponent of the Vietnam war and endorsed four straight Democratic presidential candidates, Kennedy, Johnson, McGovern, and Carter.

---

[14] This is clearly implied in Bradlee.

Nixon and the Media

It was the decision of the *New York Times* editors to publish the *Pentagon Papers* that brought open confrontation between the Nixon administration and the press. The Nixon–Agnew administration felt that its ability to govern the nation and successfully prosecute a war was being frustrated by what the Vice President called "the nittering nabobs of negativism." For their part, many prominent figures in the press felt threatened by the government. (Thus the managing editor of the *New York Times* publicly announced that he expected to go to prison for his decision to publish the *Pentagon Papers* if Nixon and Agnew were reelected in 1972.) As President, Nixon believed that he was entitled to the same respectful treatment that had been afforded President Eisenhower. He seems to have believed that newspapers should naturally be supportive of the government and that their failure to be so was a kind of treachery.

Convinced that the press was an opponent (many of the people on the so-called enemies list were from the media), the President counterattacked by authorizing Vice President Agnew to launch an unprecedented assault upon the nation's press. And one of the revealing comments on the Watergate tapes was President Nixon's promising to "get" the *Washington Post,* to which a still subservient John Dean replied, "What an exciting prospect."

Agnew charged that the press was now dominated by "eastern establishment liberals," and he directed his attack particularly at the highly vulnerable television networks as well as the *New York Times* and the *Washington Post.* Despite the heavy-handed Nixon–Agnew assault on the press, the vast majority of American newspapers that editorialized in favor of a presidential candidate in 1972 supported Mr. Nixon. Moreover, if the press ever had a liberal candidate to support, surely it was the President's 1972 opponent, Senator George McGovern. Yet the major media virtually ignored Watergate during the 1972 campaign and concentrated instead upon McGovern's difficulty in finding a running mate, his proposal to give every American $1,000, and his troubles controlling a young and inexperienced staff. McGovern's problems were publicized to the point where millions of Americans became convinced that he was bumbling fool.

Meanwhile President Nixon was portrayed as bringing peace to the world through personal diplomacy in China and Russia. On the other hand, and at the same time, the unraveling of the Watergate story had begun, however haltingly. It would destroy the Nixon administration.

As chronicled in the book and film *All the President's Men,* the investigation into Watergate was spearheaded by two young police reporters for the *Washington Post,* Bob Woodward and Carl Bernstein, covering a "routine" burglary. What became a journalistic coup was, then, the work of two obscure reporters, not regularly assigned to politics. Why wasn't the story

"Woodstein"—Two young reporters who changed American history.
[Newsweek/Susan T. McElhinney.]

unearthed by one or more of the famous and well-paid reporters assigned
to cover Washington politics? Perhaps the press was intimidated by the
Nixon–Agnew attack; perhaps experienced political correspondents were
leaning over backward to avoid even the appearance of conducting a ven-
detta against the White House. At any rate, the Watergate story remained
muted until the Woodward–Bernstein revelations made this virtually impossible.

The "Woodstein" phenomenon may have opened an entirely new phase
in the history of American print journalism. For many years it has been the
custom of Washington correspondents to maintain a sort of "old-boy" code
regarding the exposure of certain indiscretions by prominent politicians.
But shortly after Watergate, two of the most prominent men in the Congress, Wilbur Mills and Wayne Hays, found their private love affairs
splashed across the nation's front pages. In pre-Watergate days, such
stories would have been ignored or displayed far less prominently. President
Kennedy himself became a kind of post mortem victim of "Watergate
morality" when the press gave prominent attention to the claims of several

women that they had been Kennedy's lovers while he was in the White House. (It is unlikely that "respectable" news media would have printed or broadcast such "news" prior to Watergate.) The Watergate syndrome, and how people and institutions reacted to it, played a strong role in the media's approach to the 1976 campaign. President Ford's pardon of Richard Nixon was a source of continuing press comment, although neither Ford nor Carter alluded to it in the campaign except in response to direct questions. On the other hand, Carter may also have been an indirect victim of post-Watergate fallout. Some professional newsmen have suggested that much of the skepticism that characterized the press's coverage of the Carter campaign may have been because the national press, guilty about having failed to develop the Watergate story in 1972 and feeling that it had been fooled by the Nixon campaign in that year, was particularly diligent in exploiting overy Carter mistake and/or ambiguity. The *Washington Post,* for example, gave Carter a very tepid endorsement that amounted to his being "damned with faint praise."

Television

Television has obviously changed politics, particularly national politics, but no one really knows quite how or in what way. The precise impact of TV coverage upon the presidential campaign of 1976 is not clear, for example. Perhaps the results might not have been very different had there been no television at all.

One thing does seem clear, however, and that is that mistakes on TV tend to prove very damaging indeed. Nixon's apparent loss of the first TV debate to Kennedy in 1960 is usually credited with having turned the campaign in Kennedy's favor. George Gallup has asserted that President Ford's remark about Poland's not being dominated by Russia in the course of the second debate between Ford and Carter was the critical element in giving Carter victory in a very close election.

The free-swinging Democratic Conventions televised in 1968 and 1972 almost certainly contributed to Richard Nixon's victories in those two campaigns. The combat between Governor Rockefeller's forces and those who supported Senator Barry Goldwater in the Republican Convention of 1964, also televised to millions, probably paved the way for the GOP's defeat in that year.

By 1976, the leaders of both parties had learned this lesson well. The Democratic Convention was carefully managed and staged. There was very little public discord. Although the Republican Convention was almost evenly divided between Ford and Reagan forces, both sides were aware of

226

the danger of an all-out party brawl conducted before tens of millions of TV viewers. The most memorable demonstrations were relatively good-natured tributes to the candidates' wives. The need to present an image of party unity on television is one reason major-party candidates have usually been chosen on the first ballot ever since the advent of TV coverage of party conventions. Thus, although television began by covering the national political conventions, now the conventions are largely managed for television.

The American people had six full hours of prime time to judge the relative merits of the presidential and vice-presidential candidates' responses to newsmen's questions in 1976. The general consensus was that the TV debates were "dull." What was wanted was a sharper confrontation, which might have made for more interesting viewing. The candidates, aware that a single serious mistake could prove fatal, were not disposed to accommodate this desire. They did, however, present a fairly clear and coherent account of their respective views on economic policy, on "social issues" such as abortion and amnesty, and on the problems posed by pollution of the environment and in their respective conceptions of the role of the President in managing the nation's affairs. For the careful viewer, and listener, their differences would appear to have been sufficiently substantial to offer a reasoned basis for making a choice.

The debate between vice-presidential candidates Walter Mondale and Robert Dole was generally described by the media as more satisfactory, because the conflict between Mondale, a classic and soft-spoken liberal, and Dole, a rather salty-tongued and traditional conservative, seemed clearer. The failure of the debates to generate a great deal of public discussion and enthusiasm tell us more about the media and the public than it does about the candidates. Those who viewed the campaign as a kind of political Superbowl were inevitably disappointed.

Postelection surveys indicated that about 70 million Americans watched one or more of the debates in full. These same surveys indicated that the public generally found the debates useful in helping them to make up their minds about how to vote. The most persistent criticism of the debates among the general public was a desire to see more face-to-face confrontation of the candidates and less time given to the reporters.

Although still a relatively new and dimly understood force in politics, television has amply demonstrated its power to shape events. The first dramatic evidence of this came in the 1950s with the live broadcast of Senate hearings into charges that Senator Joseph McCarthy had been exerting pressure on the U.S. Army on behalf of a young staff assistant who had been drafted. McCarthy responded to these charges with his now familiar allegation that high-ranking army officials were coddling Communists. A fascinated public watched what became a mortal struggle. By the end of the hearings six weeks later, McCarthy's power to rally support from the people and hence to intimidate important public officials, had been broken. In a sense, the press created McCarthy. Television destroyed him.

Another highlight of television's impact upon politics came with the first Nixon–Kennedy debate in 1960. Nixon had been favored to win the election, but his poor performance in this debate is generally credited with having turned the tide in Kennedy's favor.

In the spring and summer of 1973 the nation watched a Senate select committee, led by Senator Sam Ervin, investigate a range of presidential abuses generally grouped together under the heading of Watergate. Support for President Nixon, which was substantial at the beginning of the hearings, seemed to erode with each day of the investigation. Television had, in effect, prepared the nation for Nixon's resignation.

In January 1977 a televised version of Alex Haley's book, *Roots,* absorbed the nation's attention for a total of eight evenings and twelve hours. Although it is too soon to judge the political consequences of this event, many, including author Haley, have expressed the belief that the television program "Roots" may prove as important to race relations in America in this century as the novel *Uncle Tom's Cabin* was in the nineteenth century. That is, it might represent a turning point in history.

Finally, in May 1977, former President Nixon chose to submit to a series of interviews with David Frost about his conduct while in office. The interviews were broadcast, through syndication, world-wide, although all three of the major television networks declined to air them. For the first time, Nixon admitted wrongdoing, although not legal culpability. "I let down my friends. I let down the country. I let down our system of government, and the dreams of all those young people that ought to get into government but think it's too corrupt," Nixon told Frost. It was a unique finale to the career of a man whose political life had often turned on a whole series of dramatic encounters on television, beginning with his celebrated "Checkers speech" in 1952.

Few serious students of politics, and even fewer politicians, doubt the power of television not only to portray but also to shape events. But that power can be used negatively as well as positively. An example of how the voters can be manipulated by sophisticated exploitation of television's inherent tendency to focus on image rather than substance is detailed by Joe McGinniss in *The Selling of the President, 1968.* McGinniss describes a strategy to sell a "New Nixon" (the old one had been somewhat tarnished by his defeat in the presidential campaign of 1960 and a subsequent loss to Governor Pat Brown of California in 1962). The essence of this strategy was outlined in a memo circulated among Nixon's close advisors, authored by Raymond K. Price, who subsequently became a presidential speechwriter.

> The natural use of reason is to support prejudice. [The Nixon campaign should focus on a] gut reaction . . . unarticulated, non-analytical . . . it's not what's there that counts, it's what's projected . . . voters are basically lazy, basically uninterested in making an effort to understand.

Hence, Price argued, the Nixon campaign should concentrate on an emotional appeal, "saturation with film" that "can be *edited*" (italic's ours). Price concluded, "So let's not be afraid of television gimmicks . . . get the voters to like the guy and the battle's two-thirds won." [15]

In all fairness, Nixon was certainly not the first or the only presidential candidate to rely largely upon "gimmicks" and "prejudice" or to assume that most voters are intellectually lazy. Virtually all nationally prominent politicians strive to create a favorable "image" and seek to use television's power to communicate on a nonverbal level. Thus President Carter has been reported to have instructed his speech writers to try to limit the words used in his speeches to the vocabulary of a ninth grader.

As Niccolo Machiavelli said long ago in *The Prince,* "Everyone has eyes to see but few are capable of understanding." Or as Marshall McLuhan has more recently noted, the rule in television is "Describe the scratch but not the itch." That is, tell what happened, but not *why* it happened.[16]

As sources of information about politics have changed, so the mass of voters have changed. A candidate such as George Wallace (before he was crippled by an attempted assassination)—appearing on television with his jaw thrust out, his body poised like the boxer he once was, preparing to give or take a verbal blow, challenging the "hippies" who turned out to heckle him, promising to give the plain man relief from the pointy-headed intellectuals and government bureaucrats—had an instant and obvious appeal. Spiro Agnew had the same sort of appeal. On the other side of the political spectrum, John Kennedy with his lordly, patrician air of disdainful pride and Bobby Kennedy with the image of a bemused saint were equally able to communicate with masses of people on a level that transcended mere logic.

"In countless ways," noted Halberstam, "John Kennedy wrote the book on television and the presidency . . . he and the camera were born for each other. He was [television's] first great superstar; as he made TV bigger, it made him bigger. Everyone using everyone. The President using the media, the media using the President." Lyndon Johnson and Richard Nixon "studied the book carefully," noted Halberstam, but were never able to comprehend its essential message.[17]

---

[15] Joe McGinniss, *The Selling of the President, 1968,* (New York: Trident, 1969), pp. 30–33.

[16] Marshall McLuhan, *Understanding Media* (New York: McGraw-Hill, 1964).

[17] Halberstam, "CBS," pp. 63–64.

229

I AM LOVED.

PEOPLE NEED ME, WORSHIP ME, CAN'T LIVE WITHOUT ME—

GO CRAZY WHEN I DON'T COME ACROSS WITH WHAT THEY WANT.

I SHAPE LIVES. I TEACH: HOW TO SHOOT. WHAT TO BUY.

I DRAIN EMPTINESS FROM LIVES. FILL THE VOID WITH JUNK. PEOPLE ARE GRATEFUL.

I AM THE GIVER OF NEWS. OPINIONS DON'T EXIST WITHOUT ME.

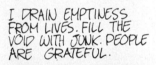

I AM THE INSIDES OF YOUR HEAD.

IF YOU WANTED A GROSS NATIONAL PRODUCT, YOU GOT IT.

That message was simply that the media now had the power to define reality for the American people. Prior to TV, the people necessarily depended upon their leaders to tell them about the world. If FDR described the Japanese attack on Pearl Harbor as a "dastardly, sneak attack," no one but a handful of Asian scholars had any basis for challenging this simplistic view of the culmination of a series of complex historical events and forces.

Lyndon Johnson tried to follow John Kennedy's lead in making confidants and allies of the media. But whereas Kennedy tended to cultivate the friendship of reporters and commentators, Johnson sought intimacy with the high brass. He particularly wooed Frank Stanton, president of CBS. When CBS used a film showing American Marines burning down the thatched huts of Vietnamese villages, Americans were shocked. We had grown up with the notion that American GIs went around the world giving chewing gum to children. Only Nazis burned villages and slaughtered poor peasants. But there were the pictures on television of Americans doing the same thing that the Nazis had done in a hundred World War II movies, complete with crying babies and terrified old women. At two that morning, notes Halberstam, LBJ called CBS President Stanton and subjected him to a classic "chewing out," complete with the kind of vigorous Johnsonian four-letter words that were an integral part of what Washington reporters called "the treatment." [18]

Johnson was learning that the Vietnam war was different from World War II or the Korean War. And that difference was at least partially attributable to the fact that the Vietnam war was on television.

President Nixon's response to unfavorable TV coverage was less direct but even more threatening. Typically he would ask Charles Colson to call top CBS executives and threaten to "bring CBS to its knees on Wall St. and Madison Ave." [19]

It should be noted that most TV executives do not seek or welcome confrontation with Presidents or even with Congress. On the contrary, in most instances they do everything in their power to avoid it. The great television networks are in the entertainment business. They earn hundreds of millions of dollars annually, and their executives a measure of fame and high social status, principally by giving the people a constant diet of innocuous melodrama, game shows, music, and comedy. Their income comes not from the viewers but from advertisers, almost always large, conservative American corporations that prefer not be involved in any sort of controversy that might result in lower sales or unpleasant political flak. Moreover, the networks, unlike the print media, are not specifically

[18] Ibid., p. 72.
[19] Robert Metz, *CBS: Reflections In A Bloodshot Eye* (New York: New American Library, 1975), p. 269.

231

covered by First Amendment guarantees of freedom. On the contrary, they are licensed by the government, and what government gives, government can take away. Also they are subject to all manner of government regulations, so that even a relatively minor policy change by the Federal Communications Commission (appointed by the President) could cost the networks millions of dollars.[20]

For all these reasons the policy of network television toward news has been to regard it as a necessary evil, a dangerous and highly vulnerable threat to a profitable entertainment business. Usually the networks have tried to select as news "anchor men" people, like Walter Cronkite, who project an air of both objectivity *and* authority. The rule is and has been that if the audience can tell whether the anchor man is a Republican or a Democrat, a liberal or a conservative, he is not suitable for the job.

But television is such an inherently powerful medium that despite the frantic efforts of executives not to influence public opinion ("There is always a Vice President in charge of fear," notes Halberstam) particularly on political matters, the slightest half-smile, the lifting of an eyebrow, the choice of a given word or phrase can and does have consequences. Which is to say that television newscasters are human beings, after all, and cannot help but react to the events they describe for the American people, and occasionally some of that reaction slips through the supersensitive eye of the camera. Thus when Walter Cronkite was broadcasting the 1964 Republican Convention in San Francisco, he began unconsciously using the word *erosion* repeatedly in describing the strength of Senator Barry Goldwater's supporters. A note came down from the executives, nervously watching the proceedings and worried about charges that their network was anti-Goldwater, instructing Cronkite to stop using the word *erosion*. Whereupon the exasperated Cronkite wrote a note in reply that simply said, "I quit," and he began to dismantle his earphones and prepared to leave on the spot. The frantic executives prevailed upon Cronkite not to walk off in the middle of the broadcast.[21]

The power of television has transformed American politics and American society. A film such as *Network* satirizes this and, at the same time, raises serious questions about the future of an industry that increasingly dominates the nation's collective vision of itself and of its leaders. Can and should such power continue to be exercised by a small group of private individuals operating on the basis of largely commercial motives?

[20] The FCC-imposed "family hour," requiring programming "suitable for family viewing" during the key prime-time hours of 7 to 9 P.M., has resulted in many major problems for the networks, among others, a multi-million-dollar lawsuit from Norman Lear (producer of "All in the Family" and "Mary Hartman, Mary Hartman").

[21] Halberstam, "CBS," p. 78.

The Fourth Estate: An Assessment

As we have noted, both Presidents Johnson and Nixon tried to manipulate the press, ultimately failed, and attributed many of their problems in office to that failure. President Ford, on the other hand, managed to maintain warm and friendly relations with the media. Part of Ford's success may have been because both the government and the major Washington media were somewhat traumatized by Watergate and were anxious for a cease-fire, if not for a permanent peace. CBS, for example, fired one of its most aggressive reporters, correspondent Daniel Schorr, after he "leaked" certain documents alleging CIA improprieties. Schorr described himself as a victim of "the swing of the pendulum."

Another factor in the relative civility that marked relations between the brief Ford administration and the media was that Gerald Ford happens to be a man not easily disliked, even by those who disagree with his politics. Several times during presidential press conferences reporters arose and, after an introductory reference to some recent Ford gaff, asked the President, in effect, "Do you really think you are smart enough to be President?" Nixon or Johnson would almost certainly have exploded at such a question and, probably, would have sought retribution against the offending reporter. Ford usually replied by smiling and pointing out that, after all, he had graduated in the upper third of his class at Yale Law School and had been elected to lead his party in Congress for many years. It was hard to be hostile to a man who seemed so at peace with himself.

President Carter has clearly studied these matters carefully. He has pledged an open administration and has promised to hold at least two press conferences a month and, thus far, has kept this promise. Indeed when a reporter asked the President if he were not in danger of overexposure, the President replied "attendance at press conferences is not mandatory." Thus, although the press's and particularly television's reaction to Carter has been friendly in the early months of his administration, there remains a certain icy edge to the new President's response, despite the famous smile, which may suggest that the "honeymoon" will not last forever.

If the press has become a de facto "fourth branch of government," should not its powers be defined and regulated by law, as is true of the other three branches? Not everyone agrees that the press should be free to "print the truth and raise hell" as Mark Twain urged. In only about 20 percent of the countries of the world are newspapers and radio and TV stations even marginally free. Third World countries, by and large, do not believe that their countries can be developed while the people are permitted the luxury of a free press. They have even sponsored a United Nations resolution that would make each nation's government "responsible" for what its newspapers print and its radio and TV stations broadcast. This resolution would put the United Nations in the position of officially advocating that the press be controlled by the state. In totalitarian states, of course, the government runs the media. And in those states virtually nothing can be printed or broadcast that runs counter to the wishes of the ruling clique.

Even among those who remain committed to the idea of free expression of opinion there is serious, perhaps growing, criticism of what the media actually do. Among the most common complaints are the following:

Although, particularly in the post-Watergate era, the press does a generally good job of investigative reporting, it remains largely hostile to serious ideas. Television, by its very nature, tends to stress the physical at the expense of mental activity. The printed press, which might do otherwise, is infatuated with headline-making "hard news" and often does a very shabby job of explaining the meaning of that news. Early in the 1976 campaign, Governor Carter told *Playboy* interviewer Robert Scheer, "The traveling press has zero interest in any issue unless it's a matter of making a mistake . . . there's nobody on the back of this plane who would ask an issue question unless he thought he could trick me into some crazy statement." Carter's observation turned out to be an accurate forecast of how the media would handle the 1976 campaign, with their extraordinary emphasis upon the candidates' occasional gaffs rather than the substance of what they were saying, a process that Pulitzer Prize winner Harry Ashmore summed up in the *Los Angeles Times* as "the trivialization of the campaign."

A related problem is the media's preoccupation with the "star system." Certain individuals are deemed by the media to have "star quality" and are elevated to virtual demigods. An example was Secretary of State Kissinger, who was treated as a diplomatic Superman by the media until about the time of the fall of Richard Nixon. Later the press apparently tired of him, as it often does with "stars" who are overexposed, and there was very little that Kissinger could do that seemed to be right. In short, the press too often seems to try to measure the men and women who hold the nation's most awesome responsibilities by the same standards used by groupies in judging rock musicians.

Finally, the most powerful medium, television, remains essentially committed to "entertainment values," even in its handling of news. A recent fad, perhaps still another overresponse to the "bad news" of Vietnam and Watergate, has been the spread of "happy news." Under the happy-news formula, two or three attractive young people try to joke with each other and generally look cheerful while reporting the latest round of famines, murders, and political scandals. It is a formula for reducing the news to what Shakespeare called "a tale told by an idiot, full of sound and fury signifying nothing."

Edward R. Murrow was one of the first to see and effectively use the power of radio, and then of television, to enlighten and inform the American people about the people and events that controlled their lives. He saw television as a means to "alter and illuminate our times." Returning to America after World War II, where his coverage of the European Theater had made him the nation's most famous and respected reporter, Murrow gathered about him at CBS News perhaps the most distinguished group of correspondents in the history of journalism. (Among them were such men as Eric Sevareid, Howard K. Smith, and Charles Collingwood.) Murrow's news broadcasts and even more his weekly public-affairs programs were classics of journalistic clarity and intelligence. But the audience for his public-affairs programs remained small, whereas another Murrow program, which featured the reporter engaged in trivial gossip with celebrities, mostly movie stars, was a popular success.

In 1954, Murrow made broadcasting history when he attacked Senator Joseph McCarthy on CBS. McCarthy received equal time, which he used to imply that Murrow was a Communist. Although Murrow's broadcast is often credited with having marked the beginning of the end for "McCarthyism" in America, it also represented a turning point in his career and in television history. For as the result of this broadcast Murrow had become "controversial," therefore tainted from the standpoint of CBS, and his influence steadily declined until he quit broadcasting to join the Kennedy administration.[22]

No one has succeeded in rivaling Edward R. Murrow's preeminence in news broadcasting. It seems unlikely that anyone ever will. For it appears unlikely that any national network will again permit an individual reporter to speak to the American people so vigorously and forcefully about whatever is on his mind. (The film *Network* turns on this point.)

To be sure, there have been some excellent special news broadcasts from those done by Murrow down to the present. But perhaps too often the bland, noncontroversial aura that characterizes other TV programming influences TV news. A serious but characteristic example of this deficiency took place in 1967, when CBS decided not to broadcast live former Ambassador George F. Kennan's critical views on Vietnam before the Senate Foreign Relations Committee and instead provided viewers with a rerun of the "I Love Lucy" comedy series.[23]

We saw earlier that no American President since Eisenhower has enjoyed a "normal" tenure of office. This, it can be argued, is at least in part because of the growing power of the media. Indeed, some have speculated that effective leadership in any free society has become enormously complicated, if not rendered impossible, by the existence of a free press. Can a

[22] See Alexander Kendrick, *Prime Time* (Boston: Little, Brown, 1969).
[23] Ibid., p. 4.

President govern without lying to the people (even for their own good)? But if he lies, he will almost assuredly be exposed and suffer the ensuing "credibility gap." Is it possible to conduct foreign policy in these thermonuclear years through "open covenants, openly arrived at," as President Wilson urged? Former Secretary of State Kissinger would almost surely say, "Regrettably, no." But the power of the press is such today that diplomatic "secrets" are frequently revealed through "leaks." (President Carter's decision to make public, during a televised press conference in early 1977, his negotiating position on the SALT talks in Moscow between Secretary of State Cyrus Vance and the Soviets appears to have contributed to the failure of those talks.)

Recent history provides two models, neither altogether satisfactory. There is the Truman–Johnson–Nixon model: in all three cases these Presidents aroused withering attacks from the most powerful media of the day and subsequently were either driven from or chose not to remain in office. Then there is the Eisenhower–Kennedy model. In both cases, these Presidents enjoyed widespread support from the press and a highly positive image with the people, but at some sacrifice to truthful reportage.

Perhaps there is a third alternative, which is neither unrelenting combat nor uncritical admiration but instead, to use a term much favored by JFK, a dialogue. Is it possible to arrive at a condition in which it is normal to have, between political leaders and the media, a continuous and critical exchange and review of one another's performance without a lapse into all-out conflict? Perhaps too it is possible for the public to approach the media in much the same way, that is, in a spirit of critical examination. There may be no greater or more important goal for the consumer movement in the United States than that the American people should learn to use the media intelligently and skeptically.[24] For the interested, well-informed, and relatively enlighted reader or viewer, the mass media represent a treasure of information and an opportunity to become aware of his or her government leaders, their policies, and their behavior that is unequaled in human history.

[24] Ralph Nader has suggested that citizens be given the right to air their views on television or in the press.

Economics:
The Prevailing Smell
of Money

Capitalism
•
Socialism
•
The Welfare State
•
Inflation Versus Unemployment
•
Welfare for the Rich or the Poor?
•
Is Less More?

Where Vanderbilt sits, there is the head of the table; teach your son to be rich.

Author Unknown

What is all this growing love of pageantry, this effusive loyalty, this officious rising and uncovering at a wave from a flag or a blast from a brass band? Imperialism? Not a bit of it. Obsequiousness, servility, cupidity roused by the prevailing smell of money.

George Bernard Shaw
Preface to Man and Superman

The English essayist Thomas Carlyle once called economics "the dismal science." Carlyle had been reading a treatise on economics and population growth, published by Thomas Malthus at the very end of the eighteenth century, that undertook to prove with mathematics and logic that efforts to improve the lot of the poor in Europe were doomed to failure.[1] As we have seen, the eighteenth century was generally a time of optimism in both Europe and America, an optimism rooted in the belief that through the use of reason and the relatively new insights and tools created by the natural sciences, it would be possible to create a much more just and bountiful society.

There was a belief that science, the spread of education and knowledge, and the political liberation of the Western world from many ancient forms of tyranny over the minds of men would result in a better, happier, and more productive future. European intellectuals of that era wrote the first dictionaries and encyclopedias, and crusading reformers created hospitals for the sick and penitentiaries for the wayward.[2] In America, men like Franklin concerned themselves not merely with politics and abstract philosophy but also with paving and lighting the streets of American cities, organizing fire departments, inventing better stoves for housewives, and exploring the mysteries of that arcane and powerful but then useless new force called electricity.

[1] Thomas Malthus, "An Essay on the Principle of Population As It Affects the Future Improvement of Society," 1789.
[2] The penitentiary was an eighteenth-century idea. It was conceived as a place where criminals could be made "penitent" for their sins rather than as a place of punishment.

The publication of Malthus's essay did not, of course, bring all such activity to a halt. But it had a sobering effect upon many intellectuals, particularly in Europe. Malthus argued that the universe was arranged in a manner that made the idea of progress simply a short-term delusion. Improving the conditions of life for the masses, he asserted, must inevitably lead to an exploding birth rate. Because human beings increase their numbers geometrically, whereas the earth, the ultimate source of all wealth, is finite, population growth must inevitably outrun economic progress, with the end result that "progress" will sooner or later lead to famine, war, and even greater misery for mankind. The logic of Malthusian economics was that it was better to leave "the poor and wretched of the earth" to their misery than to tamper with "natural law."

Until fairly recently, experience seemed to prove Malthus wrong. The world's population, for example, has grown from approximately 1 billion to about 4 billion in the past century alone. This phenomenal growth has been accompanied, at least in most of the Western world and in such nations as the Soviet Union, China, and Japan, by an improvement in the material standards of life for most people. And the "underdeveloped" world, rather than rejecting economic and demographic growth, has usually tried to follow in the path set by the richer nations.

But in one form or another, the Malthusian argument keeps reemerging. A recent advocate is Paul Ehrlich, author of such influential books as *The Population Bomb* and *The End of Affluence,* whose works prophesied impending famine, dictatorship, and war if drastic and immediate limits were not placed upon population growth. Other eminent and respected scientists have foreseen various ecological catastrophes, such as the end of all life in the oceans of the earth, poisonous smog's forcing the abandonment of whole cities, and destruction of the earth's atmosphere, which protects us from deadly radiation.

Inevitably these arguments have found their way into the political dialogue. Perhaps the most conspicuous advocate of this point of view in American politics has been California's Governor Jerry Brown, who refuses to live in the state's governor's mansion and instead occupies a simple rented apartment; who drives a Plymouth to work instead of the customary Cadillac limousine; and who has won popularity in California by calling for austerity, self-control, and lowered material expectations.

Moreover, during the 1976 presidential campaign Jimmy Carter was given higher ratings than any other candidate on environmental issues by such ecology oriented groups as the Sierra Club and the League of Conservation Voters.[3]

[3] The League of Conservation Voters ranked Jimmy Carter "outstanding," higher than any other presidential candidate of either party. (*Los Angeles Times,* July 8, 1976, p. 3).

In the early 1960s a politician expressing concern for the preservation of the natural environment would probably have been thought eccentric.[4] In the late 1970s, most candidates' standard speeches included at least one passage designed to show some ecological sensitivity, however perfunctory. As has often been the case with economic issues in the past (such as the right of labor unions to organize and the establishment of Social Security), what began as an idea propounded by a few, has gradually penetrated the mainstream of American political thought and has become a major concern to millions of voters.

Before attempting to examine current economic and environmental issues, we will define certain fundamental terms that dominate much of the public debate about economic and environmental policy.

Broadly speaking, there are three economic "systems" that exist among the developed nations of the world in the second half of the twentieth century: capitalism, socialism, and the welfare state. None of these systems is "pure." For example, there is some free enterprise (capitalism) in the Soviet Union, but it is marginal and uncharacteristic of the larger economic system. There are many nominally "socialist" (that is, publicly owned) institutions in the United States, like the army and the navy or the public schools. But most goods and services produced in the United States are produced by private individuals and corporations. Thus we may speak of the USSR as a socialist state and the USA as a capitalist state, although neither is a perfect example of either socialist or capitalist ideals and ideas in this imperfect world.

Capitalism

Capitalism, referred to as "free enterprise" by those who wish to stress its superiority to other, competing economic systems, is often confused with democracy or representative government. There is good historical reason for such confusion because the growth of free political institutions has frequently been associated with free trade. Democratic political institutions and traditions developed in France, in England, and in America side by side with capitalism, and hence it is not surprising that many people regard the two as inseparable. But strictly speaking, the two are not the same thing, because capitalism, like socialism, is primarily an economic system. *Democracy* and *dictatorship,* on the other hand, are political terms. Thus there are avowedly socialist states—Sweden and Norway, for example— that boast a highly developed political democracy, including such demo-

[4] While serving as an aide to the then lieutenant governor of California, one of the authors frequently attempted to introduce environmental and aesthetic issus into the political debate of the early 1960s, with the usual result of being roundly roasted by the press.

240

cratic characteristics as the multiparty system, free speech, a free press, and freedom from arbitrary arrest and imprisonment.

On the other hand, there have been dictatorships, such as Nazi Germany or Fascist Italy or Japan, where the economic system was at least nominally capitalist.

It might be assumed that most Americans, having spent their lives in a capitalist society, would understand the fundamental assumptions of that system. But as the leading capitalists themselves frequently remind us in full-page advertisements in newspapers and magazines, this is not necessarily the case. Capitalism begins with the premise that humans are naturally acquisitive and competitive creatures, fundamentally motivated by self-interest.[5] In seeking to gratify these instincts, people trade with others, hoping thereby to make a profit, that is, a net gain. The result of this trade will be the creation of a market. Because many individuals and companies (which in theory are simply groups of individuals banding together to trade more efficiently) will participate in this market, competing with one another as both buyers and sellers, those who produce the best goods at the cheapest prices will thrive, and the less efficient producers will gradually disappear. Thus the market is effectively governed by an "unseen hand" (the law of supply and demand), which assures survival of the economically fittest.

Freedom in the market place (freedom to buy and/or sell at the best price, terms, and conditions one can wangle) is the heart of capitalist economics. Profit, for the capitalist, is the reward for economic wisdom and efficiency and for having the foresight, the ability, or the luck to produce goods that other people want at a price they are willing to pay. To a capitalist, profit is good and healthy, the prime stimulant to economic activity, and the driving force that makes capitalist economies more productive and creative than their socialist rivals. Profit also provides the wherewithal for future investment to make the business enterprise larger, more productive and efficient, and hence even more profitable.

Proponents of capitalism argue that this system of economics is superior to its rivals because:

1. Capitalism, particularly in the United States, has provided more people with more goods and services (hence a higher standard of living) than any other system.

2. An economic system that honors and rewards private initiative and ownership of goods is conducive to personal freedom, free political institutions, and cultural and artistic freedom.

3. A system based upon the private ownership of property is in keeping with human nature, and hence under it, more people will be happy and

---

[5] Adam Smith's *The Wealth of Nations* is widely regarded as the definitive work of capitalist economic theory. It was published, curiously, in 1776.

productive than under a system that compels men to practice an altruism that in fact can only be imposed bureaucratically and that would rob most people of any incentive to excel.[6]

Critics of capitalism, on the other hand, contend:

1. Capitalism makes it impossible to approach the ideals of justice and equality for all people because those few who possess great wealth will inevitably control the lives of those who do not.

2. The competitive ethic makes it impossible to build a society based upon cooperation and brotherly love. Greed and selfishness dominate capitalist societies.

3. Although in theory capitalism is based upon equal competition, in practice capitalist economies inevitably develop huge corporations that crush their competitors and control the market, manipulating prices and the flow of goods to their own advantage and thus robbing the general public.

4. Free, democratic government in capitalist states is an illusion, just one more variety of the consumer fraud that is normal in capitalist ethics.

Socialism

Although theories and forms of socialist thought have existed for many centuries, the nineteenth-century German philosopher Karl Marx codified the principles of modern socialism and was the creator of communist economics. While a refugee from his native Germany living in London, Marx, a relatively obscure, ailing and impoverished revolutionary, struggled to support himself and his family from sporadic earnings as a writer (including a brief term of employment as a commentator on the American Civil War for the *New York Tribune*) and with loans and gifts from his friend and collaborator, Friedrich Engels. Marx spent much of his time haunting the London libraries, studying not only economics but also history, philosophy, and virtually every other area of human culture. As a result, he created a body of ideas that has had enormous and steadily growing influence on the course of history in the ensuing 125 years. Two of the world's three great powers, China and Russia, today affirm that Marxism is the basis for the political and social organization of their societies. At the present moment, perhaps half of the earth's population lives under governments at least formally committed to Marxist ideology. The triumphant sweep of Marx's ideas, particularly since the Russian Revolution of 1917, has had few parallels in human history. What are the essential Marxist ideas?[7]

[6] Robert L. Heilbroner's *The Worldly Philosophers* (New York: Simon & Schuster, 1961) presents an excellent and highly readable introduction to the usually difficult subject of economic theory.

[7] Although Karl Marx's *Das Kapital* is the definitive work of Marxist economic theory, a shorter, more interesting, and less foreboding insight into Marxism can be

242

1. *Scientific socialism*. Although, as noted earlier, socialist thought was not original with Marx, he was the first to attempt to build a coherent economic system out of socialist idealism. Using an intellectual formula borrowed from the German philosopher Hegel (thesis versus antithesis equals synthesis), Marx proclaimed that he had discovered the key to human history. For just as Newton's laws explained the movements of the planets, as Darwin would explain the course of biological evolution, so Marxists believe they have discovered the principles that scientifically explain the course of human history. Marx rejected the idealism of earlier socialist writers, who essentially staked their hopes on persuading people that cooperation was better than competition, and attempted to prove scientifically that the triumph of Marxist socialism was inevitable. This sense of certainty about the ultimate victory of their cause has helped to imbue Marxists with a sense of revolutionary zeal—comparable perhaps to the zeal of the early Christian martyrs, who were certain that they were destined to go to heaven—that has proved a powerful political weapon.

2. *Economic determinism*. Human history, Marx declared, is controlled not by ideas or ideals or spiritual, religious, or cultural values but by "the prevailing means of production," that is, economics. Man, Marx said, is an economic animal. (In this he basically agreed with capitalist Adam Smith.) That is, before he is a liberal or a conservative, a Catholic, a Protestant, or a Jew, he is a creature who struggles for food, clothing, and shelter. The struggle for the necessities of life precedes, defines, and controls all other human behavior. It is not men's creeds that determine what men do, it is how they earn their livelihood. Thus the key to understanding human history can be found in what people must do to secure wealth, for in the long run, economic interests determine behavior, hence "economic determinism." Consequently, those forces in a society that control the means of production and the distribution of goods (the landed aristocracy in the middle ages, corporation capitalists in the modern Western world) are not only the wealthiest members of society and its upper classes, but they also determine the culture of society and dominate its social and political life to their own advantage.

3. *Class conflict*. Whereas the capitalists see economic struggle being waged by individuals in competition with other individuals, Marx saw people banding together into social classes. Throughout human history, Marx argued, we are presented with a continuing drama: master against slave, lord against serf—and in the capitalist stage of production, owner against worker. Everywhere the picture is essentially the same: a small minority of powerful people who band together into an upper class for the purpose of exploiting a vast and miserable lower class. The property-

gained by a reading of *The Communist Manifesto,* published by Marx and Engels in 1848.

owning class own virtually everything, including the government, which acts as their agent; the propertyless masses own nothing—not even the fruits of their own labor. Because this arrangement is inherently unjust, there is certain to be conflict between the privileged few and the impoverished many. Sometimes this conflict is half-hidden, as in labor–management "negotiations"; sometimes it flares into open combat, as in a strike or a food riot. But it always exists behind the veil of ruling-class propaganda and management's "employee relations."

From the Marxist standpoint, democratic politics is essentially a fraudulent con-game designed to give the workers an illusion of power and to divert attention from their true condition of absolute dependence upon the ruling class. Religion too is "the opiate of the people."

However, despite the efforts of the capitalists to conceal the reality of power from the people, ultimately the workers will cease to be fooled and will rise up in revolution, a revolution that *must* prove victorious because the workers are the immense majority.

4. *The theory of capitalist crisis.* Because all capitalist states are rooted in the exploitation of the majority by the minority, they contain inherent "contradictions." These contradictions must manifest themselves in periodic crises, such as depressions, wars, and civil conflict. With the passage of time, growing injustice and exploitation will result in greater and greater crises until the system itself is facing collapse. At this point, modern Marxists argue, the capitalists will give up trying to fool the workers and will resort to naked force. Thus there will usually be a fascist interlude between the collapse of a capitalist state and the birth of a socialist society.

5. *The greatest good for the greatest number.* Although the Marxists agree with the capitalist that business takes place as the result of a desire for profit, they regard the profit motive as inherently evil rather than as a force for good. To a capitalist, profits imply greater production and investment; hence they are necessary and useful to society. Marx saw profit as inherently unjust, derived through monopolistic robbery of consumers and the exploitation of workers and by "grinding the faces of the poor." The ideal communist state would not allow profits to exist. Goods and services would be produced for the welfare of the whole community. Thus houses would be built because people need shelter, and the question of whether or not people could afford to pay for these houses would be irrelevant. The economic watchword of such a society, Marx proclaimed, would be "From each according to his ability; to each according to his need."

Most Marxists acknowledge that a true communist economy does not yet exist (although China may be approaching the ideal). In the Soviet Union today, for example, profit-making enterprises still exist. Marxists explain this by affirming that before communism is achieved, it is necessary to first pass through a socialist stage of economic development. Under Marxist socialism, the capitalist class is abolished and the state assumes control of the economy, replacing the capitalists. This is supposed to be an interim phase en route to the goal of communism.

6. *The dictatorship of the proletariat.* Marxists foresee that during a period of transition from one economic and social system to another, there will be great confusion and struggle. The old ruling class will seek to re-establish its power (through counterrevolution). Many persons educated under the old bourgeois (business) system will be unable or unwilling to change to the new way of life. Hence during this interval between capitalism and socialism, there will be a need to establish a temporary dictatorship of the proletariat (or working class). Marx was somewhat vague about how this dictatorship would work. His theory was further elaborated by the Russian revolutionary leader, V. I. Lenin. According to Lenin the Communist party, which is the party of the working class and the party that understands scientific socialism, is charged by history with leading the dictatorship of the proletariat. As "the vanguard of the working class," Communists, who may represent only a small minority of the total population, must take the responsibility for directing the state, guiding the transition to true socialism, reeducating the people, and creating the new "socialist man."

Proponents of Marxist socialism believe that their system will prevail because:

1. It is more "scientific" than capitalism, hence destined to win out over a system based upon superstition and ignorance.

2. It will provide a more just and equal way of life.

3. As socialist states, unlike capitalist states, are not engaged in competition for world markets and resources, there will be no reason for international war.

4. Under socialism, human values, such as culture and the arts, will flourish because the artist and the intellectual will no longer be subservient to the wealthy. Art will become, "a weapon of the people."

Critics of Marxism, on the other hand, argue:

1. History has proved Marx wrong. Capitalist states have not destroyed each other but are stronger and more prosperous than ever. The working classes in most Western capitalist societies have not been ground down by the capitalists to steadily deeper misery and deprivation but, on the contrary, have enjoyed rising incomes and more and more benefits (such as private autos, television sets, guaranteed pensions, and health care). In fact, Western Europeans and Americans enjoy a far higher standard of living today than do the people of the Soviet Union, sixty years after the Bolshevik Revolution.

2. The "temporary" dictatorship of the proletariat becomes the permanent dictatorship of the Communist party bureaucracy, which becomes, in effect, a new ruling class. In no Communist country is there any sign that the party dictatorship is preparing to yield control of the state to the

245

people through democratic and free elections, even though all Communist states have constitutions that proclaim this to be their objective.

3. Socialist states are no less warlike and aggressive than their capitalist counterparts. China and Russia are just as apt to go to war as any capitalist countries. And the Soviet Union today is as imperialistic and aggressive as any nineteenth-century colonial power.

4. Marxist states dare not give their people freedom to speak, to write, to criticize the government. They wall in their people, will not allow free emigration, and maintain prison camps and "psychiatric hospitals" where dissenters are persecuted in a fashion that outrages any person with a sense of human decency and dignity. Minorities (such as Jews or Lithuanians in the Soviet Union) who wish to preserve their own cultural identity are persecuted.

5. The materialist interpretation of human history, which is the foundation of Marxism, is simply an inadequate explanation of the whole range and depth of human experience in that it ignores or diminishes the spiritual, psychological, and cultural roots of human beings.

The Welfare State

There is an alternative to capitalism and socialism that has emerged in the twentieth century and characterizes much of Western Europe. It is variously referred to as the "welfare state," "democratic socialism," and "social democracy." In essence, it involves a mixture of what its proponents believe are the most desirable features of both capitalism and socialism. States that embraced democratic socialism—such as Sweden, Norway, Holland, and, to a lesser extent, England, Israel, Italy, France, and Germany—are characterized by democratic political and social life, including respect for most of the freedoms encompassed by the first Ten Amendments to the American Constitution, plus a substantial degree of free enterprise operating side by side with public ownership of many basic industries, such as transportation, oil, the manufacture of automobiles, and coal and steel. A part of this system is the "welfare state," under which the government takes responsibility for managing the economy, and guaranteeing employment, health care, and pension programs for all.

Perhaps the most famed exponent of the welfare state was Lord John Maynard Keynes, like Adam Smith an Englishman, whose book *The General Theory of Employment, Interest and Money* [8] contained many of the fundamental ideas later incorporated into various welfare-state systems. Keynes traveled to Germany after World War I as part of a commission

[8] Keynes wrote to English dramatist George Bernard Shaw upon completion of his manuscript, "I have written a book . . . which will revolutionize the way the world thinks about economic problems." Quoted in Heilbroner, p. 234.

246

of British economic experts to help reorganize the shattered economies of the various nations of Western Europe. He returned home convinced that the victorious allies had made a mistake in seeking to impose a vengeful peace upon the defeated Germans and to give themselves a competitive advantage as the result of their military triumph. His book argued that what the Allies had failed to grasp was that economically Europe was a single community and that Germany was one of its most important members. If the German economy was deliberately weakened, the Allies would also suffer. When the Depression came, many, including U.S. President Franklin D. Roosevelt, were willing to listen to Keynes. Keynes proposed what was then considered a heretical notion for meeting the crisis. Nations should literally seek to spend their way out of poverty (rather than trying to save by cutting back on expenditures as many were doing), if necessary on credit. The Depression, Keynes argued, had been caused by *too much saving,* thereby creating a lack of purchasing power; hence it could be remedied only by a governmental spending spree.[9]

Keynes's ideas were reflected in the general New Deal assault upon the Depression and even more directly in the economic policies adopted by the nations of Scandinavia. World War II drove still another lesson home to many European and American economists. Nazi Germany, mobilizing for war, was able to achieve full employment and a generally rising standard of living for her people (at least until well into the war).[10] There was little or no unemployment or economic deprivation. In the United States too, there was general prosperity during the years of World War II. Why couldn't a nation's economy be as prosperous in peacetime as it was in times of war?

In Western Europe, many states undertook to do just that. They set out to reduce or eliminate poverty and insecurity and to provide a new level of prosperity for their people. To a considerable extent they succeeded. In the United States too, an "affluent society" was created, but here it was based more on the production of goods for private consumption, such as autos and TV sets, plus enormous spending for defense. (One study estimated that "military spending never exceeded 1 percent of the Gross National Product before World War I." By 1970 it was about 10 percent of the total GNP.[11])

By the late 1970s, the welfare state had become the dominant economic system in Western Europe and was playing a steadily larger role in what most regarded as the earth's last bastion of capitalism: the United States. Even President Nixon, a lifelong spokesman for conservative business cor-

[9] Heilbroner, p. 237.
[10] John Kenneth Galbraith, *Money* (Boston: Houghton, 1975), p. 225–226.
[11] Michael Reich and David Fenkelhor, "Capitalism and the Military Industrial Complex: The Obstacles to Conversion," in *Economics: Mainstream Readings and Radical Critiques,* 2nd ed., ed. by David Mermelstein (New York: Random, 1973).

porations in the United States, declared midway in his administration, "I am a Keynesian." [12]

Proponents of democratic socialism pointed out that in states such as the Scandinavian countries and West Germany, productivity levels had risen steadily and the per capita income in most of these nations had about equaled and in some cases exceeded that of the United States. There was, strictly speaking, no dire poverty in these lands anymore, no sprawling slums, no class largely excluded from the economic mainstream and struggling to get sufficient food or pay for decent shelter. Unemployment was minimal, far below that in the United States. There was medical care for all. (And by such standards as the infant mortality rate, *better* medical care than most Americans could get at any price.) All this had been done without purges or the destruction of fundamental property rights, such as the right to own a home or to go into business for oneself. (Indeed the percentage of people, relative to the total population, engaged in their own businesses was higher in most of the Scandinavian states than in the United States.) Finally, it was still possible for some people to get very rich.

But the welfare state had not achieved economic utopia. There were many who found the system oppressive for a variety of reasons. Perhaps the most persistent and serious problem afflicting those states committed to democratic socialism was inflation. For reasons not entirely understood, inflation seemed built into the welfare-state economy. For many years this inflation tended to hold at or below a level of about 5 percent annually, considered by most economists to be troublesome but bearable. In the mid-1970s, however, inflation rates suddenly began to soar throughout the non-Communist world, perhaps touched off by a decline of confidence in the United States dollar, stemming from the Vietnam war debacle, and aggravated by an oil embargo and then a massive boost in oil prices imposed by Arab states as a consequence of the 1973 Arab–Israeli War. Inflation rates in some of the economically weaker welfare states, such as England and Italy, soared to 25 percent and even 30 percent annually, reaching about half that in even the strongest economies. At these rates, inflation threatened to destroy the economic and social gains made by Western Europe in the thirty years since the Marshall Plan helped bring about recovery from World War II. For the first time in the postwar era, unemployment became a serious problem throughout Europe. The weakness of various currencies, including the American dollar (twice devalued during the Nixon era), became a threat to international trade. In 1970, Harry Browne, an amateur United States economist, had written and published a book, *How You Can Profit from the Coming Devaluation*,[13] which

[12] James Tobin and Leonard Ross, "Living with Inflation," *New York Review of Books* (May 6, 1971).
[13] New Rochelle, N.Y.: Arlington, 1970.

advised people to turn their dollars into gold, silver, and Swiss francs and predicted worldwide famine, depression, and economic chaos. Browne suddenly found himself a best-selling author; so many Americans took his advice that the price of gold began a spectacular rise, and Swiss banks were so flooded with depositors that instead of paying interest on savings accounts, they charged depositors for the privilege of having their money held!

However, in the late 1970s, most of Europe and the United States seems to be recovering from the threat of another major depression, inflation rates have moderated,[14] gold prices have dropped, and even the weakest of the welfare states—England and Italy—seem likely to weather the storm with the help of loans from the United States and Germany.

Another major burden of the welfare-state economic system is very high taxes. In return for "cradle-to-grave" security for all, productive citizens of the welfare state usually pay at least half of their income in taxes, and the rich often pay higher percentages. This taxation causes some people, such as the celebrated Swedish film director Ingmar Bergman, to leave their homelands and migrate elsewhere, where "tax loopholes" permit retention of a far higher proportion of earnings.

Finally, an argument often heard in the United States is that life in the welfare states, such as Sweden and Denmark, has become drab, boring, and colorless because the incentive of people to work hard and make more money has been destroyed. President Eisenhower once ventured the opinion that the high suicide rates typical of Scandinavian nations were attributable to the fact that people were unhappy about having too much security. Scandinavians replied that perhaps the real reason they killed themselves more was because they killed each other less than did Americans.

The debate over "big government" and the "bloated bureaucracy" that has been a dominant theme of America's domestic politics ever since the New Deal is, fundamentally, a debate over the merits of Keynesianism as opposed to the traditional concepts of nineteenth-century capitalism. In the late 1970s, this debate bears little relevance to the practical economic problems facing the United States. For if Republican presidents, such as Nixon, were willing to borrow Keynesian ideas from the Democrats, Democratic leaders such as Jerry Brown and Jimmy Carter were borrowing from the Republican rhetoric about the evils of "big government," that is, government that, in accordance with Keynesian principles, undertakes to plan, control, and manipulate the economy. The real question is not whether the government should control the nation's economic activity (under both Democratic and Republican administrations it has done just that for four decades) but rather whose interest and whose welfare the state is serving.

[14] Although, partly due to an exceptionally cold winter and increased energy prices, the inflationary rate for the United States in early 1977 was over 10 percent.

Inflation Versus Unemployment

Although some Americans would cite inflation as America's chief economic problem, others could argue as persuasively that it is unemployment. At the depth of the mid-1970s recession, unemployment exceeded 10 percent of the labor force. Among young people, it was at least twice that high, and among young blacks it was 42 percent. In the middle of the election year of 1976, business made a strong recovery, but unemployment remained at 7.5 percent, almost twice what was considered "acceptable" by economists during the 1960s. Even the improved figure represented an unemployment rate far higher than existed in most industrialized, non-Communist states. (In the Communist world, theoretically at least, there is no such thing as unemployment because all are required to work.)

Apart from the obvious consequences of unemployment—an inability to participate in America's largely consumption-oriented society—there were social consequences as the result of high and prolonged joblessness, particularly for young people. Karl Marx and Adam Smith agreed that work in an industrial society is more than a means to earn money. For most people, work is a principal means of self-identity and self-value. Work is how most of us enter into the life of our times meaningfully. It defines us and our value in the eyes of others. A person who seeks and cannot find gainful employment is likely to experience feelings of rejection and alienation. In the chronically depressed ghettos of the nation's big cities, the absence of work condemns many young people to crime, prostitution, narcotics addiction, and a general sense of hostility to a society that seems not to need or want them.[15]

Even in the more affluent suburbs, the absence of useful work represented a major problem to young people and was perhaps a prime factor where efforts to socialize the young failed.

Whether or not the government should take responsibility for bringing unemployment down to "normal" levels (3–4 percent in the 1960s) became a major issue in the 1976 presidential campaign.

President Carter presented the Ninety-fifth Congress with a modest $31-billion two-year program aimed at reducing unemployment. Many liberal Democrats argued for a less "timid" program.

Conservative Republican orators, although loath to appear to endorse high unemployment rates, opposed direct government intervention in the job market. Republicans generally stressed the dangers of inflation, which, they point out, affects far more people. And inflation might well result from a surge of new government spending, more people earning more money,

---

[15] David Gordon, *Class and the Economics of Crime, Political Economy* (Boston: Allyn, 1972). Gordon argues that crime is often a *rational* choice for the slum dweller.

and a less competitive job market, thereby pressuring employers to raise wages and hence prices.

Again it should be pointed out that the real argument was less a matter of economic philosophy than a question of whose ox was being gored. When large corporations, such as Lockheed Aircraft Company, faced bankruptcy, the Republican administration found no overwhelming philosophical objection to using its power to guarantee loans of hundreds of millions of dollars to keep that corporation afloat. Questions of the possible inflationary impact of such actions, or of creating a bad example for other businesses and hence undermining their incentive to produce more efficiently, were simply not considered relevant. On the other hand, the disastrous effect upon the morale of a black teen-ager that might ensue from a federally created job seriously troubles many conservative economists.

Would the Carter administration succeed in halving the unemployment rate within a few years, or would it follow in the wake of many Great Society programs pushed through Congress by President Lyndon Johnson, which largely failed to achieve their stated goals?

A provocative study that questions the assumption that spending money will result in socially desirable objectives' being met has been made by economists Colin and Rosemary Campbell. The Campbells compared expenditures and tax rates of two New England states, New Hampshire and Vermont. Vermont, they pointed out, was one of the most heavily taxed states in the union, ranking third. New Hampshire was among the most lightly taxed, ranking forty-seventh. The average New Hampshire resident paid $1,340 per year in state and local taxes, the Vermont resident $1,990, or 48 percent more. And yet by virtually any statistical measure, the level of public services in New Hampshire was at least as good as in Vermont. Educational achievement by residents of both states was virtually the same, with New Hampshire pupils actually slightly outscoring their Vermont neighbors. Welfare benefits were likewise virtually indistinguishable. There was little discernible difference in such things as highways. And schoolteachers in lightly taxed New Hampshire were actually paid substantially more than in heavily taxed Vermont. What, then, were the people of Vermont getting for the 48 percent higher state taxes they were paying each year ?[16]

Welfare for the Rich or the Poor?

Closely related to the persistent problem of high unemployment is the matter of welfare. There is perhaps no American institution more widely

[16] The Campbell report, entitled "A Comparative Study of the Fiscal System of New Hampshire and Vermont, 1940–1974" is published by Wheelbrator Foundation Inc., Hampton, N.H. 03842.

and vigorously condemned by political orators, more deeply resented by tens of millions of people, more frequently held up as prima facie evidence of the failures of American government over the past few decades than the welfare system. To say that the present welfare system is unpopular and unsuccessful in America is to exaggerate its achievements. *All* recent candidates for the Presidency, regardless of party, have run for office promising a fundamental overhaul of the various welfare programs. That the nation's welfare program as constituted in 1977 was a failure is one of the few political propositions on which Senator McGovern, Senator Barry Goldwater, President Gerald Ford, former Governor Reagan, and President Jimmy Carter would all agree.

The welfare system is unpopular for a number of reasons. Working people resent having to pay taxes to support those who do not work. It is widely believed that self-reliance and economic independence (which to the average person means being self-supporting) are essential to the mental and social health of any individual physically and mentally able to work. Hence welfare often destroys the people it was intended to help. Finally, it is argued that welfare has become a way of life for millions of Americans, many of whom have been on welfare for two or three generations.

Defenders of the welfare system, growing fewer in number and perhaps less confident of their own cause each year, usually retort by pointing out that most of the people on welfare are the aged, the sick, children, and mothers of small children. Even the most severe efforts to "crack down on welfare chiselers" by the most conservative politicians have usually been at best marginally successful, sometimes totally unsuccessful.

Clearly the welfare system does need fundamental reform, and it seems likely that President Carter will attempt to make major changes in both the welfare and the Social Security systems.[17]

Welfare for the poor is widely disparaged, not only because of the economic burden it imposes on the rest of us, but also because it is associated with failure and with ethnic minorities (although, in fact, the majority of America's welfare recipients are white). Perhaps it reminds too many Americans that their society is imperfect and damages the credibility of the myth of all-pervading affluence and opportunity.

Less widely advertised is what many call "welfare for the rich," which enjoys a much more favorable image. For example, a study of the cost of sending a student to two kinds of public institutions for higher education in California in the mid-1960s revealed that the cost to the taxpayers per

---

[17] In May 1977, President Carter proposed to scrap entirely the welfare system by abolishing three assistance programs—food stamps, Supplemental Security Income, and Aid to Families with Dependent Children—and substitute a guaranteed annual income for those unable to work or earn an adequate income.

student was about $5,000 at a branch of the University of California and $1,000 per student at a typical California community college.[18]

Similar studies have demonstrated that the average student at the state university tends to come from a relatively prosperous, upper-middle-class family, whereas the typical community-college student is more likely to be from a working-class family.

Translated from statistics, this means that a student who lives in plush Westwood, Bel Air, or Beverly Hills, California and attends the nearby campus of UCLA is costing the taxpayers five times more than a student who lives in the barrio of East Los Angeles and attends East Los Angeles City College. That example, clearly, constitutes a kind of welfare for the rich. Finally, there are those who simply cannot afford any form of higher education.

Another example of the same kind of subsidy to the affluent can be found at any airport. By and large, the business and professional classes use airports far more than do the unemployed or the hourly-wage earner. But the cost of building and maintaining airports and keeping them safe is shared by all. As a result, there is usually little fuss made about proposals to improve and expand airports (except on environmental grounds). On the other hand, expansion of public transport, such as subways and busses, which serves primarily the less affluent, is almost invariably controversial.

Unquestionably the greatest and most flagrant example of government subsidy to those least in need of charity lies in the tax structure. By now it has become fairly common knowledge that there are hundreds of multi-millionaires and wealthy corporations that pay little or no taxes.[19]

The well-publicized case of President Nixon's paying a smaller percentage of his total income in taxes than do most Americans earning a fraction of his salary spotlighted this problem. The rich manage to pay a far smaller share of their taxes than ordinary working people,[20] simply because they can afford to employ the services of lawyers, accountants, and tax consultants to take advantage of "loopholes" in the law *and because the laws are written in a manner designed to give them these advantages.*

For example, a recent change in the tax laws effectively permits a company engaged in the export business to cut in half the profits they earn from the sale of American products abroad for the purposes of computing their taxes. On the surface this sounds like a reasonable idea, because it would encourage American businessmen to compete more vigorously for foreign markets. But closer examination reveals that only a handful of America's

[18] W. Lee Hansen and Burton A. Weisbord, *Benefits, Costs and Finance of Public Education* (Chicago: U. of Chicago, 1969).

[19] Phillip Stern, "How 381 Super-Rich Americans Managed Not to Pay a Cent in Taxes Last Year," *New York Times Magazine* (April 13, 1969).

[20] Michael Parenti, *Democracy for the Few,* (New York: St. Martin's, 1974), p. 87.

253

Cartoonist Ray Doty gives an impression of how some companies "wash dollars" for the purpose of avoiding taxes. [Copyright © 1976 by Ray Doty.]

three hundred thousand manufacturing enterprises are engaged to any significant degree in the export trade. This handful of companies are mostly very large corporations with assets in excess of $100 million, and the net result of this policy will be "a massive giveaway of taxpayer's money" to a few superrich corporations, with little or no effect upon American exports.[21]

The tax laws are shot through with such loopholes. Almost anything a physician or a businessman does that is remotely related to his business is deductible. The newspapers and magazines he reads, the trip he must make every few months to attend a "convention" or "meeting" in Paris or Las Vegas, the car he drives, the entertaining he "must" do—all are valid deductions. The workingman cannot normally claim any of these as a "business expense." If an executive takes his secretary to an expensive lunch at the best restaurant in town, the taxpayers help pick up the tab. If a worker brings his lunch in a brown bag and eats it in his car, he pays for the privilege himself.

Such laws obviously constitute a kind of indirect welfare that, in aggregate, probably costs the taxpayers far more each year than all forms of direct welfare combined.

Still another form of governmental compassion for those least in need can be found in various "subsidies." Gigantic corporations and immensely wealthy individuals receive checks ranging from hundreds to millions of dollars annually as gifts from a grateful government for *not* growing certain crops on their immense landholdings. One highly publicized example of

[21] John Cuniff, Associated Press business analyst, in a syndicated column, July 22, 1976.

this was a government subsidy of over $200,000 to millionaire film star John Wayne for not raising cattle on his Arizona ranch. Ironically Wayne has been in the forefront of those supporting political candidates, such as California's former Governor Ronald Reagan, who rise to heights of eloquence denouncing "welfare chiselers." (Reagan himself paid no taxes one year while serving as Governor of California, although he too is a millionaire.)

Although the welfare debacle and the tax scandal are not normally perceived as related (liberals usually denounce tax chiselers; conservatives denounce welfare chiselers), the fact is that the development of a coherent, workable, and just economic policy by the government requires attention to both problems. It is not very convincing to argue that the poor must "get off the back of the middle class" in order to make even more room for the very rich.

Is Less More?

Attending the 1976 Democratic National Convention in New York, California's Governor Brown chose to stay in a low-cost hotel instead of the luxurious suites customarily commanded by presidential candidates. One evening the governor spied a rat running around his room. The governor was not bothered by the rat. Rather it made him feel "right at home."

Brown's cozy feelings toward rats perhaps reflect a new style and a new perspective in American politics. Gone is the elegance of Kennedy's Camelot, the "country-gentleman" ambience of Eisenhower's Gettysburg estate, Nixon's pseudo-Spanish palace at San Clemente, California, and Johnson's racing around his ranch in white Cadillac convertibles at one hundred miles per hour. Within the past few years politicians have learned a new word: ecology.

In 1958, John Kenneth Galbraith published *The Affluent Society,*[22] a book whose title became a synonym for America between 1950 and 1968. Galbraith pointed out that the overriding concern of America's economic planners, particularly since FDR, had been to increase the gross national product every year. Bigger was presumed better. As the torrent of goods coming from America's factories had to be purchased if they were to continue to be produced profitably, a system had been created, largely by the manipulation of credit terms, so as to make it possible for more people to buy at "no down" or very little cash down. As a result, Americans were building and buying more and larger cars, houses, and appliances each year. At the same time, he noted, public services, supported by taxes, were being constrained. Hence the anomaly of the American family's going off to enjoy a vacation in a $10,000 air-conditioned mobile home with all the

[22] (Cambridge, Mass: Houghton, 1958).

255

most luxurious amenities, only to fight for a place to park in an over-crowded campground alongside a polluted stream.

Galbraith was among the first to raise the "quality-of-life" issue ("The Gross National Product has gone up, but what of Gross National Plea-sure?"), but other, more radical critics of capitalism and even of the whole idea of industrial civilization soon went far beyond him in their criticism. At the heart of the prevailing American economy, charged writers like Ehrlich and Barry Commoner,[23] was the idea of growth. A capitalist economy, noted Keynes, was like a spinning top: it could accelerate and decelerate, but it could not maintain its equilibrium without a change in velocity. Because the innate tendency of the capitalist was to seek ever greater profits, "pollution," concluded Commoner, "is an unintended con-comitant of the drive to increase productivity." As our economic capital (gross national product) goes up, so our *biological capital* (pure air, clean water, minerals in the land, and so on) is diminished. Thus, despite "ap-parent prosperity," argued Commoner, "the system is being driven into bankruptcy." "Growth," noted Robert Theobald, "while essential to cor-porate profits, may not be compatible with the interests of society." [24]

"You [the United States] could very comfortably have stopped growing after World War I," noted British economist Ezra Mishan. ". . . there was enough technology to make life quite pleasant. Cities weren't overgrown. People weren't too avaricious. You hadn't really ruined the environment as you have now." [25] Surveying the American economy a number of prominent British observers openly questioned the wisdom of England's attempting to follow a similar path. "Affluence creates more problems than it solves. . . . Little England would be a much better place to live than Great Britain," was a frequent response to governmental requests for greater efficiency and productivity.

More traditional economists responded with a vigorous defense of the social and political benefits of economic growth. Economic growth has, to some degree, become the modern psychic equivalent of the frontier in early America. It provides a safety value, particularly for the poor. As the result of affluence, the number of Americans below the poverty level has diminished from one third of the nation in FDR's era to less than one fifth by the mid-1970s, and even these were probably better off in a material sense. (Although some 40 million Americans were still officially classified as very poor.[26]) After allowing for inflation, the bottom 10 percent of the population had increased its income by over 55 percent since 1950.

[23] *The Economic Meaning of Ecology in the Closing Circle* (New York: Knopf, 1972).
[24] *The Challenge of Abundance* (New York: American Library, 1962), p. 111.
[25] See Peter Passell and Leonard Ross, "Don't Knock the $2 Trillion Economy," *New York Times Magazine* (March 5, 1972), pp. 14–15, 64, 68–70.
[26] Citizen's Board of Inquiry, *Hunger, U.S.A.* (Boston: Beacon, 1958).

A tree struggling to survive in an atmosphere polluted by factory smoke symbolizes industrial America as seen by many environmentalists. [Photo by Dean Immenschuh, Upland, Calif.]

"Twenty more years of growth," argue economists Peter Passell and Leonard Ross, "could do for the poor what Congress won't do." [27]

Moreover, the real victims of a "no-growth" policy in the United States

[27] Passell and Ross, p. 70.

257

and other industrialized states would be the underdeveloped peoples, who needed our tractors and technology and food far more than they did the pools of oil and mountains of ore buried in their earth. Because the West needed oil, the people of Kuwait, for example, had been transformed in a single generation from impoverished nomads into the residents of an economic paradise, with free education, free utilities, no taxes, and the highest per capita income in the world. Other underdeveloped nations were not so fortunate, but most depended upon the sale of their raw materials to the West for the wherewithal to meet the most fundamental human needs of their peoples.

Whether as the result of "no-growth" ideology or poor management of the economy or some other factor or all three, the fact was that the United States economy did slow down during the 1970s. The postwar era between 1945 and 1970 produced phenomenal increases in the GNP, but in the current decade, the growth rate has slowed to less than half of what it had been.[28]

In sum, a little- or no-growth economy seemed to contain within it certain social by-products perhaps as undesirable as pollution is to a rapidly growing economy: among these are higher unemployment rates than had traditionally been considered acceptable to America; a lack of social mobility, particularly afflicting the least-educated and least able to compete; an end to the idea of continually expanding and improving economic life-styles. Some argued that it would mean the end of the dream of America as the land of boundless opportunity.

There was still one other factor to consider. While Americans debated about the environmental and social price of economic expansion, other societies were racing ahead. By the mid-1970s, the Scandinavian nations and West Germany had about equaled the per capita income of Americans. The Japanese economy grew at an astonishing 12 per cent annually, and even the French were not very far behind. The American worker could no longer lay undisputed claim to being the best paid in the world. In mid-1975, total average compensation per hour in the United States was $6.22 (including fringe benefits). In Sweden it was $7.12, in Canada $6.20, and in West Germany $6.19. And while the rate of gain (adjusted for inflation) was still climbing rapidly in all of these nations, it had remained virtually static in the United States for several years.[29] Many large foreign corporations were opening factories in the United States at least partially because the cost of wages was less in many cases, particularly in the rural South, than would be the cost of producing the same products at home.

A decade of war in Vietnam, the uncertain and often contradictory economic policies of the last decade, and the growing foreign competition for

[28] Robert Samuelson, *Los Angeles Times* (July 18, 1976), Opinion Page.
[29] *Newsweek,* Business Section (July 12, 1976).

increasingly scarce raw materials and energy sources had combined to reduce the United States economy from a position of clear preeminence in, say, 1965 to something substantially less than that by 1975.[30] These economic statistics translated into practical terms meant that jobs were harder to find, particularly if the job paid well; most Americans were unable to afford to buy a home of their own at prevailing prices; gasoline, electricity, and other sources of energy grew more expensive and scarce rather than cheap and plentiful; the cost of such things as education soared to the point where going to college—which during the 1950s and 1960s was widely thought to be virtually a natural "right" for Americans—was now economically beyond the reach of many young people.

Americans were often told that they faced a hard choice: an end to affluence and the dream of abundance for all or suffering from smog-choked air, polluted water, dirty and crowded cities, and a ravished countryside.

To many it seemed that in the early 1970s we were experiencing the worst of both worlds: economic decline coupled with environmental pollution that seemed to reduce the quality of life steadily.

As if to underscore the economic challenges facing the administration, President Carter had hardly occupied the White House before the nation was engulfed by the coldest winter in American history. An economy still struggling to recover from the recession of 1975–1976 was hit by a loss of jobs because factories were forced to close down by a shortage of fuel. Most of the nation east of the Mississippi River learned the hard way that the warnings of impending shortages of energy could prove all too accurate.

By the spring of 1977 the Carter administration began to move on the energy front. In April, quoting from a freshly completed study of anticipated world energy supplies and demands, the President said that by the mid-1980s demand would far exceed supply, raising the possibility of runaway inflation and economic collapse. He labeled this "the greatest challenge, with the exception of preventing war, our country will face during our lifetime."

These were strong words from an American President. Reporters quickly labeled the President's remarks as his "Doomsday," speech.[31]

The President expressed confidence that the American people would respond by meeting the challenge. But then Lyndon Johnson had never publicly expressed doubt about the outcome of the Vietnam war. Undoubtedly, President Carter faces a long and difficult battle to gain the cooperation of the Congress, large elements of Big Business, and organized labor. And without such cooperation it seems unlikely that the program of calling for substantial and gradually increasing cuts in American use of

[30] John Kenneth Galbraith, *Money*, pp. 274–275.
[31] *Los Angeles Times* (Apr. 19, 1977), p. 1.

energy can succeed. Despite repeated warnings on this subject in the past, the nation's powerful thirst for oil has continued and indeed has increased through the 1970s. A powerful symbol of this is that American auto manufacturers are reporting buyer resistance in their efforts to market small, fuel-efficient automobiles, whereas they are selling the large "gas-guzzlers" at a record-breaking pace. Either the people do not believe the warnings or have decided to live it up now and let tomorrow worry about itself. Like the French aristocracy in the years prior to the French Revolution, some Americans seem to adopt the motto, "After me, the deluge."

If the crisis is indeed as grave as the President said, Carter will need first to convince the American people of that fact and second to find or invent the means to rally their support. In World War II President Franklin D. Roosevelt managed to unite the country behind the war effort (with a notable assist from the Japanese at Pearl Harbor), and the United States accomplished wonderous feats of war production. Carter's task may prove more difficult; he is not trying simply to change the American political and economic system to meet the challenges of depression and war, he seems to be faced with the necessity to change the American character. For many, perhaps even for most, Americans personal mobility *is* freedom and independence. And the symbol of this freedom and independence, and still the foundation of America's largest and most important industry, is the huge American car. When the former Secretary of Defense and former President of General Motors, Charles Wilson, said, "What's good for General Motors is good for the country," he was simply stating what many took as an article of faith. In a certain sense, General Motors was the country.

For Carter to reverse the habits of a nation accustomed to a throw-away economy and a throw-away culture, for him to succeed in making a large, air-conditioned auto a symbol, not of success or of freedom and happiness, but of what De Tocqueville called "a narrow and unenlightened selfishness," will require nothing short of a revolution in American values. Whether or not he succeeds, the effort is likely to provide fascinating drama for the balance of this decade and perhaps for the next as well.

Yet, despite the apparent urgency of the energy crisis, the general tenor of Carter's proposals were hopeful. Essentially, he proposed that Americans conserve existing but diminishing energy sources, particularly oil and natural gas, until alternative sources could be developed. Admitedly this would take some time and cost some money, but according to a Ford Foundation study released in March 1977, the development of geothermal, solar, and fusion (considered safer than fission nuclear power) energy could conceivably provide us with unlimited yet clean sources of energy. This was encouraging to a nation confronting a triple crisis in energy, the environment, and the economy.

It seemed unlikely that America could or would embrace the Malthusian notion that improving the lot of mankind was simply not possible. On the contrary, it would be the test of statesmanship in the decade of the 1980s to find a way to keep the United States economy strong and vital and its people working, while halting or at least reducing the gradual degradation of the earth, water, and air that must determine our destiny.

The issues discussed in this chapter lead us to a fundamental question: Can corporate capitalism, as it has developed in the United States, meet the economic needs and problems of the nation? Can poverty be gradually eliminated and inequality of opportunity and environmental deprivation be brought within tolerable limits? Can we at least maintain a reasonably comfortable standard of living for the mass of Americans while remaining competitive with foreign nations and conflicting economic systems?

A positive answer to these questions will require, at a minimum, legislation to change existing inequities in the tax laws, much lower levels of unemployment, and far greater social, human, and environmental sensitivity on the part of both the political and the economic leaders of the country. Short of this, it seems likely that the United States economy will fulfill the prophecies of Malthus, despite the strength and vigor displayed thus far by the most productive society the world has ever known.

America in the World: Big Brother or Brotherhood?

Nationalism
•
War
•
Foreign Policy and Diplomacy
•
Making Foreign Policy
•
American Diplomacy: Principles, Perceptions,
and Policies
•
From Cold War to Realism
•
Lessons from the Past
•
The Future of American Foreign Policy

War is politics continued by other means.
> *Carl Von Clausewitz*
> *On War*

Justice is as strictly due between neighbor Nations as between neighbor Citizens.
> *Benjamin Franklin*

[Reprinted with permission from *Intellect,* Feb. 1977.]

Nationalism

The fundamental fact of international life is the power of nationalism, which is reflected in the doctrine of the sovereignty of nations. That is, each of the world's nations is a sovereign power, at least in theory, with the almost absolute right to do whatever it pleases. Unlike civil life within the confines of a nation, where the individual's behavior can be and often is guided, and if necessary forcibly restrained by such agencies as the police, the military, the courts, and—perhaps more important than any of these—the tradition of respect for other human beings and the law, there is no comparable international police force, military organization, or court system. Respect for law and the rights of other nation-states is, unhappily, still a relatively weak factor in international affairs, although it may be growing.

An example of international lawlessness occurred in the summer of 1976. The President of Uganda, Idi Amin, apparently cooperated with Palestinian and German revolutionaries in the hijacking of a French plane carrying mostly Israeli tourists. The hijackers demanded the release of imprisoned revolutionaries in exchange for the tourists. The government of Israel had to choose between submitting to the demands of the hijackers—permitting many of its citizens to be killed—and resorting to another, probably illegal act: sending an armed force of commandos into Uganda to kill the hijackers and free their prisoners. The Israelis chose the latter course.

Despite international organizations such as the United Nations, most countries of the world have come to the conclusion that their safety and their continued national existence ultimately depend not upon international law or the United Nations but rather upon their own military, economic, and diplomatic power.

As a consequence, the wonder is not that diplomats so often fail to keep peace among nations but that they frequently succeed.

It would be wrong to create the impression that callous disregard for international law is confined to small, relatively undeveloped nations. The United States government has not hesitated to plot the murder of unfriendly heads of state, like Cuba's Fidel Castro; to conspire for the overthrow of legally elected governments that happen not to suit Washington's taste, such as Chile's Allende regime[1]; and to send troops onto foreign soil in an attempt to control the internal affairs of countries such as Vietnam and the Dominican Republic; even to bomb countries with which we were not at war, such as Cambodia, and then to mislead the American people and the world about what we had done.[2] Most if not all of these actions

---

[1] *Los Angeles Times* (Nov. 21, 1975), Part 1., p. 1.
[2] *Los Angeles Times,* (Aug. 8, 1973), Part 1, p. 6; (Aug. 9, 1973), Part 1, p. 1; (Aug. 10, 1973), Part 1, p. 1.

were probably taken in violation of international law and also may well have been unconstitutional. That is, they were illegal and wrong not only by international standards but by our own law and tradition as well. This fact did not seem to act as an effective deterrent to America's doing whatever it chose to do in the light of what certain government officials determined to be the interests of the United States.

The Soviet Union has likewise not hesitated to use force when international developments occurred that it chose to regard as hostile. Thus when the people of Hungary in 1956 and of Czechoslovakia in 1968 attempted to rid themselves of pro-Soviet regimes, Russian tanks smashed any illusions that may have continued to exist about a socialist state's behaving any less ruthlessly than any other kind of state when it perceives a threat to its vital interests.

Whether one is talking about a capitalist power like the United States, a socialist state like the Soviet Union, or a Third World state like Uganda or Libya or India, when the chips are down many, perhaps most, nations behave with contempt for international law and make a mockery of their signatures to solemn treaties professing a devotion to the peaceful settlement of international disputes. Indeed, if an ordinary citizen of Los Angeles, St. Louis, or Moscow were to act toward his fellow citizens in the way that nations commonly act toward other nations, he would be branded a criminal and locked up.

War

The most effective check on the behavior of nations is not fear of offending international opinion or United Nations sanctions but fear of war. Anytime a regime chooses to "throw the iron dice," it is gambling with its own existence. The most frequent casualties of wars are the governments that initiate them. The next most frequent casualties are the illusions of the people who support their government's decision to resort to force. The Vietnam war offers an example. Both President Johnson and President Nixon can be regarded as indirect victims of the Vietnam war. And for millions of Americans, the war represented a lesson in the limits of American power. World War I brought about the liquidation of the czarist regime in Russia, the Kaiser's government in Germany, and the Austro-Hungarian Empire. It probably finished forever the centuries-old power of monarchs in Europe. World War II brought about a transformation of the social system in Europe, divided a Germany that had been unified for less than a century, helped usher in a Communist regime in China, and destroyed the power of the ruling military class in Japan. Nothing is more likely to bring about a revolution within a nation than war, particularly if one happens to choose the losing side.

266

In addition to political changes, war usually results in social dislocation. Casualties, particularly in modern warfare, are enormous. Whole cities are destroyed. There is often hunger, sometimes famine. All that people have spent a lifetime, even centuries, to construct may be destroyed in a few minutes. Now that at least half a dozen states possess nuclear weapons, every war breaking out anywhere contains the added danger of a local conflict's escalating into a worldwide holocaust that might end man's precarious life on this planet.

Ever since the first atom bombs dropped on Hiroshima in World War II, the existence of nuclear weapons has permanently altered the nature of war and hence of foreign policy. An all-out nuclear war might not be the end of human life on this planet. The experts disagree on this question, and no one will really know the answer until it is too late to worry about who was right and who was wrong. But certainly in view of what we know of the economic, social, and political consequences of the past two world wars, which were fought with conventional weapons, the survivors of such a war would be condemned to living a life that we should be hard put to recognize as human, let alone civilized. Even if the "optimists" are right and we could manage to rebuild civilization in a hundred or a thousand or a million years, it is, to paraphrase Shakespeare, "a consummation devoutly to be missed."

A heightened awareness of the nuclear sword hanging over all our heads was therefore the earliest and clearest characteristic of the Carter administration's foreign policy. In his inaugural address, Carter pledged that he would eliminate the threat of nuclear war. It was and is a mind-boggling promise. If it can be realized, surely Carter's place in history as one of the supreme benefactor's of the human race will be secure.

It is not unusual that few statesmen today speak glowingly of war. This was not always true. As recently as the pre-World War II era in Europe, Italy's Fascist leader Benito Mussolini proclaimed that "war is the health of the state." Adolph Hitler asserted that war "was not forced upon the masses. It was desired by the whole people." Both statements contain important half-truths that have become somewhat obscured in recent years. In a certain sense, war is man's oldest and most honored profession. Most of the men history labels "great"—Caesar, Alexander, Napoleon—were warriors whose "greatness" largely resided in drenching whole continents with blood. Shakespeare, who was not unaware of the terrible human cost of war, nevertheless described many of his heroes as "warlike"; and he meant it as a compliment.

That is, war has been a popular and honored human activity, the ultimate sport of both kings and commoners. One of the great causes of tension in the modern world may be that technology has raised the price of war so high that nations can no longer indulge themselves in periodic bouts of bloodletting with anything like the old relish. One of mankind's favorite activities—the one that fills the pages of our history books, that suffuses the lyrics of national anthems, that thrills the imagination of poets, prophets, and politicians, and that is still the world's number one industry—is in some danger of being priced out of the market.

Foreign Policy and Diplomacy

When diplomacy fails, the military takes over. In war, the military leaders are charged with carrying out the orders of the government; in peace, it is the diplomat who must carry out his government's wishes, often a complex and sometimes contradictory set of short-term goals and long-range objectives. So *diplomacy* is what a nation uses in negotiating with other nations in the international community. It involves diplomats representing nations. A war may break out when countries cannot reach agreements by diplomacy. A *foreign policy* refers to a nation's aims within the international community—such as the containment of Communism, the expansion of trade, and so on. A foreign policy normally is carried out by diplomacy, but it may be pursued through warfare, subversion, or other methods. For example, in the United States in the years since World War II, two of the government's most important foreign policy objectives have been to contain the spread of Communism and to avoid war with the Soviet Union.

If the United States did not fear, or at least wish to avoid, war with the Soviet Union, our foreign policy would be much simpler and easier for the average person to understand: we would simply oppose the Russians everywhere and, when we failed to get our way, use force. If, on the other hand, we were indifferent to the spread of Communism and/or Soviet influence and power, there would be little basis for conflict. As matters stand, our diplomats must walk a careful line, trying not to precipitate World War III on the one hand, while maintaining America's power and prestige relative to that of the Soviets on the other. Thus the American government since World War II has employed a variety of techniques, including limited warfare (Vietnam and Korea), propaganda (via the U.S. Information Agency), economic pressure (the Marshall Plan, the sale of food to Russia), subversion (in Chile and Guatemala), mutual-defense treaties (as NATO and SEATO), and diplomacy (as represented in the Helsinki agreement of 1975)—all with the common objective of checking the growth of Communism while avoiding a major war.

Making Foreign Policy

In the United States, there is a complex bureaucracy responsible for developing foreign policy and conducting diplomacy.[3] This bureaucracy and

[3] See John H. Esterline and Robert B. Black, *Inside Foreign Policy* (Palo Alto, Calif.: Mayfield, 1975).

268

its activities are directed by the President, with varying—but normally limited—input from the Congress. As we have seen in earlier chapters, the Congress declares war, appropriates money, and discusses foreign policy, but the President (or his designated agent) is the only person who can communicate officially for the United States with other nations. As chief diplomat and as Commander in Chief of the Armed Forces, his power in foreign policy is immense.

The oldest agency responsible for conducting our diplomacy is the Department of State, and its head, the Secretary of State, is considered the ranking member of the President's Cabinet. The Secretary is aided by diplomatic and consular establishments throughout the world. Normally there is a single diplomatic mission in the capital of each of the countries recognized by the United States, and there may be several consulates in the same country.

Although the President, with the consent of the Senate, appoints the Secretary of State and subordinate officers down to Assistant Secretaries (there are "Undersecretaries," then Assistant Secretaries who are divided geographically and functionally) and the heads of diplomatic missions (Ambassadors), most other important jobs in the department are held by foreign-service officers, who gain their jobs by passing a difficult civil service exam. Foreign-service officers work up in rank, and are rotated among various posts about every three years.

Since World War II, the State Department has increasingly had to share its role of making and conducting policy with other agencies in the national bureaucracy. In 1947, Congress created the Department of Defense to absorb all the functions of defense and warmaking. The DOD now represents our largest bureaucratic entity, comprising about 40 percent of those working for the federal government and absorbing close to the same proportion of the national budget.

In addition, the Central Intelligence Agency, which coordinates all federal and foreign intelligence activities, has come to be important in policy implementation. Going much further than simply gathering intelligence information, the CIA has been involved in covert activities to overthrow other governments and assassinate foreign leaders. Congressional revelations of these latter activities have led to increased demands for more stringent controls over CIA operations.

The National Security Council coordinates all of these agencies and activities under a Presidential Adviser for National Security. Formed by Congress in 1947, the NSC combines all the elements that go into the making and conducting of foreign and national security policy, pulling together the views of the Department of State, Defense, Treasury, and Commerce, and the CIA and the Joint Chiefs of Staff. Before becoming Secretary of State, Henry Kissinger presided over the NSC as President Nixon's Special Adviser on National Security Affairs. Because the Congress

269

does not confirm appointments to this post, Kissinger was able to conduct a vigorous and at times novel foreign policy outside normal constitutional constraints. Such a development during the Nixon administration underscored the power of the President in making and conducting foreign policy.

American Diplomacy: Principles, Perceptions, and Policies

In 1939, the U.S. Army contained less than two hundred thousand volunteers. America had a defense budget of about $0.5 billion, no military alliances, and no American troops in any foreign country. Today our army numbers over 1 million, we have an enormous air force and navy as well, alliances with over two score nations, military personnel stationed around the world, and an annual defense budget of well over $100 billion.[4] Clearly, in the space of one generation, America's perception of her place in the world has changed considerably. So too has her foreign policy. The traumatic events of World War II were at least partially responsible for these changes.

World War II had brought us into a struggle of great powers for a second time this century but this time under different circumstances. The Axis powers—Germany, Italy, and Japan—were all military dictatorships dedicated to values alien to principles shared by the American people. The events leading up to World War II, climaxing as far as Americans were concerned with the attack on Pearl Harbor, convinced a generation of Americans that the war had been caused by the failure of free and democratic nations to stand firm against the challenge of the dictatorships. Americans denounced "isolationism" as unworkable and resolved never again to be "caught sleeping."

The image of World War II as a struggle between peaceful democracies on the one hand and fanatical dictatorships on the other was marred by one hard fact. The Soviet Union, certainly a dictatorship, was fighting on the side of the Allies. Moreover, the Soviets faced about two thirds of the German army and suffered by far the cruelest casualties of the Allies in the war.

When the war ended, it was clear that the ranks of great powers had been thinned to just two nations, henceforth called "superpowers": the United States and the Soviets. The Russians had the largest and most powerful army in the world. The United States had at least a temporary monopoly on nuclear weaponry plus the world's strongest economy.

President Roosevelt had hoped that the United States and the Soviets could find a means, despite their ideological differences, to work together

---

[4] See Stephen E. Ambrose, *Rise to Globalism* (Baltimore: Penguin, 1971), pp. 11–22.

peacefully. He had proposed the United Nations, which would inevitably be dominated by the United States and Russia, as an instrument for securing world peace and international order. However, FDR died shortly before the collapse of the Axis armies, and his successor, Harry S. Truman, was less committed to United States–Soviet cooperation in the postwar world.

At about the same time, the Soviet dictator, Joseph Stalin, always suspicious of the possibilities of peaceful collaboration with capitalist states, appears to have concluded that postwar Soviet–American cooperation was not going to happen. (Whether or not either Stalin or Truman even *wanted* it to happen is a question historians continue to debate.[5])

Russia, which had suffered 20 million casualties in the war, was understandably determined never to voluntarily allow anti-Soviet regimes in that part of Europe through which she had been attacked twice in one generation. The Soviet regime now had the world's strongest army and decided that it would be prudent not to rely for her future safety on vague American promises of future friendship, particularly as America was now ruled by a man largely unknown to the Soviets. Instead it established in the various Eastern European nations that had been occupied by Russian forces Communist regimes dependent for their survival upon Soviet power and closely following the Soviet model.

The United States saw the establishment of this "buffer zone" as evidence that the democratic and capitalist world, now led by America, was threatened by another form of totalitarianism not very different from the Nazi dictatorship. There were fears that a Communist tide might sweep over Europe.

Moreover, America had emerged from World War II as virtually the only large nation in the world whose homeland had not been devastated by the war. United States leaders foresaw that much of the Western world would inevitably become an economic dependency of American business, with only the spread of Russian-led Communism representing a major threat to American economic hegemony over much of the world.

Thus, for a number of reasons, the United States began to consider the world in *bipolar* terms; that is, other nations were either on our side, and thus dedicated to democracy and some form of capitalism, or on the Russian side, and thus (like the East European countries) puppets of the Soviet Union. There was, then, a two-way struggle between a vaguely defined Americanism and international Communism directed from the Kremlin. And because there was no "hot" shooting war between Moscow and Washington, we described this bipolar tension as a Cold War. When in

---

[5] The debate over the origins of the Cold War has created an explosion of literature. A useful collection of conflicting views is Thomas G. Paterson (Ed.), *The Origins of the Cold War,* 2nd ed. (Lexington, Mass.: Heath, 1974).

1949 China came under the dominance of the Chinese Communist party and Mao Tse-tung, the official United States position was that the new Chinese regime was subservient to Moscow and that the real Chinese government was temporarily residing on the island of Taiwan. In varying degrees, the same sort of "temporary" position was accorded Fidel Castro in Cuba and Ho Chi Minh in Vietnam. For almost twenty-five years after World War II, this *Cold War bipolar* view of the world was shared by virtually all political figures in America and by most of the American people. The only difference between so-called liberals and conservatives was in what to do about this situation. The liberals (normally Democrats) maintained that we should *contain* Communism wherever it was and stop it from spreading to other countries, hoping that it would one day liberalize itself.[6] Thus NATO, formed in 1949, was intended to hold the line in Europe; the Korean War, after some initial confusion, was explained as containing Communism at the thirty-eighth parallel in Korea; and similarly, we desired to "contain" Communism at the seventeenth parallel in Vietnam. The conservatives, led by Eisenhower's Secretary of State John Foster Dulles and Senator Barry Goldwater, among others, talked about ultimate victory over Communism and, in fact, the possibility of "liberating" the slave peoples behind the Iron Curtain.[7]

From Cold War to Realism

There were, of course, many problems with this analysis. For one thing, how was one to classify a revolution in a Third World country against a colonial imperial power? Or a revolution in a poor country for a larger economic share of that country's resources? John Kennedy shared most of the assumptions of the bipolar Cold War view of the world, but he understood the implications of Third World revolutions and so sought a more imaginative solution to the problem, which he called *counterinsurgency*. This involved attempts to win people of a country over to our side (or to the side of nationalist leaders favorable to us) by countering revolutionary forces with their own techniques. Thus he instigated the Green Beret program in Vietnam, where tough antiguerrilla Americans would dress up in green outfits and go out in the jungles and conduct covert activities against Southeast Asian revolutionaries.

But even this did not work, and Kennedy's successor, Lyndon Johnson, was forced to use much more power to thwart the advance of "Commu-

[6] The classic statement of containment was the article by "X," actually State Department member George Kennan, "The Sources of Soviet Conduct," *Foreign Affairs,* 25:566–582 (July 1947).
[7] See Barry Goldwater, *The Conscience of a Conservative* (New York: Hillman, 1960), Chapter 10.

nism" in Southeast Asia. As a result, by 1968, the United States had 525,000 ground forces in South Vietnam, costing the country close to $30 billion a year.[8]

A corollary to the bipolar Cold War view of the world was the *domino theory.* As President Johnson's Secretary of State, Dean Rusk, once said, "Aggression feeds on success." [9] That is, once an aggressor was in the least successful, he would seek ever more satisfaction. So, as President Eisenhower emphasized, if Vietnam "fell" to the Communists, so too, in rapid order, would other "free" nations in Southeast Asia, eventually Australia, and perhaps on and on until most of the world was engulfed.[10]

By the late 1960s, the evident failure of American policy in Vietnam confronted policy makers with a dilemma. If the Cold War bipolar perception of the world was correct, then the other side was about to score an important victory, the line had not been held, and other Communist aggressions would surely soon take place. We had either to anticipate doom or change our perception of the world. We did the latter.

Henry Kissinger, a professor from Harvard, brought to the Nixon administration a different way of looking at the international scene. This view we will call *realism.* It is associated with various academicians, perhaps the most famous (other than Kissinger) being Hans J. Morgenthau.[11] Although there are differences among realists, the essential lines of their thought are the following.

First, aggression on the part of one country against another country (like Germany's invasion of Poland in 1939) is different from a civil war (like Vietnamese Communists fighting other Vietnamese *in* Vietnam).

Second, an international ideology, like Communism, may well not be as important a factor in motivating individuals and governments as we have thought. Indeed, the most important factor in the contemporary world may be *nationalism,* that is, the desire of people to achieve national independence (whether from Western colonial powers or from others) and, if possible, national greatness. Maybe Vietnam was distinct from Moscow, or Peking. In fact, among Communist states themselves, there are great differences in both national aims and ideology. For example, China and Russia, rather than being closely aligned because they are both ostensibly Marxist–Leninist states, actually are more suspicious of and hostile to one another than either is to the United States.

[8] For details see *The Pentagon Papers* (New York: Bantam, 1971).
[9] Dean Rusk, "Guidlines of U.S. Foreign Policy," *Department of State Bulletin* (June 28, 1965), pp. 1032–1034.
[10] *Public Papers of the President . . . Dwight D. Eisenhower, 1954* (Washington, D.C.: G.P.O., 1960), pp. 382–383.
[11] See Hans J. Morgenthau, *In Defense of the National Interest* (New York: Knopf, 1951); *Politics Among Nations* (New York: Praeger, 1967); and *A New Foreign Policy for the U.S.* (New York: Praeger, 1969).

Third, according to realists, a nation should pursue its *interests,* not conduct diplomacy on the basis of ideology. That is, a country should understand its limitations, its own economic and defense needs, and avoid a foreign policy based on "spreading democracy," or "preserving freedom," or "fighting communism." These latter aims are vague and lead to bizarre and occasionally disastrous consequences. How, for example, could the United States legitimately say that it was upholding freedom and democracy by bringing the dictatorship of Portugal into NATO or by fighting on the side of the corrupt government of South Vietnam?

Ironically, Richard Nixon, one of the most implacable and vocal of the early Cold Warriors, became the first President to break with the old bipolar view of the world and, under the influence of Kissinger, proclaim realism as the basis of our foreign policy. An important 1970 speech to Congress by President Nixon marked this transition: "The postwar period in international relations has ended . . . international Communist unity has been shattered . . . by powerful forces of nationalism." From now on "Our objective in the first instance is to support our *interests.*" [12]

When Mr. Nixon followed this speech with diplomatic trips to Russia (to begin negotiations for arms limitations) and China, the American people seemed to respond positively, demonstrating the popularity of the new approach in foreign policy. Particularly in our relations with the Soviet Union, we began to pursue a policy of *detente,* which simply means a thawing of the old Cold War and a vigorous effort to achieve diplomatic understandings wherever possible, rather than to seek success through threats. In the context of detente, the United States left Vietnam and, mainly because of the efforts of Henry Kissinger, launched an intense diplomatic effort to begin solving the Mideast crisis. In each of these instances, we did so without having to invoke the old Cold War bipolar slogans.

In a sense, the ongoing foreign policy debate in the United States is a debate between those who believe that the Cold War view of the world is correct and those who believe that the realist view is correct. In 1976, the most fundamental difference in the Republican party between Ronald Reagan and Gerald Ford was over foreign policy, with Mr. Reagan campaigning basically as a Cold Warrior, whereas Mr. Ford continued to carry on the policies of Henry Kissinger.

Still, there are many challenges in the contemporary world that cannot be addressed by either the Cold Warriors or the realists. For example, what should America's policy be toward Southern Africa? Here there still remain two countries—the Republic of South Africa and Rhodesia—with a minority of whites ruling a vast number of black Africans. (In May 1976,

---

[12] *U.S. Foreign Policy for the 1970's: A New Strategy for Peace,* A Report to the Congress by Richard Nixon, President, Feb. 18, 1970.

Henry Kissinger, the "lone ranger" of international diplomacy, rides into the sunset at the end of his years as Secretary of State. [Sandy Campbell, The Tennessean.]

Secretary of State Kissinger, in Lusaka, Zambia, announced that the United States favored majority rule—that is, black rule—in these countries.)

What should U.S. policy be toward the undeveloped Third and Fourth World nations, which are characterized by economic poverty? (Third World nations are "developing nations" such as most of the countries in Africa. Fourth World nations are those with so many problems—chiefly large-scale hunger—that for them even to begin "developing" seems impossible at the moment. Bangladesh would be an example.)

What should be United States policy toward energy-producing nations, such as the members of the Organization of Petroleum Exporting Countries (OPEC), who, though not economically developed as are Western nations, nevertheless have considerable influence over the flow of indispensable raw materials, especially oil?

Moreover, the emergence of a realist foreign policy has not resulted in the end of some of the more unacceptable techniques used by Cold Warriors. For example, in the early 1970s, the CIA apparently spent large amounts of money to help overthrow the legitimate, constitutional government of Salvadore Allende Gossens in Chile. Allende's government was replaced, following his assassination, by a military dictatorship. Does this represent a pursuance of American "interests"? Where, indeed, do morality and a sense of values fit into foreign policy? "Morality" was one key to

Cold War views of the world because we considered Communism ruthless and immoral. Yet this view led us to drop napalm and antipersonnel weapons on civilians in Vietnam. On the other hand, realists discount as unwise the insistence on morality in foreign policy and emphasize instead "interests." But should not our foreign policy be moral? This is the question Jimmy Carter asked during the 1976 campaign, and he insists that he will restore morality to United States foreign policy.

Thus there remain unanswered questions about the principles, perceptions, and policies of our country's foreign policy. How we got into this situation and where we might go from here can perhaps best be understood from a brief, impressionistic look at our history.

Lessons from the Past

Let us return for a moment to the definition of diplomacy. It means negotiating in the international community in order to get what you want, or at least as much as possible. That is, diplomacy may be the chief means used by nations to implement their foreign policy.

What does a country use to conduct diplomacy? There are three potential tools. First, physical power. That is, you can threaten an adversary until you get your way. If you have superior military power, this may work. In the generation after World War II, Cold Warriors believed that this was the best means to achieve diplomatic goals. John Foster Dulles developed the theory of "massive retaliation," which meant that if problems arose anywhere in the world, we would threaten the Communist enemy with wholesale attack until the problem ceased.[13] Other examples are Kennedy's and Johnson's attempts to impose favorable solutions on Vietnam by using military force.

A second kind of tool is economic power. When the United States emerged as a rich nation in the early twentieth century, she frequently followed a policy called *dollar diplomacy*. President William Howard Taft used to talk about substituting "dollars for bullets." Thus, to maintain America's security in Central America, he sent United States bankers to various countries to control customs collections and national budgets there in order to thwart potential intervention by European powers. He also authorized the organization of a large group of American financiers to loan money to the Chinese government so that it, in turn, could build railroads and other public works and avoid influence from other great powers. In recent years, foreign-aid programs have represented America's attempt to use economic power to further diplomatic ends.

But what if a country docs not have a large, powerful, and threatening

[13] Ambrose, pp. 224–227.

military establishment? Or what if the country is not rich? Like Vietnam? Or the United States in 1776? What tools then can be used? The third kind of tool is wily, wise, and skillful diplomats. That is what the Vietnamese had in Paris in 1972, and that is what the Americans had, also in Paris, in 1776 through 1783.

Let us look at American diplomacy in the first generation following our Revolution, when diplomats were used at least as much as other tools. From 1776 to 1823, the United States had a perception of its role in the world, based on certain principles, and conducted a foreign policy on the basis of those principles and that perception.[14]

To be sure, Ben Franklin, John Adams, John Jay, and later George Washington and John Quincy Adams had differences of opinion, but there were certain essentials in their foreign policy. For example, Americans believed that they could develop a new diplomacy based on the new principles of the eighteenth century. The diplomacy of each of the states of Europe, not unlike that of the realists today, sought to further the interests of that nation, even (sometimes hopefully) at the expense of other nations. On the contrary, Ben Franklin said that nations should conduct diplomacy with other nations in the same spirit as a person should treat a neighbor. Thus did Franklin create the concept of good neighborliness in diplomacy.

Moreover, the Americans believed that their most important asset was a potential, growing market, and so they encouraged trade among nations in contrast to the typically nationalist policies of mercantilism then in vogue. Also, the Americans, who contained a Puritan strain, believed that cunning, adventurous diplomacy was characteristic of a decadent government. John Adams was repulsed by secret maneuverings and espionage and preferred what has been called shirt-sleeve diplomacy, that is, diplomacy that is open and down to earth. Finally, the originators of our diplomacy were, in the best sense, internationalists. Franklin, for example, while in Europe, devised a scheme for international arbitration to replace warfare as a means of settling disputes among nations. He would have liked to establish such an ongoing, almost permanent procedure of arbitration following the wars of the American Revolution.

If we look at a few select items of the period from 1776 to 1823, we can detect the characteristics of this early diplomacy. These items include the "model treaty" of 1776, approved by Congress, influenced by John Adams, and intended to be a guide for our relations with other countries; Thomas Paine's *Common Sense,* which influenced Americans' view of their place in

---

[14] The following few paragraphs are based in part on material in Felix Gilbert, *To the Farewell Address: Ideas of Early American Foreign Policy* (Princeton, N.J.: Princeton U.P., 1961); Gerald Stourzh, *Benjamin Franklin and American Foreign Policy,* 2nd ed. (Chicago: U. of Chicago, 1969); James Truslow Adams, *The Adams Family* (New York: Literary Guild, 1930); Samuel F. Bemis, *John Quincy Adams and the Foundation of American Foreign Policy* (New York: Knopf, 1949).

the world; the two treaties with France in 1778, which created a trade relationship between the two countries and a military alliance (the latter was terminated officially in 1800—we did not join another military alliance until the twentieth century); the Peace Treaty of 1783 ending the Revolutionary War; Washington's Farewell Address of 1796; the Louisiana Purchase of 1803; and finally, the great accomplishments of John Quincy Adams: the convention with Britain in 1818, the Adams–Onis Treaty of 1819, and the Monroe Doctrine of 1823.

Without attempting to explain each of these documents in detail, we can note that they contain certain basic characteristics that define our early diplomacy.

First, with the exception of the French Alliance, the United States acted in diplomacy *unilaterally*—that is, on its own—not in alliance with other nations. Second, in the items listed, the United States pursued a policy of *noninterference* in the internal affairs of other countries and *nonentanglement* in the affairs of other continents, particularly Europe. Third, the United States gave *de facto recognition* to governments—that is we recognized the governments that in fact existed, whether we agreed with their form of government or not. Fourth, we pursued policies of *economic and commercial expansion* with as many portions of the world as possible. Fifth, we sought to solidify our *continental* boundaries, creating an empire to stretch across North America, but an empire (unlike that of Rome or Britain) that contained self-governing republics (states) of equal citizens rather than colonies. Finally, we sought to be an *example* to the world of a proper, republican form of government that other countries, on their own volition, would try to imitate.

In 1846, in violation of some of the principles of the early period, the United States went to war with Mexico, and by the Treaty of Guadalupe Hidalgo in 1848 ending that war, we appropriated half of what had been Mexico. Henceforth, the thrust of American foreign policy would be different. The continent was filled and America was growing more prosperous. Now we would look forward to an isthmian canal and, concomitantly, hegemony in the Caribbean and control of Hawaii. It was fifty years before these implications of 1848 were fulfilled, but as a result of the war with Spain in 1898, the United States eventually got her canal in Panama, gained control of the Caribbean, and annexed Hawaii.[15] Also, however, in contrast to our traditions, we annexed the Philippines, which threw us into the cauldron of East Asian international diplomacy. The world wars in the twentieth century and the subsequent Cold War (as we have seen) sucked America more firmly into world affairs.

We should keep two things in mind about American diplomacy during all

[15] See Charles S. Campbell, *The Transformation of American Foreign Relations* (New York: Harper, 1976).

this history: first, the United States was never in any definable sense "iso-lationist," and secondly, we never avoided being involved in conflicts once they became international in scope. The American Revolution was itself a world war. The War of 1812 was a rump action in the international wars following the French Revolution. A century of relative peace in the world kept America and the world out of sustained warfare, but once war again became worldwide in the twentieth century, America again became involved.

The Future of American Foreign Policy

Thus the crucial question is not whether the United States should be iso-lationist or internationalist. The former is and has always been impossible. The question is what should our international role be? Should we be Cold Warriors or realists? Or something else?

Radical critics of American foreign policy find both Cold Warriorism and realism inadequate. Many of them would argue that America's foreign policy is based not on ideology or vague "national interests" but on ex-panding the markets and the available resources for large United States corporations. We seek the overthrow of governments, like Allende's in Chile, and control of other governments, like those in the Caribbean, in order to protect and expand the interests of American corporate capitalism. Applying a kind of power-elite thesis to international affairs, these critics argue that United States foreign policy is chiefly influenced by and bene-ficial to big business, ignoring the needs of the peoples of other countries as well as those of the majority of Americans. Thus, in order to eliminate American imperialism, according to these critics, it would be necessary first to make fundamental alterations in the economic system within the United States.[16]

But as wholesale revision of the American economy, on the face of it, seems unrealistic, how can America best pursue her interests without aban-doning her sense of morality? That is, is there a foreign-policy alternative to that promoted by Cold Warriors, realists, and radical critics?

One way of answering this question is by investigating once again the principles, perceptions, and policies of the first generation of American diplomacy to see how appropriate they might be for our day.

First, as Ben Franklin might say, we should be good-neighbor inter-nationalists. We could do this in a number of ways. For example, we can seek solutions to international problems, whenever feasible, through inter-national organizations. Our economic policy could be to encourage inter-national trade, and particularly we should be willing and able to provide

[16] See, for example, Gabriel Kolko, *The Roots of American Foreign Policy* (Boston: Beacon Press, 1969); Harry Magdoff, *The Age of Imperialism: The Economics of United States Foreign Policy* (New York: Monthly Review Press, 1969).

exports in food to countries desperately in need of it. Also, we could end unilateral foreign-aid programs (which were designed to create diplomatic allies in the Cold War, not to aid countries) and encourage the substitution of an internationalized aid program. Thus each country would be taxed a small percentage of its gross national product, perhaps on a progressive scale (the richest nations would pay more—this is the case now anyway). The money thus accumulated would be administered by an international organization on the basis of need rather than political alliance.

There are, of course, several formidable barriers to such international cooperation. First and foremost is the perennial problem of nationalism, which, as we have seen, militates against international law and collaboration. Moreover, as long as the world remains divided into two, three, or four blocs, each struggling for increased power and prestige for itself and a diminution of the power and prestige of others, any effective and sensible program of cooperation will be difficult to organize. For example, a recent international conference on women's rights held in Mexico City was reduced to a kind of absurdity when the conference turned into an assault by the representatives of Arab states (where women have few legal rights and in some cases may not even show their faces in public) upon Israel (where women participate actively in virtually every sphere of national life). Heedless to the purpose of their conference, most countries voted not on the question of those for and against women's rights but on whether or not they were pro-Arab or pro-Israeli.

Another serious barrier to international cooperation lies in the differences of the various countries. We are all prisoners of history. The Western states carry with them into conferences the vestigal remains of policies that were frankly racist and colonial. Others carry memories of centuries of exploitation and racial arrogance. The United Nations has grown from 51 member nations in 1945 to 146 today. Most of the states to join the United Nations in the past two decades were former colonies of Western nations. It would be unreasonable to expect delegates from countries that have just emerged from centuries of struggle against foreign domination not to view white faces and hear Anglo-Saxon voices with a certain suspicion. Moreover, the leadership of many of these states is Marxist because Marxist doctrine has often played a strong intellectual role in organizing resistance to colonialism, and the Soviet Union has often contributed at least sympathy and sometimes material aid in the struggle for independence.

Thus we must realize that the nonwhite world, unlike many Western European nations, may not regard the United States as a generous, well-intentioned nation. Some see us simply as the current bosses of the same gang that stole their country centuries ago, enslaved or colonized their people, expoited their resources, and only withdrew when the business of international robbery (imperialism) stopped being a paying proposition.

Moreover, if the developed and underdeveloped nations cannot co-operate to engage in even such an innocent and joyous thing as the Olympic Games (as they could not in 1976), one may well doubt that we could achieve global cooperation on fundamental problems like poverty, lack of food, population control, and holding down the arms race.

But policies of confrontation and war have not solved these problems either and, in some instances, have made them worse. America is a rich and powerful nation, born, after all, out of revolution against a colonial power. We have an obligation to keep trying international cooperation. President Carter's support of the United Nations, at least symbolically, is a step in this direction (he gave his first major foreign policy address before the General Assembly).

There are other elements of that first generation of American diplomacy that may also be worthy of consideration.

Second, we could return to the policy of recognizing countries de facto (those that in fact actually exist) rather than de jure (those that we think should exist). De jure recognition has created enormous problems for the United States. From 1917 to 1933 we did not have an ambassador in Moscow. For a generation we refused to recognize mainland China (though it contained about 20 percent of the world's population) and instead recognized the Chinese on Taiwan; we refused to recognize Ho Chi Minh's government in Vietnam and got bogged down in a disastrous war. In each instance, we may well have been better off to have recognized the real government.

Third, we could return to the earlier policy of noninterference in the internal affairs of other countries. Almost every time we have intervened in the twentieth century we have been unsuccessful and the intervention has been harmful to our interests—in Russia from 1918 to 1920, in China in the late 1940s, in Cuba in 1961 (the Bay of Pigs invasion), and in Vietnam.

Fourth, we should limit considerably, if not end, the international covert activities of espionage agencies. The accumulation of important data is indispensable for framing and conducting a foreign policy, but the surreptitious assassination of foreign leaders and the purposeful internal disruptions of other countries is inexcusable for a country dedicated to law and republican institutions. Franklin, Adams, and Jefferson would be horrified at these kinds of activities.

The United States would have been saved considerable international embarrassment if the CIA, for example, had abided by the U.S. Constitution as interpreted by the Warren Court.

Fifth, we should rely more on diplomacy and less on military blustering to achieve our foreign-policy aims. We have had some recent successes in this regard in the SALT negotiations, the Helsinki agreement, and Middle

East talks. The credibility of the United States as a leader in the international community would be greatly enhanced by our continuing in this direction.

Sixth, we should return to the Founding Fathers' image of our being an example to the world rather than physically trying to create little (or big) American-style democracies around the world. As John Quincy Adams so well knew, if we kept our own house in order, others would be much more likely to follow our example.

Does such a program as that outlined above make sense in the late twentieth century? Only if it can take account of the cultural, economic, and political diversity of nations better than other programs. It must prove more fruitful and less costly than the policies that have dominated the nation's foreign affairs for the past three decades, leading to two unpopular, expensive, and bloody wars and innumerable military and diplomatic confrontations. The United States can and does exercise considerable influence and therefore must accept a large measure of responsibility in world affairs. There are a number of nations in the world (usually called the Western world) who share with the United States a common commitment to personal freedom and respect for fundamental human rights. These are countries whose social system is rooted in the ideas that emerged out of the Renaissance and the Enlightenment. America's aims tend to converge most easily with the aims of these nations.

Other nations have other heritages and different views of the Good Society. China and Russia are examples. Perhaps less well understood is that the developing countries of Africa and Asia come out of quite a different historical experience and tradition, so that efforts of the United States to shape the policies of such nations are likely to prove marginally successful (as in countries like Kenya) at best or totally disastrous (as in Vietnam or Cambodia or Angola) at worst. What we are suggesting is that if, as most Americans now agree, military adventures in the Third World should be avoided, so too should efforts aimed at teaching these nations to live and think like Americans.

In recognition of this approach, United States policy in the early months of the Carter administration began to show two departures from that of the Kissinger era. The United States moved toward a normalization of relationships with Fidel Castro's Cuba and at the same time seemed to strengthen its previously announced support for the black African majorities in those remaining nations in Africa where white men continued to rule largely black nations. (As we have noted, toward the end of his tenure, Kissinger was moving in these areas.)

President Carter's National Security Adviser, former Columbia professor Zbigniew Brzezinski, emphasized that the foundation of American foreign policy would be "trilateralism." That is, the United States, Western Europe, and Japan—nations sharing similar political and social systems

282

and the major consumers and providers of technology—would henceforth work more closely together in an effort to influence global affairs. Implicit in this principle seemed to be an acknowledgment that the world would remain diverse for the foreseeable future, that the United States might well concentrate its overseas efforts among those nations that share its values, and that our influence on other kinds of societies must remain marginal or even negligible. In short, if we can achieve a polite and correct relationship with countries like Cuba, Cambodia, and Libya, this is probably the best that we might reasonably expect.

What, then, becomes of President Carter's heralded "human rights" offensive, the first major foreign policy initiative to bear the stamp of the new administration? The question, like most foreign policy matters, does not admit of an easy answer. Certainly the President's decision to speak out forcefully in favor of human rights is in keeping with the best American tradition. Yet, in the past such pronouncements usually intensified the Cold War. After all, we had ostensibly been upholding the rights of certain Vietnamese during our ill-fated involvement in their country. The Carter policy, at the outset at least, appeared to have strong support from the American people and the Congress. But it touched a sensitive nerve in Moscow and almost certainly played a role in the Soviet Union's decision to let the first serious negotiations between the Carter administration and the Soviets (over arms reduction) lapse into failure. Presumably, Carter meant to apply this policy impartially to friends and trading partners as well as to less friendly states. What then of nations like Iran, a major supplier of oil to the United States and an authoritarian state? Or of Asian nations like the Philippines, or of African states like Zaire?

In fairness to Carter, he did make efforts to apply human rights standards across the board, even to the United States itself. His administration removed travel restrictions on American passports, and, in a dramatic speech before the United Nations in March 1977, the President announced that he would sign a bill repealing the so-called Byrd Amendment and thus bring the United States into compliance with United Nations trade sanctions against minority white-ruled Rhodesia (which he did), and he promised to seek congressional approval of the United Nations covenants on economic, social, and cultural rights, the covenant on civil and political rights, the United Nations genocide convention, and the treaty for the elimination of all forms of racial discrimination.[17] For some critics the United States could hardly pretend to be the world's foremost advocate of human rights while continuing to refuse to participate in these agreements.

But it should be noted that for the President of the United States to speak

---

[17] "Remarks of the President at the United Nations," Office of the White House Press Secretary, March 17, 1977. We should note that Carter's predecessors in the White House supported the genocide and racial discrimination agreements but that the Senate refused to approve them.

President Carter's avowed determination to work for improved human rights in other countries has angered the Russian government. [Editorial cartoon by Paul Conrad. Copyright © 1977, Los Angeles Times. Reprinted with permission.]

out forcefully in behalf of human rights, sending, for example, a personal letter to a prominent Soviet dissident (Andrei Sakharov) as Carter did, is quite a bit different from another citizen's doing the same thing. An American President is not an ordinary citizen. He is a person who commands vast power. When he speaks out firmly in favor of a certain policy or idea he officially represents the nation, and it is reasonable to assume that he will follow his pronouncement with action. Thus the Soviets understandably were rather agitated that the President of the United States was taking an inordinate interest in their domestic problems. What, they must have wondered, is the President going to *do?* And if the answer is "nothing," then why did he raise the issue in the first place?

College professors and people who write books like this one enjoy a certain divine irresponsibility. They can state their opinions, but since they normally have little power to translate these opinions into concrete acts, such as moving troops or imposing trade sanctions, they are permitted a certain latitude. The President of the United States is not in this position.

He cannot presume to lecture others, particularly other sovereign states, unless he is also prepared for certain consequences to ensue from his words.

This leads us back to the more fundamental question. In a world that is, in fact, divided into competing power blocs, a world where each of 146 sovereign states seeks to pursue its own interests and enhance its own position, usually at the expense of others, a world divided by race, religion, history, economics, and ideology, a world where nuclear weapons are a fact, not a futuristic nightmare, what is the best way for the United States to conduct its foreign policy? Shall we be open, moral, and idealistic? Or shall we be pragmatic, secretive, and realistic? Or is it possible to have the best features of both morality and realism?

Although clearly we are committed to human rights, these rights can probably better be promoted if we work to relax international tensions and encourage increased communications between peoples than if we loudly proclaim to the world our own superiority in such matters. The latter is too reminiscent of the worst features of the Cold War.

Like the world outside, America internally is a diverse people—more diverse than virtually any other nation. (We can hardly expect all Americans to act "like Americans.") Although that diversity is a challenge to us domestically, it is our great advantage in world affairs, for as we proceed to fulfill our own promise, so the world can better hope for progress in international relations. We are, Lincoln said, "the last, best hope of the world." That is an audacious assumption unless we understand it in terms of trying to make our own society workable and just. In this way we can be the example our founders wanted us to be. Our historic mission, if there is such a thing, can be understood only in this way. What is needed is a foreign policy that is finite, modest, and consistent with our traditions.

Politics and the
Pursuit of Happiness

Government: The Cause or the Cure?
•
The Individual and Politics
•
Of Politics and Americans

If one really feared democracy, if one really feared the people, one would not waste time discrediting a Democrat against a Republican, a liberal as against a conservative; one would simply discredit them all. . . . One would impute base motives to the politicians and mundane motives to the people. One would teach them to despise themselves . . . to have contempt for the political process [so that] something—anything—look[s] superior to the political motive."

Henry Fairlie
The New Republic,
Nov. 13, 1976

We cannot win good lives for ourselves in peacetime by the same methods we used to win battles in wartime. The problems of peace are altogether more subtle.

Kurt Vonnegut, Jr.
Player Piano

History affirms that no human institution more quickly subverts an established and successful social order and political system than war, particularly an unsuccessful war. Marx notwithstanding, it was war, not communism, that haunted and ultimately destroyed the social order of nineteenth-century Europe.

Two unpopular and unsatisfactory wars and the three decades of tension implicit in the Cold War have left the United States with a cluster of related problems, no one of which, perhaps, is as emotionally charged as was the question of slavery in the nineteenth century, or as socially catastrophic as the Great Depression of the 1930s, or as militarily dangerous as the rise of fascism in that same period, but which together do raise fundamental questions about the continuing viability of American society.

The United States, which only two decades ago could easily command support of the majority of representatives at the United Nations, now finds itself in a position somewhat analogous to the right wing of the Republican party here at home—that is, a minority of a minority. As the leader of a shrinking block of "pro-Western" states, the United States increasingly finds itself awkwardly alone in international affairs. (For example, the United States was the only state to cast a vote opposing the entry of Vietnam into the United Nations in 1976.) An enormous gulf seems to have opened between the aspirations of a majority of mankind and the rhetoric of the

American government. No leading American statesman has thus far even proposed a method whereby that gap might be closed. We must bear in mind that "isolationism" is not always a matter of simply trying to withdraw from the affairs of the world. One can be isolated by too great a dependence upon sheer military and economic power. (Witness Nazi Germany, surely the strongest military power on earth at a certain point in its history, and also the most isolated.)

Domestically, the past three decades have left most Americans more prosperous than ever before, perhaps freer to follow their own paths in daily life, but visibly less certain of their own success as a society. At the core of the domestic crisis has been the decline of America's great cities, plagued by the threat of bankruptcy, crime, corruption, racial conflict, and declining educational achievement. (In 1976, for the first time in our history, the schools of a major American city—Toledo, Ohio—were closed for lack of funding.)

Government: The Cause or the Cure?

Notwithstanding the currently fashionable belief in the inability of government to resolve problems, most of these conditions have come about at least partially as the result of political acts or failure to act and hence can be resolved only through political action.

Our course in Vietnam, for example, was not preordained. We might have chosen from a whole range of possible options, from complete noninvolvement on the one hand to all-out warfare, including use of nuclear weapons, at the other extreme. The course we did choose turned out to be the wrong one in the opinion of most Americans. Instead of spending thirty billions of dollars each year for many years upon that useless struggle, we might have chosen to devote the same funds to eliminating poverty in America, as nations such as Germany have done for themselves, or to creating alternate sources of energy.

Policy options in purely domestic matters, although not as dramatic as matters of war and peace, are still very real and their consequences no less so. Witness the contrast between two communities in Southern California: Orange County and Watts.

Orange County today is a booming area of over 1 million persons, most of them enjoying significantly higher than average incomes, social mobility, and a high level of material abundance. It is difficult to find a single family home in Orange County that sells for less than $50,000 ($90,000 was the *average* price of new homes in 1976). New shopping centers loaded with expensive merchandise sprout like mushrooms to accommodate the needs and wants of a population that grows steadily larger and more prosperous. The *average* level of education is one year of college, and this average is

289

gradually rising as the several colleges and universities that serve Orange County expand to meet the demands of both the young and the adults seeking to upgrade their education and their earning power.

A few minutes' drive from all this lies Watts, an older, largely black community, plagued by the familiar problems of high unemployment, poor housing, crime, and urban decay. No one has built a major shopping center in Watts in years. Indeed, many chain stores have closed their operations there and moved into the more profitable suburbs. Houses are cheap, but loans are difficult to obtain. Many students do not finish high school.

How does one account for the difference between these two American communities? One might argue about the relative importance of such factors as racism, cultural heritage, the "work ethic," and family stability. All, perhaps, have contributed to the disparity. But there is one fact that simply cannot be disputed and that surely accounts for some of the difference. In the past three decades, the United States government has poured tens of billions of dollars into Orange County in the form of lush defense contracts, guarantees for housing loans, and various subsidies, direct and indirect. At the same time, the number of federal dollars going to Watts can only be described as anemic. There are no defense plants in Watts. Until recently, the Federal Housing Administration and the Veterans Administration virtually refused to grant housing loans in the area, thereby encouraging building activity, not in Watts, but in suburbs like Orange County. There have been a few small, highly publicized but largely symbolic efforts by the federal government to provide business loans in Watts—but all of these together would not begin to equal the funds pouring into Orange County's sophisticated and expensive war industries.

The result can be seen in the contrast of living conditions in the two communities. Suppose, for example, that the federal government had decided three decades ago to spend its billions subsidizing soul music instead of missiles and electronics? More realistically, suppose instead of going to the moon we had decided that it was in the highest national interest to make the older sections of our largest cities prosperous and viable. In that case, Watts today might be as prosperous as Orange County is, and Orange County might still be largely rural and "undeveloped."

The point is that the rise of one community, and the decline of another, may be the result of specific decisions made by political and governmental leaders as much as it is the product of "natural" economic and social forces and/or the character of the people. If the people of Orange County are highly motivated and optimistic about their own and their community's future, it is because, on the basis of recent experience, they have little reason to doubt that the federal government will continue to shower them with its largess. If the people of Watts are less motivated and optimistic, it is because experience has taught them to expect little and settle for less.

290

Two views of America. *Top:* **A new suburb in Southern California's booming Orange County.** *Bottom:* **A few miles away, an aging house in Watts.**
[Photos by Dean Immenschuh, Upland, Calif.]

The Watts–Orange County pattern has its counterpart in most large industrial areas of the nation. Everywhere the cities, particularly the older sections of the cities, are being systematically starved and the suburbs are growing. Private capital, anxious to follow the most lucrative markets, has joined the flight to the suburbs, compounding the problems of the cities. At some point, the trend may become irreversible. Some argue that that point has been reached and that the great cities of America simply can no longer be saved.

The human, social, and economic costs of this decline have already been enormous and will doubtless become even greater as the problems grow worse. And the question naturally arises, Can the United States remain a great and strong political and economic power if its cities gradually collapse and disappear? If New York, for example, is ultimately forced into bankruptcy, what will be the effect upon the great New York banks, upon Wall Street? And if they follow the city into collapse, what would the consequences be for the nation? The Western world? No one really knows, because there has never been a great nation without great cities. No one can imagine France without Paris, Italy without Rome, England without London.

Historically the cities have been not only a great marketplace and a reservoir of capital but a repository of talent, a center of culture and communications. The very word (and the idea of) *citizen* means, literally, someone who lives in the city. Like most of the ideas that have propelled humanity upward from barbarism, democracy is a concept born in and nurtured by the urban life.

Thus the decision by a government official or a committee to fund a shiny new electronics plant thirty miles outside the city, because land is cheaper and there are fewer messy human problems, can and does have enormous social consequences—consequences perhaps not envisioned by those who make such decisions on the basis of hard, "objective" data. The Federal Housing Administration, presumably, did not intend to contribute to the destruction of America's cities. But that has been one effect of a policy of denying loans in urban areas.

In his book *The End of Liberalism,* Theodore J. Lowi argues that the crisis of American life "is at bottom a political crisis" stemming from the collapse of "interest group liberalism." [1] Lowi's thesis is that the result of many of the "liberal" programs of the government, such as housing, welfare, and highway building, have often been the opposite of what those who originally sponsored such proposals intended. That is, these programs have tended to make the already prosperous and powerful more so and the poor poorer.

Lowi believes that what he calls "interest group liberalism" [2] has in fact

[1] New York: Norton, 1969.
[2] For a discussion of interest groups see Chapter Eight.

292

already failed. Its programs survive not because anyone believes they are working but because of bureaucratic inertia and the inability of politicians to think of something better to do about the nation's problems.

Even those who may not share Lowi's gloomy assessment of liberalism's failures might be inclined to acknowledge the decline of public support for and patience with the liberal approach to government. The Carter administration may well represent the last opportunity that liberals will have to meet and solve the nation's most urgent problems: achieving peace without the sacrifice of fundamental American interests or principles, restoring health to the economy, reducing unemployment, reversing the decline of the cities, and preserving the environment.

One way that these goals might still be achieved is by reversing the perspective of many governmental programs of the past few decades. Liberals have tended to put their faith (and their resources) in programs—in dollars expended—rather than in people. Conspicuous examples are so-called urban-renewal projects, which frequently turn out to be simply an excuse for large corporations to get federal help in building huge complexes of office buildings and shopping centers while driving the people who once lived there away. An urban-renewal program that begins with people, rather than buildings, might have happier results. The question is not how we can tear down all these depressing old stores and tenements and replace them with shiny new buildings—but how we can help the people of this area solve their problems and live better lives. That is, of course, a far more difficult question, which is perhaps one reason we have tended to avoid it.

The federal government has spent substantial funds on education in recent years. Much of this has gone to pay for "pilot" programs, special equipment, new facilities, and more administrators. Relatively little has gone to improve ordinary classroom instruction. Critics, such as Christopher Jencks, have pointed out that more money has not always meant better education and that efforts to achieve equal opportunity through integrated education have proved disappointing.[3] This assessment has led other critics to support the premise that the government is simply impotent —that it cannot "do good" in the sense of solving our problems in the same way that it helped solve problems in the past.

We would not agree. If political decisions made by finite human beings have created or contributed to such national problems as educational inequality, urban decay, environmental pollution, unemployment, and crime, then surely other decisions made by other human beings can help remedy these problems. In foreign affairs, one has only to look at such matters as the reversal of America's Cold War policy toward mainland China to see

[3] Christopher Jencks and Mary Jo Baine, "The Schools and Equal Opportunity," *Saturday Review of Education* (Sept. 16, 1972).

a concrete instance of how a change in policy can produce, relatively quickly, a much improved relationship between ourselves and another nation. Despite the uncertainty and the ambiguity that are implicit in every political problem, wise political policies can and do produce beneficial results. It is true, as many conservatives argue, that government cannot and should not try to do everything for everyone.[4] There are many areas of personal and social life that are simply none of the government's business. But government can and does influence certain directions and thrusts of our national life and hence of our personal lives as well. The huge federal budget and how it is dispensed will inevitably benefit some people but not others. A subtle change in tax policy may be responsible for redirecting billions of dollars in private capital from, say, housing to manufacturing, or vice-versa. The most financially astute men and women in the nation, those who earn their living buying and selling on the New York Stock Exchange, ceaselessly search out the newest government statistics, examine statements by the President or his close advisers, and monitor the ebb and flow of federal monetary and fiscal policies, seeking to capture the slightest hints as to future trends and policies. They do this because they understand perfectly well that such things will very likely have a decisive impact upon the future of their investments. The average working man or woman will also be affected by such shifts.

The Individual and Politics

On the other hand, Plato and other utopians notwithstanding, there are limits to the power of politicians. It is doubtful if even philosopher–kings or philosopher–presidents could make us happy and good. The Declaration of Independence speaks of the right of individual to *pursue* happiness. Delivery thereof is up to the private person.

This, of course, is a tricky point. Can we all, equally, pursue happiness without getting in one another's way? Too often we expect the government to smooth the way for us, but not our neighbor. *We* should get the tax break or the tax incentive. Others should pay the price, either in getting fewer services or in paying higher taxes.

Still, we expect the government to run efficiently and justly (whatever our idea of justice is) and hopefully to allow all of us to compete. What we must emphasize is that the government, as important as it is, is nothing without us.

It is wise to remember a theme we have earlier touched upon: the concept of government as initially developed in America in the eighteenth

---

[4] See, for example, M. Stanton Evans, *Clear and Present Dangers: A Conservative View of America's Government* (New York: Harcourt, 1975).

century emphasized the rights *and responsibilities* of the individual. Contrary to Hegelian or fascist statism, our form of democracy ostensibly promotes the individual as of the first importance, not the state. Thus a two-way relationship is implied. First, the state is here to promote the good of individuals (to aid us all, we might say, in pursuing happiness); and second, and equally important, we, as individuals, have responsibilities to see to it that the state stays on the track.

The eighteenth-century *philosophes* believed that human beings were rational, that they could weigh evidence and make sensible judgments, that they did not need to be told by abstract and mystical institutions what was right and wrong. Accordingly, enlightened individuals, working together, could further the progress of the society.

This is not such an old-fashioned notion today. Whether we like or dislike Jimmy Carter, we cannot sit back and wait to see if he will save us. That is asking too much of him and, by implication, gives him too much power. We too have responsibilities. Politicians, properly, react to their constituencies. And a constituency of well-informed, sensitive, and broadminded individuals is a better guarantee of what Jefferson meant by a "virtuous" government than the election of a "good" President or a "good" Congressman.

Thus, the "pursuit of happiness" is more complex than it might originally seem, for it involves much more than gaining material well-being. It involves, above all, *participating* in the important activities of one's society.

Of Politics and Americans

Henry Fairlie, an English observer of the American scene, has said that "It is not in an art gallery, not in a church, not on a stock exchange, not even in bed, that man is whole. It is in the ballot box." [5] Fairlie argues that politics is more than an argument about "who gets the cookies." It is also about how human beings interact with one another; about man's capacity to create and preserve civilization; about our age-old, frustrating, and yet indomitable quest for justice; and about human efforts to make meaningful our brief sojourn on this earth. Aristotle stressed that "a state exists for the sake of noble actions." This is a lofty, if not a very modern idea.

Clearly, however, not everyone who participates in the political process —whether as office seeker, activist, student, partisan, or simply sometime voter—is spurred by noble motives. Ambition, fear, and greed are common and powerful political impulses. Many enter actively into the political process because they find it an enjoyable pastime. Although the

[5] *New Republic* (Nov. 13, 1976), p. 12.

stakes are high—money, power, and even life or death—politics is a game that people play, like football, sex, or business. Winning, as we have noted, is terribly important. One of the reasons it is important is that it keeps you in the game. (The Vice Presidency has been described as a "splendid misery," not because the Vice President is denied a handsome salary and other emoluments of high office but because he is usually not permitted to participate fully in the day-to-day struggles of the administration.) Playing well, with verve, commitment, and style, is also important. Presidents who elicited strong emotional support (and dislike) from Americans, such as Franklin D. Roosevelt and John F. Kennedy, loved politics and took pleasure in high office, and they communicated that pleasure to the people. On the other hand, men who have fallen short of achieving the highest office—such as Senator Barry Goldwater and Hubert Humphrey, one a conservative Republican and the other a liberal Democrat—have also won a certain affection and respect for having devoted their lives to fighting hard and well for their respective causes, and both have seemed to enjoy themselves in the process.

One of the common characteristics of the political fanatic and the demagogue is a certain joylessness. Hitler, of course, is the classic example of the neurotic personality who turns to politics out of certain inner compulsions. It is hard to imagine Hitler laughing, particularly at himself. To be sure, tears and disappointments are part of politics. But joy and laughter are also indispensable to a humane politics.

If the ultimate consequences and aims of political action are important, the practice of the art on a day-to-day basis is also interesting. The rise and fall of certain individuals and factions, the making and unmaking of careers, the shifting alliances and changes in public opinion, the struggle to reach an easily bored and distracted people, the occasional success of a bold strategy (the Carter campaign of 1976, for example), or the failure of prudent, careful planning (Nelson Rockefeller's inability to win his party nomination for the Presidency, for example)—all of this is a continuing source of interest, pleasure, and excitement to the political devotee. On one level, it is a kind of soap opera. At times, it achieves the authentic grandeur of high tragedy. Surely the assassinations of the Kennedys or Martin Luther King, Jr. lack only a Sophocles or a Shakespeare to make their stories as timeless and exalted as the death of Caesar or the fall of Oedipus.

Through politics, the American people struggle to survive, to achieve social order and a measure of justice, and to express their values, fears, and aspirations. The successes or failures of 215 million Americans—in business, agriculture, sports, science, the arts, or education—may exist independently of government. Moreover, history, music, art, literature, gossip, myths, and popular culture may tell us a good deal about a given people, past or present. But none of these speaks quite so clearly as does how a people are governed and/or how they govern. Whether or not the United

States is "the world's last, best hope," as Lincoln believed, or a "naked and arbitrary power intent upon enforcing crackpot definitions upon the world," as C. Wright Mills charged, remains arguable. What is not arguable is that this government has had and will continue to have enormous impact on the lives of its own people and on all mankind.

Appendix

Glossary
•
Suggested Readings
•
The Declaration of Independence
•
Constitution of the United States

Glossary

Within definitions, words in italics are also defined in the glossary.

aggression: An attack upon one nation by another.

alienation: A term used in the United States to describe those individuals who have psychologically "dropped out" of the political system. Persons who take no interest in working with others to solve common problems are "alienated."

anchorperson: The central person responsible for coordinating and delivering the flow of news on television. See Chapter 9.

appellate jurisdiction: The authority to try cases on appeal, after they have been tried in a lower court. See Chapter 6.

arbitration: Resolving a dispute between two parties by appointing a third party to act as a judge or arbitrator.

bicameral: Composed of two houses. The U.S. Congress is bicameral. See Chapter 5.

bipolar: A view of the world as essentially divided into two sides, ours and theirs. Also see *Cold War* and Chapter 11.

bureaucracy: The institutions and people, usually within the executive branch, who administer the laws and services of the government. Bureaucrats sometimes acquire great power because they do not come and go, as elected officials tend to do. See Chapter 8.

capitalism: An economic system in which there is private and corporate ownership of the means of producing and distributing goods. See Chapter 10.

charisma: Originally a term employed in Greek drama, the word has been widely used in politics to describe a certain "star quality" that is projected by some leaders, such as the late President Kennedy.

Checker's speech: In 1952, vice-presidential candidate Richard Nixon was faced with the possibility of being dropped from the Republican ticket (headed by Dwight Eisenhower) as a result of the widespread publication of certain financial irregularities. Senator Nixon went on television and delivered an emotional speech, capped by a reference to "my little dog Checkers," that succeeded in turning public opinion in his favor and saving his political career.

civil service: Government employees who obtain their jobs through examination rather than through political appointment. See Chapter 8.

Cold War: The period between the end of World War II and the advent of a new *foreign policy* created by President Richard Nixon and Secretary of State Henry Kissinger in the late 1960s. Relations between the United States and Russia, and between the United States and China, were characterized by political, economic, and diplomatic hostility, often leading to the brink of an outbreak of military hostilities. See Chapter 11.

communism: A social and economic system in which there is an absence of classes and a common ownership of the means of production and distribution. See Chapter 10.

compact: An agreement between consenting parties. Comparable to a contract between individuals, a compact is normally an agreement between states or governing bodies.

consensus: An attempt of conflicting parties and interests to agree on a common course of action. President Lyndon Johnson's supporters believed that he had achieved a national consensus after his great victory in the 1964 election. However, the consensus, if it ever existed, soon collapsed.

conservatism: A point of view favoring political and social policies that preserve the existing order. See Chapter 7.

constitution: A written law describing the organs of *government,* their power, limitations on them, and the relationship between citizens and the government. See Chapter 3.

containment: The U.S. *foreign policy* of not allowing *Communism* to spread. See Chapter 10.

convention: Each of the major political parties holds a national party convention during the summer of every presidential election year. Here the party nominates its presidential and vice-presidential candidates and draws up and approves a platform. Each state is represented at the convention by delegates. The number of delegates is determined by a formula that is based on the population of each state, the number of public officials in that state who are members of the party, and other criteria. Some delegates to the convention are pledged to particular candidates as a consequence of a state presidential *primary* or of a commitment made at a local caucus or state convention. The convention should not be confused with the *Electoral College*, which elects Presidents. See Chapter 7.

counterculture: A term that became popular during the late 1960s. It was used broadly to describe large and sometimes quite different groups of Americans, such as *hippies,* radicals, or various exotic religious cults, who adopted a set of values and a style of life that rejected the established patterns and values of the American middle class.

countervailing force: A source of power that is opposite to and acts as a check upon another source of power. For example, the Congress is often a countervailing force to the Presidency. Labor is a countervailing force to corporations.

culture: The totality of socially transmitted institutions, beliefs, art, and behavior patterns of a community. See Chapter 2.

depression: See *Great Depression.*

detente: A relaxing of tensions between nations. The Nixon–Kissinger policy opened the door to somewhat better relationships between the

United States and the two Communist superpowers, Russia and China. Under the policy, trade between the United States and the Communist powers has expanded, and cultural and other contacts have been increased. Also, efforts have been made to limit the arms race, particularly between the United States and the Soviet Union. See Chapter 11.

devaluation: A reduction in the relative value of one nation's currency in exchange for the currency of other nations. Devaluation lowers the value of a nation's product on the export market and concurrently raises the price of imported goods.

diplomacy: The practice of conducting international relations. See Chapter 11.

dissidents: Those who disagree with the ruling powers.

domino theory: The belief that if Communists took over one country they would shortly take over all adjacent countries. See Chapter 11.

doves: Those favoring a peaceful solution short of military victory in the Vietnam war. See *hawks.*

due process of law: A clear, understandable procedure that must be gone through before a person can be convicted of an offense or a crime. See Chapter 6.

ecology: The study of the relationship between organisms and their environment.

Electoral College: A body of electors chosen every four years by the states and the District of Columbia to elect the President and the Vice President. The framers of the Constitution, unwilling to have the President elected by the people as a whole or by the national legislature, settled on an indirect system. Each state would provide a method to select electors, who would meet in an electoral college and choose the President and the Vice President. The system still exists. Each state is assigned a number of electors equal to its total of U.S. Representatives and Senators. The District of Columbia has three electoral votes. The candidate who receives a majority of electoral votes wins the presidential election. Currently it is the practice that the candidate who wins the most popular votes (not necessarily a majority) within a state receives all that state's electoral votes. Thus it is possible that the candidate receiving the most popular votes nationwide could actually lose the election. On three occasions (in 1824, in 1876, and in 1888), this has happened. It almost happened in 1976. Although Jimmy Carter had a 2-million-vote lead over Gerald Ford in popular votes, the switch of only about 8,000 votes in Ohio and 10,000 in Mississippi would have given the electoral votes of those states—and thus the election—to Ford. President Carter has suggested eliminating the Electoral College and electing the President strictly by popular vote. The Electoral College should not be confused with national party *conventions,* which nominate candidates.

elitism: See *power elite.*

Enlightenment: A period in the eighteenth century in western Europe of intellectual and critical examination of social and political institutions. See Chapter 3.

escalate: In the 1950s and 1960s, a theory emerged from Pentagon war games called *escalation.* The theory held that international conflict, including war, could be held to manageable limits in a nuclear age by a process of gradual diplomatic, economic, or military pressure—like the stakes' being gradually raised by poker players until one party or the other is forced to quit. The theory had its greatest test in the Vietnam war and did not work.

executive: Describing the authority to carry out the law. See Chapter 4.

Existentialism: A philosophy that has come in vogue among some twentieth-century intellectuals and artists. It stresses subjective rather than objective truth and the freedom to create the meaning of one's own life.

fascism: A theory of government developed by Benito Mussolini, dictator of Italy in the 1920s and 1930s, and later adopted by Adolph Hitler in Germany and the ruling military clique in Japan before and during World War II. The fascist state is characterized by totalitarian government, extreme *nationalism, racism,* militarism, and glorification of war and the merger of government and business leadership.

federalism: A dual form of government whereby there are *sovereign* regional governments (such as states) as well as a sovereign national government. See Chapter 3.

filibuster: Unlimited talking during debate in the U.S. Senate. Used to delay the passage of a bill that the majority favors. The House of Representatives does not allow filibustering. See Chapter 5.

foreign policy: A nation's aims and goals in relations with other countries and the international community. See Chapter 11.

Founding Fathers: The writers of the U.S. Constitution and early statesmen. See Chapter 3.

free enterprise: An economic system that has a free market and in which the laws of supply and demand determine prices and levels of production. See Chapter 10.

genocide: The systematic destruction of a people or a race. The classic example is the Nazi government's efforts to impose a "final solution" to "the Jewish question" by wiping out the Jewish people in Europe.

government: The institution or authority that creates and administers public policy.

Great Depression: The period of high unemployment and lack of economic growth that began with the stock-market crash in 1929 and continued into the 1930s.

Great Society: The slogan created by the Johnson administration designed to project an image of boundless achievement.

hawks: Those favoring strong military measures during the Vietnam war. See *doves*.

hierarchy: A system of leadership by which authority passes from the top down to the lower ranks, usually modeled in one form or another on the military.

hippies: A widely used term in the late 1960s and the early 1970s, often used indiscriminately to describe young people who espoused alternate life styles, including long hair, unkempt clothing, heavy use of drugs, and a good deal of rhetoric about "peace" and "love." Most hippies were non-political.

honeymoon period: After a new President takes office, there is traditionally a brief period, lasting from a few weeks to a few months, when both the press and the opposition are expected to refrain from serious criticism and show a spirit of national unity.

ideological: Based on a system of ideas, usually reflecting a coherent philosophy.

impeachment: A charge of malfeasance in office; that is, an accusation of a public official. Only the House of Representatives can bring impeachment charges against a President (by a majority vote). Impeachment does not mean conviction. The President is tried by the Senate, and a two-thirds vote is necessary for conviction and removal from office.

imperialism: Domination of one nation by another, either directly through the use or threat of military force, or indirectly, when economic, political, or diplomatic power are used to manipulate the affairs of a sovereign nation.

implied powers: Authority conceded to the *government* based on the Constitution, although not explicitly stated in the Constitution.

inflation: A rapid rise in prices and hence a lowering of the value of money.

interest group: A group that comes together because of a common goal or interest and that tries to influence *government*. See Chapter 8.

interstate compact: An agreement between or among two or more states to act jointly in some matter of public policy.

judicial review: The power of the courts to determine whether or not a state law or constitutional provision or a federal law is in violation of the U.S. Constitution. Judicial review occurs only if a case is brought into court. The U.S. Supreme Court normally invokes judicial review only if a case is successfully appealed to that court. See Chapter 6.

juridical: Of a legal nature.

left or left-wing: Very *liberal*. See Chapter 7.

legislative: Describing the authority to make law. See Chapter 5.

liberalism: A point of view favoring political and social policies of non-revolutionary change, progress, and reform. See Chapter 7.

limited warfare: A conflict fought for certain specific and limited objectives and with something less than the use of all possible force, such as the Korean War. In contrast, in World War II, for example, the Allies insisted upon the unconditional surrender of enemies and used virtually every weapon available, including the two atomic bombs dropped on Japan.

litigation: Legal action.

lobbyist: A representative of an *interest group* who works in Washington or in a state capital and tries to influence *legislative* and *executive* action to the advantage of the interest group.

Marxism: A theory of history and a program of revolutionary *socialism* derived from the writings of Karl Marx (1818–1883). See Chapter 10.

media: Mass communications, such as magazines, newspapers, radio, TV, film, and books. See Chapter 9.

military–industrial complex: Combination of the U.S. Department of Defense and large corporations that produce weapons under contract from the Defense Department. See Chapter 8.

nationalism: Devotion to the interests of one's nation above other nations. Also, a desire for national independence from foreign political or economic domination. See Chapter 11.

New Frontier: The slogan created by the Kennedy administration to characterize itself and its legislative program. It intended to project an image of courage, action, and exploration of new ideas.

oil-depletion allowance: For many years, oil companies, and others engaged in finding, developing, and marketing natural resources, were allowed a special tax incentive based upon the theory that they were selling a nonrenewable commodity.

original jurisdiction: The authority to try a case for the first time. U.S. district courts have original jurisdiction over cases arising under the Constitution. U.S. courts of appeal have no original jurisdiction. The U.S. Supreme Court has original jurisdiction over a very few specific kinds of cases. See Chapter 6.

pardon: To exempt a person from punishment for an offense or a crime. The President has this authority.

parliamentary system: A governmental system in which the parliament (or representative legislature) is the primary body and the *executive* function is carried out by the leader of the Parliament, who is called the Prime Minister or the Premier. This system is different from a presidential system, in which the *executive* function rests with a President chosen separately from the legislature.

philosophes: Intellectuals during the *Enlightenment*. See Chapter 3.

plea bargaining: Admitting to a crime in exchange for taking a lesser sentence than if one had been convicted in a regular court procedure. See Chapter 6.

pluralism: The idea that public policy is influenced chiefly by *interest groups*. See Chapter 8.

political hack: A person who plods away at a political job, obeys the orders of those above him without question, and rarely or never deviates in his ideas from the prevailing platitudes of his party.

political socialization: See *socialization* and Chapter 8.

politics: An individual's or group's efforts to gain or exert power or influence, as in *government*. See Chapter 7.

power-elite theory: The idea that public policy is chiefly influenced by very powerful persons in large corporations, the military, and the executive branch of government. See Chapter 8.

pragmatism: An approach to life and politics that stresses practical results rather than ideology. Americans are often said to be politically pragmatic and hence nonideological.

primary: A method of nominating, by popular vote, candidates to run for office. Normally Democrats can vote only in Democratic primaries, Republicans only in Republican primaries, and so on. The candidate who wins the primary becomes that party's nominee to run for election. Many states use the primary system to nominate almost all local, state, and national candidates. In 1976 thirty states also held presidential primaries so that voters in those states could, in effect, choose delegates to the national *conventions* who were pledged to their favorite presidential candidate. See Chapter 7.

prior restraint: Generally there are two ways to punish people who insist upon doing things you do not wish done: one is by prior restraint, that is, preventing them from doing the thing in the first place. The second is by punishment after the fact. The U.S. Supreme Court ruled in the *Pentagon Papers* case that the government could not prevent the *New York Times* from publishing excerpts from these documents but might proceed legally against the paper after publication.

propaganda: Material (books, speeches, movies, and so on) intended to instill a particular set of values or beliefs or a certain version of reality in another's mind.

pundits: A popular term used to describe political experts, such as newspaper and television commentators.

racism: The belief that one's race is superior and/or that certain other races are inferior, and social and political practices based on that belief.

realism: A *foreign policy* that emphasizes pursuing national interests as more important than fighting Communism. See Chapter 10.

reapportionment: Rearranging congressional and state legislative districts to accommodate population changes. Normally done every ten years, after the census. See Chapter 5.

rebellion: Usually an unsuccessful attempt at political *revolution.*

recession: A time of higher-than-normal unemployment and a slowdown of economic growth. See Chapter 10.

republic: A nonhereditary government. Frequently considered to be a government with a written *constitution.* See Chapter 3.

revenue sharing: The granting of federal funds to states with no qualifications placed on the grant.

revolution: A sharp and fundamental break with established tradition.

right or right-wing: Very *conservative,* perhaps reactionary, that is, favoring a return to a condition of the past. See Chapter 7.

segregation: The system of separating white and black races that almost always involves placing blacks in an inferior or dependent position. In some American states this system was actually written into the laws. The U.S. Supreme Court and the Congress have declared segregation to be unconstitutional, but the actual practice still survives in many areas of American life.

seniority: In the U.S. Congress, the rule that the person who has the longest continuous service on a congressional committee is the ranking member of that committee. See Chapter 5.

socialism: An economic system in which there is government or group ownership or control of the production and distribution of goods. See Chapter 10.

socialization: The conditioning of a person to behave in a certain way, a way usually considered normal by that person's family, peers, and associates. See Chapter 8.

southern strategy: A strategy by which some of President Nixon's advisers believed that the President could transform the Republican party from a minority to a majority party by wooing the votes of *conservative* southern white people who traditionally had voted Democratic.

sovereignty: The power to command all others.

substantive: Having to do with the substance or content of an issue or a subject rather than with its appearance.

subversion: An undermining from within.

superpower: A large and powerful nation. Generally the United States, the Soviet Union, and China are considered the superpowers.

totalitarianism: The doctrine, propounded especially by Fascist rulers such as Hitler and Mussolini, that an entire nation is a single organism, a totality, ruled by a single individual.

United Nations: International organization established after World War II, with worldwide membership, for the purpose of avoiding war and improving the condition of the world's peoples. See Chapter 10.

vital interest: A nation is presumed to have certain interests, such as its territorial integrity, the protection of which is important enough to warrant extreme measures, up to and including war.

War on Poverty: The term commonly used to describe President Lyndon Johnson's highly publicized legislative campaign to eliminate extreme poverty in America through various governmental programs.

WASP: Literally, white Anglo-Saxon Protestant. In practice, the term usually is meant to describe the dominant English-speaking groups who often tend to assume that they are the "real Americans."

Watergate: A hotel–apartment complex in Washington, D.C. where burglars, associated with the Committee to Reelect the President, were caught breaking into the Democratic National Headquarters in 1972. It became a generic term used to describe the various offenses of the Nixon administration.

witch hunt: A term deriving from the practice of hunting down suspected witches in Colonial America. Used as a synonym for baseless accusations of innocent but unpopular persons or groups.

Suggested Readings

The following suggestions, arranged by chapter, are only intended to whet the appetite of the serious student of American government, politics, and culture. The student should also refer to the footnotes within each chapter.

There are other aids as well. Periodicals are important. *The Reader's Guide to Periodical Literature* indexes popular magazines (such as *Time* and *Newsweek*). The *New York Times Index* is very useful. It is organized yearly and by topic. Helpful scholarly journals, each with its own index, are the *American Historical Review, American Journal of Political Science, American Political Science Review, American Quarterly, Journal of American History, Journal of Politics, Journal of Popular Culture, Political Sci-*

ence Quarterly, and *Public Opinion Quarterly.* The Congressional Quarterly, Inc. is an editorial research service that publishes yearly *Guides to Current American Government,* a *Weekly Report,* and several other publications of interest. Additionally, students will find useful the *United States Government Manual,* published annually by the office of the Federal Registrar, and the *Almanac of American Politics,* published annually by E. P. Dutton & Co., Inc.

Some scholars of political science believe that the serious student should start with the ancient Greek philosophers. Plato's *Republic* (trans. Benjamin Jowett [New York: World, 1946]) is a seminal work of political thought, written in the form of a dramatic dialogue. Aristotle's *Politics* (trans. Benjamin Jowett [Oxford: Clarendon Press, 1967]) is a classic examination of many themes still important to political scientists and politicians.

Finally, the student should be alerted to two novels, often cited as the greatest works of American literature. Herman Melville's *Moby Dick* (New York: Dell, 1960) is, among other things, a prophetic song of an imperial democracy. Mark Twain's (Samuel L. Clemens) *The Adventures of Huckleberry Finn* (Glenview, Ill.: Scott, Foresman, 1960), although superficially simply a youthful adventure story, contains a powerful critique of American society and values. The Scott, Foresman edition contains critical abstracts designed to help the reader understand Twain's caustic views, which are often masked as frontier humor.

Chapter 1: Shine, Perishing Republic

Carnoy, Judith, and Marc Weiss. *A House Divided: Radical Perspectives on Social Problems.* Boston: Little, Brown, 1973. A series of critical essays from the perspective of the political left.

De Grazia, Alfred. *Eights Bads Eight Goods: The American Contradictions.* Garden City, N.Y.: Anchor, 1975. A putative series of lectures to a Chinese reader outlining the good and bad aspects of American culture and society.

Evans, M. Stanton. *Clear and Present Dangers: A Conservative View of America's Government.* New York: Harcourt, 1975. A conservative criticism of contemporary America.

Putney, Snell. *The Conquest of Society.* Belmont, Calif.: Wadsworth, 1972. A somewhat unorthodox analysis of America, stressing that "systems" are no longer under the control of people.

Revel, Jean-Francois. *Without Marx or Jesus: The New American Revolution Has Begun.* Garden City, N.Y.: Doubleday, 1971. An upbeat assessment contending that the United States is leading a necessary, worldwide, and peaceful social and political revolution.

309

Chapter 2: The Pursuit of Happiness

Emerson, Ralph Waldo. *Self Reliance.* (First published in *Essays,* 1841, revised 1847.) Written in the form of a personal essay, it sums up certain salient values and ideas of nineteenth-century America.

Feldman, Saul D., and Gerald W. Thielbar. (Eds.). *Life Styles: Diversity in American Society.* Boston: Little, Brown, 1972. Essays emphasizing diversity rather than uniformity in America.

Friedan, Betty. *The Feminine Mystique.* New York: Norton, 1963. An important first book in the literature of the current women's movement.

Haley, Alex. *Roots.* Garden City, N.Y.: Doubleday, 1976. The personal history of a black family, beginning in Gambia, West Africa, in the eighteenth century, extending through slavery in America and Reconstruction, and ending with an explanation of the author's research.

Hall, James W. (Ed.). *Forging the American Character.* New York: Holt, 1971. A compilation of classic and conflicting essays regarding the nature and origin of an American character.

Handlin, Oscar (Ed.). *Immigration as a Factor in American History.* Englewood Cliffs, N.J.: Prentice-Hall, 1959. Essays gathered by a major scholar.

Miller, Perry. *Errand into the Wilderness.* Cambridge, Mass.: Harvard U.P., 1956. One of many important works by the most profound student of New England Puritanism.

Morgan, Edmund S. *The Puritan Dilemma.* Boston: Little, Brown, 1958. A short and insightful analysis of Puritanism via the biography of John Winthrop.

National Advisory Commission. *Report of the National Advisory Commission on Civil Disorders.* New York: Bantam, 1968. A comprehensive study of the problems and the promise of blacks in America.

Paine, Thomas. *Common Sense.* Garden City, N.Y.: Doubleday, 1973. Containing radical views on the meaning and purpose of government, a classic defense of the American Revolution. Originally published as a pamphlet six months before the Declaration of Independence.

Reisman, David. *The Lonely Crowd.* New Haven, Conn.: Yale U.P., 1961. The character and qualities of middle-class, suburban American life examined by a prominent sociologist.

Taylor, George Rogers (Ed.). *The Turner Thesis: Concerning the Role of the Frontier in American History.* Lexington, Mass.: Heath, 1972. Contradictory essays on the meaning and importance of the frontier. Includes F. J. Turner's seminal essay of 1893.

Whitman, Walt. *Democratic Vistas.* (First published in *Galaxy* magazine shortly after the Civil War.) Whitman undertook in this essay to evaluate the condition of democracy in America and ended by writing a prose-poem of American idealism.

Chapter 3: The Constitutional Framework

Beard, Charles A. *An Economic Interpretation of the Constitution of the United States.* New York: Macmillan, 1913. The influential, classic thesis that the Founding Fathers were motivated chiefly by economic considerations in framing the Constitution.

Brown, Robert E. *Charles A. Beard and the Constitution.* Princeton, N.J.: Princeton, U.P., 1956. A critical and detailed attack on Beard's thesis.

Corwin, Edward S. *The Constitution and What It Means Today,* rev. Harold W. Chase and Craig R. Ducat. Princeton, N.J.: Princeton U.P., 1974. A careful explanation of the Constitution by a foremost scholar.

Elkins, Stanley, and Eric McKitrick. *The Founding Fathers, Young Men of the Revolution.* Washington, D.C.: Service Center for Teachers of History, 1962. A brief survey of various views on the origin of the Constitution plus a short but brilliant interpretation by the authors.

Chapter 4: The President as Superstar

Barber, James David. *The Presidential Character.* Englewood Cliffs, N.J.: Prentice-Hall, 1972. Analysis of why Presidents act as they do. Based on biographical study of Presidents from Taft to Nixon.

Corwin, Edward S. *The President: Office and Powers.* New York: New York U.P., 1957. A traditional and classic exposition of the Presidency.

Dean, John. *Blind Ambition.* New York: Simon & Schuster, 1976. A personal and revealing account of events surrounding the Watergate scandal.

Hughes, Emmet John. *The Living Presidency.* New York: Coward, 1972. A readable essay on the nature of the modern Presidency by a journalist and sometime presidential adviser.

Koenig, Louis W. *The Chief Executive,* 3rd ed. New York: Harcourt, 1975. Scholarly study of the various aspects of the Presidency.

Rossiter, Clinton, *The American Presidency,* rev ed. New York: Harcourt 1960. A slightly dated but valuable look at the many roles of the President.

Schlesinger, Arthur M., Jr. *The Imperial Presidency.* Boston: Houghton, 1973. An assessment of the growing power of the modern President by the historian of Presidents Jackson, F. D. Roosevelt, and Kennedy.

Chapter 5: Congress and Its Critics

Berman, Daniel M. *A Bill Becomes a Law.* New York: Macmillan, 1966. Comparison of passage of two civil-rights bills, one in 1960, another in 1964.

Burns, James McGregor. *The Deadlock of Democracy,* rev ed. Englewood Cliffs, N.J.: Prentice-Hall, 1972. Includes criticisms of the slowness and inadequacy with which Congress responds to national needs.

Green, Mark J., James M. Fallows, and David R. Zwick. *Who Runs Congress?* New York: Bantam, 1972. A Ralph Nader project study emphasizing Congressional weaknesses and lack of responsiveness to the American people in general.

Mayhew, David R. *Congress: The Electoral Connection.* New Haven, Conn.: Yale U.P., 1974. Brief survey of Congress emphasizing that a Congressman's chief motivation is to be reelected.

Polsby, Nelson W. *Congress and the Presidency,* 2nd ed. Englewood Cliffs, N.J.: Prentice-Hall, 1971. Useful analysis of both branches of government.

Truman, David B. (Ed.). *The Congress and America's Future,* 2nd ed. Englewood Cliffs, N.J.: Prentice-Hall, 1973. Essays on various aspects of Congress by acknowledged specialists.

Chapter 6: The Courts

Abraham, Henry J. *The Judicial Process,* 2nd ed. New York: Oxford U.P., 1968. Basic survey of state and federal systems of justice and comparison with other countries.

Bickel, Alexander. *The Supreme Court and the Idea of Progress.* New York: Harper, 1970. A critical assessment of the Warren Court.

Garraty, John A. (Ed.). *Quarrels That Have Shaped the Constitution.* New York: Harper, 1964. A series of lively essays explaining the major court decisions in America from *Marbury v. Madison* to *Brown v. Board of Education.*

Lewis, Anthony. *Gideon's Trumpet.* New York: Vintage, 1966. A readable chronology of a case from a local jail to the Supreme Court.

McCloskey, Robert G. *The American Supreme Court.* Chicago: U. of Chicago, 1960. Brief history of the Supreme Court and developing legal ideas.

Chapter 7: The Art of Politics

Burnham, Walter Dean. *Critical Elections and the Mainsprings of American Politics.* New York: Norton, 1970. A major study of the theory of critical elections, although now under increasing scholarly attack.

Chambers, William Nisbet, and Walter Dean Burnham (Eds.). *The American Party System: Stages of Political Development,* 2nd ed. New York: Oxford U.P., 1975. Essays presenting an analytical and historical survey of political parties.

Key, V. O., Jr. *Politics, Parties and Pressure Groups,* 5th ed. New York: Crowell, 1964. A classic and comprehensive study; indispensable for the serious student.

Polsby, Nelson W., and Aaron B. Wildavsky. *Presidential Elections,* 3rd ed. New York: Scribner's, 1971. Analysis of how Presidential campaigns are conducted.

Pomper, Gerald M. *Elections in America.* New York: Dodd, 1968. Study of election procedures at the state and federal levels.

Sorauf, Frank J. *Party Politics in America,* 2nd ed. Boston: Little, Brown, 1972. Examination of the roles of parties, their influence on government, party organizations, and the nature of party supporters.

Chapter 8: Who Rules America?

Campbell, Angus, Philip E. Converse, and Warren E. Miller. *The American Voter.* New York: Wiley, 1960. Comprehensive, landmark study of voting behavior compiled by the Survey Research Center of the University of Michigan.

Dahl, Robert A. *Who Governs?* New Haven, Conn.: Yale U.P., 1961. Contains theory of "pluralism" by its chief proponent.

Drucker, Peter. *The Age of Discontinuity.* New York: Harper, 1969. One of many works by an important student of bureaucracy.

Dye, Thomas R. *Who's Running America?* Englewood Cliffs, N.J.: Prentice-Hall, 1976. Recent elaboration of the "power elite" thesis.

Lowi, Theodore J. *The End of Liberalism.* New York: Norton, 1969. Critical analysis of theory and practice of interest groups.

Marini, Frank (Ed.). *Toward a New Public Administration.* Scranton, Pa.: Chandler, 1971. Essays on the study of public administration.

Mills, C. Wright. *The Power Elite.* New York: Oxford U.P., 1956. Classic statement of "power-elite" thesis.

Nie, Norman H., Sidney Verba, and John R. Petrocik. *The Changing American Voter.* Cambridge, Mass.: Harvard U.P., 1976. The latest important comprehensive study. It challenges some prevelant theories about voting behavior.

Chapter 9: Media, the Shadow Government

Kendrick, Alexander. *Prime Time: The Life of Edward R. Murrow.* Boston: Little, Brown, 1969. A probing and critical look at television news.

McGinniss, Joe. *The Selling of the President, 1968.* New York: Trident, 1969. Eye-opening account of the Nixon media campaign.

McLuhan, Marshall. *Understanding Media.* New York: McGraw-Hill, 1964. Essays by the stimulating and controversial Canadian critic.

Reston, James. *The Artillery of the Press.* New York: Harper, 1967. A newspaper journalist's view of the press and its relationship to government

Small, William. *To Kill a Messenger: Television News and the Real World.* New York: Hastings House, 1970. History of TV reportage of major social and political events.

Swanberg, W. A. *Luce and His Empire.* New York: Scribner's, 1972. Study of the influential *Time–Life* publisher.

Woodward, Bob, and Carl Bernstein. *All the President's Men.* New York: Simon & Schuster, 1974. Story of the unraveling of the Watergate scandal by the two *Washington Post* reporters.

Chapter 10: Economics

Ehrlich, Paul R., and Anne H. Ehrlich. *Population, Resources, Environment: Issues in Human Ecology,* 2nd ed. San Francisco: W. H. Freeman, 1972. An alarming analysis of problems of pollution, overpopulation, and hunger.

Friedman, Milton. *Capitalism and Freedom.* Chicago: U. of Chicago, 1962. An important explanation of conservative attitudes.

Galbraith, John Kenneth. *American Capitalism.* Boston: Houghton, 1956. Influential study containing theory of countervailing power.

Harrington, Michael. *The Other America.* Baltimore: Penguin, 1962. Well-known survey of poverty in America.

Heilbroner, Robert L. *The Worldly Philosophers,* rev ed. New York: Simon & Schuster, 1961. Readable explanations of the ideas of major economic thinkers throughout history.

Samuelson, Paul A. (Ed.). *Readings in Economics,* 6th ed. New York: McGraw-Hill, 1970. Conflicting essays over a wide range of economic issues.

Chapter 11: America in the World

"America: Still No. 1?" *Skeptic,* special issue, number 8 (1976). Views from a variety of scholars and journalists, including Henry Kissinger, James Schlesinger, Tom Hayden, and David Halberstam.

Combs, Jerald A. (Ed.). *Nationalist, Realist, and Radical: Three Views of American Diplomacy.* New York: Harper, 1972. Conflicting essays on major historical events in American diplomacy.

Jones, Alan M., Jr. *U.S. Foreign Policy in A Changing World.* New York: McKay, 1973. Collection of studies by specialists in particular geographic areas.

Kalb, Marvin, and Bernard Kalb. *Kissinger.* Boston: Little, Brown, 1974. A detailed look at the dominant figure in recent American diplomacy.

Sheehan, Neil, et al. *The Pentagon Papers.* New York: Bantam, 1971. Important collection of articles and documents on America's involvement in Vietnam from the Truman Presidency through 1968.

Taubman, William (Ed.). *Globalism and Its Critics.* Lexington, Mass.: Heath, 1973. Essays and speeches on American foreign policy from the perspective of the political right, "globalists," "realists," "liberals," and "radicals."

Chapter 12: Politics and the Pursuit of Happiness

Banfield, Edward C. *The Unheavenly City Revisited.* Boston: Little, Brown, 1974. An unorthodox and controversial analysis of the American city.

Cox, Harvey. *The Secular City.* New York: Macmillan, 1965. A fascinating and upbeat analysis of the city and its meaning for contemporary society by a popular theologian.

Putney, Snell. *The Conquest of Society.* Belmont, Calif.: Wadsworth, 1972. An analysis of contemporary American problems with recommendations for action on the part of "autonomous" individuals.

Rosenau, James N. *The Dramas of Politics.* Boston: Little, Brown, 1973. Emphasizes the parallels between the dramas of politics and those of personal life.

Toffler, Alvin. *Future Shock.* New York: Random, 1970. Influential study on the rapidity with which our world is changing.

The Declaration of Independence

IN CONGRESS, JULY 4, 1776: THE UNANIMOUS DECLARATION
OF THE THIRTEEN UNITED STATES OF AMERICA

When in the Course of human events, it becomes necessary for one people to dissolve the political bands which have connected them with another, and to assume among the Powers of the earth, the separate and equal station to which the Laws of Nature and Nature's God entitle them, a decent respect to the opinions of mankind requires that they should declare the causes which impel them to the separation.

We hold these truths to be self-evident, that all men are created equal, that they are endowed by their Creator with certain unalienable Rights, that among these are Life, Liberty and the pursuit of Happiness. That to secure these rights, Governments are instituted among Men, deriving their just powers from the consent of the governed, That whenever any Form of Government becomes destructive of these ends, it is the Right of the People to alter or to abolish it, and to institute new Government, laying its foundation on such principles and organizing its powers in such form, as to them shall seem most likely to effect their Safety and Happiness. Prudence, indeed, will dictate that Governments long established should not be changed for light and transient causes; and accordingly all experience hath shown, that mankind are more disposed to suffer, while evils are sufferable, than to right themselves by abolishing the forms to which they are accustomed. But when a long train of abuses and usurpations, pursuing invariably the same Object evinces a design to reduce them under absolute

315

Despotism, it is their right, it is their duty, to throw off such Government, and to provide new Guards for their future security.—Such has been the patient sufferance of the Colonies; and such is now the necessity which constrains them to alter their former Systems of Government. The history of the present King of Great Britain is a history of repeated injuries and usurpations, all having in direct object the establishment of an absolute Tyranny over these States. To prove this, let Facts be submitted to a candid world.

He has refused his Assent to Laws, the most wholesome and necessary for the public good.

He has forbidden his Governors to pass Laws of immediate and pressing importance, unless suspended in their operation till his Assent should be obtained; and when so suspended, he has utterly neglected to attend to them.

He has refused to pass other Laws for the accommodation of large districts of people, unless those people would relinquish the right of representation in the Legislature, a right inestimable to them and formidable to tyrants only.

He has called together legislative bodies at places unusual, uncomfortable, and distant from the depository of their Public Records, for the sole purpose of fatiguing them into compliance with his measures.

He has dissolved Representative Houses repeatedly, for opposing with manly firmness his invasions on the rights of the people.

He has refused for a long time, after such dissolutions, to cause others to be elected; whereby the Legislative Powers, incapable of Annihilation, have returned to the People at large for their exercise; the State remaining in the mean time exposed to all the dangers of invasion from without, and convulsions within.

He has endeavoured to prevent the population of these States; for that purpose obstructing the Laws of Naturalization of Foreigners; refusing to pass others to encourage their migration hither, and raising the conditions of new Appropriations of Lands.

He has obstructed the Administration of Justice, by refusing his Assent to Laws for establishing Judiciary Powers.

He has made Judges dependent on his Will alone, for the tenure of their offices, and the amount and payment of their salaries.

He has erected a multitude of New Offices, and sent hither swarms of Officers to harass our People, and eat out their substance.

He has kept among us, in times of peace, Standing Armies without the Consent of our legislature.

He has affected to render the Military independent of and superior to the Civil Power.

He has combined with others to subject us to a jurisdiction foreign to our constitution, and unacknowledged by our laws giving his Assent to their acts of pretended legislation:

For quartering large bodies of armed troops among us:

For protecting them, by a mock Trial, from Punishment for any Murders which they should commit on the Inhabitants of these States:

For cutting off our Trade with all parts of the world:

For imposing taxes on us without our Consent:

For depriving us in many cases, of the benefits of Trial by jury:

For transporting us beyond Seas to be tried for pretended offences:

For abolishing the free System of English Laws in a neighboring Province, establishing therein an Arbitrary government, and enlarging its Boundaries so as to render it at once an example and fit instrument for introducing the same absolute rule into these Colonies:

For taking away our Charters, abolishing our most valuable Laws, and altering fundamentally the Forms of our Governments:

For suspending our own legislature, and declaring themselves invested with Power to legislate for us in all cases whatsoever.

He has abdicated Government here, by declaring us out of his Protection and waging War against us.

He has plundered our seas, ravaged our Coasts, burnt our towns, and destroyed the lives of our people.

He is at this time transporting large armies of foreign mercenaries to compleat the works of death, desolation and tyranny, already begun with circumstances of Cruelty & perfidy scarcely paralleled in the most barbarous ages, and totally unworthy the Head of a civilized nation.

He has constrained our fellow Citizens taken Captive on the high Seas to bear Arms against their Country, to become the executioners of their friends and Brethren, or to fall themselves by their Hands.

He has excited domestic insurrections amongst us, and has endeavoured to bring on the inhabitants of our frontiers, the merciless Indian Savages, whose known rule of warfare, is an undistinguished destruction of all ages, sexes and conditions.

In every stage of these Oppressions We have Petitioned for Redress in the most humble terms: Our repeated Petitions have been answered only by repeated injury. A Prince, whose character is thus marked by every act which may define a Tyrant, is unfit to be the ruler of a free People.

Nor have We been wanting in attention to our British brethren. We have warned them from time to time of attempts by their legislature to extend an unwarrantable jurisdiction over us. We have reminded them of the circumstances of our emigration and settlement here. We have appealed to their native justice and magnanimity, and we have conjured them by the ties of our common kindred to disavow these usurpations, which would inevitably interrupt our connections and correspondence. They too have been deaf to the voice of justice and of consanguinity. We must, therefore, acquiesce in the necessity, which denounces our Separation, and hold them, as we hold the rest of mankind, Enemies in War, in Peace Friends.

We, therefore, the Representatives of the united States of America, in

General Congress, Assembled, appealing to the Supreme Judge of the world for the rectitude of our intentions, do, in the Name, and by Authority of the good People of these Colonies, solemnly publish and declare, That these United Colonies are, and of Right ought to be Free and Independent States; that they are Absolved from all Allegiance to the British Crown, and that all political connection between them and the State of Great Britain, is and ought to be totally dissolved; and that as Free and Independent States, they have full Power to levy War, conclude Peace, contract Alliances, establish Commerce, and to do all other Acts and Things which Independent States may of right do. And for the support of this Declaration, with a firm reliance on the Protection of Divine Providence, we mutually pledge to each other our Lives, our Fortunes and our sacred Honor.

*John Hancock**

Constitution of the United States

We the people of the United States, in order to form a more perfect union, establish justice, insure domestic tranquility, provide for the common defense, promote the general welfare, and secure the blessings of liberty to ourselves and our posterity, do ordain and establish this Constitution for the United States of America.

Article 1

Section 1

All legislative powers herein granted shall be vested in a Congress of the United States, which shall consist of a Senate and House of Representatives.

Section 2

1. The House of Representatives shall be composed of members chosen every second year by the people of the several States, and the electors in each State shall have the qualifications requisite for electors of the most numerous branch of the State legislature.

2. No person shall be a representative who shall not have attained to the age of twenty-five years, and been seven years a citizen of the United States, and who shall not, when elected, be an inhabitant of that State in which he shall be chosen.

3. Representatives and direct taxes [1] shall be apportioned among the several States which may be included within this Union, according to their

---

* The remaining signatures are omitted.
[1] See the Sixteenth Amendment.

respective numbers, which shall be determined by adding to the whole number of free persons, including those bound to service for a term of years, and excluding Indians not taxed, three-fifths of all other persons.[2] The actual enumeration shall be made within three years after the first meeting of the Congress of the United States, and within every subsequent term of ten years, in such manner as they shall by law direct. The number of representatives shall not exceed one for every thirty thousand, but each State shall have at least one representative; and until such enumeration shall be made, the State of New Hampshire shall be entitled to choose three, Massachusetts eight, Rhode Island and Providence Plantations one, Connecticut five, New York six, New Jersey four, Pennsylvania eight, Delaware one, Maryland six, Virginia ten, North Carolina five, South Carolina five, and Georgia three.

4. When vacancies happen in the representation from any State, the executive authority thereof shall issue writs of election to fill such vacancies.

5. The House of Representatives shall choose their speaker and other officers; and shall have the sole power of impeachment.

Section 3

1. The Senate of the United States shall be composed of two senators from each State, chosen by the legislature thereof,[3] for six years; and each senator shall have one vote.

2. Immediately after they shall be assembled in consequence of the first election, they shall be divided as equally as may be into three classes. The seats of the senators of the first class shall be vacated at the expiration of the second year, of the second class at the expiration of the fourth year, and of the third class at the expiration of the sixth year, so that one-third may be chosen every second year; and if vacancies happen by resignation, or otherwise, during the recess of the legislature of any State, the executive thereof may make temporary appointments until the next meeting of the legislature, which shall then fill such vacancies.[4]

3. No person shall be a senator who shall not have attained to the age of thirty years, and been nine years a citizen of the United States, and who shall not, when elected, be an inhabitant of that State for which he shall be chosen.

4. The Vice President of the United States shall be President of the Senate, but shall have no vote, unless they be equally divided.

5. The Senate shall choose their other officers, and also a president *pro tempore,* in the absence of the Vice President, or when he shall exercise the office of President of the United States.

---

[2] Partly superseded by the Fourteenth Amendment.
[3] See the Seventeenth Amendment.
[4] See the Seventeenth Amendment.

6. The Senate shall have the sole power to try all impeachments. When sitting for that purpose, they shall be on oath or affirmation. When the President of the United States is tried, the chief justice shall preside: and no person shall be convicted without the concurrence of two-thirds of the members present.

7. Judgment in cases of impeachment shall not extend further than to removal from office, and disqualification to hold and enjoy any office of honor, trust or profit under the United States: but the party convicted shall nevertheless be liable and subject to indictment, trial, judgment and punishment, according to law.

Section 4

1. The times, places, and manner of holding elections for senators and representatives, shall be prescribed in each State by the legislature thereof; but the Congress may at any time by law make or alter such regulations, except as to the places of choosing senators.

2. The Congress shall assemble at least once in every year, and such meeting shall be on the first Monday in December, unless they shall by law appoint a different day.

Section 5

1. Each House shall be the judge of the elections, returns and qualifications of its own members and majority of each shall constitute a quorum to do business; but a smaller number may adjourn from day to day, and may be authorized to compel the attendance of absent members, in such manner and under such penalties as each House may provide.

2. Each House may determine the rules of its proceedings, punish its members for disorderly behavior, and, with the concurrence of two-thirds, expel a member.

3. Each House shall keep a journal of its proceedings, and from time to time publish the same, excepting such parts as may in their judgment require secrecy; and the yeas and nays of the members of either House on any question shall, at the desire of one-fifth of those present, be entered on the journal.

4. Neither House, during the session of Congress, shall, without the consent of the other, adjourn for more than three days, nor to any other place than that in which the two Houses shall be sitting.

Section 6

1. The senators and representatives shall receive a compensation for their services, to be ascertained by law, and paid out of the Treasury of the United States. They shall in all cases, except treason, felony and breach

of the peace, be privileged from arrest during their attendance at the session of their respective Houses, and in going to and returning from the same; and for any speech or debate in either House, they shall not be questioned in any other place.

2. No senator or representative shall, during the time for which he was elected, be appointed to any civil office under the authority of the United States, which shall have been created, or the emoluments whereof shall have been increased during such time, and no person holding any office under the United States shall be a member of either House during his continuance in office.

Section 7

1. All bills for raising revenue shall originate in the House of Representatives; but the Senate may propose or concur with amendments as on other bills.

2. Every bill which shall have passed the House of Representatives and the Senate, shall, before it become a law, be presented to the President of the United States; if he approve he shall sign it, but if not he shall return it, with his objections to that House in which it shall have originated, who shall enter the objections at large on their journal, and proceed to reconsider it. If after such reconsideration two thirds of that House shall agree to pass the bill, it shall be sent, together with the objections, to the other House, by which it shall likewise be reconsidered, and if approved by two thirds of that House, it shall become a law. But in all such cases the votes of both Houses shall be determined by yeas and nays, and the names of the persons voting for and against the bill shall be entered on the journal of each House respectively. If any bill shall not be returned by the President within ten days (Sundays excepted) after it shall have been presented to him, the same shall be a law, in like manner as if he had signed it, unless the Congress by their adjournment prevent its return, in which case it shall not be a law.

3. Every order, resolution, or vote to which the concurrence of the Senate and House of Representatives may be necessary (except on a question of adjournment) shall be presented to the President of the United States; and before the same shall take effect, shall be approved by him, or being disapproved by him, shall be repassed by two thirds of the Senate and House of Representatives, according to the rules and limitations prescribed in the case of a bill.

Section 8

1. The Congress shall have the power to lay and collect taxes, duties, imposts, and excises, to pay the debts and provide for the common defense

and general welfare of the United States; but all duties, imposts, and excises shall be uniform throughout the United States;

2. To borrow money on the credit of the United States;

3. To regulate commerce with foreign nations, and among the several States, and with the Indian tribes;

4. To establish an uniform rule of naturalization, and uniform laws on the subject of bankruptcies throughout the United States;

5. To coin money, regulate the value thereof, and of foreign coin, and fix the standard of weights and measures;

6. To provide for the punishment of counterfeiting the securities and current coin of the United States;

7. To establish post offices and post roads;

8. To promote the progress of science and useful arts, by securing for limited times to authors and inventors the exclusive right to their respective writings and discoveries;

9. To constitute tribunals inferior to the Supreme Court;

10. To define and punish piracies and felonies committed on the high seas, and offenses against the laws of nations;

11. To declare war, grant letters of marque and reprisal, and make rules concerning captures on land and water;

12. To raise and support armies, but no appropriation of money to that use shall be for a longer term than two years;

13. To provide and maintain a navy;

14. To make rules for the government and regulation of the land and naval forces;

15. To provide for calling forth the militia to execute the laws of the Union, suppress insurrections and repel invasions;

16. To provide for organizing, arming, and disciplining the militia, and for governing such part of them as may be employed in the service of the United States, reserving to the States respectively the appointment of the officers, and the authority of training the militia according to the discipline prescribed by Congress;

17. To exercise exclusive legislation in all cases whatsoever, over such district (not exceeding ten miles square) as may, by cession of particular States, and the acceptance of Congress, become the seat of the government of the United States, and to exercise like authority over all places purchased by the consent of the legislature of the State in which the same shall be, for the erection of forts, magazines, dockyards, and other needful buildings; and

18. To make all laws which shall be necessary and proper for carrying into execution the foregoing powers, and all other powers vested by this Constitution in the government of the United States, or in any department or officer thereof.

Section 9

1. The migration or importation of such persons as any of the States now existing shall think proper to admit, shall not be prohibited by the Congress prior to the year one thousand eight hundred and eight, but a tax or duty may be imposed on such importation, not exceeding ten dollars for each person.

2. The privilege of the writ of *habeas corpus* shall not be suspended, unless when in cases of rebellion or invasion the public safety may require it.

3. No bill of attainder or *ex post facto* law shall be passed.

4. No capitation, or other direct, tax shall be laid, unless in proportion to the census or enumeration hereinbefore directed to be taken.[5]

5. No tax or duty shall be laid on articles exported from any State.

6. No preference shall be given by any regulation of commerce or revenue to the ports of one State over those of another: nor shall vessels bound to, or from, one State be obliged to enter, clear, or pay duties in another.

7. No money shall be drawn from the treasury, but in consequence of appropriations, made by law; and a regular statement and account of the receipts and expenditures of all public money shall be published from time to time.

8. No title of nobility shall be granted by the United States: and no person holding any office or profit or trust under them, shall, without the consent of the Congress, accept of any present, emolument, office, or title, of any kind whatever, from any king, prince, or foreign State.

Section 10

1. No State shall enter into any treaty, alliance, or confederation; grant letters of marque and reprisal; coin money; emit bills of credit; make anything but gold and silver coin a tender in payment of debts; pass any bill of attainder, *ex post facto* law, or law impairing the obligation of contracts, or grant any title of nobility.

2. No state shall, without the consent of the Congress, lay any imposts or duties on imports or exports, except what may be absolutely necessary for executing its inspection laws: and the net produce of all duties and imposts laid by any State on imports or exports, shall be of the use of the treasury of the United States; and all such laws shall be subject to the revision and control of the Congress.

3. No State shall, without the consent of Congress, lay any duty of tonnage, keep troops, or ships of war in time of peace, enter into any agreement or compact with another State, or with a foreign power, or engage in war, unless actually invaded, or in such imminent danger as will not admit of delay.

[5] See the Sixteenth Amendment.

Article 2

Section 1

1. The executive power shall be vested in a President of the United States of America. He shall hold his office during the term of four years, and, together with the Vice President, chosen for the same term, be elected, as follows: [6]

2. Each State shall appoint, in such manner as the legislature thereof may direct, a number of electors, equal to the whole number of senators and representatives to which the State may be entitled in the Congress: but no senator or representative, or person holding an office of trust or profit under the United States, shall be appointed an elector.

The electors shall meet in their respective States, and vote by ballot for two persons, of whom one at least shall not be an inhabitant of the same State with themselves. And they shall make a list of all the persons voted for, and of the number of votes for each; which list they shall sign and certify, and transmit sealed to the seat of the government of the United States, directed to the president of the Senate. The president of the Senate shall, in the presence of the Senate and House of Representatives, open all certificates, and votes shall then be counted. The person having the greatest number of votes shall be the President, if such number be a majority of the whole number of electors appointed; and if there be more than one who have such majority, and have an equal number of votes, then the House of Representatives shall immediately choose by ballot one of them for President; and if no person have a majority, then from the five highest on the list said House shall in like manner choose the President. But in choosing the President, the votes shall be taken by States, the representation from each State having one vote; a quorum for this purpose shall consist of a member or members from two thirds of the States, and a majority of all the States shall be necessary to a choice. In every case, after the choice of the President, the person having the greatest number of votes of the electors shall be the Vice President. But if there should remain two or more who have equal votes, the Senate shall choose from them by ballot the Vice President.[7]

3. The Congress may determine the time of choosing the electors, and the day on which they shall give their votes; which day shall be the same throughout the United States.

4. No person except a natural born citizen, or a citizen of the United States, at the time of the adoption of this Constitution, shall be eligible to the office of President; neither shall any person be eligible to that office who shall not have attained to the age of thirty-five years, and been fourteen years a resident within the United States.

[6] See the Twenty-second Amendment.
[7] Superseded by the Twelfth Amendment.

5. In case of the removal of the President from office, or of his death, resignation, or inability to discharge the powers and duties of the said office, the same shall devolve on the Vice President, and the Congress may by law provide for the case of removal, death, resignation, or inability, both of the President and Vice President, declaring what officer shall then act as President, and such officer shall act accordingly, until the disability be removed, or a President shall be elected.[8]

6. The President shall, at stated times, receive for his services a compensation, which shall neither be increased nor diminished during the period for which he shall have been elected, and he shall not receive within that period any other emolument from the United States, or any of them.

7. Before he enter on the execution of his office, he shall take the following oath or affirmation:—"I do solemnly swear (or affirm) that I will faithfully execute the office of President of the United States, and will to the best of my ability, preserve, protect and defend the Constitution of the United States."

Section 2

1. The President shall be commander in chief of the army and navy of the United States, and of the militia of the several States, when called into the actual service of the United States; he may require the opinion, in writing, of the principal officer in each of the executive departments, upon any subject relating to the duties of their respective offices, and he shall have power to grant reprieves and pardons for offenses against the United States, except in cases of impeachment.

2. He shall have power, by and with the advice and consent of the Senate, to make treaties, provided two thirds of the senators present concur; and he shall nominate, and by and with the advice and consent of the Senate, shall appoint ambassadors, other public ministers and consuls, judges of the Supreme Court, and all other officers of the United States, whose appointments are not herein otherwise provided for, and which shall be established by law; but the Congress may by law vest the appointment of such inferior officers, as they think proper, in the President alone, in the courts of law, or in the heads of departments.

3. The President shall have power to fill up all vacancies that may happen during the recess of the Senate, by granting commissions which shall expire at the end of the next session.

Section 3

1. He shall from time to time give to the Congress information of the state of the Union, and recommend to their consideration such measures as he shall judge necessary and expedient; he may, on extraordinary occa-

[8] See the Twentieth Amendment and the Twenty-fifth Amendment.

sions, convene both Houses, or either of them, and in case of disagreement between them with respect to the time of adjournment, he may adjourn them to such time as he shall think proper; he shall receive ambassadors and other public ministers; he shall take care that the laws be faithfully executed, and shall commission all the officers of the United States.

Section 4

The President, Vice President, and all civil officers of the United States, shall be removed from office on impeachment for, and conviction of, treason, bribery, or other high crimes and misdemeanors.

Article 3

Section 1

The Judicial power of the United States shall be vested in one Supreme Court, and in such inferior courts as the Congress may from time to time ordain and establish. The judges, both of the Supreme and inferior courts, shall hold their offices during good behavior, and shall, at stated times, receive for their services, a compensation, which shall not be diminished during their continuance in office.

Section 2

1. The Judicial power shall extend to all cases, in law and equity, arising under this Constitution, the laws of the United States, and treaties made, or which shall be made, under their authority;—to all cases affecting ambassadors, other public ministers and consuls;—to all cases of admiralty and maritime jurisdiction;—to controversies to which the United States shall be a party;—to controversies between two or more States;—between a state and citizens of another State;[9]—between citizens of the same State claiming lands under grants of different States, and between a State, or the citizens thereof, and foreign States, citizens or subjects.

2. In all cases affecting ambassadors, other public ministers and consuls, and those in which a State shall be party, the Supreme Court shall have original jurisdiction. In all the other cases before mentioned, the Supreme Court shall have appellate jurisdiction, both as to law and to fact, with such exceptions, and under such regulations as the Congress shall make.

3. The trial of all crimes, except in cases of impeachment, shall be by jury; and such trial shall be held in the State where the said crimes shall have been committed; but when not committed within any State, the trial shall be at such place or places as the Congress may by law have directed.

Section 3

1. Treason against the United States shall consist only in levying war against them, or in adhering to their enemies, giving them aid and comfort.

[9] See the Eleventh Amendment.

No person shall be convicted of treason unless on the testimony of two witnesses to the same overt act, or on confession in open court.

2. The Congress shall have power to declare the punishment of treason, but no attainder of treason shall work corruption of blood, or forfeiture except during the life of the person attained.

Article 4

Section 1

Full faith and credit shall be given in each State to the public acts, records, and judicial proceedings of every other State. And the Congress may by general laws prescribe the manner in which acts, records and proceedings shall be proved, and the effect thereof.

Section 2

1. The citizens of each State shall be entitled to all privileges and immunities of citizens in the several States.

2. A person charged in any State with treason, felony, or other crime, who shall flee from justice, and be found in another State, shall on demand of the executive authority of the State from which he fled, be delivered up to be removed to the State having jurisdiction of the crime.

3. No person held to service or labor in one State under the laws thereof, escaping into another, shall, in consequence of any law or regulation therein, be discharged from such service or labor, but shall be delivered up on claim of the party to whom such service or labor may be due.

Section 3

1. New States may be admitted by the Congress into this Union; but no new State shall be formed or erected within the jurisdiction of any other State; nor any State be formed by the junction of two or more States, or parts of States, without the consent of the legislatures of the States concerned as well as of the Congress.

2. The Congress shall have power to dispose of and make all needful rules and regulations respecting the territory or other property belonging to the United States; and nothing in this Constitution shall be so construed as to prejudice any claims of the United States, or of any particular State.

Section 4

The United States shall guarantee to every State in this Union a republican form of government, and shall protect each of them against invasion; and on application of the legislature, or of the executive (when the legislature cannot be convened) against domestic violence.

Article 5

The Congress, whenever two-thirds of both Houses shall deem it necessary, shall propose amendments to this Constitution, or, on the application of the legislatures of two-thirds of the several States, shall call a convention for proposing amendments, which, in either case, shall be valid to all intents and purposes, as part of this Constitution when ratified by the legislatures of three-fourths of the several States, or by conventions in three-fourths thereof, as the one or the other mode of ratification may be proposed by the Congress; Provided that no amendment which may be made prior to the year one thousand eight hundred and eight shall in any manner affect the first and fourth clauses in the ninth section of the first article; and that no State, without its consent, shall be deprived of its equal suffrage in the Senate.

Article 6

1. All debts contracted, and engagements entered into, before the adoption of this Constitution, shall be as valid against the United States under this Constitution, as under the Confederation.

2. This Constitution, and the laws of the United States which shall be made in pursuance thereof; and all treaties made, or which shall be made, under the authority of the United States, shall be the supreme law of the land; and the Judges in every State shall be bound thereby, anything in the Constitution or laws of any State to the contrary notwithstanding.

3. The senators and representatives before mentioned, and the members of the several State legislatures, and all executive and judicial officers, both of the United States and of the several States, shall be bound by oath or affirmation to support this Constitution; but no religious test shall ever be required as a qualification to any office or public trust under the United States.

Article 7

The ratification of the conventions of nine States shall be sufficient for the establishment of this Constitution between the States so ratifying the same.

Done in Convention by the unanimous consent of the States present the seventeenth day of September in the year of our Lord one thousand seven hundred and eighty-seven, and of the independence of the United States of America the twelfth. In witness whereof we have hereunto subscribed our names.

[Names omitted]

Articles in Addition To, and Amendment Of, the Constitution of the United States of America, Proposed by Congress, and Ratified by the Legislatures of the Several States, Pursuant to the Fifth Article of the Original Constitution.[10]

[10] The Twenty-first Amendment was not ratified by state legislatures but by state conventions summoned by Congress.

(The first ten Amendments were ratified December 15, 1791 and form what is known as the "Bill of Rights.")

Amendment 1

Congress shall make no law respecting an establishment of religion, or prohibiting the free exercise thereof; or abridging the freedom of speech, or of the press; or the right of the people peaceably to assemble, and to petition the Government for a redress of grievances.

Amendment 2

A well regulated Militia, being necessary to the security of a free State, the right of the people to keep and bear Arms, shall not be infringed.

Amendment 3

No Soldier shall, in time of peace be quartered in any house, without the consent of the Owner, nor in time of war, but in a manner to be prescribed by law.

Amendment 4

The right of the people to be secure in their persons, houses, papers, and effects, against unreasonable searches and seizures, shall not violated, and no Warrants shall issue, but upon probable cause, supported by Oath or affirmation, and particularly describing the place to be searched, and the persons or things to be seized.

Amendment 5

No person shall be held to answer for a capital, or otherwise infamous crime, unless on a presentment or indictment of a Grand Jury, except in cases arising in the land or naval forces, or in the Militia, when in actual service in time of War or public danger; nor shall any person be subject for the same offence to be twice put in jeopardy of life or limb; nor shall be compelled in any criminal case to be a witness against himself, nor be deprived of life, liberty, or property, without due process of law; nor shall private property be taken for public use, without just compensation.

Amendment 6

In all criminal prosecutions, the accused shall enjoy the right to a speedy and public trial, by an impartial jury of the State and district wherein the crime shall have been committed, which district shall have been previously ascertained by law, and to be informed of the nature and cause of the accusation; to be confronted with the witnesses against him; to have compulsory process for obtaining witnesses in his favor, and to have the Assistance of Counsel for his defence.

329

Amendment 7

In suits at common law, where the value in controversy shall exceed twenty dollars, the right of trial by jury shall be preserved, and no fact tried by a jury, shall be otherwise reexamined in any Court of the United States, than according to the rules of the common law.

Amendment 8

Excessive bail shall not be required, nor excessive fines imposed, nor cruel and unusual punishments inflicted.

Amendment 9

The enumeration in the Constitution, of certain rights, shall not be construed to deny or disparage others retained by the people.

Amendment 10

The powers not delegated to the United States by the Constitution, nor prohibited by it to the States, are reserved to the States respectively, or to the people.

Amendment 11

(Ratified February 7, 1795)

The Judicial power of the United States shall not be construed to extend to any suit in law or equity, commenced or prosecuted against one of the United States by Citizens of another State, or by Citizens or Subjects of any Foreign State.

Amendment 12

(Ratified July 27, 1804)

The Electors shall meet in their respective states and vote by ballot for President and Vice President, one of whom, at least, shall not be an inhabitant of the same state with themselves; they shall name in their ballots the person voted for as President, and in distinct ballots the person voted for as Vice President, and they shall make distinct lists of all persons voted for as President, and of all persons voted for as Vice President, and of the number of votes for each, which lists they shall sign and certify, and transmit sealed to the seat of the government of the United States, directed to the President of the Senate;—The President of the Senate shall, in presence of the Senate and House of Representatives, open all the certificates and the votes shall then be counted;—The person having the greatest number of votes for President, shall be the President, if such number be a majority of the whole number of Electors appointed; and if no person have such majority, then from the persons having the highest numbers not exceeding three on the list of those voted for as President, the House of Representatives shall choose immediately, by ballot, the President. But in choosing the President, the votes shall be taken by states, the representation from each state having one vote; a quorum for this purpose shall consist of a member or members from two-thirds of the states, and a majority of all the states shall be necessary to a choice. [And if the House of Representatives shall not choose a President whenever the right of choice shall devolve upon them, before the fourth day of March next following, then the Vice President shall act as President, as in the case of the death or other constitutional disability of the President.—] [11] The person having the greatest number of votes as Vice President, shall be the Vice President, if such number be a majority of the whole number of Electors appointed, and if no person have a majority, then from the two highest numbers on the list, the Senate shall choose the Vice President; a quorum for the purpose shall consist of two-thirds of the whole number of Senators, and a majority of the whole number shall be necessary to a choice. But no person constitutionally ineligible to the office of President shall be eligible to that of Vice President of the United States.

Amendment 13

(Ratified December 6, 1865)

Section 1

Neither slavery nor involuntary servitude, except as a punishment for crime whereof the party shall have been duly convicted, shall exist within the United States, or any place subject to their jurisdiction.

Section 2

Congress shall have power to enforce this article by appropriate legislation.

Amendment 14

(Ratified July 9, 1868)

Section 1

All persons born or naturalized in the United States, and subject to the jurisdiction thereof, are citizens of the United States and of the State wherein they reside. No State shall make or enforce any law which shall abridge the privileges or immunities of citizens of the United States; nor shall any State deprive any person of life, liberty, or property, without due process of law; nor deny to any person within its jurisdiction the equal protection of the laws.

[11] Superseded by Section 3 of the Twentieth Amendment.

Section 2

Representatives shall be apportioned among the several States according to their respective numbers, counting the whole number of persons in each State, excluding Indians not taxed. But when the right to vote at any election for the choice of electors for President and Vice President of the United States, Representatives in Congress, the Executive and Judicial officers of a State, or the members of the Legislature thereof, is denied to any of the male inhabitants of such State, being twenty-one years of age,[12] and citizens of the United States, or in any way abridged, except for participation in rebellion, or other crime, the basis of representation therein shall be reduced in the proportion which the number of such male citizens shall bear to the whole number of male citizens twenty-one years of age in such State.

Section 3

No person shall be a Senator or Representative in Congress, or elector of President and Vice President, or hold any office, civil or military, under the United States, or under any State, who, having previously taken an oath, as a member of Congress, or as an officer of the United States, or as a member of any State legislature, or as an executive or judicial officer of any State, to support the Constitution of the United States, shall have engaged in insurrection or rebellion against the same, or given aid or comfort to the enemies thereof. But Congress may by a vote of two-thirds of each House, remove such disability.

Section 4

The validity of the public debt of the United States, authorized by law, including debts incurred for payment of pensions and bounties for services in suppressing insurrection or rebellion, shall not be questioned. But neither the United States nor any State shall assume or pay any debt or obligation incurred in aid of insurrection or rebellion against the United States, or any claim for the loss or emancipation of any slave; but all such debts, obligations and claims shall be held illegal and void.

Section 5

The Congress shall have power to enforce, by appropriate legislation, the provisions of this article.

Amendment 15

(Ratified February 3, 1870)

---

[12] Changed by Section 1 of the Twenty-sixth Amendment.

Section 1

The right of citizens of the United States to vote shall not be denied or abridged by the United States or by any State on account of race, color, or previous condition of servitude—

Section 2

The Congress shall have power to enforce this article by Appropriate legislation.

Amendment 16
(Ratified February 3, 1913)

The Congress shall have power to lay and collect taxes on incomes, from whatever source derived, without apportionment among the several States, and without regard to any census or enumeration.

Amendment 17
(Ratified April 8, 1913)

The Senate of the United States shall be composed of two Senators from each State, elected by the people thereof, for six years; and each Senator shall have one vote. The electors in each State shall have the qualifications requisite for electors of the most numerous branch of the State legislatures.

When vacancies happen in the representation of any State in the Senate, the executive authority of such State shall issue writs of election to fill such vacancies: *Provided,* That the legislature of any State may empower the executive thereof to make temporary appointments until the people fill the vacancies by election as the legislature may direct.

This amendment shall not be so construed as to affect the election or term of any Senator chosen before it becomes valid as part of the Constitution.

Amendment 18
(Ratified January 16, 1919)

Section 1

After one year from the ratification of this article the manufacture, sale, or transportation of intoxicating liquors within, the importation thereof into, or the exportation thereof from the United States and all territory subject to the jurisdiction thereof for beverage purposes is hereby prohibited.

Section 2

The Congress and the several States shall have concurrent power to enforce this article by appropriate legislation.

Section 3

This article shall be inoperative unless it shall have been ratified as an amendment to the Constitution by the legislatures of the several States as provided in the Constitution, within seven years from the date of the submission hereof to the States by the Congress.[13]

Amendment 19

(Ratified August 18, 1920)

The right of citizens of the United States to vote shall not be denied or abridged by the United States or by any State on account of sex.

Congress shall have power to enforce this article by appropriate legislation.

Amendment 20

(Ratified January 23, 1933)

Section 1

The terms of the President and Vice President shall end at noon on the 20th day of January, and the terms of Senators and Representatives at noon on the 3d day of January, of the years in which such terms would have ended if this article had not been ratified; and the terms of their successors shall then begin.

Section 2

The Congress shall assemble at least once in every year, and such meeting shall begin at noon on the 3d day of January, unless they shall by law appoint a different day.

Section 3

If, at the time fixed for the beginning of the term of the President, the President elect shall have died, the Vice President elect shall become President. If a President shall not have been chosen before the time fixed for the beginning of his term, or if the President elect shall have failed to qualify, then the Vice President elect shall act as President until a President shall have qualified; and the Congress may by law provide for the case wherein neither a President elect nor a Vice President elect shall have qualified, declaring who shall then act as President, or the manner in which one who is to act shall be selected, and such person shall act accordingly until a President or Vice President shall have qualified.

Section 4

The Congress may by law provide for the case of the death of any of the persons from whom the House of Representatives may choose a President

[13] Repealed by Section 1 of the Twenty-first Amendment.

334

whenever the right of choice shall have devolved upon them, and for the case of the death of any of the persons from whom the Senate may choose a Vice President whenever the right of choice shall have devolved upon them.

Section 5

Sections 1 and 2 shall take effect on the 15th day of October following the ratification of this article.

Section 6

This article shall be inoperative unless it shall have been ratified as an amendment to the Constitution by the legislatures of three-fourths of the several States within seven years from the date of its submission.

Amendment 21

(Ratified December 5, 1933)

Section 1

The eighteenth article of amendment to the Constitution of the United States is hereby repealed.

Section 2

The transportation or importation into any State, Territory, or possession of the United States for delivery or use therein of intoxicating liquors, in violation of the laws thereof, is hereby prohibited.

Section 3

This article shall be inoperative unless it shall have been ratified as an amendment to the Constitution by conventions in the several States, as provided in the Constitution, within seven years from the date of the submission hereof to the States by the Congress.

Amendment 22

(Ratified February 27, 1951)

Section 1

No person shall be elected to the office of the President more than twice, and no person who has held the office of President, or acted as President, for more than two years of a term to which some other person was elected President shall be elected to the office of the President more than once. But this Article shall not apply to any person holding the office of President when this Article was proposed by the Congress, and shall not prevent any person who may be holding the office of President, or acting as President, during the term within which this Article becomes operative from holding the office of President or acting as President during the remainder of such term.

Section 2

This article shall be inoperative unless it shall have been ratified as an amendment to the Constitution by the legislatures of three-fourths of the several States within seven years from the date of its submission to the States by the Congress.

Amendment 23

(Ratified March 29, 1961)

Section 1

The District constituting the seat of Government of the United States shall appoint in such manner as the Congress may direct:

A number of electors of President and Vice President equal to the whole number of Senators and Representatives in Congress to which the District would be entitled if it were a State, but in no event more than the least populous State; they shall be in addition to those appointed by the States, but they shall be considered, for the purposes of the election of President and Vice President, to be electors appointed by a State; and they shall meet in the District and perform such duties as provided by the twelfth article of amendment.

Section 2

The Congress shall have power to enforce this article by appropriate legislation.

Amendment 24

(Ratified January 23, 1964)

Section 1

The right of citizens of the United States to vote in any primary or other election for President or Vice President, for electors for President or Vice President, or for Senator or Representative in Congress, shall not be denied or abridged by the United States or any State by reason of failure to pay any poll tax or other tax.

Section 2

The Congress shall have power to enforce this article by appropriate legislation.

Amendment 25

(Ratified February 10, 1967)

Section 1

In case of the removal of the President from office or of his death or resignation, the Vice President shall become President.

Section 2

Whenever there is a vacancy in the office of the Vice President, the President shall nominate a Vice President who shall take office upon confirmation by a majority vote of both Houses of Congress.

Section 3

Whenever the President transmits to the President pro tempore of the Senate and the Speaker of the House of Representatives his written declaration that he is unable to discharge the powers and duties of his office, and until he transmits to them a written declaration to the contrary, such powers and duties shall be discharged by the Vice President as Acting President.

Section 4

Whenever the Vice President and a majority of either the principal officers of the executive departments or of such other body as Congress may by law provide, transmit to the President pro tempore of the Senate and the Speaker of the House of Representatives their written declaration that the President is unable to discharge the powers and duties of his office, the Vice President shall immediately assume the powers and duties of the office as Acting President.

Thereafter, when the President transmits to the President pro tempore of the Senate and the Speaker of the House of Representatives his written declaration that no inability exists, he shall resume the powers and duties of his office unless the Vice President and a majority of either the principal officers of the executive department or of such other body as Congress may by law provide, transmit within four days to the President pro tempore of the Senate and the Speaker of the House of Representatives their written declaration that the President is unable to discharge the powers and duties of his office. Thereupon Congress shall decide the issue, assembling within forty-eight hours for that purpose if not in session. If the Congress, within twenty-one days after receipt of the latter written declaration, or, if Congress is not in session, within twenty-one days after Congress is required to assemble, determines by two-thirds vote of both Houses that the President is unable to discharge the powers and duties of his office, the Vice President shall continue to discharge the same as Acting President; otherwise, the President shall resume the powers and duties of his office.

Amendment 26

(Ratified July 1, 1971)

Section 1

The right of citizens of the United States, who are eighteen years of age or older, to vote shall not be denied or abridged by the United States or by any State on account of age.

Section 2

The Congress shall have power to enforce this article by appropriate legislation.

Proposed Amendment 27

(Proposed March 22, 1972)

Section 1

Equality of rights under the law shall not be denied or abridged by the United States or by any State on account of sex.

Section 2

The Congress shall have power to enforce, by appropriate legislation, the provisions of this article.

Section 3

This amendment shall take effect two years after date of ratification.

Index

Numbers in *italics* refer to illustrations.

A

Abortion, 143, 170
Abzug, Bella, 167
Adams, John, 2, 29, 54, 139, 185, 189, 277, 281
Adams, John Quincy, 277, 278, 282
Advertising industry, 36
Affluent Society, 39–40, 41
Agnew, Spiro, 12, 20, 32, 81, 154, 183, 224, 225, 229
Alienation, 193
Allende, Salvadore, 265, 275, 279
American character, 26–49
American Indians, 41, 52
American Medical Association, 106, 186, 187
American Nazi party, 16, 45
American Revolution, 56, 98, 184, 278, 279
Americans
  average age, 44
  as consumers, 39
  "typical," 33
  values of, 44–49
Amin, Idi, 265
Anderson, Glenn, M., *110,* 124, 125*n.*
Andrus, Cecil D., 209
Annapolis Convention, 54–55
Apathy, 204–206
Arab states, 21, 248, 280
Arendt, Hannah, 195
Aristotle, 48, 56, 152, 295

Army, U.S., 270
  constitutional provisions, 62–63
  desertions, 19
  See also Military establishment
Articles of Confederation, 54–55, 57, 59, 66
Ashmore, Harry, 234
Assassinations, 12, 18, 38, 47, 94
Attentive public, 207–209

B

Baker, Howard, 118
Baker v. Carr, 45*n.*, 120, 141, 192
Baldwin, James, 43
Bay of Pigs invasion, 97, 281
Beard, Charles, 55–56
Becker, Carl, 22
Bentham, Jeremy, 11
Bergman, Ingmar, 249
Bernstein, Carl, 91, 224, *225*
Biddle, Nicholas, 96
Bill of Rights, 58, 63, *65*
Bills of attainder, 63
Black, Hugo, 134, 141
Black Panther party, 16, 45
Blackmun, Harry A., *133,* 135
Blacks, 34, 178, 182
  discrimination against, 33–34, 40–41, 56
  political affinities of, 152, 161, 171
  population statistics, 32
Bork, Robert, 137

340

F

G

J

K

V

W